The Ulster Crisis

Related titles from Palgrave Macmillan

Peter Catterall and Sean McDougall (eds), *The Northern Ireland Question in British Politics* (1996)

Paul Dixon, *Northern Ireland: The Politics of War and Peace* (2001)

Thomas Hennessey, *A History of Northern Ireland, 1920–96* (1997)

James Loughlin, *The Ulster Question since 1945, 2nd edition* (2003)

Peter Rose, *How the Troubles Came to Northern Ireland* (1999)

The Ulster Crisis 1885–1921

Edited by

D. GEORGE BOYCE

and

ALAN O'DAY

First published 2006 by
PALGRAVE MACMILLAN
Houndmills, Basingstoke, Hampshire RG21 6XS and
175 Fifth Avenue, New York, N. Y. 10010
Companies and representatives throughout the world

PALGRAVE MACMILLAN is the global academic imprint of the Palgrave
Macmillan division of St. Martin's Press, LLC and of Palgrave Macmillan Ltd.
Macmillan® is a registered trademark in the United States, United Kingdom
and other countries. Palgrave is a registered trademark in the European
Union and other countries.

ISBN-13: 978–1–4039–4369–9   hardback
ISBN-10: 1–4039–4369–9   hardback
ISBN-13: 978–1–4039–4370–5   paperback
ISBN-10: 1–4039–4370–2   paperback

This book is printed on paper suitable for recycling and made from fully
managed and sustained forest sources.

A catalogue record for this book is available from the British Library.
A catalog record for this book is available from the Library of Congress.

10   9   8   7   6   5   4   3   2   1
15   14   13   12   11   10   09   08   07   06

Printed in China

Contents

List of Illustrations

List of Tables

Contributors

Timothy Bowman, Lecturer in History, University of Kent at Canterbury

D. George Boyce, Professor (Emeritus) in Politics, University of Wales Swansea

Graham Brownlow, Senior Lecturer in Economics, Auckland University of Technology

N.C. Fleming, Lecturer in History, Queen's University Belfast

Sally Warwick-Haller, Senior Lecturer in History, Kingston University

A.C. Hepburn, Professor in History, University of Sunderland

D.M. Jackson, AHRB-Funded doctoral student at Northumbria University

Matthew Kelly, British Academy Fellow, Hertford College, Oxford

Gillian McIntosh, Fellow, Institute of Irish Studies, Queen's University Belfast

D.M. MacRaild, Professor in History, University of Northumbria

Patrick Maume, Dictionary of Irish Biography, Dublin

Marc Mulholland, Fellow in Modern History, St Catherine's College, University of Oxford

Alan O'Day, Fellow in Modern History, Greyfriars, University of Oxford

Brian M. Walker, Professor in Politics, Queen's University Belfast

Michael Wheatley, Fellow, Institute of Irish Studies, Queen's University Belfast

1

The Ulster Crisis: A Conundrum

Alan O'Day

I

The long Ulster crisis from the mid-1880s until the 1920s is an occasion when a moment or incident in time is decisive in shaping the future. This comparatively short span of time witnessed the creation of a new state or province, Northern Ireland, a sense of common destiny among Ulster Protestants who virtually reinvented themselves as a different people, the erection of a 'national mythology', while also giving an un-expected geographical and psychological form to the modern British nation that continues to the present-day. By the same token these na-tional pioneers rocked the old foe, Irish nationalism, onto its back heels, causing it to haemorrhage perhaps even fatally in the longer term. After the better part of a century of British leaders trying to tame the thrust of nationalism, the Ulster crisis did more to undermine its self-confidence than possibly all previous machinations combined. The Ulster unionist offensive merits placement among the master-strokes of post-1918 state-construction in Europe. Yet, as Alvin Jackson points out, the victory was gained at a price for 'the Protestant past is an uncomfortable and ugly garment, and a gaudy Orange sash never fully conceals the stains of de-nominational conflict, or the patches of class division'.[1] The outcome in 1921 was fiercely contested and remains bitterly divisive. Few people in 1885 and merely a minority as late as 1911 thought in terms of a divided Ireland, of a Northern Ireland state, or of an identity part Irish, part British, but not quite Ulster or Northern Irish either. Catholics, rejected both a dramatic shift of identity and the state in which they unexpect-edly found themselves. Like minorities across Europe, though, they were

1

largely powerless in the maelstrom of the state-making enthusiasm of a local plurality. The enormous Unionist effort merits Declan Kiberd's observation that 'no generation before or since lived with such conscious national intensity or such an inspired (and in some ways, intimidating) legacy',[2] though predictably, he is referring to the formulation of Irish nationalism alone, though his observation ought to be applied even more to Ulster identity. As Gerard Delanty and Patrick O'Mahony note, 'nationalism thrives in period of rapid and dislocating social change, especially the social challenge of accommodating new classes or class factors thrown up by such change and requiring a new model of social integration'.[3] The new entity, Northern Ireland, had just such a social function and raised problems attendant upon its caesarean birth. Thereafter both the British state and Ulster Unionists searched for the means to institutionalise the product of this dislocation.

George Dangerfield's, *The Strange Death of Liberal England*, published in the 1930s charges the Ulstermen, who threatened to take up arms against the lawful authority of Parliament, and British Conservatives with major responsibility for bringing about the downfall of Victorian liberalism.[4] His view has weathered its critics and remains implanted in the historical imagination. The essays in this volume test many of the cherished nostrums of the long crisis, examining aspects of prelude to the division of Ireland, the immediate threat of upheaval along with contemporary and later perspectives. Under the umbrella of the crisis they assess the economic position of Ulster; A.V. Dicey's insertion of moral authority underpinning the Unionist case; the Irish Volunteers; the role of the aristocracy in Ulster's resistance; the position of northern Catholics; the attitude of a significant figure who clung to his Ulster Protestant, Irish and British identity; William O'Brien's attempts to strike a *modus* vivendi; how symbolic occasions such as the centenary of the 1798 rising were treated; the provincial press in the south; responses of a major Dublin daily newspaper; the impact of the crisis on the Orange Order in northern England; the actions of the Ulster Volunteer Force; and the opening of the Northern Ireland Parliament in 1921. This constitutes a major, though not complete, agenda and the pieces individually and collectively, place incidents and their outcomes in differing lights, contributing fresh insights and, as in a number of essays, considering the crisis within theoretical paradigms.[5] The mechanics of the crisis receive less attention overall than does the evolution and symbolism of what Ireland or Ulster would constitute. Themes running through many contributors include emphasis on the forces dividing the contending parties from one another and differentiating both from their respective co-religionists in the South.

II

The idea of a Protestant British nation had distant roots and was enshrined in the Act of Union which, when it came into effect on 1 January 1801, proclaimed 'the two kingdoms were "for ever, be united into one kingdom"'. Ulster was part of this new United Kingdom political nation, one that was Protestant and where Protestants, unlike in a Ireland alone, were an overwhelming majority.[6] Much attention has been devoted to the Irish Catholic challenge to the dominant culture and political state; the formation of a Ulster Protestant identity and subsequently a 'Protestant Parliament for a Protestant people' has received much less sympathetic treatment. The literature is imbued with a presumption that nationalism is a natural, if not necessarily desirable factor in modern civilisation; counter-movements, in contrast, seen as a negation of the flow of history. And, yet, what actually emerged in Ulster was a sub-species of European ethno-regional nationalism; a counter-movement that came to resemble Irish nationalism in its fundamental characteristics. Jim Mac Laughlin comments perceptively on the similar pathways of the nationalism and Ulster Unionism.[7] And, as Frank Wright observes, 'the North of Ireland was becoming during the nineteenth century an ethnic frontier between the British and Irish nations. As the settlement colonial structure decayed the two communities become opposed national peoples in conflict for the same land'.[8]

If the Irish Church act in 1869 altered the position of the Protestant Church of Ireland, it did not tamper with the reality that Irish Protestants still were a majority in the whole United Kingdom.[9] Robert Lowe expressed the ambition of the Act 'as a matter of justice and conscience'.[10] While neither that Act nor the many further pieces of legislation forged 'true union' between Protestants and Catholics, paradoxically it did mark a beginning of a political rapprochement between the hitherto divided northern Protestants who previously had been split between a minority community subscribing to the Church of Ireland who shared in the privileges of Ascendancy and others, including Presbyterians, a local plurality, and members of Nonconformist sects. They now met on terms of legal equality, old hatchets, if not buried, were put aside, in the face of the mutual enemy, Catholic Nationalism. This came just in the nick of time for Protestants had to face the fast moving juggernaut of Irish Nationalism in later Victorian Ireland. Both sides began a reappraisal of the place of Protestants in Ireland, a battle that proved unequal in the mainly Catholic south but swung in their favour in the north-east of the island.

The land agitation of the Land War between 1879–81 attracted the limited adhesion of some northern Protestants, particularly tenant-farmers. Wright argues that northern Liberals were briefly able to put Pan-Protestantism, a way of looking at society and seeing everywhere threatening Catholic power "off the streets"'.[11] But this phase was short-lived, not least because co-operation between northern Liberalism and the Land League masked underlying divergences which became manifest when the main grievances were tackled by the Gladstone government in 1881 and 1882 and Nationalists moved on to their main agenda, demanding a separate Parliament for Ireland – all Ireland – with the subtext that this could be under the control of the Catholic majority. As Alvin Jackson explains, 'home rule was important because it united Irish and British statesmen; its politics reveal much about the thought and priorities of British leaders in the late nineteenth and early twentieth centuries'. Moreover, he points out 'the importance of home rule rests, too, in its continuing emotional hold over the Irish and British people'.[12] It unites, Jackson says, the story of Irish Catholics and Protestants, Nationalists and Unionists albeit in differing ways. If in the south the Protestant community was stretched, living with the endemic fear of being overrun by Catholic irredentism, in the north, many areas had Protestant pluralities which did not fear local Catholics but nevertheless dreaded the prospect of a popish-dominated government from Dublin. Extension of the ballot and redistribution of parliamentary constituencies in 1884–85 provided the framework for two territorial polities – Nationalist and Unionist – while the Home Rule bill in 1886 ensured the division was written in stone. An electorate expanded from 222,018 to 737,965 male voters coupled with the eradication of small borough constituencies reduced Protestant representation in the southern three provinces to a trickle.[13] Instead of democratisation placing all citizens on a plane of formal equality, it meant that ethnic antagonism become increasingly difficult to restrain.[14] As the basis of representation did not change until 1918, another anomaly in the representative system appeared. By 1910 in proportion to its population Ireland as a whole, but not in northern and eastern Ulster, was vastly over-represented, having at least 30 too many seats. Within the country this distortion gave the rural south and west enormous political importance while in contrast the Protestant north-east was short-changed. This had a double distorting effect. Rural Catholics had exaggerated numbers whereas Unionists were underrepresented. A dominant creed of exclusive Nationalism, hostile to Protestants generally, supplanted the more cosmopolitan inclusive variety promoted by the older Dublin-centred elite. Ulster Unionists responded with a similar polarised world-view. Second, the imbalance inflamed Conservative and Unionist resistance during the third home rule dispute. They believed that the 'parliamentary majority' that secured passage of Home Rule was 'artificial';[15] it was built on inflated Nationalist representation. Demographic and social trends present a paradox. On the one hand, the political manifestations of Nationalism became more rural oriented after the mid-1880s just as the Ireland became increasingly urban. In contrast, Unionist politics took on a more urban hue. Industrialists, notable for their absence in the Nationalist party, began to play a larger part in Unionist politics. In 1893 representatives of commerce and industry took a leading role in the anti-Home Rule campaign while throughout the years after 1886 the economic case against creation of a Dublin Parliament was at the forefront even if a clutch of Unionist politicians showed an awareness of small-farmer radicalism and some others of the trades unionists.[16]

In the immediate context the impact of franchise and redistribution legislation in 1884–85 exposed the limitations of Unionism. Charles Stewart Parnell's Nationalist phalanx captured 17 of Ulster's 33 parliamentary seats in 1885, claiming not just a majority for Home Rule in Ireland but also a narrow one in Ulster as well.[17] The Ulster in question was not the modern Northern Ireland, but the historic province Ulster, which contained three counties with heavy Catholic pluralities – Cavan, Donegal and Monaghan. The propaganda value of a Nationalist majority of Ulster seats was not forsaken; Gladstone, who had very limited sympathy for Ulster Protestants, insisted that Home Rule was endorsed by even a majority in Ulster. In any case Gladstone held that Unionists north and south were mistaken in failing to recognise their destiny as part of the Irish nation and in later years he 'reserved his special scorn for the anti-home rule Nonconformists of Ireland...' who manifestly rejected to see their own best interests.[18]

The Ulster question, though, played a minor part in the debates on the first Home Rule bill. In his speech introducing it on 8 April 1886 Gladstone stated 'I cannot allow it to be said that a Protestant minority in Ulster or elsewhere, is to rule the question at large for Ireland'.[19] Nevertheless, he said, 'but I think that the Protestant minority should have its wishes considered to the utmost practicable extent in any form which they may assume'. He called for an 'unprejudiced discussion of Ulster options'. The new Ulster party, chaired by Colonel Edward Saunderson, was divided about a specifically Ulster dimension. Saunderson declared against an Ulster solution: 'we are prepared and determined to stand and fall, for weal or woe, with every loyal man who lives in Ireland'.[20] The foremost advocate in the House of Commons of an Ulster solution was Joseph Chamberlain. In the aftermath of 1886 crisis northern Unionism quickly gained the initiative never again surrendering its advantage.

III

The present volume takes up the story of how the Ulster dimension of the home rule episode unfolded consequent upon Gladstone's attempt to create an all-Ireland parliament in Dublin. A corner-stone of the Ulster Unionist case was the probable impact of Home Rule on Ulster's economy, particularly on its industry, and the overall finance implications of the scheme[21] Whereas previous writings have focused on the practicalities of Home Rule, Graham Brownlow's fresh approach assesses the interplay of the northern economy and the home rule issue, highlighting how recent work in the field of institutional economics – in particular the research relating to the concept of *social capability* and the literature on globalisation during the period – can better illuminate the political economy of the Ulster crisis. His insight rather confutes Wright's assertion that 'economic determinants of ethnic antagonism had disappeared...' in Ulster 'the antagonism had a life of its own...'.[22] According to Brownlow Irish economic performance between the 1870s and the 1920s improved as a consequence of the existence of widespread (if unevenly distributed) social capability. Ulster Unionism was influenced by globalisation and it was not a coincidence that many of the most politically influential opponents of home rule were also successful businessmen. Yet, he maintains, ultimately, there was some dissonance in the two related visions of Constructive Imperialist thinking on Britain's world political and economic role and the Unionist view of Ulster's political and economic relationship to Britain. The Constructive Imperialists disliked the globalisation of labour and capital flows that characterised the period.[23] Yet for instance, Belfast's shipyards relied on these sustained factor flows for their very existence.

The literature on the Ulster Crisis is studded with studies of the political dimension. There has been less attention devoted to the ideology underpinning the dispute. Yes, Home Rule, George Boyce remarks, was one of those 'sharp transitions' that brought the state to the attention of those who were involved in the working of institutions. The result was a sustained and bitter conflict, but also one of the rare occasions when the state was made the centre of political debate, its effect on those subordinate to its institutions analysed, and recommendations for its radical reform put forward. This occasion also brought into focus another absentee from British political discourse since the seventeenth century: the Constitution, or the lack of what was generally understood in the United States and Europe as a constitution, that is a written document setting out the rights, powers, and inhibitions on the power of the state. And, finally, Home Rule raised in acute form the question of nationhood and the integrity of the nation. Between 1886 and 1921 A.V. Dicey, the leading constitutional authority of the day, argued the case against devolution. By so doing he raised wider issues, including the role of Parliament in British constitutional and political life, the national identities of the United Kingdom, and the question of how most effectively to manage the force of Irish nationalism. The threat of violence between 1912 and 1914 enforced upon Dicey the necessity of identifying the core of the Constitution, which he saw as the rule of law. As Boyce demonstrates elsewhere, the work of Dicey was crucial because it gave the Unionist cause a moral dimension, not simply a dependence on raw physical force.[24] This then stands Dangerfield's thesis on its head with an alternative view of the Ulster Crisis.

The Home Rule bills between 1886 and 1920 raised political issues of a most profound kind. These have rightly retained their place in the history of the attempts by Liberal governments to satisfy the demands of Irish Nationalists while retaining the sovereignty of the United Kingdom Parliament. Less attention has been paid to the constitutional implications for the British Constitution of the attempts to bestow devolved government on Ireland, and the impact of British constitutional change on Irish Home Rule. Yet a key argument against Home Rule was that the Liberal claim that the sovereignty of the British Parliament remained unimpaired was a chimera, Boyce observes. As Dicey put it 'the fullest legislative assembly meeting in Dublin would rightly claim to speak for the Irish people. A town council, whether of Birmingham or Belfast, springs from and is kept alive by the will of Parliament, and cannot pretend that its powers, however extensive, compete with the authority of its creator'.[25] Thus, for Dicey, the moral, if not legal, check upon Westminster over-ruling an Irish Parliament was a significant invasion of British sovereignty. Local self-government meant delegation of powers; Home Rule, however curtailed, implied the constitutional recognition of a nation.

In 1886 and 1893 the question of justice for the Protestant minority in Ireland was part, but by no means the main part, of the case against Home Rule. But it did tap into the English political tradition that emphasised the freedom of individuals under the law, and the absence of the kind of powerful state apparatus that could bear down heavily on citizens that, it was a widely held, characterised government on the continent of Europe. By 1913 Dicey pushed the argument for defending the Protestant minority still further, and placed more emphasis on Ulster Unionist resistance to the 1912 Home Rule bill. Ulster Unionists were protesting against a double injustice: that of being deprived of their rights as citizens of the United Kingdom; and the compulsion to obey a Parliament in Dublin to which they owed no allegiance. There may exist 'acts of oppression on the part of a democracy, no less than of a king, which justify resistance to the law, or, in other words, rebellion'.[26]

As Boyce comments, proposed reforms – the referendum, federalism – were all the product of the intense political conflict that gripped Great Britain and Ireland between 1886 and 1914, especially in the couple of years before the outbreak of the First World War. They survived that war, but in the event they found no place in the British Constitution until a much later date. Yet they did not die without a struggle. The federal idea re-surfaced in 1918–1920, with the British government accepting that any Home Rule bill for Ireland must be seen as a prelude to, and a preparation for, the making of a federal system. Citizenship, which Rodney Barker defines as 'taking part in the selection, critical scrutiny, and pressurising of representatives and rulers' was central to Unionist rhetoric between 1912 and 1914. Now the British people reverted to their more familiar role as subjects, becoming 'the object of governmental action…'.[27] Moreover the failure of the federal idea, the secession of 26 counties of Ireland and the distancing of the six counties in the devolved government of Northern Ireland reinforced the assumption that the 'British' were indeed, to use Dicey's phrase, 'morally a nation', their organic nature no longer disturbed by Irish Nationalism and the ultra-patriotic demands of Ulster Unionism. But at least the Home Rule and Ulster questions had thrown light on the character of the British Constitution, and helped provoke a debate about its changing nature.

However, the questions raised by Boyce also resonated in Irish Nationalist circles. The question of what constituted citizenship and nationhood is examined further by Matthew Kelly whose purpose is to explore Volunteering discourse, arguing that although seeking to emulate the celebrated eighteenth century Volunteers and the achievement of the Dungannon Convention of 1782, it represented a genuine new departure in Irish politics. The Volunteers of 1913–14 can be contrasted to their eighteenth century predecessors by the strategy and political mode of the Redmondites, and the Redmondites were found wanting. The ideal of an armed citizenry, established in perpetuity, and dedicated to the protection of established, or virtually established, rights and liberties, was contrasted with the apparently emasculated representative politics of Home Rule. Perhaps because of the over-whelming support shown to John Redmond following the Volunteer split, the ideological significance of the movement has not been recog-nised fully. But the meaning of the Volunteers cannot be fixed in the image of this revived civic republicanism; at best it was the nearest the movement had to an official doctrine, at worse it masked the range of incompatible political and ideological currents at work. But the Irish Volunteers were unique in radicalising the doctrines of the constitu-tionalist agenda while presuming to remain within its bounds. To insist on the permanence of the force and the determination to provide Ireland with an independent defensive capacity was incompatible with the claim that Home Rule would reconfigure the Union in a manner that would restore the legitimacy of Westminster, the Crown and its agencies as the ultimate source of authority in Ireland. Volunteering was a cathartic experience. Here was a generation of young men granted a suggestive taste of the potential of collective action. In this there is a parallel to Fenianism which 'appealed most strongly to sec-tions of the population that were ready for an organisation that would provide members with a sense of personal fulfilment through identify-ing with a group of their peers in autonomous social activities'.[28] Involvement in the Volunteers provided retrospective justification for Fenianism and the United Irishmen, living evidence of the spirit of comradeship and empowerment evoked in countless addresses and speeches. Volunteering was an act of re-appropriation, restoring politi-cal agency to the ordinary man and woman, liberating it from the suf-focating and narrow strictures of the increasingly distant Home Rule campaign at Westminster. This was the spirit of Fenianism, a brief moment when full expression was given to an Irish national identity suppressed by pragmatism and opportunism.

This, at least, was the experience promoted by the *Irish Volunteer* and *Irish Freedom*, Kelly observes. This discourse provided a framework within which the emotional experience of volunteering was under-stood, granting it a wider political significance and meaning. Super-ficially then, the 'Machiavellian moment' of the Ulster crisis confronted Unionist anarchy with Nationalist civic virtue; ideologically the situa-tion was much more complicated. Nationalists sought to protect the sovereignty of Westminster against Unionist insurrectionism, while at the same time threatening a similar insurrectionism if the executive did not mobilise the State against militant Unionism. As volunteering discourse became increasingly influenced by Fenian polemic the meaning of the crisis for Nationalists became clearer. They asked themselves, in the light of these events, what value could be attached to their vote. If any all-Ireland settlement achieved on the basis of British constitutional principles could be wrecked by Unionist militancy on what foundations was Redmondism ultimately based?

The issue about the contest for the leadership of Ulster Unionism between a traditional landed elite and the new industrialist magnates of the north-east is a significant sub-debate. Neil Fleming addresses the controversy of whether power was shifting to the new lords of wealth, exploring the position of the landed class and concludes that landlord decline and survival within Irish Unionism during the 'long Ulster Crisis' is best understood by examining how the power relationships and authority mechanisms of northern-eastern or 'Ulster' Unionism were affected by periods of crisis, particularly the Land War (1879–82) and, from 1885, the ongoing campaign for Home Rule. For most of Ireland, these crises heralded the end of landlord dominance and confirmed the counter-elite status of the Catholic bourgeoisie and clergy. In the northeast, however, they gave fresh impetus and purpose to the local landed class who, via an accommodation with the bourgeois elite of Belfast and environs, formed new power relationships and authority mechanisms for that region that were neither exclusively traditional or legal-rational, but a hybrid of the two. In time, the internal dynamics of northern Unionism would favour the legal-rational, but traditional authority continued to be a conspicuous presence in what became Northern Ireland. The structural, economic, and social changes of the late nineteenth century set the context for landlord decline across the United Kingdom. The character of that decline differed at a regional level, and in Ireland there was a significant difference between the fortunes of the landed elite of the northeast from that of the south. This confirms Samuel Clark's paradox of successful landed elites being closer to centres of industrial and commercial growth.[29] Faced with the influence of the Land League, landlords in the northeast moved to reinforce their economic and political position by strengthening their bonds with the Belfast bourgeoisie, forging alliances with populist Orangeism, and accommodating Liberal-Unionists. In doing so, they had to appease and manage the demands of these powerful interest groups, one of which, the question of representation at the leadership level, proved almost unstoppable by the turn-of-the-century.

The declining status of landlords, throughout the United Kingdom but particularly in Ireland, and their problematic and increasingly anachronistic leadership made this transition all the more likely. Already enervated by electoral obliteration in southern Ireland, and by continuing efforts at land reform, landlords were further weakened by their faltering attempts to referee the sectional interests that constituted Unionism in Ulster. If structural and cultural factors were making traditional authority increasingly obsolete, then it would take a major political crisis, similar to that in the early 1880s, to change the power relationships and authority mechanisms within Ulster Unionism. That crisis came in 1904 and led to the formation of the Ulster Unionist Council. This did not exclude the landlords, but it reduced their influence and placed the movement firmly in the hands of the bourgeoisie, men like James Craig and J.B. Lonsdale, both from wealthy business backgrounds who in due course would accept peerages The crisis of 1912–14 allowed Unionists of all ranks throughout the United Kingdom to champion Ulster Unionism, but when this support unravelled during the First World War, those landlord-politicians still in the movement were expected to place regional (six counties) Unionist priorities above all others. A significant portion of the landed elite proved able to do this, and their families supplied leading figures to the Ulster Unionist party until the early 1970s. As a political class they had therefore survived the key moments of change that marked the long Ulster crisis, albeit precariously, and with a considerably reduced amount of influence. There the old Ascendancy forged a fresh relevance inside Ulster Unionism but its social and economic leadership neither went unchallenged nor was identical to the earlier deference accorded to inherited status. An emergent and increasingly assertive sectarian democracy extracted a price. Contrary to their southern brethren northern Ascendancy leaders presided over a completed social structure and were able to retain their nominal position but only at the cost of bowing to the will of plebeian Protestantism. Traditional authority structures looked familiar, concealing fundamental changes beneath the surface. Thus, in both south and north old deference was under attack but the ammunition employed for the assaults differed. This, then, is a nuanced story, one of adaptation and survival.

Wright, among others, reflects on the situation of Protestants and Catholics in Ulster. He concludes that the inequality in wages was dissipating, asserting that 'the greater the equalising tendencies of economic life, the more visible was the intent displayed in preserving the differences that remained. Taking a long view, antagonistic intent become more manifest as substantial inequality declined'.[30] Wright, of course, is arguing against an economic interpretation of the Ulster crisis. However, the position was more complex. Tony Hepburn adopts a less pointedly Protestant versus Catholic model; instead he looks at the internal dynamics of Ulster Catholics, observing that the differences between Irish Nationalism in the north and in the south of Ireland were pervasive and ongoing during the period. Similar to their southern colleagues as they may have seemed, Irish Nationalists in most of Ulster had to live and work in a very different environment. Whereas in southern Ireland Catholics were an overwhelming majority, Ulster Catholics and Protestants coexisted in large numbers as the following table reveals. In Ulster the Protestant proportion of the population rose at the expense of Catholics.[31]

Even though all of Ireland in the late nineteenth century was only beginning to emerge from a world in which Protestantism, wealth and power were strongly correlated, the ways and the extent to which this change came about were determined by regional ethnic balances. In the south a combination of socio-economic and political change brought about the participation of large numbers of Catholics to a high level in business and public administration; in the private sector a large Catholic market encouraged the development of Catholic professional and retail services. In most of Ulster, on the other hand, economic and political

Table 1.1   *Ulster*

Year	RC	C of I	Presb	Method	others
1861	966,613 [50.5]	391,315 [20.4]	503,835 [26.3]	32,090 [1.7]	20,443 [1.1]
1871	897,230 [48.9]	393,268 [21.5]	477,729 [26.1]	29,903 [1.6]	35,098 [1.9]
1881	833,566 [47.8]	379,402 [21.8]	451,629 [25.9]	34,825 [2.0]	43,653 [2.5]
1891	744,859 [46.0]	362,791 [22.4]	426,245 [26.3]	40,528 [2.5]	45,391 [2.8]
1901	699,202 [44.18]	360,373 [22.77]	425,526 [26.88]	47,372 [2.99]	50,353 [3.18]
1911	690,816 [43.67]	366,773 [23.19]	421,410 [26.64]	48,816 [3.09]	33,881 [3.41]

change did not put anything like the same level of pressure on the dominant Protestant society to increase the involvement of Catholics, while
the smaller and poorer Catholic community provided a relatively limited
market for professional and retail services. There was thus a broadly-
based 'north–south divide' in Catholic Ireland, which by the end of the
nineteenth century had become crucially important. Within Catholic
Ulster there was also something of an 'east–west divide', between counties Antrim, Down, northern Armagh and eastern Londonderry on the
one hand, where Protestants were in a majority of more than 3:1, and
western and south-western Ulster, where Catholics were a small majority. The city of Belfast was especially important in shaping Ireland's
dichotomous ethnic demography.

As Hepburn notes, there were two possible routes for northern
Catholic advance. Either some kind of transformation would have to
taken place, causing the ethnic connotations of religious difference to
wither away so that Catholic-Protestant differences would lose their
salience in political and social life. In practice this would have meant the
integration of Ulster Catholics to the dominant culture of their region.
A large proportion of Ulster Catholics would have had to become 'West
Britons' or 'Castle Catholics'. Some individuals did, but the abusive implication of these terms indicates the ignominy that the wider Catholic
community heaped on them. In reality the only people who could
afford to pursue such a course were those whose social and economic
status enabled them to live outside the Catholic community, amongst
middle-class Protestants who were sufficiently confident of their own
affluence and status not to seek to exclude Catholics from their neighbourhoods in the way that routinely happened in working-class areas.
Even comfortably-off Catholics, if their business or profession depended
on wider Catholic custom, would have been ill-advised to turn their
backs on their compatriots in any public way. Unlike some regions
divided by language, where bilingualism on occasion offered the basis
for a middle ground, an ethnic identity defined by religion offered no
such potential. Miroslav Hroch points out that ethnic and the ensuing
national identities were mutually more sharply defined (and perhaps also
more conflicting) where religion rather than culture stood as the criterion'.[32] In practice both the increasingly 'Protestant' flavour of the
dominant regional culture and the defensive communalism of the majority of Ulster Catholics rendered the regional integration of Catholics
and Protestants within existing state structures impossible. The only
route for group economic and political advancement that appeared to
be open to Ulster Catholics was the link to Irish Nationalist politics, as

it evolved in the more favourable ethnic demography of southern Ireland. Thus the social, economic and educational structure of Ulster Catholics developed more slowly than was the case further south, but politically, Ulster Catholics tended increasingly to take their cue from their southern co-religionists. It was a trend that had its origins in Daniel O'Connell's time, but established itself slowly and unevenly.

The Ulster Catholic minority, Hepburn suggests, does not fit easily into the theoretical and comparative literature. Part of the problem is that, unlike the multi-ethnic states of continental Europe, the United Kingdom was a victorious power in 1919. Thus, instead of Ulster Protestants becoming a national minority within an Irish successor state, like the Germans in Czechoslovakia or Poland or the Hungarians in Romania, it was the Catholics who became a minority within the devolved state of Northern Ireland. In the terminology developed by Hroch they remained a reluctant minority within the 'state-nation' of the United Kingdom, wedded to irredentist aspirations for reunion with the 'mother-nation'.[33] In one sense Ulster Catholics were newly separated from their southern co-religionists in 1921, but at another level they already had some of the characteristics of a dispersed national minority existing within a territory controlled both economically and demographically by others. It is in fact helpful to analyse Ulster's Catholics, or at least the Catholics of Belfast and the industrial towns of east Ulster, as a quasi-diasporic minority, closer in circumstances, behaviour and outlook to the Catholic Irish of British, North American and Australasian cities than to the Irish of the mother-nation. It is no coincidence that Joe Devlin, the leading northern Nationalist leader, had a greater appeal to the Irish of the global diaspora than any of his contemporaries. These diaspora were of course predominantly urban and industrial, which constituted a further difference from the prevailing ethos of the mother-nation.

Most analysts agree that there is a close relationship between nationalism and the process of modernisation, i.e. the transition from a predominantly agrarian society to an urban and industrial capitalist community.[34] Often, and as strongly in the case of the Irish as of any other nationalist movement, this relationship was a negative one. Both the Catholic Church and the lay leadership of the Gaelic revival in Ireland rejected what they saw as the moral degradation of urbanism-in-dustrialism and the concomitant emigration from the Irish Catholic heartlands. Gaelic revivalists were themselves predominantly urban, but their anti-urbanism was essentially a middle-class revulsion against the city which was typical of the *fin-de-siécle* western world – viewed through an Irish Nationalist prism but in part at least a response to the same phenomena. The two most prominent – if very different – figures in Irish Nationalist politics seeking to apply *urban* solutions to urban problems were James Connolly and Devlin. The former delivered working-class Dublin to revolutionary Nationalism for a crucial but brief interlude which brought no benefit to his socialist successors, while the latter saw in Westminster parliamentary processes and in British labour politicians a practical if more pedestrian route to industrial and welfare reform than the idealistic visions of the Gaelic revival. Interestingly Devlin who, as National Secretary of the United Irish League (1905–20), did his best to continue the policy of running the land and the national questions in harness.

The social and economic policies of the Gaelic revival and later on, Sinn Féin, offered little to the industrial north. This reluctance to come to terms with realities outside of their idealised nexus of values is also apparent in the growing lack of interest in addressing the fact of the mixed society in the north. Both Jim Mac Laughlin and Patrick O'Mahony and Gerard Delanty argue that the Catholic Church grew stronger in public life partly as a result of its reassertion of moral authority during the Parnell Split and also because of the way in which the ideologies of Nationalism and Catholicism were bound increasingly together by the writings of D.P. Moran, Patrick Pearse and others. This increased authority might in fact be traced back a further generation to Cardinal Paul Cullen's re-organisation of the Catholic Church in the years after 1850. But it does seem to have been the case that the rise of a Gaelic cultural Nationalism that was relatively free of any clear social programme did not supplant Catholicism or clerical influence but in fact strengthened it. It provided massive cultural and political reinforcement for the Cullenite religious view 'of both the virtue and the desirability of an exclusively Catholic society'.[35] Thus, some years before 1914, the ideologies of both clerical Catholicism and lay Gaelic revivalism had become implicitly partitionist. On the one hand the 'island of Ireland' constituted the territory of the nation, but on the other hand there existed no ideological tools for relating the Protestant quarter of the population of Ireland to the Irish nation-building project. Among the chief victims of these developments were to be the Catholic minority of Ulster, Hepburn believes. The differences between Irish Nationalism in the north and in the south of Ireland were therefore pervasive and ongoing during the Home Rule and revolutionary periods. The years between 1906 and 1914, when Devlin was a successful Party secretary, running the United Irish League headquarters in

Dublin and injecting the Ancient Order of Hibernians with organisation and energy, is the closest that Ulster Nationalism came to an effective and integrated role in the national movement. During the winter of 1913–14 Devlin discovered the limitations on his own position and that of Catholic Ulster.

As Fleming suggests, during the first two decades of the twentieth century, Ulster Unionist underwent subtle but significant change. Brian Walker expands upon this development from the perspective of the political identity for many Unionists moving from an Irish to an Ulster self-identification. Political activity changed from purely parliamentary means to include non-constitutional action. Walker explores these changes through the career of J.B. Lonsdale. Lonsdale tackled local issues and patronage, improved party organisation and responded positively to constituency concerns. An issue strongly backed by Lonsdale was tariff reform (see Brownlow) which he believed would cause closer union of the empire and bring advantages to Ireland and Great Britain.

From Lonsdale's speeches it is clear, remarks Walker, that both Ireland and Ulster were important to him, in different but complementary ways. During the second reading of the Home Rule bill in May 1912, he made a rare reference to himself as 'an Ulsterman and the representative of an Ulster constituency for many years', in order to justify his claim to understand feelings there.[36] Three months earlier in the House of Commons, he had stated that there was not one nation in Ireland, but two, 'sharply divided in race, in religion, and in character'; this statement was made in response to an argument that the Irish nation was exclusively Nationalist.[37] He never again made this particular argument about two nations, although he elsewhere referred to two sections in Ireland – those sympathetic and those hostile to the empire.[38] He retained a strong all-Ireland perspective. He continued to refer to himself and his followers as Irish Unionists or Loyalists. Lonsdale saw Ireland as a partner in the United Kingdom and believed that the country benefited greatly from this link.[39] He continued to speak for both southern and northern Unionists. More importantly, Lonsdale was concerned with the fate of all of Ireland as vital for the defence of the Union and the integrity of the United Kingdom.

Lonsdale defended Unionist non-parliamentary activities in a number of ways. He insisted that Irish Unionists were men of peace who sought to uphold law and order, but because their 'rights and liberties' were now seriously in jeopardy and they faced political tyranny, they had a duty to offer 'stern and unyielding resistance' to the proposals.[40] Here his view bears comparison with Dicey's reflections considered by Boyce. At the end of Lonsdale's career, he gave backing to the new Northern Ireland Parliament, but this outcome had not been his goal. His overriding concern in politics had been the United Kingdom and the empire. At the same time it is clear that he retained a strong Irish perspective. He continued to speak for Irish Unionists and to argue for union for all of Ireland. For Lonsdale this Irish dimension arose largely because he regarded all of Ireland as an essential part of the United Kingdom and the empire. His case serves as a reminder of the Irish identity that persisted among many northern Unionists. While for most an Ulster identity became strong, a British dimension in the form of citizenship of the United Kingdom and membership of the empire, was also important. In the case of Lonsdale and others, British identity remained paramount, in spite of their regard for Ulster Unionism. After 1914 he began to see new ways of formulating this British identity. There were more references to the idea of a British or United Kingdom nation.[41] Some Unionists now called themselves 'Britishers' or 'British', while previously they said they were 'British subjects' or 'British citizens'.[42]

Walker's analysis of the indefinite notion of nationality and ethnicity among a section of the Protestant elite corresponds to Don Handleman's four levels of ethnicity – ethnic category (a loose level of incorporation, where there is a perceived cultural difference between the group and outsiders), an ethnic network (where there is regular interaction between the group; ethnic association (where members develop political organisations to express common goals), and an ethnic community (which possesses a permanent, physical or more appropriately in this case a mentally bounded territory, over and above its political organisations).[43] Many northern Unionists glided between these categories during and consequent upon the Ulster Crisis.

On the other side of the confessional divide, William O'Brien, affords an insight into the tensions and contradictions induced by the crisis. Sally Warwick-Haller observes that O'Brien was a committed Nationalist, but his Nationalism, unlike the vast majority of his fellow-Nationalists, was not founded on recognising a separate ethnic identity for Catholic Ireland. His Nationalism, transcending ethnic boundaries, had been inspired by Thomas Davis's vision of an Irish nation that brought together all classes and creeds. O'Brien's Nationalism emanated from a strong sense of place, that of the whole island – a single state, but one that must make significant concessions towards minority interests. Even though O'Brien had, since 1910, operated on the margins of Irish political life, and his political influence had been but a shadow of his role in the Land War, his efforts as a conciliationist over the 1911–14 crisis deserves acknowledgement. He had recognised the bitter sectarian feelings that were gathering force in North East Ulster. O'Brien's Nationalism cannot be categorised; it did not preach primordial or modernist theories, but he did lean towards modernism in that he argued that the Irish nation could be constructed and that a 'new' nationalism embracing all classes and creeds could be forged.[44] At the same time he recognised the ethnic identity of Unionists, but did not see this in terms of seeking to remain with Britain; he sincerely believed that most Unionists could be persuaded to feel more Irish than British as long as Unionist opposition could be forestalled and Protestant fears allayed before they were aroused. In this context Wright maintains, 'to break the pan-Protestant process was to take pre-emptive action that prevented the polarisation from occurring and opened up different horizons, instead of enforcing sectarian choices'.[45] O'Brien anticipated and tried to forestall this and the factors J. Milton Yinger cites as essential for the existence of 'full ethnicity'; self-identification; identification by others; and shared activities.[46]

In a more narrowly gauged but conceptually challenging essay, Marc Mulholland, assesses newspaper coverage of the 1898 commemoration of the rising of 1798. As he notes, newspapers have generally been thought of in two ways in media theory. Structuralists argue that the interests of a socio-economic elite delineate the bounds of acceptable news reporting and colours its tone. Protestations of neutrality or even subversive intent mask an acceptance of societal norms as interpreted by a hegemonic governing interest. A less top-down version of the same approach suggests that news media reflect and reinforce culture, rather than generating it. Historians of particular newspapers or other discrete media organs are more inclined to highlight the particular proclivities of individual journalists, or schools of journalism, or editors, or proprietors. There have been productive attempts to combine this genre, with news output being analysed as a product of tension between individual reporters, newspaper businesses, and the pressures of social environment. More recently, the idea of multiculturalism has focussed attention on the fracturing of homogenous national audiences in an era of globalisation. This, it is argued, has given rise to numerous media forms that address subaltern niche-markets. This latter perspective invites consideration of places and periods in which nation-states were yet in the process of formation. Ireland and particularly Ulster, in the run up to partition, might be considered analogous. Benedict Anderson, prominent amongst theorists of nationalism, has asserted the role of print culture in unifying audiences around a common language, set of cultural reference points and, often, a map image of the nation.[47] Ernest Gellner emphasises the generation of vertically bonded societies on the basis of homogenising markets.[48] Such processes are taken to have spontaneously spread national consciousness from an intellectual minority to, by the First World War, the mass of European populations. Recently Mac Laughlin has tested such theories in the context of Ireland. He argues that Irish Nationalist and Ulster Unionist traditions should be understood as rational expressions of regional interests rather than as merely irrational manifestations of social forces driven blindly by literacy, print culture and the market. In stressing regionalism in his explanation of the formation of identities, Mac Loughlin pays particular attention to the provincial press of Ulster. Mulholland, however, notes that the newspapers did not simply address regional audiences but also were aimed at class-based niche markets. While he takes on-board Mac Laughlin's point about Unionism and Nationalism being rational political interests in specific geographical settings, he points out significant variations of interest within these blocs. The uses made by the Ulster press of an event commonly acknowledged across of Ireland – the 1798 rebellion – but variously received by region, religion, political persuasion and class, sheds light on the reproduction of two polarised and antagonistic identities, Nationalist and Unionist that clashed in the 'Ulster crisis'.

Two further articles by Michael Wheatley and Patrick Maume examine the role of the press during the Ulster Crisis. Wheatley analyses 18 weekly newspapers, from the autumn of 1913 until the outbreak of war in August 1914, published in five politically-linked counties in the Irish midlands and East Connaught – Leitrim, Longford, Roscommon, Sligo and Westmeath. Such newspapers remained the most important forum for the dissemination of opinions among the intertwined commercial, professional and political elites of 'small town' Ireland. In the middle and west of Ireland, the Ulster crisis came to dominate local political life only from the autumn of 1913 – before that time, the paramilitary Ulster campaign against Home Rule was not seen as a looming and ever-growing physical threat, but primarily as a political and propaganda campaign, 'a bluff' to undermine British support for the Home Rule bill before it could pass.[49] For a long time, Nationalists' confidence in their ability to defeat Ulster's political challenge remained intact. Complacent apathy was a far more typical response to events than either wild enthusiasm or paranoia. It was only in the autumn of 1913, when Ulster's 'bluff' of England seemed suddenly to be working, undermining the resolve of Liberal politicians and making Ulster exclusion a serious prospect, that the crisis in provincial, Nationalist Ireland become a reality. When the Ulster crisis did break out in provincial Ireland, it transformed local politics. 'Parish pump' rivalries and considerations were subsumed into the pervasive, national issue of whether the Home Rule bill would fail. Large numbers of people, formerly quiescent, were mobilised into political and paramilitary activity through their participation in the Irish Volunteers. Whereas David Fitzpatrick maintains that 'the party vampire' was at 'its most incisive' when it took control of the Volunteers in mid-1914,[50] Wheatley finds that 'vampirisation' worked in reverse – it was the Irish party rather than the Volunteers who were losing blood. This was particularly apparent in the party's main local organisation, the United Irish League, whose historic stimulus to activity from land disputes and agitation had largely receded. The eve of the First World War, therefore, saw provincial Nationalist opinion almost totally absorbed in the Home Rule crisis, experiencing a mass political mobilisation, militarism and a bellicosity of language unseen in recent times.

For Maume the growth of the *Irish Independent* indicated the Irish party's waning ability to impose its dominance on Nationalist civil society, and the potential for a consumer-driven commercial press to displace more explicitly political party-related newspapers. This did not, however, mean that the *Independent* could advance an agenda of its own for outright opposition to the Irish party could trigger a damaging boycott by party loyalist readers and advertisers. The *Independent*, like most Nationalist papers, initially mocked the martial rhetoric of Ulster Unionists as a 'bogey'.[51] Resistance to partition was so central to the *Independent*'s editorial politics in the following years that it is important to consider why the issue provoked its owner, William Martin Murphy, so fiercely. Murphy's suspicion that the Irish party leaders were mediocrities, incapable of obtaining Home Rule or making it work if they got it, was not merely the product of personal bitterness at the defeat of Healyism and the Irish party's long-running suspicion of his influence; it reflected the long history of post-Parnellite factionalism and the mixed record of local government, not to mention Redmond's disastrous management of the Parnellite *Independent* in the 1890s was widely shared by middle-class Nationalist as well as Unionists.[52]

If the main thrust of the volume is on events in Ireland, its impact elsewhere should not be overlooked. The popular campaign against the Third Home Rule bill in the major northern British cities has escaped attention, write D.M. Jackson and Donald MacRaild. Such neglect relates to a perceived lack of importance attached to the issue of Ireland's constitutional status by 1912. Driven by what some have perceived as the 'Crisis of Conservatism' and others have dubbed the 'apathy of Great Britain',[53] it has become commonplace to infer from scanty evidence that, unlike in 1885–86, the populace of the larger island cared little for the political struggle that so exercised their counterparts in the 'sister isle'. Yet during the high water mark of constitutional opposition to a Dublin Parliament, the cause of Protestant Ulster actually mobilised hundreds of thousands of supporters outside of Ireland, particularly in the industrial areas of northern England. This may have been fired by the substantial Irish component of those places; a degree of turbulence may also have been a function of the staunch factionalism of urban politics. Whatever the cause, the politics crowds came out in force to denigrate the potential disintegration of the United Kingdom. The fact that there was no general election in this period ensured additional importance for this series of massive popular demonstrations against Home Rule.

Mark Harrison, who distils and re-assesses some of the most important recent thinking on the subject of crowds, convincingly argues that nineteenth century crowds were in point of fact rarely violent, and that their function lay in their role as 'vehicles for the expression of cohesion', and for participants to perceive themselves as 'bearers of messages' and to be accepted as such.[54] The work of David Cannadine also demonstrates the utility of applying techniques from other disciplines to the study of public ritual.[55] Through his concept of 'circularity' Cannadine provides perhaps the best definition of the importance of ritual in this period, albeit in a different context: 'it may well be that these spectacles were not just the expression of this sense of community: perhaps they were the community'.[56] Jackson and MacRaild apply this new methodology to the study of Edwardian anti-Home Rule demonstrations which may have spelled the only way that support for Ulster could be articulated. In such a context, the most effective means of making their case was by expressing the continued dominance of their own urban territory, by taking to the streets. For, as one historian of the Orange Order has argued, 'claiming physical space entailed also claiming political and ideological space'.[57] It was the combined decorum and quietude of these demonstrations that makes the crucial point. These peaceful yet grimly determined protests denote the importance attached to the struggle against Home Rule. The meetings in Liverpool and Wallsend were a manifestation of popular inclusive politics; they were not last-gasp meetings of desperate, marginal men and women. Though the politics of Unionism was unpalatable to many, it had certainly involved people in the political process on a scale not seen since the great radical demonstrations of earlier times. This was an issue bigger than party politics: people were genuinely concerned about the disintegration of the Union and what they perceived to be the encroachment of the Catholic Church into British affairs. In this last respect, the Unionist crowds of the 1910s sounded faint echoes of the enormous meetings that had been held to protest against the re-establishment of the Catholic hierarchy in 1851, but which, despite their size and fervour had engendered relatively little open violence. Similarly, despite the passions aroused by Carson's sojourns away from Ulster there were negligible instances of violent behaviour. This is unsurprising in many respects, for one historian notes that the worst instances of sectarian violence 'occurred when the Irish question was in abeyance'.[58] And although one author stresses that the widely held belief in the orderliness of Victorian society is a 'gross misconception' he is quick to acknowledge that even when rioting, nineteenth-century Britons abstained from serious violence, and remained almost instinctively decorous.[59] This was certainly still true in 1912.

As Jackson and MacRaild point out, the organisers of these events also updated the traditions of carnival by utilising modern technological advances, for instance, the heightened drama created by the use of 'arc-lights' at both events. The Newcastle demonstration updated the ancient tradition of cavalcade by deploying motorcars by the score. This ability to choreograph was the particular skill of the Unionist party in this period, as they proved that they had the capacity not only to address their supporters' concerns over Ireland, but also to offer them the visceral thrill of participation in parades and ceremonies. Indeed, in many ways this emotive, visual, quality is the most important point, as being before the days of amplifiers, not many in these great audiences would have heard what was being said. Thus to ask whether F.E. Smith's claim that 10,000 armed Liverpool men really would sail to Belfast to fight, was endorsed by his audience, or whether the good people of Wallsend really were 'breathless[ly] interest[ed]' in what the Conservative party leader, Andrew Bonar Law, had to say would be missing the point. In this sense it is far more likely that the demonstrators were transported to such rapturous appreciation by a combination of a sense of tribal affirmation, religious fervour, and theatrical histrionics.

Women, too, played an important role in all of these demonstrations. This is interesting considering the contemporaneity of the Suffragette movement, for these female enthusiasts espoused a cause that was at best ambivalent, but usually hostile, towards the political rights of women. The number of female Orange lodges in Liverpool grew enormously before the First World War, from three in 1881 to 43 in 1915. And this was mirrored by the growth of the Liverpool Women's Unionist Federation, who were important enough for a prominent member of the Ulster Unionist Women's Council to come to Merseyside earlier in 1912 to address a large meeting of these same ladies, at which it was noticed, by the Liverpool press, that the applause was most vociferous.

These demonstrations, Jackson and MacRaild suggest provide evidence of the health of a polity in which concepts of community and sectarian allegiance were still paramount: a political culture that many had assumed to be moribund by the end of the Edwardian period. Some would argue that religion, and even locality, as a political determinant was dying before 1914, and that the only residue of that culture was confined to Liverpool. However, even on Tyneside, a Liberal bastion which escaped the worst excesses of sectarianism, provided the location for probably the biggest *indoor* anti-Home Rule meeting ever held, certainly the largest Bonar Law ever addressed. So to put it baldly, therefore, it is obvious that Home Rule *did* have resonance outside Ulster, because an English city could get more supporters out onto the streets than even Belfast itself. Sometimes, moreover, political rituals could speak louder than political oratory. Even if those marchers had not thought too deeply about the larger significance of their actions, or had not cared that much, the symbolism of parades, music, and flags would have provided psychological satisfaction for those serried ranks of Unionists, without which the rhetoric of the platform would have added to relatively little in terms of popular appeal. But this in turn would have fortified those very same people who felt such obvious discomfort over recent plans for the future of Ireland: for crowd activity such as this can act 'as a means of preserving communal identity or re-casting it in the face of external pressure and underlying social change'.[60] Between 1912 and 1914 people were being asked how much the Union of the three kingdoms meant to them – a question that was rarely considered openly. Common opposition to anything is often the most potent method of achieving solidarity. And, as Emile Durkheim's integrationist approach has it, the 'conscience collective' was often a product of crowd assembly 'where the individuals, being closely united to one another, reaffirm in common their common sentiments; hence some ceremonies such as those afforded the Ulster leaders do not differ from regular religious ceremonies, either in their object, the results which they produce, or the processes employed to attain those results'.[61]

Notwithstanding the Protestant overtones of Orange bands and battle hymns, it is essential to look beyond that orthodox religiosity to employ the term 'religious' in a broader Durkheimian sense (which he took to mean anything considered *sacred*). Jackson and MacRaild ask, what was more sacred to those saturated stalwarts on the Pier Head, or the torch-bearers in Wallsend than the Act of Union?

A key element in the Ulster Crisis between 1912 and 1914 is the role of the Ulster Volunteer Force. Whether the threat to take up arms was real if Home Rule were imposed remains a perennial debate. One leading Liberal complained in June 1914, 'The whole present trouble of course is largely due to the fact that the Ulstermen have sufficient arms and ammunition to make themselves unpleasant'.[62] He believed, 'the Ulster Volunteer Force, if armed today only with sticks and dummy rifles, would be a factor in the situation leading to a reasonable instead of an unreasonable settlement'. Timothy Bowman takes a new look at this organisation, assessing its leadership, membership and regionalism. Whereas, previous historians have tended to view the UVF as little more than a party militia, which was under the authority of the Ulster Unionist political leadership Bowman suggests that ascertaining the re-lationship between the UVF and Ulster Unionist party is rather complex. While Paul Bew states that Carson raised the UVF to prevent disgruntled Unionists resorting to rioting, Bowman observes there is slender evidence to support this hypothesis.[63] In reality the UVF was a bottom up rather than top down force in many areas.

Overall the UVF in this period was more popular and, indeed, more democratic in its organisation than some historians have allowed, Bowman points out. Indeed, in many areas it appears that it was retired 'other ranks' rather than the landed gentry who were the drivers behind much paramilitary activity. The UVF was strongly influenced by re-gional factors, with the initial impetus for its formation coming in areas of Ulster where Unionists were in a slight majority of the population. Reaching its highest membership, of around 100,000 men in late 1913 the UVF appears to have gone into a rapid decline with the outbreak of the First World War and its attempted re-formation in 1920 was marred with recruiting difficulties though the formation of the Ulster Special Constabulary clearly involved former UVF personnel.

Fittingly, the volume concludes with the visit to Belfast in June 1921 by King George V and Queen Mary to inaugurate the Northern Irish Parliament. Gill McIntosh examines the episode. As Elizabeth Hammerton and Cannadine maintain, she writes, 'the planning, staging and celebration of a ritual is not just a means by which people explain society to themselves: it is also, of itself, an expression, a product, of tensions and conflicts, links and shared assumptions of that society'.[64] In the twentieth century royal visits to Northern Ireland have followed clear symbolic strategies. However, as was evident from the public response to the 1921 visit there are no such easy conclusions. One could generalise that northern Nationalists associated the monarchy with the British state, and resented their visits on the basis that they underlined Northern Ireland's separation from the rest of Ireland, and emphasised the link to Britain through the Crown. Unionists on the other hand found security in the visits of monarchy to the State, and reassurance from the presence of royals, seeing them as a symbol of unity and stability. Of course there was no such simple opposition, and all sections of the community found the pageantry and ritual associated with royal visits, with the novelty and excitement they generated, entertaining, particularly at times of social austerity and political stress.

Amidst the strict security the policing of this royal visit symbolised in a broader way the changes in Northern Ireland and the attitude of those who governed the new state. The response of the Belfast press to the royal visit split along predictable political lines. More significantly, with the symbolic inauguration of the Northern Ireland Parliament in 1921 by the King the embryonic state's position within the empire was made tangible in a high profile way to both a domestic and foreign audience. This was of course aided by the press, which conjured up interest and excitement about the event in the public sphere, and gave the population at large (in particular the Protestant population) a sense of involvement. Additionally, focus on Ulster's part in the First World War, throughout the visit and in the press, allowed Unionists to claim their position in the empire in terms of sacrifice. Ostensibly the visit may have been Lloyd George's way of providing his government with another option in terms of Irish policy, but for Craig and his constituency it was the symbolic endorsement of the new state and its government. In a high profile way, with northern Catholic and Nationalist elites absenting themselves from the proceedings, it underlined the separation of the north from the south, and internally the distance between the Catholic and Protestant communities. This royal ritual united Unionists in a display of strength, while at the same time betraying their continuing defensiveness in the face of serious civil unrest within and without the state.

IV

Neither the evolution of self-government in both parts of Ireland nor the Irish problem ended in December 1921. The Union between Great Britain and Ireland was dissolved partly, not completely, for the larger part of Ireland. As in other end games, the conclusion was not tidy; it was not truly satisfactory for any of the participants. But, the Ulster problem as an integral feature of British political culture was over, the experiment of an all-British Isles united state at an inglorious end. When Ulster reared its head in British politics thereafter it did so under different conditions, never becoming so central or the stuff of party warfare again. Irish difficulties no longer galvanised ideological concerns; its symbolic status was a relic of the past. There were important new challenges posed by Ulster difficulties both within the two Irelands and for Great Britain but they were genuinely different in kind. O'Mahony and Delanty point out in such situations there is a conflict between cultural ideas of the nation and rights of citizenship and, also explain that, 'national identity is located in the space between collective cultural identity of the nation's people – what they consider themselves to be and desire to become – and the political identity that transfers the substance of national identity into values that underpin political activity'.[65] It is worth recalling without necessarily an endorsement, Wright's observation that this was a crisis emanating from a 'one-time settlement colonial structure which had decayed'.[66] What emerged was a national conflict and 'in national conflict there is in the end no agreement about contexts'.

2

The Political Economy of the Ulster Crisis: Historiography, Social Capability and Globalisation

Graham Brownlow

> The modern case for the Union rests mainly on the abnormality of Ireland, and that is precisely why it is such a formidable case to meet. For Ireland in many ways is painfully abnormal. The most cursory study of her institutions and social, economic and political life demonstrate that fact.[1]
>
> Ulstermen ask, what is industrial prosperity without freedom?[2]
>
> Above all, Unionism was accepted by those who conceived their prosperity as being linked to the British economy.[3]

1. Introduction: Challenges to constructing a political economy of the Ulster crisis

Arguably the major analytical challenge to the scholar examining the role of economic factors in the context of the Ulster crisis is a methodological one shared with economic historians of other topics. The foremost challenge in applying economics to the past lies in selecting the economic tools that are most relevant to the historical issue under consideration.[4] In terms of the Home Rule crisis, A.T.Q. Stewart's measured evaluation of Unionist thinking on the relative roles of economic, religious and political factors and has much to commend it as he highlights the ideological ferment of the period:

> At the time of the Home Rule controversy, religious passion in Ireland still burned with a white-hot intensity…It is doubtful if the Ulster Protestant

had much desire to persecute his neighbour because of the way he wor-
shipped, but he certainly had an excessive fear of being persecuted by him,
or, to be more accurate, by his church. He did not fear his fellow
Ulsterman, but the powerful and world-wide organisation behind him.
Much of this suspicion arose from ignorance, for ordinary people had wildly
exaggerated ideas of papal influence in Ireland, and thought of the Pope as a
personal and inveterate enemy, who spent all his time scheming to get his
hands on the Belfast shipyards...in a changing world Ulster required that the
guarantees of its commercial interests should remain unchanged. Nevertheless, religion was the dynamic in Ulster, and not merely a cloak for other
motives: historians have sometimes underestimated it, but politicians never.[5]

The 'white hot intensity' associated with the Home Rule debates
intensified religious polarisation and social division in Ireland. The militancy of one group raised the intransigence of the other.[6] Consequently what has become known as 'the Ulster Crisis' (1912–14) was
ultimately a conflict between competing 'visions' of Ireland's constitutional, and hence its institutional, future. These competing perspectives
gave rise to an ideological 'tug of war' between those attempting to use
the political process to support institutional reform (the Nationalist-
reformists) and those (Unionist-conservative groups) using it to defend
the *status quo*.[7] Philip Ollerenshaw has noted the role of business
interests in the in the debates on Irish independence:

> As the third Home Rule Bill proceeded successfully through Westminster
> just before the First World War it had become clear that the business com-
> munity in the north-east would use its wealth to support a campaign to
> maintain the union or, failing that, to defy any attempt to force this region
> into an independent Ireland. In this sense, industrialisation helped to pave
> the way for the partition of Ireland and the creation of a Northern Ireland
> state in 1921.[8]

Yet despite the economic element, the political and institutional
nature of the Home Rule debate has also made it difficult for cliometri-
cians, a term which covers economic historians that utilise economet-
rics and neo-classical price theory, to apply their normal range of tools
to historical issues for which until recently no economic data or theory
has existed.[9] There is by way of illustration, no entry in the index under
'Home Rule' in Cormac Ó Gráda, *Ireland a New Economic History:
1780–1939*.[10] Economic historians of Ireland have instead focused their
attention on other topics concerned with post-famine economic
adjustment that are easier to analyse via econometric techniques.
Ó Gráda has recognised the importance of issues connecting polity to

the economy, but he noted the difficulty in empirically measuring many of the most important economic consequences of sectarian politics. These economic effects included the impact of selective emigration and the higher transaction costs due to mutual distrust. He added that such an enterprise had to be left to some future research agenda.[11]

This study does not pretend to provide the culmination of such a research agenda, it merely aims to highlight how recent work in the field of institutional economics (in particular the research relating to the concept of *social capability*) and the literature on globalisation during the period can better illuminate the political economy of the Ulster crisis. In section two the concept of social capability is briefly outlined. In section three contemporary views of Irish political economy made by political and academic commentators are surveyed. In contrast, to the opinions of later political and social historians, as summarised in section four, it is suggested that the economic aspect of the Home Rule debates were well understood. Section five surveys the modern academic literature on Irish economic performance between the 1870s and the 1920s, it is suggested that the existence of widespread (if unevenly distributed) social capability raised Irish economic performance. In section six evidence from the banking sector is used to support this assessment of Irish social capability. Section seven considers how Ulster Unionism was influenced by globalisation and section eight offers some conclusions.

2. Social capability as a concept in political economy

The term 'social capability' was first used in relation to Japanese economic development, but it has become widely used in the contemporary literature on economic development.[12] Social capability has been defined as 'those attributes, qualities, and characteristics of people and economic organisation that originates in social and political institutions and that influence the responses of people to economic opportunity'.[13] The basic insight is that a country with lower productivity can exploit the technological gap with respect to the leader, as best practice technology can be imported or imitated and, hence living standards can be raised in the productivity laggard. Economic leaders cannot benefit from this process; a technological leader's productivity increases are necessarily limited to applying new (domestic) technology to production. The more relatively backward a country is, the greater the technological gap will be, and hence the faster is the potential ability to attain convergence: the concept of social capability nevertheless recognises that this potential may not be fulfilled. Social capability is the capacity that relatively backward economies have towards actually converging on richer economies.

In the short run, social capabilities can hinder the ability to exploit the opportunities afforded by best practice technology. Yet over the longer-term, social capabilities associated with technical change adjust to render them more complementary to the prevailing technical trajectories. For instance, educational curricula and training modify, new methods of business management replace traditional forms and legal codes such as company law change. In the even longer-term, experience in using new technical and organisational forms increases the technical and managerial competencies that serve it. Factors such as improvements in education, business administration and capital markets all tend to promote the functioning of a market-orientated economy. These kinds of 'positive feedbacks' support further cumulative advances along the same growth path as social capability promotes development and development promotes social capability.[14] In other words, there are often substantial obstacles for getting 'take-off' into sustained economic growth, because initially inadequate levels of social capability may frustrate the pursuit of economic growth. Yet after a while if the level of social capability is adequate to initiate a 'take-off', then the trend growth rate can become firmly embedded in an economy's technological path.

Conversely, while a nation's stock of technology is relatively flexible and adaptable, its cultural attitudes, social norms, organisational structures and institutional rules are not so adaptable. This lack of 'plasticity' suggests that institutional change is much slower than technical progress. In extreme cases the lack of plasticity can actually block an otherwise technologically progressive society.[15] A country's potential for sustained economic growth is accordingly strongest when it is technically backward but socially advanced.[16] Technological backwardness provides the potential for achieving catch up growth based on the introduction of best practice technology, while social advancement promotes innovation and experimentation. It is assumed that as economic growth leads to structural changes, so there is a potential for political and social discontent. An effective and stable government is required that softens resistance to economic change and correspondingly promotes social capability. In this framework, political independence can only be said to promote social capability if it is associated with the appropriate levels of governmental strength and stability.[17]

3. Contemporary Nationalist, Unionist and academic views on the institutional economics of the Union

Contemporary propagandists and politicians utilised the rhetoric of economic logic in debates on the costs and benefits of Home Rule. Yet it seems safe to claim that many political actors on both sides had already established their positions on the Home Rule issue and only then considered the (often tenuous) economic arguments that would lend weight to their political beliefs. During the period, this tendency was especially strong among Nationalists; this finding echoes Kennedy's interpretation of the triumph of political over commercial values in earlier Nationalist economic thought.[18] In contrast academic economists largely stood aside from the debate on Ireland's constitutional future. Rather than being due to political agnosticism, this silence instead reflected the desire of most Irish economists to transform the traditional politically-loaded 'political economy' debated in Ireland into a formalistic and apolitical 'economic science'.

Nationalist writers either suggested that institutional reforms and policy measures made possible by Home Rule would stimulate Irish economic development or alternatively they argued that the economic costs associated with Home Rule could be understood as a necessary price of gaining what Erskine Childers termed 'moral independence'.[19] Rather inconsistently, Childers also suggested that the Union had damaged Irish economic development.[20] Table 2.1 shows that nominal public expenditure on Ireland doubled between 1893/4 and 1911. In 1907/8 there was a balance of £1,911,000 available for Imperial Services, while local expenditure exceeded 'true' revenue levels in 1910/11 by £1,312,500. The principal cause of the growth in public expenditure was the Old Age Pensions Act of 1908.[21]

Between 1896 and 1911, as the value of government intervention in the British economy began its ascent, so it became clear that breaking the financial connection with Great Britain would have considerable economic costs attached.[22] Childers considering the need to reconcile financial balance with political independence saw short-term economic sacrifice as an inevitable feature of political independence:

> If there were no alternative between financial independence without a farthing of temporary aid, and permanent financial dependence without a permanent loss of liberty, it would pay Ireland a thousand fold in the future to choose the former, remodel taxation promptly to meet the initial deficit, and with equal promptitude set on foot such a drastic reduction of expenditure as would ensure the rapid attainment of a proper financial equilibrium.

Table 2.1   *Comparative public finances of Britain and Ireland*

	Ireland 1893/4	Great Britain 1893/4	Ireland 1910/11	Great Britain 1910/11
Population	4,638,000	33,468,000 (estimated)	4,381,951	40,834,790
'Collected' Revenue (including non tax revenue)	£9.65m	£88.72m	£11.70m	£156.57m
'True' revenue (including non-tax revenue)	£7.56m	£89.28m	£10m	£155.14m
Local Expenditure	£5.60m	£30.62m	£11.34m	£60.54m
Contribution to Imperial Services	£1.97m	£58.69m	Nil	£94.59m

Source: Based on E. Childers, *The Framework of Home Rule* (London Edward Arnold, 1911), p. 260.

When once the Irish realized the issue, they would accept the responsibility with all its attendant sacrifices, which would no doubt be severe.[23]

Yet the 'attendant sacrifices' he associated with accepting political independence would have been too severe for the island as a whole, even in the short-term. Any rapidly attained 'proper financial equilibrium' would have necessarily involved reduced public expenditure.[24] Childers did however make an exception for the case of education, he argued much more had to be spent in that area.[25] This feature of Childer's economic thinking can be viewed as a strategy to raise Irish social capability. However, Childers ignored the observation that a reduction in public spending associated with Home Rule would have left Ulster Protestants losing both their national identity and living standards into the bargain. It would be inaccurate to describe such a potentially serious situation as any kind of equilibrium. In modern terms, Childers was prepared to support independence even if it damaged Ireland's overall social capability.

The volume by the 'Irish Essays Committee' entitled *Against Home Rule* (1912) is also of direct relevance.[26] The book is worthy of note not just for the range of its religious, political, military and constitutional objections to Home Rule but also for its identification of a specifically Unionist analysis of institutional and economic relationships within the British Isles. The possible net economic costs of constitutional change figure in a range of essays.[27] As Arthur Balfour noted, Unionists saw social and economic factors outside of the control of political leaders as the prime barrier to Ireland's economic development.[28]

For contemporary historians of economic thought the precise institutional-economic arguments advanced in *Against Home Rule* are notable for three main reasons. First, they are far from supportive of unfettered *laissez faire*. The writers repeatedly recognised that market forces alone would not bring either economic diversification or development to Ireland. This rejection of an extreme pro-capitalist position was in line with wider intellectual and political trends. Second, the essays were wide ranging in their focus, involving discussions of the economics of rural, industrial and regional development, transport, social welfare and public finance. Third, the essays are technically sophisticated for the period. In fact, with the Unionist focus on the technical and institutional advances supposedly associated with the Union, they could be viewed as forerunners of social capability type arguments.

In *Against Home Rule* the important issue of income convergence was discussed. The writers in the book suggested that Ireland as a whole by 1912 was converging on Britain's income per head because of increased efficiency within Irish agriculture. Yet the writers also considered that this convergence was delicate and conditional in nature, and required further fiscal transfers in order to be sustained.[29] Evidence presented in section five may nevertheless bring into question their assumptions on agricultural development. There are undoubtedly echoes of Joseph Chamberlain's 'municipal socialism' in the interventionist leanings of the essays. For instance, the emergent British welfare state was highlighted as offering a major financial advantage to Ireland.[30] Redistributive schemes such as the Congested Districts Board, Land Purchase Scheme, cheap labourers' cottages and old age pensions were viewed as tangible benefits of the Union.[31] Sir Edward Carson, responding to the kind of argument made by Childers, suggested that Home Rule would lead to these income guarantees being removed and thereby prevent the amelioration of Irish poverty.[32] L.S. Amery further argued that industrial expansion in an independent Ireland could only offset the loss of scale economies, which he suggested were inherent in separating from Britain, by following relatively lax standards in the area of worker health and safety: 'There will thus not only be an inevitable falling back for want of means, but, in addition, a continual temptation to the weaker and more backward state to meet superior industrial efficiency by the temporary cheapness of inferior social conditions'.[33] In modern parlance, Unionists claimed that Irish workers after the introduction of Home Rule would bear the brunt of 'social dumping'. This line of argument anticipates modern concerns with ensuring the harmonisation of working conditions in situations of trade and economic integration.

Unionist economic objections to constitutional change were also efficiency-based. For instance, it was predicted that the removal of rail subsidies, implicit in the pursuit of Irish independence, would mean that Irish railways would lose an important source of investment finance.[34] Recent research, to be discussed later, suggests that indeed fears over the possible adverse effects of Home Rule on the profitability of railway investments, did damage the value of holdings of Irish rail shares. Furthermore, without additional investments in the railway system, it was predicted that tourism would not be developed in a way that would promote diversification. Similarly, it was suggested that agricultural producers would find it more difficult to increase their export levels without the existing British subsidies.[35] It was additionally claimed that further moves towards Home Rule would depress industrial production in Ulster by promoting industrial unrest and the emigration of skilled workers.[36]

Of perhaps most relevance to contemporary work in economic history, the depreciation of leading Irish stocks of between 15 and 20 per cent was attributed to the uncertainty associated with Ulster's constitutional future.[37] By linking the existence of political uncertainty to reduced investment levels these arguments anticipate H.J. Voth's econometric findings for the effects of political uncertainty on industrial activity in inter-war Europe.[38] Moreover, C.R. Hickson and J.D. Turner's recent quantitative paper on the performance of the Irish stock market between 1865 and 1913 finds that political uncertainty indeed affected the performance of the stock market.[39] Hickson and Turner constructed an index of stock prices to examine the trends in the economy, they state that:

> [F]rom 1865 up to until the end of the 1890s market capitalisation doubled and our stock market indices rose over 50 per cent. Thereafter, the market declined steadily until the end of our sample period, with market capitalisation falling by over 30 per cent and the indices falling by over 40 per cent. The decline is the more curious as it cannot be explained by macroeconomic conditions', nor does it mirror the performance of the overall British market. We argue that the decline in the market may be attributable to revised expectations as to the future earnings streams of companies, arising from the growing threat of populist and anti-big-business nationalism. It is suggested that the downwards decline [sic] in the stock market was sparked by the passage of the Local Government Act in 1898. Despite its limited

taxing and regulatory empowerment, we suggest that this act may have signalled to investors the inevitability of a future redistributive populist national regime.[40]

Unionist fears over the effects of Home Rule on rail development were justified. Hickson and Turner demonstrate that in the 1880s railway securities constituted between 50 and 60 per cent of total equities held.[41] Moreover they show that the fall in market capitalisation, which they date after 1898, was most dramatic for firms having appropriable and non-fungible assets such as rail and canals.[42] While the emphasis that Hickson and Turner place on the 1898 Act may be questioned, the broad thrust of their empirical work is convincing: Hickson and Turner have provided a tangible link between political and economic developments in Ireland in the decades leading up to the Ulster crisis.

One can go beyond their economic conclusions and consider some wider political economy implications. Insofar as Nationalist agitation tended to depress stock prices, by threatening the holdings of assets such as railway securities, it tended also to reduce the available resources on which a substantial segment of investment in Ireland was based. Hence Hickson and Turner's findings imply that any weaknesses in Irish economic performance that Nationalist writers identified were, at the very least, as much the consequence of their own political agitation as any industrial backwardness due to the Union.

In spite of scepticism about the quality of some of the economic arguments presented in *Against Home Rule*, it could for instance be suggested that economic concepts were merely used by Unionists to cloak objections based on religious and ethnic identity in more acceptable 'scientific' garb, it nevertheless is notable that arguments based on economic considerations were made at all. In contrast, apolitical academic 'economics' made little running in public debates on the issue of Irish independence. Mary Daly's official history of the Statistical and Social Inquiry Society of Ireland is useful in indicating how contemporary academic economists responded to the political convulsions of the period.[43] The experience of the dismal scientists is thus a useful contrast to the notable response by overtly Unionist and Nationalist commentators. Daly repeatedly notes the liberal and scientific objectives of the Society which ensured that it pursued only objectively scientific policy conclusions.[44] Yet in the face of the Home Rule debates in the 1880s the liberal consensus on which the Society had been run was damaged by the political divisions associated with the constitutional issue.[45]

The legacy of this breach was that the Society between the 1880s and the 1910s became Dublin centred and committed to theoretical (and hence apolitical) economics rather than the more contentious policy issues associated with political economy.[46] By 1913 no MPs or members of Dublin corporation were listed as members, and nor did any member give a Belfast address.[47] Daly suggests that the dominance of Dublin in membership accounted for the lack of interest in Ulster, though she does not attempt to explain why Ulster's businessmen, policy makers and academics did not find it worthwhile becoming a member of the Society.[48]

4. The treatment of political economy in subsequent academic writings

Stewart's influential *The Ulster Crisis*, in contrast to the arguments in *Against Home Rule*, did not provide a clear explicit account of the Unionist economic objections to Home Rule.[49] By way of illustration, Stewart did not develop the observation that senior figures in the Belfast shipyards had differing opinions on Ulster's political destiny. While Lord Pirrie, director of Harland and Wolff was involved in the pro-Home Rule Ulster Liberal Association, his business rival Sir George Clark, a partner in Workman and Clark, was heavily involved in the Ulster Volunteer Force's [UVF] import of arms.[50] Clark was head of the Ulster Provisional Government's 'business committee', which was responsible for arms importation; he was also a substantial donor to the UVF's indemnity guarantee fund, guaranteeing £10,000 to compensate members and their dependants for active service.[51] Moreover, he was also a member of the Ulster Unionist Council.

The economic aspect, when it has featured at all in the work of political or social historians, has been confined to the details of financial provisions of the various Home Rule bills or to the margins of the main discussion. J.J. Lees explicitly nationalistic account of the campaign against self-government very much sidelines the economic aspect.[52] Lee's emphasis on a supposed Unionist obsession with racial superiority, an attendant 'siege mentality' and 'sacred egoism' unfortunately distorts his discussion of Unionist actions during the period.[53] In an otherwise critical assessment of nationalistic economic thinking, Lee strangely avoids any extended account of Unionist economic thought.[54] His observation that 'Home Rule is Rome Rule' was a slogan that grabbed public attention in a way that other issues in political economy could not is incontestable, Stewart had made the same point earlier; Lee was however simply incorrect when inferring that economics was not a topic that Unionists had considered.[55]

The neglect of the economic aspect can also be seen in less nationalistic accounts. For instance the index of English and Graham Walker's impressive set of essays entitled *Unionism in Modern Ireland* has no entry for 'economics' or 'finance'.[56] Walker suggested that Sinclair's contribution to opposition to Home Rule was to contribute to the creation of an Ulster identity that was vital to the Unionist case.[57] Moreover, without Sinclair's Liberal Unionism, Walker contended that Ulster's (largely Presbyterian) business community would not have been so eager to oppose Home Rule.[58] Again Walker's valuable paper does not integrate the literature on Ulster's economic development that would explain the role of the business community in the story of opposition to Home Rule.

Paul Bew's recent paper on Home Rule follows the neglect of the economic dimension.[59] Bew notes Stewart's approach continues to 'provide the template for our understanding' of the topic of Home Rule.[60] Just as Stewart's template downplays the economic backdrop so does Bew downplay the links between industrialisation and the political process. Bew's article suggests that the two traditions were merely talking past one another. The Irish language issue was for Bew the key to creating Protestant alienation from the Nationalistic objective of an independent Ireland.

Marxian or dependency school writers have been far more willing than other historians of the Ulster crisis to highlight the economic aspects of the Ulster crisis. But even the Marxians relegate the importance of Home Rule, preferring instead to ruminate on the historical relevance of the leftist concepts of 'labour aristocracy' and 'dependent development'.[61] It is notable that the issue of Home Rule is barely discussed in the most recent extended dependency account of long-run Irish economic development.[62] Marxists (and dependency theorists) contend that the debate on the national question preserved capitalistic privileges and workers exploitation behind the veil of existing ethnic and religious hatreds.[63] This kind of determinism has led to some quite astonishing assertions. Roland Munck claims, for instance, without producing any supporting historical evidence, that 'northern capitalists' as a bloc threw their collective weight behind the Unionist case solely out of pure naked economic self-interest.[64]

5. Interpreting economic performance in Ireland, 1870–1920

The prosperity of Ireland under the Union is an important part of a wider assessment of Ireland's net benefits of membership of the Union.[65] Hence the estimation of Irish national income for the late nineteen and early twentieth century has profound implications for the assessment of Irish social and political conditions. For instance, the greater the level of over-taxation under the union, the less economically rational was it for Unionists to support the financial *status quo* of membership of the UK and hence the more rational institutional reform would have been. The report of the 1896 Royal Commission, which mainly focused on the revenue side of the public finances, for instance took a Nationalist line that Ireland was overtaxed by a minimum amount of two million and three-quarters. Unsurprisingly, therefore the committee concluded that there was a need for institutional reform in the area of public finance. It was claimed that a tax system suitable for an advanced industrial economy like Britain was not necessarily the best system for a less developed area such as Ireland.[66] This politically charged conclusion stemmed from a comparison of actual tax revenue with an equitable share of the UK's tax revenue based on Ireland's estimated taxable capacity relative to Britain.[67]

Yet as Louis Cullen observed, no reliable estimates could be said to exist of the relative incomes of the two countries in the 1890s. Hence the commission's findings were 'based therefore on premises which would warrant only very tentative deductions'.[68] Cullen noted that the other half of the public finance story was also germane to an economic appraisal of the Union circa 1896. He noted that government expenditure in Ireland exceeded revenue in the decade or so before the First World War.[69] Cullen suggested that it was the incidence rather than the level of taxation that gave rise to the allegations of inequity. In particular Ireland's indirect tax rates on consumer goods such as tea, tobacco and whisky were high relative to Britain. Given that Ireland's poor spent a disproportionately high share on these kinds of goods it follows that Irish over-taxation was more the consequence of backwardness than its cause.[70]

The political ramifications of the debate on tax levels arise from the observation that the greater (lower) Irish relative economic backwardness was compared to Britain the more onerous (generous) was its financial treatment based on a common tax system relative to Great Britain and equally the more (less) it would have required financial subventions to close the gap in living standards.[71] The estimation of Irish national income has involved a range of statistical methodologies; regardless of the methods used, most of those economic historians that have empirically estimated Irish national income, have tentatively suggested that Ireland became a richer place over the period.[72] Yet even those economic historians that accept that Ireland grew richer differ on the causes of this increased income per head as well as on its distributional implications. They can be thus contrasted with Royal Commission's members who did not believe that Irish growth during the nineteenth century was more rapid than Britain's.[73] The three respective modern positions (extreme pessimists, moderate pessimists and optimists) can be illustrated in Table 2.2 below.

The extreme pessimists either discern no evidence of Irish economic convergence on Britain levels or suggest that post-famine Irish National Income was extremely low to start off, so any growth should not be confused with successful economic development. The moderate pessimists do suggest that convergence towards the economic development levels of other places occurred. Yet these writers attribute Ireland's economic convergence to the contraction of labour supply associated with post-famine emigration rather than being due to genuine productivity advances in Irish economic organisation. Only the optimists regard the observed convergence as being due to efficiency improvements.

A. Maddison's (1995) series for the area of the Republic of Ireland between 1820 and 1913 assumes no convergence on the rest of the UK.[74] His extreme pessimism echoes the earlier findings of N. Butlin and C.H. Feinstein.[75] Most recent writers have not accepted this interpretation. The more moderate pessimistic view is contained in Kieran Kennedy et al suggestion that Irish income per head grew faster than Britain and Europe.[76] Ó Gráda also accepts that Irish income per caput grew faster than Great Britain.[77] Jeffrey Williamson concentrating on

Table 2.2   *Did Ireland's economy converge on Britain in the post-famine period?*

NO (Extreme Pessimists)	YES Due to Emigration *(Moderate Pessimists)*	YES Due to Efficiency Improvements *(Optimists)*
Crotty (1966)	Kennedy et al (1988)	Cullen (1972)
Butlin (1968)	Ó Gráda (1994)	Geary and Stark (2002)
Feinstein (1972)	Williamson (1994)	
Maddison (1995)		
O'Hearn (2001)		

real wages, rather than income, also detects a convergence of living standards with Britain.[78] All these writers suggest that Ireland's convergence of income per head was primarily due to emigration rather than to increased productivity. Williamson has indeed claimed that Ireland's convergence was driven solely by exporting labour:

> Ireland did undergo an impressive catch-up on both Britain and the United States after the Famine. Economics as old as Adam Smith can explain why: emigration made labor more scarce in Ireland, thus raising real wages and living standards at home even compared with conditions overseas and living standards at home where immigration made labor more abundant...Although the movers may have been able to escape to higher wages abroad, the now-scarcer stayers found conditions improving at home.[79]

It is important to note that Williamson accords little role in the late nineteenth century development process to the economic benefits from increased schooling. Williamson suggests that in this period all technical knowledge could be transmitted without cost.[80] Moderate pessimists suggest that the observed convergence of incomes merely reflected the existence of strong push and pull factors that tended to encourage the Irish to look elsewhere for work.

The suggestion that Irish income levels converged because of emigration rather than due to productivity improvements is one that F. Geary and T. Stark have strongly contested.[81] Geary and Stark, following Cullen's thesis, place the sources of convergence on the real gains connected with factors (tending to be associated with social capability) such as structural change, capital accumulation, technical progress and the increased trade that occurred in the second half of the nineteenth century.[82] These writers suggest that the Irish economy of 1911 was not just the Irish economy of 1861, albeit with fewer people, they suggest economic organisation had profoundly changed in the intervening half century.[83] Following Cullen's earlier work, Geary and Stark contend that the ability to diffuse innovation within Ireland was high due to an increasingly diversified industrial base, large foreign trade and developments in banking, commerce and transport.[84] Geary and Stark's calculations indeed suggest that in terms of the growth of both GDP per capita and GDP per worker Ireland outpaced British growth rates in the period 1871 to 1911.[85]

Geary and Stark's figures suggest that Ireland's prosperity slipped however only relatively when comparisons with other advanced economies are made. Measuring levels in a league table of 16 advanced economies Ireland's GDP per caput rated seventh in 1871 and fell to eleventh in 1911. The corresponding rankings for GDP per worker were seventh and tenth. This slippage in relative Irish economic performance was indicative of Ireland sharing in the UK's relatively poor growth performance between the 1870s and the 1910s.[86] In Geary and Stark's calculations only Great Britain performed worse than Ireland in terms of growth of GDP per caput.[87]

Crafts forthcoming paper has extended Geary and Stark's methodology to all the regions of the United Kingdom for the period 1871–1911.[88] The resulting evidence suggests that in the pre First World War era, regional income divergence was driven by increased economic integration; by way of illustration, globalisation, by lowering the cost of transporting agricultural products from the New World, reduced agricultural rents in the UK. Moreover, as the global economy integrated so urban incomes increased as the trade in invisibles grew. Crafts emphasis on the economic importance of globalisation to the economy will be developed later in section 7 of the paper. It will be suggested that in the case of Ulster, uneven growth had political repercussions.

Crafts further demonstrates that Ireland's share of UK GDP fell from 10.7 to 6.3 per cent between 1871 and 1911, but its regional GDP grew from £129.3 million to £146.8 million in the same period.[89] However, while N. Crafts does not explicitly discuss the topic of regional differences within Ireland in his paper, it is clear that further calculations would suggest that Ulster's commercial and especially industrial power was disproportionately responsible for the increase in Irish national income between 1871 and 1911. Ulster was an undoubted beneficiary of globalisation, it developed heavy industry without local supplies of coal and iron and its imports of raw materials were supplemented by importing also skills and technical knowledge. Even many of Ulster's entrepreneurs outside of the linen sector were from England and Scotland.[90] Likewise, Ireland's overall declining share of UK national income was due to the continued importance of agriculture in the Irish economy. Crafts calculations imply that Ireland's falling share of British national income looks similar to the pattern of decline experienced in agricultural East Anglia during the same period.

Concluding this section it can be observed that if the optimistic view of Irish development is correct, then further historical investigation should provide substantial evidence of considerable levels of social capability. Likewise, if the more pessimistic interpretations are right, then convergence did not require a good set of institutions: it merely would have required a sufficient degree of factor mobility that allowed labour supply (and wage levels) to adjust to economic conditions. At the time of writing, the optimistic argument is in the ascendancy. Globalisation, as was clear from Ulster, did affect the Irish economy beyond stimulating emigration, for instance it encouraged technical, organisational change in industry as well as financial diversification. Supporting evidence on banking will be produced in the following section. This evidence suggests there was an emerging social capability in Ireland, albeit this capability was undermined by social division.

6. National aspects: Applying social capability to Irish banking

While the discussion of the previous section should have made clear that a consensus on the empirics of Irish growth is still awaited, the concept of social capability has insights into the possible interactions between political and economic development. One way of applying the social capability effects of political agitation to Irish economic development is to consider the then existing institutional framework and how it could have helped or hindered the level and distribution of social capability on the island. A number of areas could be considered in this regard, developments in educational and business organisations spring immediately to mind, but due to lack of space the discussion will be restricted to the possible role of banking and finance on social capability.

Properly functioning financial institutions enable capital (and hence new technologies) to flow into burgeoning areas of industry. A well functioning banking system will give successful investors access to savers funds. Formal legislation can help or hinder this flow of finance, as can the cultural attitudes of those making investment decisions and the ethics of the government under which these decisions are made. The pace at which economic growth is realised will depend on the degree to which the response of the government, financial community and the public proves adequate to support the industrial organisation that technology requires.[91]

Ireland was not backward in regard to access to bank created funds, even if political factors affected securities; Ireland had more bank branches per head than either France or England on the eve of the First World War. Moreover, the growth of savings within Ireland kept pace with Britain.[92] As early as 1886, Ulster certainly had a high degree of social capability in the area of business finance; this is demonstrated by Hickson and Turner's work on the trading of unlimited liability bank shares between 1868 and 1879.[93] They empirically establish that shareholders in the Ulster Banking Company were wealthy individuals living within ten miles of the nearest branch and were consequently well able to monitor the health of the business. This case study suggests a well-functioning capital market existed. When this is combined with Ó Gráda's observation of the low propensity of Ulster investors to take up British government securities it suggests that, in Ulster at least, a class of financially sophisticated business leaders existed. These investors participated in globalisation by investing in Britain and abroad.[94]

What is clear in this regard is that Ulster's social capability in the 1880s was stimulated by financial development and by the end of the period the island as a whole had an effective financial system. One complication in this optimistic story however was the segmentation of finance by religion. Banks in Ireland tended to be strongly Unionist or Nationalist in ethos and hired accordingly.[95] This suggests that while economically efficient at one level, Irish banking also reflected deeper social divisions. Persistent social conflict thus coexisted with a relatively high level of social capability. This co-existence must have impaired the creation of further social capability. The extent of social division suggests that to some extent two economies, separated by religious affiliation rather than by formal legislation, existed prior to formal partition.

7. International aspects: Ulster Unionism, constructive imperialism and globalisation

The modern approach to the historical development of international trade has specific implications for interpreting the economic backdrop to the Ulster crisis. It was not a coincidence that many of the most politically influential opponents of Home Rule were also successful businessmen.[96] No less a political figure than James Craig was from a distilling background. Craig's father was a millionaire director of Dunville's.[97] To some degree Ulster's reliance on industrial exports hence created an overlapping business and political elite, but the extent of this overlap and the possibility that this intersection led to excessive rent-seeking in Northern Ireland after 1920 requires further research.[98]

Within the literature on international economic history written in the last decade there has been a widespread recognition that globalisation was feature of the world economy in the early 1900s just as surely as it has been in the early 2000s.[99] The late nineteenth century was the period in which the largest decline in inter-continental barriers to trade and factor mobility was recorded.[100] Many economic historians have begun to accept the claim that, measured in terms of the convergence of prices rather than income per capita, the period between 1870 and the First World War was the most impressive period of international economic integration that world commerce has yet experienced.[101]

As the empirical evidence from Crafts in section 5 implies, this process of globalisation undoubtedly influenced Irish living standards. The world economy, in stark contrast with later periods had little restraint on immigration. This combination of flows of products and labour promoted convergence, but this process was reversed in the 1930s.[102] The recent work on the economic history of globalisation suggests that it is possible that this era of economic liberalism sowed the seeds of its own destruction, as it threatened long established political equilibria that had existed in the developed world.[103] Additionally, it has been suggested that the desire to restore old economic and cultural certainties, exemplified by older institutional forms, lay behind the revival of nationalistic forms of trade policy. For political actors the rational response in terms of securing power was to advocate economic alternatives to the 'destabilising' forces of liberal trade policy. In the 1930s these alternatives could be found in a variety of concepts including nationalism, corporatism, demand management and state (or national) socialism. Such a perspective on globalisation is tentative. As yet there has been no explicit empirical test of the role of policy and war in explaining the end of convergence.[104] Where Kevin O'Rourke and Williamson's interpretation is least satisfactory for understanding changes in the Irish economy is their contention that Ireland's convergence was solely the result of migration without any reference to alterations in Irish social capability.[105]

Stewart's *The Ulster Crisis* does not discuss in any detail that the period of Ulster Unionism's emergence as an independent force coincides with the rise of protectionism in British politics. However, more recent writers have noted how Unionism was shaped by support for the empire.[106] Burnett, echoing Gibbon's Marxist account, goes so far as to link Unionism to the development of pro-imperialist groups in British politics.[107] Indeed in Britain there was strong links between support for empire and support for protectionism.[108] In Britain protectionist sentiments were a response to the decline in arable agriculture and the onset of import penetration in manufactures. Manufactures were only 3 per cent of imports by value in 1860 yet by 1900 they were a quarter.[109] In the early part of the period, Chamberlain was both a staunch critic of free trade and of Gladstone's Irish proposals; it should be recalled that

Chamberlain actually resigned from Gladstone's government in 1886 over Ireland.[110] More generally, in an uncertain world where Britain's economic rivals were gaining ground, the 'Constructive' or 'Social' Imperialists who favoured tariff reform viewed protection as a means to preserve and extend a world-wide British community.[111] The Constructive Imperialists saw the preservation of British industrial might as a way of sustaining military influence in the world.[112] Ulster's reliance on manufacturing rather than services for its economic development was in line with the Constructive Imperialist vision for the British economy as a whole.[113]

Ultimately, however there was some dissonance in the two related visions of Constructive Imperialist thinking on Britain's world political and economic role and the Unionist view of Ulster's political and economic relationship to Britain. The Constructive Imperialists diverged from Unionist experience in that the former identified Britain's Industrial Revolution with the pre-existence of a mercantilist state; yet the Unionist's were consciously aware that Ulster's economic improvement was the result of free trade rather than being due to a mercantilist framework. The Constructive Imperialists disliked the globalisation of labour and capital flows that characterised the period.[114] Yet for instance, Belfast's shipyards relied on these sustained factor flows for its very existence. On balance, it is difficult to see how Ulster Unionists of the time could have agreed in the Constructive Imperialists claim that free trade was the consequence not the cause of economic prosperity. Ulster's trade-led path to industrialisation stood in stark contrast to any such diagnosis.

With lower incomes than Britain, despite convergence, an overtly protectionist economic strategy created the increased possibility of the 'dear loaf', and the Unionist industrial working classes, like those in Britain, would hardly vote for a tax on eating.[115] Thus in the early twentieth century just as Ulster Unionism was out of sympathy with Arthur Griffith's protectionist proposals inspired by Irish Nationalism, so was it also implicitly critical of the protectionist designs inspired by British mercantilist thinking. It was Ulster Unionism's fate that by the 1930s the free trade that had been so instrumental in guiding their political and economic fortunes was merely a distant memory. Ireland's political and economic fate as a whole was perhaps especially tragic in that it was driven apart at a time of global economic integration. Later these same ethno-religious divisions became entrenched as protectionism gained force.

8. Conclusion: Towards a political economy of the Ulster crisis 1886–1920

It has been suggested that the performance of the multiple compo-
nents of social capability were in all probability uneven. For instance, while banking in Ulster was developed in the 1880s in other
areas, such as access to education for instance, the relative level of
social advancement throughout the island was far less impressive.
Following Ó Gráda's findings, it is clear that the output growth that
did occur was skewed towards industrial activities such as linen, en-
gineering and shipbuilding overwhelmingly concentrated in
Ulster.[116] Ulster's level of social capability was probably higher than
the rest of Ireland given the vitality of its manufacturing sector in
promoting technological progress and business finance. It is also reasonably safe to suggest that on balance political agitation tended to
act as a moderate brake to growth as it impeded social advancement
and discouraged certain forms of investment. Yet perhaps a far
greater impediment to long-term economic development was the
underlying social divisions that blighted business and cultural life on
the island. The quantitative impacts of these divisions are debatable,
but are worth further investigation.

As the empirical uncertainties surrounding Irish national income
are reduced over the next decade, so attention in Irish economic
history will necessarily shift away from cliometrics, though that set of
tools will continue to have an important role in economic history.
On balance, as identified by Ó Gráda, there will need to be a shift
towards the research agenda concerned with the institutional economics of social division.[117] It is now well recognised that across con-
tinents and historical period, endogenous institutional and technical
changes, such as social capability, are the central themes of long-run
economic history. The price theoretic tools of the earlier cliometric
work are inadequate to the task of investigating these issues.[118] For
these reasons the tools required for future research in Irish economic
history, regardless of period, will increasingly be inspired by the 'new'
institutional approach to economic history.[119] The literature on the
economic analysis of politics, or 'public choice' as it is more commonly known, may provide further insights on the economic and
political development of Ulster in the run up to the Home Rule
crisis. To borrow a well-worn word in Irish historiography, a new
stage in 'revisionism' is needed if a complete political economy of the
Ulster crisis is ever to be written.

3

The State and the Citizen:
Unionists, Home Rule, Ulster and
the British Constitution, 1886–1920

D. George Boyce

When the Unionist Peer, Lord Selborne, in his book *The State and the Citizen*, was trying to explain why the British constitution was now, in 1909–1912, a matter of profound dispute between the political parties, he quoted the Conservative writer Sir Henry Maine's explanation of the conflict occasioned by the 1884 Franchise Reform bill. 'Political history', Maine wrote, 'shows that men have at all times quarrelled more freely about phrases and formulas than even about material interests, and it would seem that the discussion of British constitutional legislation is distinguished from all other discussion by having no fixed points to turn upon and therefore by irrational violence'. Maine advocated safeguards against 'surprising and hostile' alteration of the constitution and for all men to know for certain under what laws they were living.[1] Modern political scientists, for their part, have commented on the fact that the British lacked a conception of the state as it was found on the Continent, of what Matthew Arnold called ' the nation in its collective and corporate character, entrusted with stringent powers for the general advantage, and controlling individual wills in the name of an interest wider than that of individuals'. The state, Professor Rodney Barker argues, 'does not exist in British political thought', and the explanation for this was that the history of government in Britain, 'whilst characterised by more or less distinctive phases, has rarely been marked

by sharp transitions of a kind which bring institutions sharply to the attention of those who are involved in or subordinate to them'.[2]

Irish Home Rule, however, marked one of those 'sharp transitions'
which brought the state to the attention of those, at least, who were involved in the working of institutions. The result was a sustained and
bitter conflict, but also one of the rare occasions when the state was
made the centre of political debate, its effect on those subordinate to its
institutions analysed, and recommendations for its radical reform put
forward. This occasion also brought into focus another absentee from
British political discourse, at least since the seventeenth century: the
Constitution, or the lack of what was generally understood in the
United States and Europe as a constitution, that is a written document
setting out the rights, powers, and inhibitions on the power of the state.
And, finally, Irish Home Rule raised in acute form the question of
nationhood and the integrity of the nation in this stateless and non-
constitutional (but not of course unconstitutional) entity, the United
Kingdom.

The Home Rule bills between 1886 and 1920 raised political issues
of a most profound kind. These have rightly retained their place in the
history of the attempts by Liberal governments to satisfy the demands of
Irish Nationalists while retaining the sovereignty of the United
Kingdom Parliament. Less attention has been paid to the constitutional
implications for the British Constitution of the attempts to bestow devolved government on Ireland, and the impact of British constitutional
change on Irish Home Rule. Yet a key argument against Home Rule
was that the Liberal claim that the sovereignty of the British Parliament
remained unimpaired was a chimera. As the great Victorian jurist, A.V.
Dicey put it in his *England's Case against Home Rule*, published in 1886,
'the fullest legislative assembly meeting in Dublin would rightly claim
to speak for the Irish people. A town council, whether of Birmingham
or Belfast, springs from and is kept alive by the will of Parliament, and
cannot pretend that its powers, however extensive, compete with the
authority of its creator'. Thus, for Dicey, the moral, if not legal, check
upon Westminster over-ruling an Irish Parliament was a significant invasion of British sovereignty. Local self-government meant delegation of
powers; Home Rule, however curtailed, meant the constitutional
recognition of a nation.[3] Such a profound constitutional change must
not be left to the will of politicians or even Parliament. Dicey in May
1886 told the Liberal James Bryce that he wanted a plebiscite on Home
Rule, with the 'simple question an independent Parliament for Ireland
or not. Were there a vote in its favour I would then have a constitu-

tional convention to draw up a Constitution fairly carrying out this popular vote, and the Constitution itself I wd. then submit to the people aye or no'.[4]

Dicey argued that Gladstonian Home Rule initiated a new Constitution for (as he put it) England. The complete withdrawal of Irish MPs from Westminster, included in the first Home Rule bill but abandoned thereafter, created a new Parliament, different in composition from the present one, and ended the concept of one sovereign legislature for the whole kingdom. But equally important was the question of the place of minorities in this new constitution. Dicey did not doubt that a strong government in Dublin would enforce the law. But the 'energy of a strong government in carrying out the laws which it approves is a different matter from the zealous maintenance of even-handed justice'. Landlords enjoyed no security from the activities of the Land League. And so among the arguments in favour of defending the Union Dicey listed one that was part of the 'current of English history' and 'the tendencies of modern civilisation': that the Union, as matters now stood, provided 'the only means of giving legal protection to a large body of loyal British subjects'. Home Rule, under whatever form, 'whilst not freeing England from moral responsibility for protecting the rights of every British subject, does virtually give up the attempt to ensure to those rights more than a nominal existence, and thus gives up the endeavour to enforce legal and equal justice between man and man'.[5]

In 1886 and 1893 the question of justice for the Protestant minority in Ireland was part, but by no means the main part, of England's case against Home Rule. But it did tap into the English political tradition that emphasised the freedom of individuals under the law, and the absence of the kind of powerful state apparatus that could bear down heavily on citizens that, it was widely held, characterised government on the continent of Europe. In 1886 Dicey noted in passing that 'it is hardly an exaggeration to assert that even now we have in the United Kingdom nothing like what foreigners mean by an administration. We know nothing of that official hierarchy which on the Continent represents the authority of the State'. Englishmen were accustomed to the notion that the fact that the business of the country was conducted by 'unconnected local bodies' should 'be the subject of unqualified approval'. This was based on the English respect for privilege, which had preserved English freedoms, while, Dicey acknowledged, making her slower than other civilised countries to adopt ideas of equality.[6]

By 1913 Dicey pushed the argument for defending the Protestant minority still further, and placed more emphasis on Ulster Unionist resistance to the 1912 Home Rule bill. Ulster Unionists were protesting against a double injustice: that of being deprived of their rights as citizens of the United Kingdom; and the compulsion to obey a Parliament in Dublin to which they owed no allegiance. There may exist 'acts of oppression on the part of a democracy, no less than of a king, which justify resistance to the law, or, in other words, rebellion'. Unionists must press for a general election on the bill to avert this danger, otherwise the Home Rule bill lacked 'constitutional authority'.[7]

Parliamentary sovereignty was not the sovereignty of the House of Commons merely; it was the sovereignty of the King in Parliament, and Parliament still consisted of both Lords and Commons, each with its own role in legislation. But just as Home Rule would have an impact upon the English Constitution, so did the English Constitution impact upon Home Rule. When Dicey published the eighth edition of his great and highly influential work on the Constitution, *Introduction to the Study of the Law of the Constitution* (1915) he inserted a new introduction 'whereof the aim is to compare our constitution as it stood and worked in 1884 with the constitution as it now stands in 1914'.[8] In this 'work of historical retrospection' Dicey selected five main topics for discussion: the sovereignty of Parliament; the rule of law; the law and conventions of the constitution; new constitutional ideas, and general conclusions.[9] In all these areas important changes had been wrought since 1884. The nature of the sovereign Parliament had been modified by the 1911 Parliament act which destroyed the Lords' veto on money bills and reduced its powers over other bills to a 'suspensive veto' only. Legislative authority had been transferred from the King and the two houses of Parliament to the House of Commons.[10] The rule of law had declined: recent acts had given 'judicial or quasi-judicial authority to officials who stand more or less in connection with, and therefore may be influenced by, the government of the day' and thus had diminished the authority of the law courts (for example the power given to officials by the Insurance Act of 1911).[11] The Parliament Act of 1911 enabled a majority of the House of Commons to overcome the will of the electors – and therefore of the nation. That the 1912 Home Rule bill was opposed by a large number of the electors, and was hated by a powerful minority of Irishmen was certain; yet the widespread demand for an appeal to the will of the people received no attention from the majority in the House of Commons.[12] It was now possible to place the control of legislation and the whole government of the country in the hands of the Cabinet, which was the only instrument through which a dominant party could exercise its power 'and the only body in the state which can lead and control the parliamentary majority of which the Cabinet is the organ'.[13] It was for this reason that in his section on the new constitution Dicey advocated the referendum which, by checking the 'omnipotence of partisanship' might 'revive faith in that parliamentary government which has been the glory of English constitutional history'. In his 'conclusions' Dicey drew consolation from the fact that, while the Parliament act represented the 'last and greatest triumph of party government', the Crown had not only maintained, but had increased its 'moral force' and authority because the Crown stood outside the party system.[14]

Dicey was a prejudiced, if incisive, observer of the British constitutional affairs. But he reflected the opinion of other experts, such as A.W. Lowell and Sydney Low, that great and lasting changes had been wrought in the working of the Constitution because of the way that Party had fastened its grip upon the system, and had facilitated the emergence of the Cabinet as the great, central engine of power.[15] For Dicey and for Unionists generally, these developments deepened the crisis over the third Home Rule bill of 1912; for they placed the power-hungry party machine and the all powerful Cabinet in opposition to the high moral ground which Unionism occupied in its fight, not only against Irish Home Rule, but against the new tyranny. Selborne believed that the Parliament act had removed all constitutional safeguards; and he drew a contrast between the British and American systems, where the disestablishment of the Church of Ireland in 1869 might have been passed by Congress and President, but would have been checked by the protection of the law courts, which would have pronounced the act of Congress to be unconstitutional ' and immediately the act would have become so much waste paper'.[16] The waning of constitutional understanding also set the power of the modern state against the rights of individuals and minorities. Selborne gave the example of the National Insurance bill which was passing 'almost entirely undisguised' through the House of Commons. Yet this Bill, he alleged, damaged (to take 'one minute instance') those people who worked in the glove trade and who as a result of the bill were now going to lose their livelihood.[17] Dicey drew attention to the Irish Home Rulers in the Commons voting for the Old Age Pensions and National Insurance acts 'which they did not think desirable for Ireland' as part of their bargain with the Liberal government over Home Rule. English Nonconformists were induced 'not one suspects without qualms' in Parliament at least to 'turn a deaf ear to the bitter cry of all Protestants, whether Nonconformists or not, in Ireland'. The 'revolutionary purposes' of the government filled 'men of sense' with intense fear because the Parliament act, and it alone, meant that Ministers could pass into law proposals 'which Ministers themselves dare not submit to the judgement of the nation'.[18] Thus would Unionist Ulster be pushed to the fore as the sharp edge of the defence of the rights of all British citizens against party and executive oppression.

The difficulty for Unionists was that it was hard to persuade the British people that there had indeed been a major shift in the traditional balance of the Constitution between King, Lords and Commons. The British people were not inclined to think much about these matters. In 1912 Lord Lansdowne described the constitutional question as the key issue of the day, and claimed that the constitution was 'in abeyance'. It was now not just one of a number of questions, but was 'the master question'; yet audiences did not respond to this master question as they did to other political topics. The former was seen as requiring from the speaker an 'apology for their dryness'.[19] Dicey argued that it was a characteristic of the British democracy that 'fundamental changes in the Constitution are matters which may be undertaken with a light heart, and may be carried through as thoughtlessly as laws of merely temporary importance'.[20]

The Conservative and Unionist party has often been presented in these crises as having weakened or perhaps even lost its belief in constitutional methods and principles.[21] The Unionist leader, Andrew Bonar Law's assuring the Ulster Unionists in July 1912 that there were 'things stronger than parliamentary majorities', and that he could imagine 'no lengths of resistance to which Ulster will go in which I should not be ready to support them' suggested that Unionism was now entering dangerously unconstitutional waters.[22] Selborne argued that the demise of the Constitution began with Lloyd George's 'People's Budget' of 1909, when the 'less reflecting portion of the electorate' was misled by the cry of 'Peers versus People'. Within six months the House of Commons had passed a Bill 'to repeal the Constitution of England'.[23]

Certainly the language of British politics was embittered by the budget crisis of 1909, the Parliament act of 1911, and the third Home Rule bill which, Bonar Law claimed, revealed the 'despotic power' which the Liberals were now exercising.[24] A Constitutional Conference held in June 1910 between the Government and the Opposition (with the Irish Parliamentary Party excluded) failed to resolve the deep divisions between the parties because the Unionists could not wrest guarantees that future conflicts over finance issues and other matters by a conference of representatives of both Houses of Parliament would not include Home Rule.[25] Unionist political rhetoric reached new heights of indignation, with the party claiming that it was standing in the way of revolution and arbitrary government. There was also the by no means insignificant consideration that the loss of the general election of 1906 ('an amazing catastrophe' as one Unionist put it) followed by two further reverses in 1910 seemed to show that the political system was no longer working in favour of Conservatism.[26] And this system was itself being undermined by the 'corrupt bargain' which had been struck after the 1910 elections between the Liberals and the Irish Home Rulers whose votes, it was held by Unionists, kept the Liberals in power. This was an oversimplification of the balance of forces in the Commons: the Liberals could depend on the support of the Home Rulers, but need not give in to their every whim; who else would they support if not the Liberals. And the Labour party contingent likewise found natural allies in the Liberal party. Nevertheless this was the corrosive background to the introduction of the third Home Rule bill in April 1912. Selborne, usually no partisan figure, in 1907 characterised the Liberals as unfit to govern the Empire, because of the influence of the large radical element in the party whom he described as 'malignant lunatics'.[27]

In his new introduction to his attack on the 1893 bill, *A Leap in the Dark*, which was re-published in 1911, Dicey warned Unionists and the nation that 'we stand on the brink of a precipice'. Unionists were engaged in a 'revolutionary movement' and the 'construction of a Constitution', in neither of which English statesman had much experience.[28] Dicey foresaw the danger that Ulster Unionist resistance to the legal authority of the British Parliament would bring, and in his attack on the 1912 Home Rule bill, *A Fool's Paradise*, he sought a way out: if the bill were placed before the British electorate than it would elicit an 'incontrovertible answer'.[29] He believed that the British public would oppose it, if they were told that the issue at stake was 'whether the United Kingdom is morally a nation, and whether as a nation it has a right to insist upon the supreme authority belonging to the majority of its citizens'.[30]

The phrase, 'morally a nation' was a profoundly significant one. It was upon this that the Federal Government in the United States of America justified its decision to go to war with the Confederate states in 1861 to enforce Union. The North decided then to resort to the 'arbitrament of battle' – a 'terrible calamity' – but one that must not be repeated in the United Kingdom.[31] The problem was that the British Constitution worked on the assumption that it clothed a nation that was fundamentally at one with itself. There were of course class and regional differences; but these were never regarded as insuperable, or as threatening the search for consensus that, it was held, characterised the working of the Constitution. Ireland challenged this assumption. But it challenged it in two ways: first by the claims of Catholic Nationalists that Ireland was a nation; second, by Ulster Protestant rejection of that claim. Even Walter Bagehot, who in 1866 referred without qualification to the 'English Constitution' noted in 1867 that Irish Nationalism, or at least the Fenian version of it, found its true analogy, not in the revolt of the Poles, but in Bohemia, with 'four millions of Czechs, controlled by an immutable geographical position, vainly trying to destroy the power of a million and a quarter Germans quartered among them'. Irish Catholics were the Czechs; Ulster Protestants the Germans.[32]

English constitutional assumptions divided into two parallel themes: that the Constitution rested upon consensus and agreement; and the recognition that there was disaffection in Ireland, a kind of double disaffection, that might not be held within the compass of consensus politics. These were by 1912 seen by some observers to be intersecting and interacting. As Josef Redlich predicted in his volume *The Procedure of the House of Commons* (1908), the Commons had been transformed from an institution which could facilitate decision by 'consensus rather than by majority' into one firmly biased towards the majority.[33] This provoked Unionists into seeking an alternative to the majority biased Commons, and the one they favoured was the referendum. Lord Salisbury suggested this as long ago as 1884, arguing that the Liberal government's franchise reforms must be placed before the people who had 'in no sense been consulted'; though he added cautiously that the referendum device was 'a matter of feeling and judgement.[34] In 1893 Dicey added his voice to the cause, and he continued to argue that the referendum was necessary because the House of Commons was no longer the home of free debate because of the growth of party loyalty.[35] Selborne, believed that it would restore stability to the constitution. He acknowledged that there might be the danger of the 'bribery'; of the electorate, but 'your Lloyd Georges and Winston Churchills' would offer bribes without the referendum; and it was 'at its lowest...a court of appeal from the tyranny of the caucus'. Selborne held that the ultimate authority...in the state, whose legal existence 'differentiates a civilised from a barbarous state', was the partnership of Crown and people, which Unionists must strive to rescue from the Liberal betrayal.[36] In April 1912 the Southern Irish Unionist, Lord Midleton, pointed out an additional advantage of the referendum to Selborne: it would enable the King to say to Asquith, 'I am bound to stand by the people's opinion; the referendum takes the people's opinion and does not enable the House of Lords to disturb the Administration'.[37] Lord Curzon (an unlikely convert) argued that the referendum would not diminish Parliament, but, on the contrary, would enhance its sense of responsibility because MPs would feel 'that they might be called to account by a referendum of the people at no short date afterwards'.[38]

What F.S. Oliver, the leading political pamphleteer of his day, called 'constitution making' was now at the heart of Unionist political rhetoric.[39] And these reform proposals all had in common several themes: the restoration of 'balance' to the Constitution, which had been destroyed by the Parliament act of 1911, and which was the root cause of the Liberal/Nationalist alliance's ability to push Home Rule through the Commons and the Lords; the reconnection of the 'people' with government; the rights of citizens against the over-mighty state, and, in particular, the right of the British citizens of Ulster not to be placed under a government against their will; and the defence of the nation against the secession of Nationalist Ireland. Most of these aims were perfectly compatible with constitutional behaviour. But the large exception was Unionist Ulster and its rights of citizenship. The question posed by the inevitable passage of the third Home Rule bill through Parliament was whether or not Ulster Unionists had the right to resist its imposition upon them by force of arms. This was still rather theoretical in 1912. But it was raised by Lord Hugh Cecil in his *Conservatism* (1912). Citizens' opposition to controversial policies so far (tariff reform, Women's suffrage, the Nonconformist refusal to pay the educational rate) had aroused hardly any public discussion of the limits of legitimate resistance to the authority of the state. He held that obedience to that authority was a fundamental principle of the Constitution. When he looked at the history of Toryism, Cecil observed the old Tories' argument that no active resistance by the subject to the ruler could be right. But in the time of James II this proved no longer feasible. Yet too ready a resistance could make rebellion 'too much an ordinary political resonance', detracting from the 'sacred authority' of the state. Conservatives, he concluded, would naturally lean more to the side of authority than did radicals; but, he added, 'as the case of Ireland shows, circumstances might arise strong enough to produce a reversal of the attitude of the two parties'.[40]

By 1913–14 the 'reversal of attitudes' was well under way. This particularly exercised Dicey, whose great corpus of work on the British Constitution stressed the centrality of the power of the sovereign

Parliament and the rule of law. He continued to seek a way out by demanding a referendum or an election fought on the single issue of Home Rule. But if this failed, and it seemed increasingly likely to fail, then the question must be faced: when if ever, was an Ulster Unionist rebellion justified?

Dicey pondered on this in his 1915 edition to the *Law of the Constitution*. He remarked on what he saw as a 'new doctrine of lawlessness' in England, whereby 'large classes of otherwise responsible persons now held the belief that it is not only allowable, but even highly praiseworthy, to break the law of the land if the law-breaker is pursuing some end which to him or to her seems to be just and desirable'. He once more blamed the rise of party for this, because the 'rule of a party cannot be permanently identified with the authority of the nation or with the dictates of patriotism'. But he was troubled by the consequences of this doctrine. For while 'no sensible man can refuse to admit that crisis occasionally, though very rarely, arise, when armed rebellion against unjust and oppressive laws may be morally justifiable', yet 'this concession is often misconstrued; it is taken sometimes to mean that no man ought to be blamed or punished for rebellion if only he believes that he suffers from injustice and is not pursuing any private interest of his own'.[41]

The question then was whether or not an Ulster Unionist rebellion was justifiable, or could be 'misconstrued' in this way. And there was another constitutional issue raised here: what would be the position, morally and legally, of that instrument of the state which the Government must turn to if it were to suppress rebellion: the British army?

Unionist claims to be the defenders of the Constitution and the protectors of citizens' right stood at odds with their serious consideration of a tactic that seemed to contradict the whole warp and woof of the fabric of British history, with its hostility to any attempt to bring the armed forces into politics. The question was whether or not the Liberal government's Parliament act of 1911, and now their determination to push the Home Rule bill through the Commons and Lords, was of such a nature that it called for an equally radical response. There was the precedent of the Glorious Revolution of 1688, when the danger of royal tyranny had been met with rebellion, and the armed forces of the Crown subverted. But this episode had only served to copper fasten the notion that the army, which in the seventeenth century had been a very significant political instrument, must never be allowed to play that role again. Selborne did not deny that there were occasions when it was right to take up arms, for example for the monarchy against a republic;

but civil war was the 'ultimo ratio and the last party in the world that ought to turn to arms if it can possibly avoid it or go outside legal and constitutional forms is the Conservative and Unionist party'.[42] Sir Robert Sanders accepted that Bonar Law's claim at Blenheim Palace that if Ulster resisted, the sympathy of the Unionist party 'as a whole' was with him, but he confessed that he had not yet been able to find out who she was going to fight or 'or what form resistance can take'.[43] Dicey, for his part, held that oppression might justify what was (as he put it with some delicacy) 'technically conspiracy or rebellion', but he hoped that Ulster Unionists would resort to moral resistance only, and pay 'extreme attention to the preservation of order', though he feared that they might not possess such a degree of fortitude and patience.[44]

But some Unionists believed that the predicament was so desperate, and the danger of civil war in Ireland (and possibly in Great Britain as well) was so great that it called for desperate remedies. They came up with a proposal to amend the annual Army act, whereby the military were subjected to the authority of Parliament. It also maintained military discipline for, as Dicey himself put it, 'if this act were not in force a soldier would not be bound by military law.[45] The annual act was placed before Parliament each April as a bill which could be amended or rejected; but to reject it, or delay it by amendment would mean that the legal status of the army would be in abeyance. But, R.J.Q. Adams, Bonar Law's biographer points out, the British Constitution was 'whatever Parliament said it was, as the passage of the Parliament act proved, and to suggest that amendment would have been judicially unconstitutional was to go too far'.[46]

Unionists were aware of the dangers of amending the Army act; but they were alerted to its advantages by Lord Hugh Cecil in a memorandum of 5 June 1913. Cecil put the moral case for amendment. It would be a 'grave and even intolerable responsibility' if the Unionist party did not exhaust 'every conceivable means' of preventing the passage of the Home Rule bill 'and the consequent immediate rebellion of North-Eastern Ulster'. Even if Ulster Unionists' determination to set up a separate government on the day that the bill passed would not necessarily lead to 'violence and the effusion of blood', it was a very great risk, especially in the border areas of the province. Moreover, it would be dangerous, if Unionists won a general election in the United Kingdom, for them to repeal the Home Rule bill once passed; the Nationalists of the south and west of Ireland would never acquiesce in this. And so it was imperative that the bill should never reach the statute book. Amending the Army act in the House of Lords could 'compel the government to refer the question of Home Rule to the people'. The Lords had 'clearly the right to insist that before the standing army is used to establish Home Rule in Ireland against the will of a large section of the Irish population, it should at least be certain that the electorate approve of Home Rule and of such use of the King's armed forces'. The Liberal government might resign or accept a referendum. In fighting an election they would be obliged to deal with the Ulster question and 'explain how they proposed to get over the resistance of Ulster'. Thus, 'discredited by their reluctance to appeal to the people, they will have to attack the House of Lords for having merely insisted that security should be taken against using British soldiers to shoot down Ulstermen before the British people had an opportunity of expressing their will'. The Liberals' best defence would be to claim that the Lords were only using Ulster as a pretence, and were 'really anxious to wreck the land programme of Ministers'. For this reason Cecil preferred a referendum rather than a dissolution of the House of Commons; the referendum was 'not exposed to the imputation of some indirect motive of party advantage to be gained by a General Election'.[47]

Cecil's anxiety about the Unionist party's vulnerability to the charge of seeking party political advantage was well founded. J.S. Sandars, A.J. Balfour's private political secretary confessed in December 1912 on the Unionist demand for a referendum that 'Personally I don't care a bit one way or the other....All I care about is the party advantage; and I should rejoice to hear that we have gained by the new move'.[48] But this was not a typical Unionist opinion. Professor Adams has no doubt that Bonar Law believed that 'forced alienation of the loyalist Ulster minority from the United Kingdom and their subjection to the power of an unsympathetic authority they did not recognize – a Dublin Parliament – would do violence to the constitution of the United Kingdom'.[49] Law supported attacking the government through amending the Army act. Not all Unionists shared Law's convictions. Lansdowne, Balfour and Curzon were reluctant to follow this radical path; Selborne, at first positive to this strategy, changed his mind, and Bonar Law admitted on 20 March that it would be 'quite fatal' to amend the bill if there were any serious opposition to this in the party.[50] The plan was abandoned when in February and March 1914 the Liberals considered some special treatment for Unionist Ulster, suggesting that there might be exclusion for six years of those Ulster counties that wished to opt out of the Home Rule Parliament's authority. But Unionist efforts to alert the Army to the duty of refusing support for any 'despotic intention' of government,[51] emulating the army of James II, had resonance in the 'Curragh Incident' of March 1914, when a combination of Ministerial mismanagement, the precautionary movement of troops to Ulster, and, perhaps, a desire on the part of some Cabinet Members to test the resolve of the Ulster Volunteer Force and the Ulster Unionist Council led to confusion and the real possibility that some Army officers would refuse to obey orders. The Unionists' hopes of using the Army to prevent what they called 'unconstitutional' behaviour by the government turned out to be less effective than the Army's own anxiety about being used for what a significant proportion of the officer cadre regarded as an unconstitutional and even immoral political purpose.

It was for these reasons, and despite serious misgivings, that Dicey found himself in March 1914 signing the 'British Covenant' which was drafted on the lines of 'Ulster's Solemn League and Covenant' of September 1912 which pledged the signatories to resist the imposition of Home Rule on Ireland by all means that might be found necessary. The British Covenant declared that it was designed to prevent 'the armed forces of the Crown being used to deprive the people of Ulster of their rights as citizens of the United Kingdom', and Lord Milner justified it by asking 'when before, in our lifetime, have thousands upon thousands of sober steady-going citizens deliberately contemplated resistance to an act of Parliament, because they were sincerely convinced that it was devoid of all moral sanction?'.[52] Dicey, despite his earlier misgivings about seeming to endorse rebellion, signed the Covenant because it was 'now or never' for the Union.[53] But he feared the consequences for the constitution if British Army officers were encouraged to resign their commissions as a protest against 'an attempt which they condemn, to coerce Ulster'. In no free country would the army be allowed to demonstrate against the 'legally expressed orders of the nation'. 'The plain truth' was that 'the English nation will never stand any tampering with the army'. Even in France the army 'during a series of revolutions has hardly ever acted without orders from a civil authority' and had 'thus saved France from sinking into the condition of Spain'.[54] In articles published in the *Nineteenth Century* in April and May 1914 he warned that, while many thousands of British soldiers sympathised with the Ulster covenanters, he was 'personally assured that British soldiers will, in any case, do their duty, and not forget that the primary duty of a soldier is obedience to lawful orders'.[55] He asked the question: 'Does the Army owe obedience to the King or to the House of Commons? Are there cases when men who detest all lawlessness must recollect that a law itself may be iniquitous?' But 'to these ill-omened problems', he concluded 'I absolutely refuse to give an answer'.[56] But privately he warned Milner that he was 'certain that the English public will never tolerate the dictation of the Army. I think the public are in this right'.[57]

That the foremost legal and constitutional expert of the day was now alarmed that Unionist efforts to save the Constitution might end up, if not destroying, then certainly undermining it, showed how far Unionists had advanced into what they themselves called a 'revolutionary situation'. As part of their counter-revolutionary tactics they turned to the third element in the constitution, the Monarchy. Lord Milner in 1914 claimed that 'Nobody except one blinded by party prejudice can fail to realise the appalling danger with which this country is confronted. Surely it is the duty of our King, acting strictly within the Constitution, to do his utmost to save his country from such deadly peril?'[58] Lord Willoughby de Broke claimed that the King 'still has the legal right to refuse assent to any act of Parliament; and one tendency of the natural desire to restore the balance of the Constitution may well be that those over whom the House of Commons rides roughshod will bring their grievance to the King himself'.[59] Certainly Bonar Law made it his business to inform the King that it was his duty to intervene and refuse to give the royal assent to the Home Rule bill without first asking the government to place it before the public in order to prevent his Irish subjects from engaging in civil war.[60] The Unionist attack on alleged Liberal flouting of the law and conventions of the Constitution embarked upon dangerous waters; but at least it brought forth what J.A.R. Marriott called ' a revision of the whole British Constitution without any precedent or parallel'.[61] Yet Unionists stand open to the accusation of looking backwards to an era whose end was perhaps implicit in the 1832 Great Reform act, which, though at the time was meant to cure the Constitution, sowed the seeds of the rise of the Commons as the directly elected body, as against the powers of the Crown and the House of Lords. The Duke of Wellington confessed that he did not know how the 'encroaching power of the people out of doors on the House of Commons, and the encroaching powers of the House of Commons on the House of Lords and the Crown, is to be checked and brought back to its fair balance'.[62] But Unionists also produced modern ideas of reform, especially the proposal of a federal United Kingdom. Here was a reform that would have both Irish and British dimensions, and correspond to, and yet stabilise, the multi-national regime that was the United Kingdom. The creation of devolved governments throughout the United Kingdom would answer this difficulty and also accommodate the Ulster Unionist complaint that Ireland was being accorded special treatment, with Home Rule acknowledging the so-called national identity and history of Ireland.[63] Federalism, or 'Home Rule all Round' would, by treating all the countries of the kingdom in a uniform way, not only deny Irish Nationalists' claims that they were a separate nation, but also mollify Ulster Unionists, since all British citizens would be treated alike: thus avoiding any form of partition which some Unionists regarded as a 'catastrophe...certainly the worst solution short of civil war'.[64]

These proposed reforms – the referendum, federalism – were all the product of the intense political conflict that gripped Great Britain and Ireland between 1886 and 1914, especially in the couple of years before the outbreak of the First World War. They survived that war, but in the event they found no place in the British Constitution. Yet they did not die without a struggle. The federal idea re-surfaced in 1918–1920, with the British government accepting that any Home Rule bill for Ireland must be seen as a prelude to, and a preparation for, the making of a federal system. Sir Edward Carson wrote to Selborne in February 1918 that the best way forward for Ireland 'seems to me to lie in a system of federation for the whole United Kingdom. Averse, as I am, from any change in the present Constitution with its single Parliament for all purposes, I do not deny that the Union, which I regard as the keystone of the British Constitution, may nevertheless be preserved upon the principles of a true federation'. If such a policy were adopted 'it is easy to see that a settlement of the Ulster difficulty could be found, either by making Ulster a unit or by providing for its particular needs within another unit'. The south and west could have their act, with necessary safeguards, 'and let Ulster stand out until such time as England and Scotland can be brought in'.[65] F.E. Guest, the Coalition government's Chief Whip, estimated in May 1918 that the 'Tory federalists', led by Walter Long and Austen Chamberlain, numbered between 80 or 90 and 120.[66]

When in April 1918 the government responded to the failure of an Irish Convention (established in 1917 to see if Irishmen could settle their differences amongst themselves) by drawing up another Home Rule plan, it set up a committee under Long to work out a new bill. Long assured the Cabinet on 23 April that 'there was considerable and increasing evidence to show that, if a beginning could be made with the establishment of a federal system for the United Kingdom, it would be easier to pass the Government of Ireland

Amendment bill through the House of Commons. He was receiving many representations daily in favour of the federal solution from both Liberals and from Unionists'.[67] By late June 1918 Long's committee had drafted a proposal for a federal reorganisation of the United Kingdom which proposed the simultaneous establishment of national Parliaments for England, Scotland, Wales and Ireland; the supremacy of the Imperial Parliament was to remain undiminished, although the House of Commons was to be reduced to 350 members.[68] This languished because of the government's decision to abandon its policy of introducing Home Rule and military conscription in Ireland (though it always denied that the two were complementary). Lloyd George in April 1918 gave notice of his doubts about federalism, remarking that he 'would not, however, make the Home Rule bill dependent on the acceptance of a general scheme of federalism'.[69] But even the 'Partition Act', the Better Government of Ireland act of 1920, was drafted, and certainly presented, in terms of its compatibility with an overall federal reorganisation of the United Kingdom. The first report of Long's Cabinet committee on the Irish Question of 4 November 1919 noted that the giving of 'state rights' to the Northern and Southern Irish Parliaments had the advantage that Ulster, if she could 'persuade Nationalist Ireland to its views, will be able to secure that Ireland forms part of a United Kingdom federation at the price of agreeing to Irish unity themselves'.[70]

Federal thinking applied outside the Irish case. In 1920 the government set up a committee under the Speaker of the House of Commons to examine the possibility of applying Home Rule all Round, with a 'view to enabling the Imperial Parliament to devote more attention to the general interests of the United Kingdom, in collaboration with the other governments of the empire, to matters of common imperial concern....The time has come for the creation of subordinate legislatures within the United Kingdom'. The committee drew up a plan for a federal constitution, but the Speaker confessed that he was 'frightened' by the prospect of a multiplicity of elections and the cost of creating four new sets of parliamentary buildings.[71]

Lloyd George confirmed his dislike of federalism, arguing that in any case England did not want it.[72] But in truth it – like the referendum – was seen as out of step with the whole trend of English constitutional theory, with its stress on the need for strong, stable administrations and the all-powerful sovereign parliament. These traditions were more in keeping with the real needs of politicians in power and not, as were the Unionists between 1912 and 1914, in frustrating opposition. It was Ireland that drove the engine of reform, raising also questions about the rights of citizens and the authority of the state when faced with a minority's opposition to an act of Parliament. But Ireland was not interested in the federal idea, for, as Reginald Coupland put it in his exploration of Welsh and Scottish nationalisms, Ulster Unionists 'were anti-nationalist and anti-federalist in Britain because they were anti-nationalist and anti-federalist in Ireland'.[73] The Ulster Unionist members of the Speaker's Conference objected that it was considering the relationship between devolution and nationalism, arguing that its proper remit was to consider devolution as a way of reducing parliamentary congestion.[74] British federalists talked increasingly about the 'British Problem' and the need even to call any Irish Home Rule bill a 'United Kingdom' bill or a 'bill for the Better Government of the United Kingdom'.[75] When Ireland disappeared from British politics as a divisive and dangerous force, then federalism and other constitutional reforms were soon uncoupled from the political engine that had driven them. The expressions 'citizens' and 'the state' were once more elided from British constitutional discourse. Parliament returned to the centre of that discourse, reinforced by its perceived 'success' in defeating the General Strike of 1926, which was taken – wrongly – as a direct challenge to its authority; its victory seemed to demonstrate that there was nothing very wrong with Parliament, and that most Englishmen, at any rate, meant, in the words of the Unionist Lord Birkenhead, to 'go muddling on tolerably well'.[76]

Citizenship, which Professor Barker has defined as 'taking part in the selection, critical scrutiny, and pressurising of representatives and rulers' was central to Unionist rhetoric between 1912 and 1914. Now the British people reverted to their more familiar role as subjects, becoming 'the object of governmental action…'.[77] Moreover the failure of the federal idea, the secession of twenty-six counties of Ireland and the distancing of the six counties in the devolved government of Northern Ireland reinforced the assumption that the 'British' were indeed, to use Dicey's phrase, 'morally a nation', their organic nature no longer disturbed by Irish Nationalism and the ultra-patriotic demands of Ulster Unionism. But at least the Home Rule and Ulster questions had thrown light on the character of the British Constitution, and helped provoke a debate about the changing nature of that Constitution in the late nineteenth and early twentieth centuries; even if it could do little to influence the direction in which it was heading.

4

The Irish Volunteers:
A Machiavellian Moment?

Matthew Kelly

As the title of this essay suggests, the argument deployed owes a great deal, albeit in a diffuse way, to J.G.A. Pocock's classic study of Enlightenment political thought *The Machiavellian Moment. Florentine Political Thought and the Atlantic Republican Tradition*[1] The purpose is to explore Volunteering discourse, arguing that although seeking to emulate the celebrated eighteenth century Volunteers and the achievement of the Dungannon Convention of 1782, it represented a genuine new departure in Irish politics. The Volunteers of 1913–14 contrasted their eighteenth century predecessors with the strategy and political mode of the Redmondites, and the Redmondites were found wanting. The ideal of an armed citizenry, established in perpetuity, and dedicated to the protection of established, or virtually established, rights and liberties, was contrasted with the apparently emasculated representative politics of Home Rule. Perhaps because of the over-whelming support shown to John Redmond following the Volunteer split, the ideological significance of the movement has not been fully recognised.[2]

But the meaning of the Volunteers cannot be fixed in the image of this revived civic republicanism; at best it was the nearest the move-ment had to an official doctrine, at worse it masked the range of in-compatible political and ideological currents at work. On the one hand, volunteering provided cover for the increasingly effective and determined members of the rejuvenated Irish Republican Brotherhood [IRB]. On the other, a large proportion of the members were channelled into the ranks by the Ancient Order of Hibernians [AOH], the decidedly Catholic mass organisation of Irish constitutional Nationalism. Just as volunteering was an attempt to rejuvenate and embolden constitutional Nationalism through popular mobilisation, it was also an attempt to re-make Irish Nationalism on the basis of civic republican principles. As with every other constitutionalist Nationalist movement in Irish history, it is near impossible to judge the balance between these influences. But the Irish Volunteers were unique in radicalising the doctrines of the constitutionalist agenda while presuming to remain within its bounds. To insist on the permanence of the force and the determination to provide Ireland an independent defensive capacity was incompatible with the claim that Home Rule would reconfigure the Union in a manner that would restore the legitimacy of Westminster, the Crown and its agencies as the ultimate source of authority in Ireland. Consequently, the passage of the Parliament bill, the curtailing of the House of Lords' unrestricted veto, and the success of the Ulster Volunteer Force [UVF] in both staving off and diluting the scope of Home Rule were seismic moments in Irish history. According to the advanced Nationalists, the illusion underpinning the Home Rule campaign was finally and unambiguously exposed. Parnell's 1882 commitment to constitutional activity was revealed as a sham by the crisis provoked by the end of the Lords' veto. The Irish could behave responsibly and constitutionally but ultimately Westminster would not deliver. This, then, was one of those moments, identified by Pocock, 'at which the formation or foundation of a "republic" appears possible or the moment at which its formation is seen to be precarious and entail a crisis in the history to which it belongs'.[3]

The significance of these external pressures on Volunteering needs to be related to the internal history of Irish nationalism. The little evidence there is that Nationalists in the provinces had begun to imitate the UVF in the autumn of 1913 was not very significant to the metropolitan launch of the organisation in November. More pertinent were the machinations of the IRB since the passage of the Parliament act in 1911.[4] The internal politics of the IRB should be patterned against these wider political developments. With the launch of the unambiguously Fenian newspaper *Irish Freedom* in 1911 – a product, effectively, of a coup in the IRB supreme council – John Redmond's old Fenian collaborator Fred Allan was marginalised and the final ascent of a younger cohort under the spiritual leadership of Tom Clarke occurred. *Irish Freedom* simultaneously marked a repudiation of Arthur Griffith's assumption of the role as principal spokesman for Irish separatism. Griffith's ideological flexibility, his promotion of an open separatist movement, and the increasing attention *Sinn Féin* paid to constitutional politics angered the purists who regarded these tendencies as a form of apostasy. As P.S. O'Hegarty later writes, Griffith had been the dominant force in separatist politics until 1911 but with the advent of *Irish Freedom* his pre-eminence ended. Contemporary Fenian correspondence, saturated with provincial resentment of Griffith, corroborates O'Hegarty's argument. Sinn Féin, declining from it high point in 1907–8 when it benefited from a series of high profile defections from the Home Rule party, was reduced by 1911 to little more than a mouthpiece for Griffith. Griffith's attempt to reconfigure the centre ground in Irish politics appeared to have failed;[5] instead, a revived constitutionalism was met with a resurgent Fenianism.

That said, although the IRB were better placed to influence the course of events than they had been for a generation or more, and although they had outmanoeuvred Griffith personally, mainstream Volunteering discourse, in strongly identifying with their eighteenth-century exemplars, was clearly greatly influenced by Griffith's prose-lytism. It is notorious that the 1916 rising was immediately identified with Sinn Féin despite it being an IRB and Irish Citizen Army insurrection. As striking, following the Volunteer split the anti-Redmondite minority were immediately labelled by the police 'Sinn Féin Volunteers'. Reflecting Griffithite success in creating a new corporate identity for 'advanced' Nationalism, this also gave notice of the influence of the Griffithite agenda in the ideological conflicts of 1913–14.

For the IRB volunteering was an undeclared New Departure, and as with that of the late 1870s, they provided the organisational prowess that drove the new movement. There is no need to exaggerate their influence in 1913–14 in order to recognise the dividends the crisis paid them in the battle of ideas. The increasing receptiveness of Irish Nationalists to 'advanced' Nationalism can only be understood as part of the post-Parliament act dynamic that saw Unionism adopt the uncompromising politics of the street. Had the new cohort not taken control of the IRB, the organisation would not have been so well placed to respond effectively to the opportunity. As in 1879–82, 1890–91, and 1898, Irish politics was awash with Fenian sentiment, so much so, that Redmond precipitated a split in the movement in the hope this would restore his authority.

I

The resurgent activism of the Volunteers ended a period of political quiet; the police had earlier observed an absence of enthusiasm for the Home Rule debate conducted at Westminster. 'The introduction of the Home Rule bill has evoked little or no enthusiasm throughout the country', it was noted in April 1912. Moreover, 'In connection with the measure there seems to be considerable dread of extra taxation'.[6] The Inspector General was similarly sanguine in November although he did draw attention to 'a seditious newspaper called "Irish Freedom"' circulating in country towns.[7] Recent work by Michael Wheatley affirms this description of Irish Nationalists as apathetic in the face of the Home Rule bill.[8] Political participation was at low ebb and the introduction of the Home Rule bill clearly shifted the focus to the Westminster arena. The widespread assumption that the mobilisation of the UVF was a political bluff left Irish Nationalists with little choice but to await the outcome of the parliamentary process. Redmond's insistence that the partition of Ireland was impossible provided further reassurance. The eventual trigger for the foundation of the Volunteers was only indirectly the Ulster crisis. In the aftermath of Sir Edward Carson's declaration of a Provisional Government Liberal moves in the autumn of 1913 suggested that the Unionist mobilisation was finally endangering the Home Rule bill and demanded a Nationalist response. Michael McDermott-Hayes, secretary of the South Westmeath United Irish League and editor of the *Westmeath Independent*, concocted a story of 5000 men parading, with buglers, drums, and cavalry, and formed into 20 companies. Such reports were greeted with scorn in Dublin Castle circles but the story was picked-up by the Dublin press, and J.P. Farrell (Nationalist MP for Longford) airily encouraged drilling in a series of speeches[9] – by May Farrell was back in Redmondite line, saying the time was 'not opportune'.[10] IRB activity in late 1913 formed part of this general atmosphere of mounting unease. By the summer of 1914 the authorities had changed their tune. The County Inspector for Tyrone noted the evident fillip given to the advanced men. 'The impunity with which the Ulster Army of 100,000 men enrolled, drilled, and armed themselves, has given an immense stimulus to the Physical Force party. They say it is proof of what they always asserted, that England will yield everything to force, and nothing to other considerations'.[11] Preoccupied with attempts to create an alliance with the IPP that would not compromise the non-political principles of the Volunteers, Eoin MacNeill was similarly concerned by the political complexion of the organisation. He wrote to Darrell Figgis in May 1914:

> In launching such a movement one had only to hold up a finger & naturally every physical force man & every Sinn Féiner would come in. At the same time, in the absence of a lead from the Irish party at the time when no such lead would be expected, it was very difficult to attract men of standing from among the party's adherents.[12]

From the outset, the IRB were the largest single group on the Volunteer Provisional Committee, with 12 of the 30 representatives. They were bolstered by men of more ambiguous political identity like MacNeill and Michael O'Rahilly, while six further men identified as 'advanced Nationalists', including Roger Casement, Michael J. Judge of the AOH, and Colm O'Lochlainn, assistant master at Patrick Pearse's school, St Enda's.[13] Pearse later identified six of the members with the AOH.[14] As David Fitzpatrick however comments, 'no simple definition can do justice either to the richness or to the amorphousness of the new force'.[15] This was reflected in the different emphases in contemporary and retrospective responses. The veteran Fenian Clarke was ecstatic ('Tis good to be alive in these times'), detecting a transformation in 'the young men'.[16] William O'Brien, taking another step in his journey from Parnellism to Sinn Féin, retrospectively identified the Volunteers as an expression of the desire to throw off the influence of the AOH.[17] Although, as will be shown, the AOH was the largest source of Volunteer recruits throughout 1914. Among the separatists, their strategies ranged from the insurrectionism of the professional revolutionaries (Tom Clarke, Seán MacDermott and the IRB), through the passive resistance republicanism of Bulmer Hobson (who in opposing the 1916 rising showed himself loyal to the democratic exactitudes of the IRB constitution), to the cultural separatism of Eoin MacNeill, Gaelic League leader and opponent of IRB insurrectionism.[18] Conversely, in the Volunteers the Redmondite Tom Kettle sought salvation for the dignity of Irish manhood; Colonel Maurice Moore, brother of George, son of a Catholic landowner and Volunteer Inspector-General, regarded volunteering as an extension of his commitment to the Gaelic League. To ascribe some form of collective political identity to these diverse Nationalists invites recourse to the unsatisfactory but inclusive appellation 'advanced': regardless of how numerous were Volunteers who retained membership of constitutional Nationalist organisations, and regardless of how carefully described and delimited their Volunteer allegiance was, adherence to the Volunteers inescapably bespoke a critique of the shortcomings of Redmond's strategy and constitutional Nationalism more generally. As Edward Martyn brusquely telegrammed Casement when invited to attend the Galway meetings of December 1913: 'Not coming believe volunteers will kill Home Rule'.[19]

Clearly then, the Nationalist militia had identity problems. Were they the National Volunteers, the Irish Volunteers, or, even, the Irish National Volunteers? Casement recognised the importance of these differences. To be a member of either the National Volunteers or the Irish National Volunteers was to align with a particular section of the Irish population, whereas the Irish Volunteer believed in an Irish nation that transcended the political divisions not just within Irish Nationalism, but also between Irish Nationalism and Unionism. To be a National Volunteer implied a loyalty to the sectional political identity of the IPP. Casement reminded Moore in June 1914: 'Please always bear in mind the correct title of Irish Volunteers not "National" or "Nationalist" Volunteers (the latter wholly damnable)'.[20]

A close reading of the manifesto approved at the inaugural meeting of 25 November 1913,[21] the benchmark against which all future developments of the movement were measured, shows it to be a highly ambivalent document.[22] Volunteering was not merely an imitation of the UVF, nor simply a means to defend Home Rule. It was a defence of the 'semblance of civil government' that the Ulster Unionist-Conservative nexus threatened. The over-arching danger was the sacrifice of 'the future control of all our national affairs' to this form of mobilisation. Westminster could no longer be even partially relied upon and Irish Nationalists were forced to consider whether they were to 'rest inactive in the hope that the course of politics in Great Britain may save us from the degradation openly threatened against us?' Ultimately, British politics were judged to be 'controlled by British interests' and the British would not help the Irish if they were 'quiescent' or 'unworthy of defence'.

The permanency envisaged for the force was declared in this founding document: 'But the Volunteers, once they have been enrolled, will form a prominent element in the National life under a National Government. The nation will maintain its Volunteer organisation as a guarantee of the liberties which the Irish people shall have secured'. Constitutionalist support for this aspect of the Volunteering agenda represented a radicalisation of the Redmondite project. This went some way toward recognising Sinn Féin's insistence that Ireland acquire the means to pursue an independent foreign policy and high-lighted

just how far Home Rule fell short of this.[23] Patrick Maume argues that
Irish receptiveness to advanced Nationalist rhetoric generated wider
adherence only when allied to specific grievances.[24] Unionist obstruc-
tionism generated just such a grievance, and the claim that to bear
arms for the protection of the 'rights and liberties common to all the
people of Ireland' was a civic duty had a widespread resonance.

The precepts of the Volunteer constitution were elaborated in their
official newspaper the *Irish Volunteer*. In particular, volunteer polemic
celebrated dissent, recognising it as characteristic of a mature political
democracy. In promoting the Volunteers as a 'national' rather than a
'political' body the organisation actualised a distinction dear to advanced Nationalist thinking. This analysis found its clearest and most
forceful exposition in an article on 'Politics and Patriotism' in *Irish
Volunteer* by Peter Macken.[25] Macken, ex-Alderman, Labour leader,
and member of the Gaelic League and Sinn Féin, considered politics
in 'a self-governing country' to be shaped by class and economic
rivalries filtered through personality. He argued that the Gaelic
League taught Nationalists to distinguish between 'Nationality', that
is Irish identity, and 'Party Politics', the machinations of the political
process. Political disagreement should not impugn the claim of an individual to his Irishness. According to Macken, volunteering developed these distinctions further, teaching the difference between
'Patriotism' and 'Party Politics'. Threats to Home Rule identified a
clear patriotic agenda that provided common ground for all
Nationalists. When Ireland finally experienced 'real politics' as a 'free
country' they would discover that the system of two parties,
Nationalist and Unionist, was unsustainable and would fragment
along other lines. Embedded in this was the socialist thesis that the
advent of normal politics would ensure the replacement of sectarian
with class divisions. Vertical class integration would crumble as politics matured, bringing Ireland into the European mainstream. To
some extent this had happened already. While the Home Rule party
was the party of (newly-acquired) Catholic property, working class
politics subsisted in the Fenian-influenced workingmen's clubs of
urban Ireland: The tardy development of Irish trade unionism can in
part be attributed to the existence of this alternative political culture;
James Connolly's socialist republicanism had quite precise sociological
origins. Consequently, the principal function of a permanent volunteer force would be the maintenance of patriotic unity. 'An army is
not a political organisation. We can in a Volunteer corps drill and
march and learn to shoot without forfeiting our individual views and

without giving offence to or shewing [sic] intolerance for the man who drills beside us'. Macken closed by suggesting that patriotism may even be 'the privilege of the man who is of no party, who is simply a Volunteer'.[26] Barring this closing ambivalence, Macken's argument, intentionally or not, resonated with Mandevillian claim that the pursuit of self-interest ('private vice') through the political sphere generates 'public virtue'. The broader revolutionary implications of Macken's argument only became clear with the progress of the war of independence. Here were intimations of the apolitical culture of the Irish Republican Army [IRA] flying columns analysed by Peter Hart; their disregard for political control originated in the pre-war political identity of the Volunteers.[27]

Fenians believed that through the UVF the Tories had inhibited Westminster's ability to devolve political rights to Dublin and for Liberals submission to Unionist 'Fenianism' meant Westminster had ceased to be the principal forum for the determination of the great political questions. This left Nationalist loyalty to the parliamentary party predicated on false assumptions. After the Curragh incident of March 1914 a front-page commentary in *The Irish Volunteer* starkly delineated these implications, displaying their Fenian affinities. 'We sacrificed "unconstitutional" methods for constitutional, and if at the last minute England tells us that her constitution is a sham we must take her words and take back the arms we dropped'.[28] The question was not whether Home Rule would get onto the statute book, but whether England was sufficiently determined to enforce its provisions. It was to ensure implementation that the Volunteers, armed and drilled, were essential. 'The time for mere empty talk is past, and on behalf of an armed Irish nation leaders will speak with the consciousness of power that will make their voices of the utmost weight. Behind the ballot box is the rifle, behind the Irish Parliamentary party must be the army'.[29] Mounting evidence of the failure of the Westminster strategy increasingly justified its rejection. In March, Casement discarded Volunteer proprietary giving full expression to the supposed implications of this scenario.

> The freedom of Ireland was not going to be won at Westminster. If the people of Ireland wanted it as much as the people of Ulster did not want it they must be prepared to fight for it. They must put revolution in the place of resolution as they had enough resolutions already. If they meant to have Home Rule they should be prepared to shed their blood for it. No nation could ever win its freedom without fighting for it. Unless they fought for it they would not get it.[30]

The mounting evidence of English perfidy invited a more defiant separatist polemic and this worried moderate volunteers. Casement provided Moore ambiguous reassurance: 'I am not a "revolutionary" an "idealist" – beyond the limit of most of my countrymen – or anxious for "rebellion"'.[31] But the increased threat of partition permitted a departure from orthodox Volunteer rhetoric. In Tullamore Casement was adamant, the Volunteers stood for 'a united Ireland, and in the end for a free Ireland'. Casement's intimation of revolution had been given a wider purchase by the Ulster crisis.

Augustine Birrell, Chief Secretary of Ireland, was sensitive to the subtle nuances of Irish Nationalist discourse. In a confidential Cabinet memorandum of April 1914 he noted that the 'word "volunteer" in Ireland is full of historical significance, and touches the national sentiment in all parts of the country'. Although consisting of 'somewhat ragged regiments, ill-equipped as yet and not particularly well disciplined', the Volunteers were 'daily increasing in number and may become a formidable force in the future'.[32] Birrell, however indolent, knew his brief. The advanced Nationalists of the 1900s had invested the historic Volunteers with particular significance. Griffith regarded their disbanding as the essential precursor to the passage of the Act of Union, denuding Grattan's Parliament of the source of its essential patriotic defence;[33] MacNeill put the same case in his seminal essay 'The North Began';[34] and on a fund-raising tour in the US, Pearse told a Philadelphia crowd in March: 'Had the Volunteers not handed back their arms, the horrors of '98 would never have come. The Union would never have been accomplished. The sacrifice of Emmet would not have been needed'.[35] In separatist historiography, the call in 1782 by the convention at Dungannon for the repeal of constitutionally limiting legislation was the moment *par excellence* when popular pressure reinforced the demands of the politicians. The achievement of the legislative independence of Grattan's Parliament was directly attributed to the existence of this armed body of patriotic Irishmen and although motivated by a very particular form of Ascendancy patriotism, twentieth-century advanced Nationalists aspired to their civic and martial spirit. The Dungannon Convention was proof the battle could be won by taking a determined stance on a series of well-articulated demands. It was the ambiguous historical legacy of the eighteenth-century Volunteers that provided much of the ideological justification for Sinn Féin's nimble quickstep between constitutionalism and Fenianism. Unlike the republican abstractions of Fenianism, the eighteenth-century volunteers suggested practical solutions rooted in the specificities of England and Ireland's constitutional relationship.

As Charles Townshend shows, although the legality of the Volunteering movement was dubious, drilling in defence of 'rights and liberties' was an established right.[36] Not only was the constitutionalism of the force complicated by the fact that the 'rights and liberties' they proposed to defend were yet to be granted, but the permanency claimed for the Volunteers surpassed these anticipated 'rights and liberties'. But the problem was knottier still. Volunteering embodied a further paradox that went to the heart of the Home Rule strategy. Was Home Rule a pragmatic response by a coherent and fundamentally separatist Nationalist community to the overwhelming military and commercial superiority of the colonising power, or, was it a sincere attempt to reconfigure the Union so as to ensure that it was compatible with the interests of that same nationalist community? Home Rule cannot be reduced to either and the tension is clear. On the one hand, Irish Nationalists regarded themselves as a national community with the right to self-determination, on the other, their support for the constitutionalism of Home Rule represented the ceding of this right to the sovereignty of Westminster. In 1798, 1848, 1867, and 1913–14, *and for quite disparate reasons*, sections of the Nationalist community reclaimed that right to self-determination.

Tom Kettle's participation in the movement emblematised the home rule paradox. A loyal Redmondite, Kettle emerged as one of the firmest advocates of full Irish involvement in the war against 'Prussian tyranny'.[37] With his brother Laurence he was a member of the Volunteer 'Provisional Committee', giving credence to its non-partisan identity. Kettle's writings in the *Irish Volunteer* were underpinned by his belief that Irish liberties were should be rooted in abstract notions of citizenship rather than the provisions of the constitution. His desire to put the Irish question into an international context[38] reflected his positioning of the Volunteers in a world dominated by 'the strange reversion to the gospel of the force'.[39] This applied equally to the international arms race, the violence of class conflict (the 'prologue to passionately desired rebellion'), and, presumably, the UVF. Fenian expectations that disappointment with Home Rule would generate a rebirth of national sentiment were to some extent affirmed by Kettle's assertion that the programme of the Volunteers was the product not of 'logic' but of a 'sudden illumination'.[40] Kettle's constitutional credentials were further stretched by his distrust of the forces of the Crown. The delegation of responsibility of defence to a professional (mercenary?) army was not only unmanly but, in Ireland's particular case, not 'safe'. The 'Castle-controlled policeman' or the 'London-controlled soldier', those officially responsible for the maintenance of law and order, could not be relied upon to arbitrate fairly between the competing claims on their authority. Kettle's fear that it was 'something too much of a gamble whether the baton...will crack the right skull or the wrong one' recalls Pearse's notorious (if ironic) apologia of November 1913 ('we may make mistakes in the beginning and shoot the wrong people; but bloodshed is a cleansing and sanctifying thing'), demonstrating the ambiguous rhetorical currency images can gain.[41] Ultimately, Kettle argued, military organisation in Ireland was 'created not to defend the nation against invaders, but to defend the Government against the nation'. The fraught circumstances of 1914, compounded by the Curragh incident, saw Kettle tell a Tullamore crowd that they, 'were not going to rely...for their national security upon the whims or the fancies of some old fellow with gold braid down the seams of his breeches (laughter). Irishmen were going to take care of themselves, and they meant to do it (cheers)'.[42] Kettle saw the movement radicalising the Home Rule demand. 'Whoever is responsible for the government of the country will be forced to regularise and adopt' the Volunteers. The Home Rule bill contained no provision for an Irish defence or military capacity, yet Kettle regarded the Volunteer opportunity as restoring to him his 'self-respect as a citizen' by enabling him to efficiently fulfil those attendant obligations, rather than relying on 'inadequate proxies'. These were the essentials of the classic defence of an armed republican citizenry.

Kettle's highlighting of the restoration of self-respect reflected more generalised Volunteer polemic. Volunteering relied upon the nurture of a martial spirit that drew on the Fenian discourse that linked revolution with the restoration of Irish manliness.[43] If the experience of colonial subjugation had rendered Irish manhood feminised, subservient and dependent, this was enhanced by the secondary dependency on the Parliamentary Party. Volunteering answered the Fenian complaint that the role of ordinary Irishmen had been reduced to voting pointless res-olutions and paying subscriptions. Griffith's doctrine of self-reliance had at root sought to emancipate the Irish from this emasculating political culture, Volunteering aimed to do the same.

Inseparable from this was the firearm. The linkage of arms and mas-culinity was a strong theme in *Irish Volunteer* discourse. Every Volunteer 'loves a rifle' claimed the newspaper, and a number of writers of greatly differing temperaments addressed this theme. Casement, advocating the celebration of the 900th anniversary of the Battle of Clontarf, argued that 'to be a good Irishman means also to be a good Christian, and that it is only the strong man armed who keepeth his own house and

Church'.[44] Joseph Plunkett also argued along muscular Christianity lines: 'it is at once the duty and the dignity of Christian manhood to bear arms, even if only for their symbolism, and if there were to be no likelihood of the necessity for their use'.[45] This chimes with Michael Laffan's observation that Pearse's claim that 'nationhood is not achieved otherwise than in arms' was qualitatively distinct from F.S.L. Lyons's paraphrase 'Nationhood could not be achieved other than by arms'.[46] Again, the shortcomings of the Home Rule bill were indicated. By failing to extend to Ireland the power of self-defence it failed to render 'Ireland a nation' and to restore to Irishmen their masculinity: 'A man is not fully a man, nor is a nation a nation without the power to direct a policy and to ensure civil and religious liberty to those who demand those blessings. For this reason conscription is the prevailing military policy among the Powers of Europe. The whole nation must bear arms'. Passing over the confusion expressed here between an armed citizenry and a conscripted army, this argument nonetheless departed from the cultural nationalist conception of the nation as the embodiment of a culture rooted in an ethno-linguistic specificity to one in which the nation could only be realised through the achievement of political liberties. Without the capacity to conduct an independent defence of these liberties the nation and its manhood remained incomplete.

After the Curragh incident in March and the UVF gunrunning at Larne in April this discourse became more strident. In May the *Irish Volunteer* proclaimed the 'man who has once handled a rifle and is not smitten with a desire to own one is not an Irishman'.[47] In defiance of the acceptance of Redmondites onto the Executive Committee, the paper made its priorities clear in July. 'We must have rifles. Whether the proclamation [against importing arms] is torn up or not the rifles must come....All the rest, uniforms, equipment, standards, could be dispensed with, but the rifle is the soldiers arm'.[48]

A subsidiary aspect of the talk of arms was their role in tempting young men into the movement. It is difficult to demonstrate how effective this was as a recruiting strategy, but there is evidence that young men coveted rifles and revolvers. Moreover, the increase in the circulation of arms and the incidence of gun-related crime before 1913 acted as a further conditioning factor in the reception given the Volunteers. By allowing the Peace Preservation act of 1881 to lapse in 1906 the limited legal restrictions on the importation of arms to Ireland were removed.[49] One melodramatic witness later suggested a clear causal link between this Liberal move and future events: 'The Arms act was dropped. The Irish party and their cause were swept into oblivion in consequence'.[50] The remaining 1870 Gun Licence act did not provide an adequate legal basis to control the circulation of arms and this was of particular concern to the police.[51] Equally worried was the *Irish Catholic*, it lamented, 'the foolish and irresponsible farmers boys and village youths to whom the prospect of acquiring revolvers in payment of a shilling a week has been an irresistible temptation'.[52] Of the many newspaper advertisements for firearms in this period a typical example was carried by the *Weekly Freeman* for a Birmingham company offering the aptly named Davis's Original & Genuine 'Defiance' Gun for 50/.[53]

After 1906 there was a marked rise in the number of offences committed with firearms. Historically, times of political unrest brought an increase in indictable offences. This becomes clear if a series of five-year periods are examined:[54]

1848–1852	annual average	139
1858–1863		55
1868–1872		58[55]
1878–1882		157
1888–1892		72
1908–1912		90[56]

There appears to be a strong correlation between the lifting of the restrictions on the purchase of arms and the increase in the incidence of gun-related crime. Second, since 1848 the increases and decreases in agrarian and non-agrarian crime tended to coincide, suggesting that there was a general increase in lawlessness at times of agrarian agitation. That said, during the Land War agrarian gun-crime of a threatening nature far out-stripped the non-agrarian equivalent.[57] The signs of a trend away from agrarian gun-crime after 1912 suggests that with the decline in UIL agitation there was a general decline in rural lawlessness. On the other hand, the increase in non-agrarian gun-crime continued and it seems this both conditioned the emergence of the Volunteers and was symptomatic of this development. Indeed, recognition of this seems congruent with the Inspector General's characterisation of the Volunteer threat as chiefly one to law and order. Pearse's notorious demand of November 1913 that, 'We [the Irish] must accustom ourselves to the thought of arms, to the sight of arms, to the use of arms',[58] gave an ideological gloss to a process already at work. The existence of a section of Nationalist Ireland pre-disposed to the ownership and use of firearms helps explain the apparently spontaneous drilling. More than this, although such activity was not the product of political organisation, in a culture that celebrated Fenian daring-do it seems hard to dispute that ownership of non-essential firearms had political significance. The UVF may have returned the gun to Irish politics, but it was not responsible for bringing it to Irish society.[59]

II

The very existence of the Volunteers represented the partial realisation of its doctrinal aspirations. Another marker of its success was the extent to which its social complexion reflected the support of all social classes. Paradoxically, as the Redmondite/AOH influence on the organisation grew so did it more fully fulfil these ideological objectives – of particular note was the cadre of upper class Catholics and Protestants that took a leadership role. Where the Volunteers obviously failed was in making common cause with the UVF in the interests of national unity.

It has been established that the Volunteers did not become a large body until the summer of 1914 when the Redmondites extended their influence on the controlling committee. According to the police, the total membership in March was 10,489, by late April it had reached 19,206, and in May 25,000.[60] This rapid increase reflected the reaction to the Curragh incident, increased organisational effectiveness, and the decision by the AOH to order its branches to establish Volunteer companies[61] – this came pretty close to the organisation receiving, whether the leadership liked it or not, official Redmondite approval. O'Rahilly, appealing to Devoy for money for rifles, claimed there were 25,000 members by the beginning of April with the potential to build a force of 200,000.[62] Moore, the Volunteer Inspector-General, imagined an eventual force of 200,000 defending Ireland against a German invasion force of 20,000.[63] The detailed police figures available for March 1914 report the following. There were 4,390 Volunteers in Ulster organised into 18 branches; about 993 in Leinster with eight branches; approximately 2,333 organised into 11 branches in Munster; 1,638 in Connaught in 11 branches; and 1,140 in the Dublin Metropolitan Police area in nine branches.[64] To achieve these modest figures was not easy. An early meeting broke up in Cork and little initial success was observed in Limerick, Galway, Kerry and Wicklow. In East Limerick the local MP Thomas Lundun poured cold water on the initiative at an UIL meeting explaining that the Volunteers were not yet necessary and in time the political leadership would give the order. Richard Hazelton was similarly negative to his Galway constituents.[65] Nonetheless,

February saw rapid proliferation, with branches soon reported in 17 counties. A renewed Nationalist 'vitality' was widely noted but all County Inspectors agreed that the movement would only grow rapidly if it were supported by the IPP: nationalist Ireland, however, was in 'general sympathy'.[66]

The indicators of the social complexion of the Volunteers suggest that the bulk of the membership was of the lower middle classes and the labouring class. However, Nationalists from across the social spectrum increasingly associated with the movement, particularly from the end of May. 'The rank and file consist so far of farmer's sons, shop assistants, and servant boys, but the Catholic clergy, professional men, County and District Councillors, magistrates…and a very few ex-military officers, have identified themselves with the movement'.[67]

Class tension was reported in Carlow where the 'labour and corner boy element' was resented by the shop assistants and the farmers' sons. Class and sectarian divisions combined in Donegal: while 'farmers and their sons drill in the Unionist hall their labourers drill in the opposite camp', illustrating how sectarian identities over-lapped class position. In Armagh, where 3,000 had joined, it was noted that 'the better class of Nationalists' had kept their distance, whereas in Mayo not only did the Volunteers attract support from across the class spectrum but was also supported by persons who were not known to have joined Nationalist organisations before. In Westmeath no Nationalist section opposed, in Waterford the O'Brienites held aloof.[68] In Galway college students joined up, possibly reflecting the strong Gaelic Athletic Association and secret society presence. Sir Roger Casement reported that they could barely cope with the initial rush of 4–500 recruits: 'every section of the populace was there (but no gentry) of the town and all parties' he wrote to Maurice Moore. 'If one resolute, clearheaded Irishman who cared for Ireland, as an Irish gentleman should, lived here and took the boys up he could have a splendid National Corps in six months. So far I can see no man'.[69]

Casement was a little too pessimistic. 'There is a tendency recently of persons who heretofore regarded as strong Catholic Unionists to support the Movement', reported the Galway county inspector, 'They have not come forward in public, but doing so is only a matter of time'.[70] It seems the apparently apolitical stance of the Volunteers and the emphasis on discipline appealed to those who had previously identified with Unionism and the landowning class. Volunteering invited retired soldiers to take a leadership role, successfully appealing to a patrician instinct otherwise denied expression.[71] Hobson later joked of his embarrassment at having attracted 'as many members of the House of Lords as the Ulster Volunteers.'[72] Particularly in Galway, where the campaign against the graziers had been especially 'advanced', the advent of the Volunteers fulfilled this particular need. That said, 'the Riding cannot be described as peaceable as it is in the grip of the Volunteers who are recruited in nearly every branch by moonlighters and other seditious and undesirable characters'.[73]

The relative numerical strength of Volunteers in Ulster owed much to the influence of the AOH. They dominated the five branches in Co. Tyrone, the largest of which comprised the 750 members in Strabane; they were similarly prominent in Fintown, Donegal. It seems probable that the AOH presence would have been as marked where branches were identified as run by 'local' and 'prominent' Nationalists, notably the 960 Volunteers of Ballyshannon, Co. Donegal and the 935 of Derry, Co. Londonderry. Strikingly the 100 members of the Falls Road in Belfast practising 'simple drill indoors' were identified with the IRB, evoking Hobson's memory of nervously promoting the Dungannon Clubs on Falls street corners with Seán MacDermott.[74]

Pearse may have hoped that he might one day see arms in the hands of the AOH,[75] but many separatists bitterly resented their presence in the Volunteers. For Thomas Ashe their high profile threw into doubt the whole Volunteer project. He was enraged that the organisation was 'practically ruled to-day by the AOH Board of Erin'.[76] MacDermott, Eamon Ceannt and the 'Dublin boys' were attempting to keep them 'straight…but their efforts will be to no avail as the preponderating majority are U.I. League and Hibs'. O'Rahilly hoped the Clan would help with the provision of rifles and tackled John Devoy's gravest doubts, arguing along classic Fenian lines: 'The men at the wheel are straight thinkers and include all the advanced and sincere who are interested in real nationality'. Given the controversies of June, there was some irony in O'Rahilly's reassurances: 'In order to be representative we include the inevitable proportion of jelly fish and of compromisers besides a crank or two, but they are keeping fairly well in line'. Ultimately, the 'objects of the men *who are running this movement* are exactly the same as yours'.[77]

Relations between the IRB and the AOH had been transformed since the factional fights of the 1890s. Of obscure origins, caught somewhere between a communal Catholic response to the Orange Order, a development of Ribbonism, and that classic nineteenth century social formation the friendly-society, the AOH had developed into the principal repository of Nationalist opinion in the north of Ireland. Under the provisions of 'New Liberal' social legislation, the AOH was formally recognised as an 'approved society' and grew rapidly after 1909.[78] Though hardly the jack-booted *squadristi* of O'Brienite lore, the 'Mollies' reputation for political rowdiness was confirmed by the notorious 'baton' convention of 1909: William O'Brien's supporters were driven from a party convention by Joe Devlin's boys, earning O'Brien's unstinting opprobrium.[79] O'Brien condemned the 'narrow sectarian intolerance' of the AOH, claiming the Volunteers reflected the 'longing of the youth of Ireland for some escape from the corrupt atmosphere of the Hibernian tyranny to a higher and more generous plane'.[80] Separatists viewed the AOH as representative of all that was most regressive about Nationalist politics in the north, regarding them as particularly threatening to the links they hoped to build with sympathetic Protestants. Earlier McCartan had written, 'The AOH in any shape or form is a barrier to the progress of real Nationalism as it fosters distrust and bigotry'.[81]

The IRB may have been repelled by the high profile of the AOH in the Volunteers, but providing their sectarian tendencies were hidden, they were tolerated. To prevent the organisation from becoming merely an adjunct of the Parliamentary party the original manifesto had prohibited individual Volunteer branches being based on individual organisations – Volunteer identity was to be regional. In practice, through sheer weight of numbers the AOH was able to make its presence felt, undermining the influence of the separatist minority in nominal command. Hobson's acquiescence in the face of Redmond's demand that 25 of his nominees be accepted onto the committee was an acknowledgement of this reality. And to regard this as a betrayal of all he had worked for since the 1900s would be to take a very narrow view of IRB strategy. Certainly Hobson was responding to immediate political pressures, but he also provided for the maintenance of an organisation the IRB could work through rather than against. A bastardised New Departure perhaps, but one approved by a majority of eventual committee of the breakaway faction.

III

Shortly before the Volunteer split, official figures suggested the organisation to be 181,732 strong. Enrolment remained highest in Ulster (59,892 members, 442 branches), followed by Leinster (47,103 / 441), Munster (42,750 / 412), and finally Connaught (31,987 / 318).[82] By December 1914 the police estimated Irish Volunteer membership to be at 9,971. As with all such statistics they are problematic, and these bring into question the revisionist analysis that follows Hobson's claim that between two and three thousand stayed with the Irish Volunteers as opposed to the traditional figure of 11–12,000.[83] In October/November 1914 the police identified 11,000 as loyal to the Provisional Committee and Sinn Féin, but added the important caveat that numbers were sufficient to form separate corps only in Cork, Belfast, Limerick, Athenry, and Enniscorthy.[84] The significance of this ready association of the Irish Volunteers with Sinn Féin was earlier observed. Further examples from October 1914 included the 120 SF Volunteers addressed by McCullough in Belfast;[85] the 160 Dublin SF Volunteers who marched to Tallaght; the 30 SF and 320 Redmondite Volunteers in Queen's County; the 40 SF Volunteers out of total of 400 in Enniscorthy (the numbers volunteering in late 1914 were 50 and 350 respectively); and the 130 SF Volunteers who marched past the Kerry meeting during which J. O'Donnell MP established a Redmondite branch and enrolled 400.[86] Given the rapid decline of the National Volunteers following the split, a generous estimate of the proportion of rebel volunteers in late 1914 might be up to 10 per cent of the overall Nationalist total.

Despite the small force the Sinn Féin Volunteers could command it was clear their influence exceeded their numbers. Redmondite speakers touring the country encouraging enlistment prompted a Sinn Féin anti-enlistment campaign. The police considered this effective, noting their 'possession of greater influence than is warranted by their numbers and position'. However, 'the correct explanation probably is that the majority of men in this country are naturally disinclined to enlist, and consequently welcome the Sinn Féin arguments as an excuse to stay at home'.[87] This is curious given that David Fitzpatrick's statistical analysis suggests that recruitment patterns did not demonstrate widespread Irish Catholic disapproval of the war because voluntary enlistment among Irish Catholics was not significantly low.[88] Arguably, police impressions were shaped by the intensifying atmosphere of disloyalty that characterised Irish nationalist communities, enhancing the perception of a population immune to the cultures of deference, patriotism and duty thought to be the characteristic of the British working class. The British or imperial agenda was tolerated in Ireland providing it did not impact detrimentally on individual lives. Taxation was a necessary evil; the demands of the recruiting officer were of a different order.[89] The police noted that, 'while the number of persons who are pro-German remains small, there is now a much greater anti-English feeling abroad than was the case at the beginning of August…and [it] is no doubt largely due to the Sinn Féin propaganda'.[90]

Explanations posited for Redmondite support for the Great War ranged from the morally dubious motivations imputed to them by the separatists (cannon fodder in exchange for Home Rule) to the internationalism of Kettle. British reluctance to impose conscription on Ireland recognised Ireland's difference, while this ongoing threat provided Sinn Féin one of its strongest political arguments. The Parliamentary party was in an impossible situation. At the upper levels its strategy was predicated on persuading men to voluntarily enlist as a means to stave off conscription, at the lower level, Redmondite MPs were reluctant to address the issue at all, well aware of the destabilising threat the issue posed.[91] Noting that by November 1914 only 11,720 Catholics had enlisted compared to 19,011 Protestants, the police observed that the Redmondite National Volunteers were 'not organised', 'practically unarmed' and few members had any 'proper military training'; having been formed for a 'political purpose' it was 'formidable only on paper'.[92] Evidently, the police did not consider the National Volunteers a basis on which to build an army. Kitchener, it seems, agreed, and the explanation for this did not merely lie in the organisational weakness of the movement. British actions, whether through their reluctance to conscript Ireland or on the Volunteers regiment issue, suggested that not only were Irish Nationalists not regarded as British, but that the British recognised they were dealing with a fundamentally disloyal population – which Home Rule pieties could not paper over. The events of 1911–14 had reinforced rather than diluted Irish Nationalist alienation from the British state.

By contrast, the 'Sinn Féin Section' was importing rifles and showing signs of determined – though numerically not very threatening – activity. McCullough and A. Heron oversaw the rifle practice of 30 Volunteers in Belfast on 14 November; on 22 November when 85 Sinn Féiners marched to a meeting at St Mary's Hall, 35 carried loaded rifles with fixed bayonets. While 14 Sinn Féiners had rifle practice on 8 November in Donegal, 850 mostly armed SF Volunteers marched from Dublin to Swords, where they met 60 local Volunteers and conducted a mock battle. In Galway, O'Neill and Judge inspected 300 SF Volunteers, 36 were armed, although only 20 turned out to hear John MacBride lecture at Tuam on 22 November. In Tralee, a disorderly march ended with two men being charged for firing shots; in Castleisland (Co. Kerry) 24 rifles were delivered from a Dublin dealer. Near Listowel a 'skirmishing drill' was practised on 8 November and 160 Limerick SF Volunteers attended rifle practice at Woodcock Hall, Co. Clare.[93] These were extra-ordinary scenes. London and Dublin Castle looked on, reluctant to inter-vene, while an avowedly revolutionary organisation, hostile to the British government and empire, conducted armed drills in preparation of rebel-lion. Much of the explanation of this must lie in the close study of the British 'Thing', of the tensions between the immediate political dangers, in Ireland, at home, and on the continent, and its underlying liberal men-talité. In December 1914 the County Inspector for Tyrone reported: 'Information has been received that a meeting of 16 local IRB members was held in a field at Mullaghmore near Dungannon on the 9th of December, with the object of encouraging the growth of the associa-tion'.[94] Marginal concern at the rate of Catholic enlistment can have been little enhanced by 16 men in a field, stamping their feet, rubbing their hands and, amid frosty breath, plotting revolution.

IV

Volunteering was a cathartic experience. Here was a generation of young men granted a suggestive taste of the potential of collective action. Their involvement provided retrospective justification for Fenianism and the United Irishmen, living evidence of the spirit of comradeship and empowerment evoked in countless addresses and speeches. Volunteering was an act of re-appropriation, restoring politi-cal agency to the ordinary man and woman, liberating it from the suffo-cating and narrow strictures of the increasingly distant Home Rule campaign at Westminster. This was the spirit of Fenianism, a brief moment when full expression was given to an Irish national identity suppressed by pragmatism and opportunism.

This, at least, was the experience promoted by the *Irish Volunteer* and *Irish Freedom*. This discourse provided a framework within which the emotional experience of volunteering was understood, granting it a wider political significance and meaning. But the political implications of this experience remained obscure. Police contempt for the ineffec-tiveness of the majority provided one marker of the uncertainty at the heart of volunteering, the recourse to secret plotting by the IRB another. But the ideological nature of this uncertainty needs to be registered. The Irish Volunteers were another example of a popular Irish political movement that blurred the boundaries between constitu-tional and non-constitutional Nationalism. More than any other, the 'advanced' edge it gave to constitutional Nationalism fundamentally challenged Home Rule orthodoxy. As significant, however, was the

evidence from the Casement correspondence that the 'advanced' leadership was determined to support Redmond while the parliamentary
strategy remained viable. In June, warning Casement against immoder-
ate language, Erskine Childers said the Home Rule party 'must be
supported till they fail'.[95] Ultimately however, the rapid disintegration
of the Redmondite Volunteers attested to the incompatibility of the
movement's civic republicanism with Redmondism. For the original
Volunteer leadership, the failure of Redmondism to sustain a Volunteer
organisation was indicative of its wider inadequacies. Orthodox Home
Rule, after all, was predicated on the conviction that the reform of
the institutions of government would reconcile Irish Catholics to the
British state. The pre-war crisis provided further reasons why they
would not be. Everything that served to reinforce Ireland's atavistic
enmities damaged the Home Rule ideal, possibly the greatest chimera
in modern British history.

Superficially then, the 'Machiavellian moment' of the Ulster crisis
confronted Unionist anarchy with Nationalist civic virtue; ideologically
the situation was much more complicated. Nationalists sought to
protect the sovereignty of Westminster against Unionist insurrectionism, while at the same time threatening a similar insurrectionism if the
executive did not mobilise the state against militant Unionism. As volunteering discourse became increasingly influenced by Fenian polemic
the meaning of the crisis for Nationalists became clearer. They asked
themselves, in the light of these events, what value could be attached to
their vote. If any all-Ireland settlement achieved on the basis of British
constitutional principles could be wrecked by Unionist militancy on
what foundations was Redmondism ultimately based? As the high level
of volunteer recruitment to the British army demonstrated, however,
questioning the efficacy of Redmondism did not generate widespread
conversion to advanced Nationalist principles. Approving the volunteer
critique of constitutional Nationalism did not a separatist make.
Nonetheless, during 1913–14 the internal politics of Irish Nationalism
experienced its gravest disruption, certainly since the Parnell split, probably since Isaac Butt first promoted the Home Rule idea. Patrick
Maume argues that we should take seriously the suggestion that the
1916 rising accelerated existing trends;[96] consistent with doing so is to
recognise that however inconclusive the battle of ideas in 1913–14, its
very occurrence on such a grand scale indicated the weakening of the
Irish party's ability to determine the acceptable boundaries of debate.
Volunteering's intimation of an alternative nationalism functioned as the
stalking horse for the more visible post-1916 radicalisation, en route

reinforcing Sinn Féin's contention that the strategic dichotomy of home rule/constitutionalism and separation/insurrectionism was false. Faced with assessing the impact of the 1916 rising on the evolution of Nationalist attitudes, Fitzpatrick admits how difficult it is for the historian to 'reassemble...the subtle process by which imagination is set free';[97] that liberation was conditioned by the 'moment' of 1913–14, in all its seismic but apparently impractical implications.

5

The Landed Elite, Power and Ulster Unionism

N.C. Fleming

The theme of decline is a central feature in examinations of all European landed elites. In the case of Ireland, the fate of the so called 'Ascendancy' is related directly to the progress of organised nationalism, a feature that has served to encourage scholarly analyses of Irish landownership. Early examples of this tended to reinforce popular perceptions of the role of class, property and politics in the Irish 'struggle', assumptions that later scholars undermined through detailed studies of estate papers and government records.[1] Their 'revisionist' approach, particularly in the late 1970s and 1980s, challenged the prevailing nationalist and Marxist analyses of the 'Land Question', just as it challenged these interpretations more generally. Accompanying this has been a steady output of popular books on Ireland's landed elite and their properties. Yet despite this considerable range of work, few have addressed the continuance of landed power well into the twentieth century, specifically in the northeast, in the six counties that after 1921 became the self-governing province of Northern Ireland. On the rare occasions when it is mentioned, usually very briefly, writers are often content to merely note that decline was slower in the northeast than in the rest of Ireland. This is attributed, often implicitly and without explanation, to the role of landlords in the Ulster Unionist movement, an explanation that appeared to ignore Peter Gibbon's 1975 study of Ulster unionism in which he argued that the Belfast bourgeoisie had effectively replaced landlords at the head of the movement in the early 1890s.[2] Unintentionally, the commonplace explanation has been given credibility by Alvin Jackson's detailed dissection of pre-1912 Ulster unionism. In contrast to Gibbon, Jackson argues that the ultimate suzerainty of the Belfast bourgeoisie was only evident in the formation of the Ulster Unionist Council in 1904 (formally established in 1905), and in the mass mobilisation of 1912 in response to the third Home Rule bill.[3]

If Jackson demonstrated that landed power and influence did not disappear in the 1890s, he still concludes that it was ultimately eclipsed by the need for greater professionalism, particularly among elected representatives. How then do we account for the presence of the landed elite in successive Unionist governments of Northern Ireland (1921–72)? Jackson's scholarship is not directly concerned with this, but it has not gone completely unnoticed by others. Among the few scholars who have taken it seriously are Amanda Shanks, a social anthropologist, and the historians John Harbinson and David Cannadine. Harbinson's examination of the Ulster Unionist party does not give specific figures for members of the landed elite, but he does note that the party at Stormont was overwhelmingly middle- and upper-class, adding that 'the influence of the "big house" in Ulster politics must not be measured by the number of seats in parliament held by the aristocracy.'[4] Cannadine devotes several pages of his *Decline and Fall of the British Aristocracy* to Northern Ireland, acknowledging both the continued presence of 'grandees' in local and regional government, and the increasing limitations on their once dominant influence.[5] Shanks also highlights the continued existence of gentry culture into the 1980s, and like the Belfast poet John Hewitt – in his 'An Ulster landowner's song' – she concludes that it was only the onset of the Troubles in 1969 that finally removed them from politics.[6] But if these writers are able to point to the continued presence, physically and politically, of the landed elite in Northern Ireland, they avoid drawing firm conclusions about why and how this situation came about.

It is argued in this chapter that these questions can be answered through an examination of power relationships and authority mechanisms, and how these were effected by periods of crisis; in particular the Land War (1879–82), the 'Invasion of Ulster' in 1883, the 'Devolution Crisis' of 1904, the 'Ulster crisis' of 1912 to 1914, and the foundation of Northern Ireland (1920–5). For most of Ireland, the earlier of these crises heralded the end of landlord dominance and confirmed the counter-elite, and later elite, status of the Catholic bourgeoisie. In the northeast, however, these same crises gave fresh political impetus and purpose to a politically active section of the landed class. Accommodating the bourgeois elite of Belfast and environs, these landlords formed new power relationships and authority mechanisms for their regionally-based movement that were neither exclusively traditional or legal-rational, but a hybrid of the two. In time, later crises would determine that the internal dynamics of Ulster unionism would favour the legal-rational, but the landed elite continued to be a conspicuous political presence in what became Northern Ireland.

I

Like other modernising societies in the latter half of the nineteenth century, politics in Ireland came to be transformed by increased public monitoring through informed and critical discourse. New elites emerged, made up of professionals, educators, clerics, businessmen and large farmers, all asserting what Max Weber identified as 'legal-rational authority'.[7] As their numbers and influence grew, they were better able to contest the economic, political and cultural dominance of the landed elite, making significant advances, as Weber found generally, at times of crisis. This had obvious consequences for 'traditional authority', but it also had an impact on the leadership style of movements challenging that authority, particularly, in the case of Ireland, organised nationalism.[8]

Neverless, it would be a gross over simplification to associate legal-rational authority exclusively with organised nationalism. It was also very much in evidence in the Irish Conservative party, particularly in Belfast. Moreover, in its attempt to create an anti-nationalist alliance of Conservatives and Liberals, it became even harder for traditional authority to resist what Weber viewed as the inevitable encroachment of legal-rational authority, especially at times of crisis when existing power relationships and authority mechanisms were viewed as inadequate. In contrast to organised nationalism, however, the early accommodation of traditional- and legal-rational authority within unionism meant that the former was never completely dismantled by the latter. Indeed, it was incubated in the structures of the UUC, the organisation that in 1921 assumed control of the devolved government of Northern Ireland. Nevertheless, the question remains, how was traditional authority able to secure a popular following, and why were the landed elite of the northeast in a relatively strong position vis-à-vis their bourgeois rivals?

To command the opposition to organised nationalism in the early 1880s, landlords began the process of placing themselves at the head of a cross-class alliance of loyalist interests, an assertion of their traditional role, but one that now acknowledged the need for a more responsive and accountable leadership. They did not, therefore, suddenly impose a specifically Unionist ideology on the protestants of the northeast; as Jim Mac Laughlin observes, the proletariat and petit-bourgeoisie of Unionist Ulster opposed Catholic Irish nationalism as active nation-builders of the protestant United Kingdom of Great Britain and Ireland. Landlords seeking to command a popular anti-nationalist movement therefore had to court the interests of these supporters as expressed by the 'organic intelligentsia', that is, the region's well-developed provincial press.[9] This meant that aspiring landlord-leaders would have to adapt to the political culture of popular politics in protestant Ulster. No longer could they rely on deference, even among traditionally Conservative supporters. Landlords now had to embrace a charismatic or 'demagogic' style of leadership more usually associated with Ulster's radicals and preacher-politicians.[10]

The question remains, however, of how the landed elite of the northeast, as opposed to landlords elsewhere in Ireland, possessed sufficient strength in the early 1880s to be a credible political force. Common nation-building has already been noted, but work on the 'British' landed elite is also instructive. In his introduction to a collection of essays published in 1975, David Spring attempted to explain the success of the 'English' landed elite by comparing their situation with that existing in the rest of Europe. He concluded that English landowners had no major competitors in the form of a 'land-hungry peasantry' or 'land wealthy state'.[11] In the same volume, in a chapter on the British landed elite, F.M.L. Thompson explained how the bourgeoisie and landed elite avoided a serious clash of values through the mutual cultivation of good relations, a process he labelled 'aristocratic embrace'.[12]

Another general explanation for landlord strength in northeast Ireland is found in Samuel Clark's 1995 survey of aristocratic power in western Europe. Clark noted a striking paradox in his study, that landed elites at the heart of centralising states, and those close to areas of industrial and commercial expansion, tended to be more powerful than those on the periphery of these modernising developments.[13] It is true that in most of Ireland the landed elite were on the periphery of industrial and commercial expansion, but not so in the northeast. Like industrial cities throughout the United Kingdom, Belfast's industrialists constituted an urban elite that not only complemented the landed elite, but also shared with it broad coincidences of interest.[14] Both, for example, patronised the Belfast Constitutional Club, a Tory organisational base and social venue for the wealthy. And grandees with local connections had an almost regal role in the city's life, gracing important civic functions and lending a sense of prestige to the growing numbers involved in local government.

What of the other aspect of Clark's paradox? It is conceded that Ireland was on the periphery of a centralising British state, but the northeast became the base of an increasingly powerful regional movement that, by 1921, achieved not only separation from the rest of Ireland, but also a parliament and government of its own. This new state centralised power in the region, and at the same time preserved a diluted form of landed influence in rural areas through district and county councils. With so many layers of government in Northern Ireland, local, regional and national, and with Unionists stressing cross-class solidarity, it is not surprising that the landed elite found a role in its politics at all levels.

II

In response to the advances of organised nationalism, especially from 1879, the landed elite of the northeast realised that they needed to harness pre-existing identities and modes of authority in order to create a coherent and landlord-led anti-nationalist alliance. A section of the landed elite, typically in the outlying frontier counties of Ulster, set about enhancing their influence in the Irish Conservative party, the Church of Ireland, and the Orange order. The very structures of these organisations, each with its own tiers of authority, often elected, meant that any assertion of traditional authority would be vitiated by the need for leaders to accountably articulate cross-class concerns. This shift to a more representative style of leadership was underscored by recent changes to electoral practices including the introduction of the secret ballot in 1872, the extension of the franchise in 1884, and the redistribution of seats in 1885. From this set of circumstances a charismatic, populist and successful landlord-leadership emerged, a striking contrast to the electoral eclipse of landlord power in the south and west of Ireland. But the influence of landlords in the northeast had limits. In order to secure and extend their popular anti-nationalist front, they had to prioritise regional concerns over those of the Irish landed elite in general. And although their efforts strengthened the already familiar overlap of Tories, Anglicans and Orangemen, they still had to win over Presbyterians and Ulster Liberals, conterminous definitions of a section of Ulster society hostile to both organised nationalism and landlord power. Nevertheless, these were not impassable obstacles.

Of the three organisations landlords utilised to enhance their authority, the Conservative party was the most suitable for absorbing discontented supporters of the Ulster Liberal party, especially in the aftermath of W.E. Gladstone's 'conversion' to Home Rule in 1886. Just as with conservatism in Britain, the Irish party had a long history of accommodating disaffected Whigs. But it was not a mere landlord party: it attracted urban support throughout Ireland and across the social spectrum. The Liberals by contrast had lost most of their Catholic support to organised nationalism, and as a consequence their urban support was largely lost to the Tories, leaving them a party of mainly Presbyterian farming interests. The Church of Ireland was not, of course, an agency for the absorption of Presbyterians, but it was no longer the obstacle to protestant co-operation that it once was. Relations had been improving throughout the second half of the nineteenth century, in part due to the perceived common threat of a resurgent Catholicism. Indeed, disestablishment of the Church of Ireland in 1869 both confirmed the potential of this threat and had a levelling effect among the protestant denominations. But if these developments paved the way for the consolidation of unionism in 1886, then landlords still needed a more popular and democratic movement to enhance their authority.

The Orange order was in several ways highly suitable for this purpose. It was historic, supplying a pre-existing political identity to what was an innovative reaction to organised nationalism. It also supplied pre-existing modes of authority that, after the extension of the franchise in 1884, were crucial to establishing a mass movement with landlord leadership. Capturing the order meant having access to lodges across Ireland, albeit with a concentration in Ulster. Even here, however, the order transcended the urban-rural divide, helping to promote a sense of common purpose in the region. Landlords had long played a prominent if marginal role in the order, particularly in the Grand Lodge at Dublin, holding senior but titular posts in what was a localised and largely plebeian movement. Orangeism, therefore, was never able to fully quell class tensions within its ranks. These were harnessed in the late 1860s by William Johnston of Ballykilbeg, an impecunious County Down landlord who became a folk hero to Orangemen for his defiant breach in 1867 of the ban on party processions. The following year he was returned to Westminster as MP for south Belfast, largely on the back of newly enfranchised working class protestants demanding a greater say in the affairs of the city's Conservative Association. Initially shaken by this new strategy, the bourgeois city fathers quickly tamed Johnston and reformed their own association to include politically active working class protestants. In this way Belfast Conservatism prefigured events over a decade later, when the landed class of rural Ulster faced a similar crisis but on a greater scale.[15]

The signal for the landed elite's change of heart was the Land League's 'invasion of Ulster' in 1883. As a means of meeting this crisis, the Orange order not only supplied a mechanism for landlord leadership, but also provided the only credible vehicle for deafening Presbyterian and Anglican farmers in the northeast to the siren calls of the Land League. From a steady trickle the number of landlords joining the order grew into a stream, with prominent names such as Somerset Maxwell and Colonel Edward Saunderson assuming a high profile in Orange agitation.[16] This in turn attracted bourgeois members and support, including the gentlemen members of the Constitutional Club. Inasmuch as this mobilisation reversed the Land League's encroachment into protestant areas of rural Ulster, the campaign was a success. But it did not kill off the sympathy of protestant farmers for land reform, a situation that would bedevil landlords who sought to retain control over this precarious alliance. It was, nevertheless, a tangible victory for the landed elite, one that supplied a new Orange martyr from their ranks: the fifth Baron Rossmore, removed from the magistracy for his defiant performance at an Orange demonstration at Rosslea.

In the aftermath of this victory, landlord–leaders came to view their connections to the Tory front bench at Westminster as a potential liability. These hitherto useful ties now risked lessening their credibility as custodians of local interests, especially as the Conservative front bench had been wavering in its attitude to C.S. Parnell, a situation that heightened pre-existing suspicions that London had little concern for Irish loyalists. In reconsidering their links to the Tory leadership, Irish landlords were also motivated by their own difficulties with the front bench. The latter had ignored their protests against extending the 1884 franchise reforms to Ireland, a situation that led on 20 February 1885 to the formation of a ginger group of 25 Irish MPs on the Conservative benches. This came to nothing in the short term, but it set a precedent. Moreover, as a result of the franchise reforms being passed, landlords in the northeast were now even more reliant on their tenantry for political support. Out of this series of setbacks came a determination to prevent the front bench from imposing candidates on Ulster constituencies. This was dramatically played out later in the year in a by-election selection battle for the Westminster seat of north Armagh. Backed by an

Orange and loyalist following he assiduously cultivated, Edward Saunderson saw off the front bench's preferred candidate to win the nomination and the seat. By January 1886 Saunderson had succeeded in creating and leading a new and lasting ginger group of Irish Tory MPs. But the general election of 1885 was far from a success for those in the northeast opposed to Home Rule. In contrast to the numerically weak Conservatives and Liberals of south and west Ireland, including County Donegal, who fought a united campaign, albeit with very limited success, the two factions in the northeast continued to stand against each other.[17] Further problems arose in Belfast where Orange populists fomented tensions between the proletariat and bourgeoisie, a familiar dynamic that emphasised the need for more effective authority mechanisms to control dissent within Belfast loyalism. But this crisis, which witnessed Gladstone's 'conversion' to Home Rule and nationalist gains in Ulster, also supplied the stimulus to successfully promote solidarity.

To this end the Conservatives created the Ulster Loyalist Anti-Repeal Union (ULARU) in January 1886, under the chairmanship of the fifth Earl of Ranfurly. The leaderships of these two bodies were almost indistinguishable, not surprising given that landlords constituted half of those recently elected to the House of Commons; the number of landlord-MPs representing Irish loyalism had actually risen from 9 in 1885 to 10 in 1886. Nevertheless, the need to consolidate their position meant accommodating other interest groups, a task made more complicated by developments at Westminster. Gladstone's decision to press ahead with Home Rule prompted the Conservative party to throw its weight behind Irish loyalism, thus papering over tensions between grandees and smaller landlords in Ulster, and between the latter and the front bench. It also led 93 Liberal-Unionists to cross the floor of the Commons and sit on the Conservative benches. Yet despite these dramatic alterations to the political landscape, the *idea* of landed leadership remained largely intact. Indeed, when the English aristocrat-politician and champion of Tory Democracy, Lord Randolph Churchill, was invited to address to ULARU at Belfast in February 1886, it appeared as if wealth and privilege on both sides of the Irish Sea could be relied upon to protect of the loyalists of Ulster.

These circumstances also made it easier for the ULARU to continue the Conservative's cultivation of Orange support, and to turn its attention to winning the co-operation of Ulster Liberals. Despite losing all their seats in Ireland, Liberals there initially hoped they might persuade Gladstone to rescind or dilute his Home Rule bill. Their failure to do so, and the example of the Liberal-Unionists, left them with little alternative other than to work with the landlord-led ULARU. But the latter paid a price for this co-operation, albeit less obvious than that stumped up by the Liberals. Landlord-leaders now had to reckon with calls for land reform from within a broad alliance they sought to lead. If not handled correctly potential divisions risked undermining their own position and the Unionist movement generally.

This was soon tested following the formation of a Unionist government under Lord Salisbury on 3 August 1886. Even before this, however, problems had been evident. During the Home Rule debates Saunderson had struggled to deal with a belligerent William Johnston, whose calls for armed resistance the former attempted to square with the need to maintain support in Britain. Landlord-MPs attitudes to land reform were also tested at this stage. Saunderson had been hostile to the Conservative government's 1885 Ashbourne Land Purchase Act, but his ambition to create a broadly based movement meant that he could not ultimately stand in the way of Tory inspired reforms. This dynamic ensured that, from 1886, Unionist supporters in Ulster could depend on the front bench to pass reforms in the teeth of local landlord opposition. If this situation diminished landlord influence, particularly when it was seen to resist this, then it also served to underscore the benefits of a pan-Unionist alliance, and this in turn helped to mitigate demands for a dramatic overhaul of party structures in the northeast.

The threat of a second Home Rule bill in 1892 prompted the organisation of an 'Ulster Convention' that year, chaired by the second Duke of Abercorn. The landed leadership still held many of the key positions within the movement, but it ensured that the Convention reflected a broad socio-economic support base. Prominence was therefore given to Belfast businessmen, including the Tory Sir William Ewart and the Liberal Thomas Sinclair.[18] The significance of their presence on the platform should not, however, be overstated, as non-landed MPs still only constituted a third of loyalist MPs returned to Westminster. Nevertheless, their desire for a greater role in leading the movement at provincial level was increasingly felt, and landlords could not stand in their way. Professionals were making an impact at Westminster with lawyers in particular regarded as better suited to dealing with the intricacies of parliamentary bills, including, somewhat ironically, reforms to Irish land law. The growing number of loyalist lawyer-MPs were not, therefore, necessarily a threat to landlord interests. Indeed, the legal profession was one of several professions that appealed to those in the landed elite who could not count on property for an income, such as the Ulster MPs W.G. Ellison-Macartney and William Moore.

Accompanying the growing number of lawyers returned to Westminster was a modest increase in the number of merchants and industrialists, from two in 1886, to five in 1892, to 10 at the 1906 election.[19] This slow advance on the preserve of landlords should not, however, belie their more significant input into the organisation and financing of unionism in Ulster. First, in a movement that elevated unity it was unlikely that landlord MPs would be deselected. Second, the owners of industrial and commercial wealth were no longer the poor relations of landed wealth, replacing landlords as the main donors to the regional movement by the Edwardian period, and building up a head of steam that would lead to a complete overhaul of party structures in 1904–5. Third, professionals, rather than businessmen, tended to be better suited to parliamentary work, for reasons already noted, and because the latter tended to be reluctant to leave their companies for prolonged periods. However, just as the professions attracted impecunious members of the landed elite, so they also attracted greater numbers of those with close kinship ties to industry and commerce. It is clear then that the Ulster Convention did not signal the end of landlord-leadership, but was instead another indicator of their steadily declining influence. This ongoing slippage was evident in March 1893, in the afterglow of the Convention's success, when Thomas Sinclair was appointed chairman of the Unionist Clubs Council, a representative assembly for unionism in the northeast that recognised implicitly the need for better structures and able personnel. And although it was traditional authority, in the form of the House of Lords, that effectively blocked Gladstone's second Home Rule bill in 1893, an increasingly critical public sphere in Britain meant that this use of parliamentary power was unsustainable, despite the best efforts of Salisbury to render it compatible with popular opinion.

III

If the forces of legal-rational authority were gradually undermining the power of landlord-MPs in the northeast, then their own mishandling of the leadership in the 1890s increased disquiet among those who viewed them as anachronistic and potentially harmful to Unionist unity. This unity had been made both necessary and more difficult by the electoral annihilation of liberalism in the northeast and its accommodation within a broad Unionist alliance. The potential difficulties of this arrangement were already evident in 1885, but they came into sharper relief in 1894–5 when the maverick Liberal-Unionist T.W. Russell attracted support from sections of Ulster's farming constituency. This allowed Salisbury's returning administration to openly commit itself to land reform – as part of its project to kill Home Rule with kindness – without fear of a popular backlash in Ulster. It nevertheless antagonised landlord MPs like Saunderson, and with Unionists certain to form the next government, he felt able to neglect the requirements of loyalist unity in favour of an election campaign in 1895 that championed an alliance of landlords and proletariat, rural and urban. Although this no doubt played to the demography north Armagh, and aspired to emulate William Johnston's success in 1868, it was a potentially disastrous stance for the leader of a movement that sought to contain Liberal farming interests.

In one sense Saunderson's position as leader was saved by his relative powerlessness in parliament. Salisbury's Unionist government were determined to press ahead with the 1896 Land bill, not least to remove the momentum from nationalism, but also in the knowledge that a section of Ulster's landlord-MPs did not express the views of all in their regional movement, nor even the views of all landlords. This was particularly evident in the attitude adopted by the professional and industrial elite of Belfast, who backed the land bill for the sake of Unionist unity in the region. This allowed Salisbury's government to retract assurances given to Saunderson during the bill's drafting stages and instead implement a measure more likely to satisfy agricultural grievances across Ireland. The landed elite's prominence in Ulster loyalism appeared to count for nothing. But it did help those landlords who sought to remain a credible political force, particularly in County Tyrone, to outwardly support land reform in the knowledge that they would a favourable hearing.[20] This outcome would ultimately thwart those in the landed elite of south and west Ireland, who at this time had begun to move in the direction of economic co-operation with organised nationalism.

Tensions within unionism were therefore exacerbated and contained during periods of Unionist government, allowing a declining number of landlord-MPs to seek re-election unopposed, and simultaneously undermining their influence and general approach to leadership. Any further decline in landlord influence would be subject to their reactions to subsequent developments at Westminster and at home. Accordingly, landlord-MPs actually sustained their *influence* by not opposing the Unionist government's 1898 local government bill, a measure that belatedly institutionalised legal-rational authority throughout Ireland at local level. But if the landed elite felt they could oversee the rolling out of a more democratic society, they could not control its rate of growth and the intensity of those who sought further reforms.

When Russell launched a second wave of agitation to coincide with the 1900 general election, Saunderson responded to this more radical campaign by echoing his earlier calls for an alliance of landlords and proletariat. But unlike the earlier agitation, Saunderson, along with several other longstanding MPs, now faced a rival pro-union candidate for the first time. These challengers articulated a critique of landlord-leadership that reflected popular disquiet about their lack of professionalism, their distance from popular concerns, and somewhat ironically, their close ties with a reforming Tory front bench that was increasingly distrusted. It was a serious attack on what remained of traditional authority, but it was only the first such attack on this scale, and so the number of Unionist landlord-MPs returned to Westminster remained at seven out of 21.

Saunderson's calls for a restoration of traditional power relationships proved sufficient to re-elect him in what was a predominantly Anglican and Orange constituency, but it only diminished his already damaged reputation among the Belfast bourgeoisie. Nor could it rival the marshalling of urban working-class and lower middle-class discontent by Thomas Sloan, leader of the militant Belfast Protestant Association. Sloan's synthesis of firebrand evangelicalism and left-leaning politics condemned almost all Unionist leaders, British and Irish, but none looked as discredited and vulnerable as the landlord-leaders of Ulster unionism. Sloan's anti-elite invective was theatrically played out in 1902 at the annual 12 July demonstration at Belfast. Tensions between landed officers of the order, now considerably expanded in membership, and populist Orangemen had been high from the year before when the government had banned some potentially violent Orange demonstrations in south County Down. Rumour had it that the decision to ban them had been taken after advice from the fourth Earl of Erne and Lord Arthur Hill, both senior members of the order. When Saunderson – as Grand Master of the Grand Orange Lodge of Belfast – spoke at the 1902 'Twelfth', hecklers accused him of defending the bans. Sloan was then hoisted to the platform to demand that Saunderson address their concerns. It proved to be a turning point, for not only did Saunderson stand down as Grand Master, but Sloan soon afterwards defeated the official Unionist candidate, Lord Arthur Hill, in a by-election for south Belfast called after the death of William Johnston. For the next decade Sloan continued to threaten Unionist unity; creating the Independent Orange Order in 1903, and three years later entering an electoral alliance with nationalists and labour representatives in

Belfast. But by 1910 his support was lagging, not least because he now had to compete with an official Unionist movement that was very different in organisation to the one he challenged in 1902.

IV

Around the time of Sloan's clash with Saunderson, a section of the landed elite in south and west Ireland were in negotiations with the more pragmatic wing of organised nationalism. The resulting settlement of the land question was framed in the highly popular 1903 Wyndham Land Act, a measure Saunderson reluctantly supported despite widespread landlord opposition to it. If his outward tolerance of the measure was a sign of powerlessness, the Act and Saunderson's support for it helped to sustain what remained of landlord influence in the northeast. For not only was the Act seen by many as resolving the long running sore of landownership, but it also had something of a levelling effect that probably fostered a greater sense of common purpose among those with wealth in the region. Nonetheless, observers in 1903 could be forgiven for thinking that landed power had been completely undermined by recent events. This, however, would have overlooked the many ways in which it continued to play a role in Ireland, particularly in the northeast. It also would have failed to register the political credit landlords had accumulated within unionism in contrast to the fate of landlords in the south and west, whose success in 1903 quickly turned sour with the rise of 'Irish-Ireland'.[21] Within a year this credit proved its worth.

Tensions between Unionists at Belfast and the British appointed Unionist administration at Dublin were not new in 1904, but they provided the excuse to overhaul the movement's structures in the northeast when it emerged that discussions had taken place at Dublin Castle about implementing a scheme of Irish devolution. In the past, many Unionists in Ulster looked to the Tory front bench to pass land reforms, often in opposition to local landlord opinion. But, with the land question largely resolved, and landlord power in the descendent, the movement's professional and business leaders moved to decisively take *control* of unionism in Ulster, not least so that they might contain working-class dissent in Belfast. Yet its structures were weak, incoherent and irregular, a reflection of its traditional authority mechanisms and parliamentary focus. However, these weaknesses had not gone unrecognised. There was a short lived attempt to address them in 1893 with the creation of the Ulster Clubs Council, and landlord MPs in Ulster had been subject to unprecedented criticism at the 1900 general election. The 'Devolution Crisis' therefore supplied the opportunity for change, and for a younger leadership to emerge that better reflected the professional and business interests now bankrolling unionism in the northeast.

The decision to create the Ulster Unionist Council (UUC) in 1904–5 formally institutionalised unionism's twenty-year old attempt to create a social and political alliance of anti-nationalists. As an assembly of 200 delegates, the UUC acquired a legal-rational legitimacy that the landlord-leaders could never fully realise on their own. Control, however, remained firmly in the hands of a cabal of leaders, notably the lawyer William Moore, and James Craig and J.B. Lonsdale, men whose considerable wealth and business backgrounds both facilitated their entry into politics and their determination to see it organised effectively. The new structures and ethos of the movement ensured that it became more reactive to grass-roots concerns, making it difficult for mavericks to work outside of it. Resuscitated local constituency associations were put on a more permanent footing, although in some localities this was more apparent than real, allowing local landlords in rural areas to continue to exercise influence as if nothing had changed. In general, however, the driving ethos behind these structural changes was, of course, for professionalism and accountability at the regional level, attributes typically associated with businessmen and professionals. But their claim on these apparent virtues did not preclude landlord involvement. Indeed, although diminished, the landed elite continued to be substantial backers of the movement, particularly, as it has been noted, in rural Ulster. And although the number of landlord-MPs returned to Westminster declined in the general elections that followed, members of the landed elite with Irish connections still had a significant presence in the House of Lords. In short, continued wealth, status and deference ensured that even in 1910, a third of the 66 nominees to the standing committee of the UUC were either peers or gentry.[22]

V

The continued presence of the landed elite at all levels of unionism also had less tangible benefits for those who now sought to shift the movement onto a more professional footing. It emphasised continuity with the past in what was a socially conservative movement, and gave an element of respectability to the UUC's increasingly militant strategies. They also proved a useful link to the British Conservative party, which in 1911 had once again wed itself to the cause of Irish loyalism. This

mutually beneficial relationship opened up opportunities for Irish landlords to campaign in Britain, and meant that grandees with Irish connections could avoid conflicts of interest between commitments to the
Tory front bench and rhetorical commitments to Ireland.

Only during the acrimonious passage of the Parliament bill in 1911
were these dual commitments severely tested. The bill proposed to
curtail the ability of the House of Lords to veto bills from the House of
Commons, and thereby pave the way for a potentially successful third
Home Rule bill. Ulster Unionists were clearly unnerved by this and
lobbied peers to reject the measure. But the Tory front bench were
activated by broader concerns, including their own divisions over tariff
reform, constitutional upheaval, and potentially dire electoral consequences. They chose instead to not oppose the bill in the Lords, and
were supported, perhaps crucially, by the fifth Marquess of Lansdowne
and the sixth Marquess of Londonderry, peers with strong connections
to Ireland, and in the case of Londonderry, to the UUC. The bill
passed by 131 votes to 114. If Ulster Unionists were disappointed by
the actions of Lansdowne and Londonderry, the vote nevertheless
affirmed the fundamental importance of the UUC, for no matter how
close the Conservative party might move towards supporting militancy
in Ulster, Unionists there knew that security ultimately lay in
their own resources.[23] In the short term, however, the effect of the
Parliament Act meant that any grievance the UUC had with British
Conservatives, and their noble stooges in Ulster, came second to the
need for pan-Unionist unity, especially as UUC strategy entered a
more militant phase.

It is partly for these reasons that the prominence of peers increased at
this time; in contrast the number of landlord-MPs continued to decline,
with five returned to Westminster in 1906, four in January 1910, and
three in December 1910 (by 1918 only one was returned).[24] The patronage of titled landlords at unionist rallies helped to create a picture
of Unionist solidarity across the British Isles, and also sustained the
image of cross-class unity in the northeast of Ireland. Theatre was a
crucial element to Unionist strategy from 1912, with the new leader
Sir Edward Carson cast in the starring role.[25] Second billing was often
given to Lord Londonderry, a leading practitioner of aristocratic
embrace; his signature followed Carson's on the Solemn League and
Covenant, the UUC's declaration of conditional loyalty to Britain,
signed with great fanfare at Belfast City Hall on 28 September 1912.[26]
This emphasis on tradition was driven home by the next seven signa-
tures, six of which belonged to leading protestant clerics, and the

seventh to Londonderry's politically unimportant son, Viscount Castlereagh. Notably downplayed on this occasion were the real managers of unionism, in particular James Craig, the highly effective director of the movement in general and this strategy in particular.

With the Liberal government pressing ahead with its Home Rule bill, the theatre of UUC protest took on a more ominous appearance. The latter made arrangements, in the event of the bill being passed into law, for a provisional government to be formed at Belfast. The landed elite supplied some of the leading members of this shadow administration, including the third Duke of Abercorn, Lord Londonderry, the third Earl of Kilmorey, the sixth Viscount Bangor, the second Baron Dunleath and the Hon. Arthur O'Neill MP. These men, and others like Sir Basil Brooke and Oliver Nugent, were also prominent in the Ulster Volunteer Force (UVF), the militia raised to emphasise the UUC's revolve to oppose Home Rule, and to assert Carson's control over potentially violent elements of his support base. The UVF even enhanced the role of the landed elite in certain localities. Many landlords had military experience and large properties in which to drill and train, whereas local businessmen were wary of taking up leading roles in the UVF for fear of nationalist customers boycotting their businesses. It is not difficult to dismiss or exaggerate landlord involvement in the UVF, but it should be borne in mind that this same class, across the British Isles, greeted the outbreak of war in August 1914 with enthusiasm, in part because it presented an opportunity to reassert one of their traditional functions: soldiering.

Somewhat less dramatically, Irish landlords and peers were also prominent in the propaganda campaign in Britain, a form of activism that particularly suited them.[27] The Irish landed elite, especially those with peerages, had always possessed strong familial, educational and economic connections to Britain. As supranational advocates for Irish Unionism, men like Viscount Templetown, the third Baron Oranmore and Brown, and Bryan Cooper could readily communicate to British audiences in a familiar accent, appearing and sounding less parochial than a more typical representative of the UUC. Their presence in this aspect of campaigning also helped to bring southern unionism and the UUC together in Britain, a break with the more pronounced trend that was pulling them further apart. Nevertheless, the role of landlords in campaigning should not be overstated. The business arguments against Home Rule and the professionalism required from campaigners meant that they were only one component of what was a well organised and sophisticated propaganda strategy.

In the co-operative atmosphere of 1912–14, as at other times of crisis, it was not difficult for landlords in the UUC to toe the party line. However, when the pan-Unionist movement began to unravel during the First World War, the multifaceted allegiances of the landed elite were again placed under enormous strain. An unmistakable indication of how far the bulk of Ulster Unionists were prepared to go in safeguarding their core area came in June 1916 when the UUC reluctantly agreed to only six-counties being excluded from an immediate Home Rule settlement. It caused enormous upset among Unionists in south and west Ireland, particularly in the outlying counties of Ulster. Southern Unionists subsequently used their influence over members of the coalition War Cabinet, in particular Lord Lansdowne, to scupper the deal, but the circumstances of this propitious opportunity for them would never again return. Moreover, with only the UUC offering Irish landlords the prospect of a political future, the landed elite of the northeast had to abide by its determinations above all other considerations.

VI

Crisis surrounded the creation and early years of the first Parliament of Northern Ireland (1920–1; 1921–25). Far from being marginalised, however, as in the south and west of Ireland, the landed elite of the northeast supplied two of the six ministers in James Craig's Cabinet, Edward Mervyn Archdale and the seventh Marquess of Londonderry. But the case of these two politicians illustrates the tightening constraints now imposed on landlord influence. Archdale was a successful minister in that he did not contest the form of Unionist government that emerged from this troubled period. Londonderry, however, did contest the government's reliance on populist policies, and in January 1926 he became the first minister to resign from the Belfast government.[28] His successor as Education Minister and Leader of the Senate, the eighth Viscount Charlemont, proved a more cautious proponent of paternalist unionism.

Having survived, somewhat battered and diminished, the major crises that attended the evolution of unionism in the northeast of Ireland, the landed elite found Northern Ireland a warm house in the relatively peaceful decades that followed its troubled beginning. Some of the landed families that played a prominent role in the pre-war campaigns continued to achieve political success in Northern Ireland. As has already been noted, the sixth Marquess of Londonderry's son was appointed to the Belfast cabinet in 1921. His own son was later elected unopposed to Westminster for County Down in 1931. The third Duke of Abercorn inherited his father's title and prestige in the movement in 1913, and went on to be appointed the first Governor of Northern Ireland. His son, the eventual fifth Duke, was in 1964 elected to Westminster as the Unionist MP for Fermanagh and South Tyrone. The family of Arthur O'Neill continued to produce MPs for mid-Antrim until the 1960s, the last of them being the Hon. Terence O'Neill, fourth Prime Minister of Northern Ireland (1963–9). He was succeeded as premier by James Chichester-Clark (1969–71), a distant relation from gentry stock in the northwest of the province. The continuance of landed influence was particularly notable in the socially conservative townlands of rural Northern Ireland, where the economic and educational status of the landed elite marked them out as natural leaders. One such family, the Brookes of County Fermanagh, prominent in local politics from the eighteenth century, supplied the third Prime Minister of Northern Ireland (1943–63): Sir Basil Brooke.

VII

The structural, economic, and social changes of the late nineteenth century set the context for landlord decline across the United Kingdom. The character of that decline differed at a regional level, and in Ireland there was a significant difference between the fate of the landed elite of the northeast from that of the south and west. This confirms Clark's paradox of successful landed elites being close to areas of industrial and commercial growth and the centralising state. Faced with the success of the Land League, landlords in the northeast moved to reinforce their economic and political position by strengthening their alliance with the Belfast bourgeoisie, forging bonds with populist Orangeism, and accommodating Liberal-Unionists. In doing so, they had to appease and manage the demands of these powerful interest groups, a careful balancing act that they struggled with throughout the 1880s and 1890s. Their efforts could not stop the transition from traditional authority to legal-rational authority, but they did at least ensure that the power relationships and authority mechanisms that emerged in the Edwardian period accommodated suitably able and co-operative members of the landed elite. Therefore, despite the UUC being under the firm control of wealthy businessmen like Craig and Lonsdale, and officered by ranks of professionals, its ethos of professionalism and retrenchment did not rule out landed participation, indeed, in some instances it was needed and encouraged. It would be wrong, however, despite the aforementioned, and despite the crossing of many younger sons from the land to the professions, to assume that what emerged in Northern Ireland was what C. Wright Mills might describe as a 'power elite'.[29] They did share broad coincidences of interest, particularly in politics, and there was an exchange in personnel and ideas, but it tended to be one way, with personnel going from land to the professions, and with ideas going in the opposite direction. As the work of Shanks suggests, there still remained a clear social and cultural divide between the landed elite and those outside its ranks; hardly the interaction and fusion of elites Mills observes in nineteenth century America. Moreover, if a 'power elite' did exist in Northern Ireland, why was the flight of land from politics in the early 1970s so noticeable? The onset of the 'Troubles' was the one crisis they did not survive as a political force, nearly a century after the first serious challenges to their power.

6

Irish Nationalism in Ulster, 1885–1921[1]

A.C. Hepburn

However similar to their southern colleagues they may have seemed, Irish nationalists in most of Ulster had to live and work in a very different environment.[2] Whereas in southern Ireland Catholics were an overwhelming majority, Ulster Catholics and Protestants co- existed in large numbers. Even though all of Ireland in the late nineteenth century was only beginning to emerge from a world in which Protestantism, wealth and power were strongly correlated, the ways and the extent to which this change came about were determined by regional ethnic balances. In the south a combination of socio-economic and political change brought about the participation of large numbers of Catholics to a high level in business and public administration; in the private sector a large Catholic market encouraged the development of Catholic professional and retail services. In most of Ulster, on the other hand, economic and political change did not put anything like the same level of pressure on the dominant Protestant society to increase the involvement of Catholics, while the smaller and poorer Catholic community provided a relatively limited market for professional and retail services. There was thus a broadly-based 'north-south divide' in Catholic Ireland, which by the end of the nineteenth century had become crucially important. It remains only to note that within Catholic Ulster there was also something of an 'east-west divide', between counties Antrim, Down, northern Armagh and eastern Londonderry on the one hand, where Protestants were in a majority of more than 3:1, and western and south-western Ulster, where Catholics had a small majority. The city of

Belfast was especially important in shaping Ireland's dichotomous ethnic demography: without Belfast, claimed John Redmond, Catholics would have comprised 55 per cent of Ulster's population.[3]

The gradual extension of parliamentary democracy between 1832 and 1885 and the implementation of elected local government in 1898 accentuated this division, as the Catholic south used its new electoral power to help improve its circumstances. This was not possible in most of the north, where male householder democracy served to strengthen the 'Protestant' nature of the dominant politics. There were two possible routes for northern Catholic advance. Either some kind of transformation would have to have taken place, causing the ethnic connotations of religious difference to wither away so that Catholic-Protestant differences would lose their salience in political and social life. In practice this would have meant the assimilation of Ulster Catholics to the dominant culture of their region. A large proportion of Ulster Catholics would have had to become 'West Britons' or 'Castle Catholics'. Some individuals did, but the abusive implication of these terms indicates the ignominy that the wider Catholic community heaped on them. In practice the only people who could afford to pursue such a course were those whose social and economic status enabled them to live outside the Catholic community, amongst middle-class Protestants who were sufficiently confident of their own affluence and status not to seek to exclude Catholics from their neighbourhoods in the way that routinely happened in working-class communities. Even comfortably-off Catholics, if their business or profession depended on wider Catholic custom, would have been ill-advised to turn their backs on their community in any public way. Unlike some regions divided by language, where bilingualism on occasion offered the basis for a middle ground, an ethnic identity defined by religion offered no such potential.[4] In practice both the increasingly 'Protestant' flavour of the dominant regional culture and the defensive communalism of the majority of Ulster Catholics rendered the regional integration of Catholics and Protestants within existing state structures impossible. The only route for group economic and political advancement that appeared to be open to Ulster Catholics was the link to Irish nationalist politics, as it evolved in the more favourable ethnic demography of southern Ireland. Thus the social, economic and educational structure of the Ulster Catholic community developed more slowly than was the case further south but, politically, Ulster Catholics tended increasingly to take their cue from their southern co-religionists. It was a trend that had its origins in Daniel O'Connell's time, but it established itself slowly and unevenly.

This essay will review the development of the relationship between Ulster Catholics and the rest of nationalist Ireland during the period 1885 to 1922. The Ulster Catholic minority does not fit easily into the theoretical and comparative literature. Part of the problem is that, unlike the multi-ethnic states of continental Europe, the United Kingdom was a victorious power in 1919. Thus, instead of Ulster Protestants becoming a national minority within an Irish successor state, like the Germans in Czechoslovakia or Poland or the Hungarians in Romania, it was the Catholics who became a minority within the devolved state of Northern Ireland. In the terminology developed by Miroslav Hroch they remained a reluctant minority within the 'state-nation' of the United Kingdom, wedded to irredentist aspirations for reunion with the 'mother-nation'.[5] In one sense Ulster Catholics were newly separated from their southern co-religionists in 1921, but in another sense they already had some of the characteristics of a dispersed national minority existing within a territory controlled both economically and demographically by others. It is in fact helpful to analyse Ulster's Catholics, or at least the Catholics of Belfast and the industrial towns of east Ulster, as a quasi-diasporic minority, closer in circumstances, behaviour and outlook to the Catholic Irish of British, North American and Australasian cities than to the Irish of the mother-nation. It is no coincidence that Joe Devlin, the leading northern Nationalist leader, had a greater appeal to the Irish of the global diaspora than any of his contemporaries. These diaspora were of course predominantly urban and industrial, which constituted a further difference from the prevailing ethos of the mother-nation.

Most analysts agree that there is a close relationship between nationalism and the process of modernisation, i.e. the process of transition from a predominantly agrarian society to an urban and industrial capitalist society.[6] Often, and as strongly in the case of the Irish as of any other nationalist movement, this relationship was a negative one. Both the Catholic Church and the lay leadership of the Gaelic revival in Ireland rejected what they saw as the moral degradation of urbanism-industrialism and the concomitant emigration from the Irish Catholic heartlands. Gaelic revivalists were themselves predominantly urban, but their anti-urbanism was essentially a middle-class revulsion against the city which was typical of the *fin-de-siècle* western world – viewed through an Irish nationalist prism but in part at least a response to the same phenomena which gave rise, for instance, to the garden city movement in England.[7] Many Gaelic revivalists were also first-generation migrants to the city,

frequently public sector or corporate employees from a farming background. But the views of revivalists like Patrick Pearse, who believed that
under independent conditions Ireland's 'population will expand in a
century to twenty millions', with 'no Glasgows or Pittsburghs', resonated
awkwardly amongst Irish Catholic communities in Belfast and industrial
Ulster and in the diaspora.[8] It may have been an attractive dream for
many thousands of industrial toilers, but it offered no immediate solace.
The Gaelic revival was indeed 'ambivalent and evasive about urban problems'.[9] The two most prominent – if very different – figures in Irish
nationalist politics who sought to apply *urban* solutions to urban problems
were James Connolly and Joe Devlin. The former delivered working-
class Dublin to revolutionary Nationalism for a crucial but brief interlude
which brought no benefit to his socialist successors, while the latter saw
in Westminster parliamentary processes and in British labour politicians a
practical if more pedestrian route to industrial and welfare reform than
the idealistic visions of the Gaelic revival. Interestingly Devlin who, as
National Secretary of the United Irish League (1905–20), did his best to
continue the policy of running the land and the national questions in
harness, did not – in contrast to Connolly – seek to integrate the urban
and national questions in the same way, except in the limited area of
ethnic discrimination. This may go some way towards explaining the
continued support of the Catholics of Belfast and urban Ulster for
Devlin's practical policies and their lukewarm response to Sinn Féin.

The social and economic policies of the Gaelic revival and later on,
Sinn Féin, offered little to the industrial north. This reluctance to come
to terms with realities outside of their idealised nexus of values is also
apparent in the growing lack of interest in addressing the fact of
the mixed society in the north. Both Jim MacLaughlin and Patrick
O'Mahony & Gerard Delanty argue that the Catholic Church grew
stronger in public life partly as a result of its reassertion of moral authority during the Parnell Split and partly because of the way in which the
ideologies of nationalism and Catholicism were bound increasingly together by the writings of D.P. Moran, Patrick Pearse and others. This
increased authority might in fact be traced back a further generation to
Cardinal Paul Cullen's re-organisation of the Irish Catholic Church in
the years after 1850. But it does seem to have been the case that the rise
of a Gaelic cultural nationalism that was relatively free of any clear social
programme did not in fact supplant Catholicism or clerical influence
but in fact strengthened it. It provided massive cultural and political
reinforcement for the Cullenite religious view 'of both the virtue and
the desirability of an exclusively Catholic society'.[10] Thus, some years

before 1914, the ideologies of both clerical Catholicism and lay Gaelic revivalism had become implicitly partitionist. On the one hand the 'island of Ireland' constituted the territory of the nation, but on the other hand there existed no ideological tools which could relate the Protestant quarter of the population of Ireland to the Irish nation-building project. The victims of these developments were to be the Catholic minority of Ulster.

I

The ethnic demography of Ulster differed from that of the rest of the country. In most rural areas there were fewer strong Catholic tenant farmers than in the south. Catholic farmers tended to predominate only in mountain districts. In villages and market towns Catholic professionals and shopkeepers were only as strong as the relative numbers and prosperity of Catholics in the nearby countryside. In the majority of areas where local government remained in Protestant hands, Catholics had more restricted access to public-sector jobs than was the case further south. In the predominantly industrial areas of Belfast, Derry City and the smaller manufacturing towns Protestants predominated in management and in the skilled trades of modern industries. The impact of Ulster's industrialisation on the Catholic portion of its population was threefold. Its most distinctive feature was a large, predominantly semi-skilled female workforce not found to anything like the same extent anywhere else in Ireland. Secondly it created a large male Catholic industrial working class, though predominantly unskilled and non-unionised until the early twentieth century, and therefore not that different from Dublin and from Ireland's other main urban centres. Third, and most important of all, it created an even larger semi-and unskilled Protestant working class. Thus the context of numerical inferiority in which Ulster Catholics lived meant that remaining ethnic barriers to their upward mobility intervened at a lower level on the ladder of opportunity than was the case in the south. Ulster Catholics existed, especially in urban areas, cheek-by-jowl with a Protestant lower working class which was, for the most part, intensely hostile towards them. This last, as much as the relatively limited opportunities for advancement, was a defining feature of the Ulster Catholic situation. Bishop Patrick Dorrian stated in 1864 that there were probably only 70 to 90 of the 45,000 Catholics then living in Belfast who could 'spare £100 a year from their incomes'.[11] In comparison to the south of Ireland, therefore, Ulster Catholics possessed a very small lay elite.

Partly for this reason, but also because it felt itself embattled in the midst of a more powerful Protestant local majority, the role of the clergy remained stronger for longer, in public life, than was the case even in the south.

This situation was not new in the nineteenth century. But it was exacerbated considerably by urbanisation, industrialisation and the Europe-wide rise of nationalism, which gradually turned Catholic ethnicity into popular Irish nationalism and at the same time solidified the unity of denominational Episcopalians, Presbyterians and Methodists into an ethnic 'Protestantism' which drew its energy from the 'religio-political institution' of Orangeism.[12] Unlike the rest of Ireland, much of Ulster had become, from the early seventeenth century, a 'settlement colony', with competing mythologies. Protestants saw themselves as extending the frontiers of civilisation and progress, while Catholics espoused a rhetoric of repression and dispossession. By the early nineteenth century, as legal and other formal restrictions on the rights of Catholics were steadily eroded, the status of Ulster shifted from 'settlement colony' to 'ethnic frontier', a zone within which two rival ethnic groups competed for ascendancy, neither of them willing to acknowledge the over-arching authority of a neutral state.[13] 'Exclusive dealing' in the sale of land and, to a considerable extent, retail trading, was established by the late eighteenth century in many rural areas, most especially in south and west Ulster where Catholics and Protestants lived in approximately equal numbers. In urban areas such Belfast and Derry City, but also in smaller industrial centres such as Lurgan and Portadown, this system of ethnic boundary maintenance became more refined and pervasive as the nineteenth century progressed. Territorial assertion and control were driven and sustained by party parades in quiet times, and by residential/workplace expulsions and inter-communal rioting when marching was not enough. High levels of residential and workplace segregation were thereby established, so that well before the 1880s the majority of people in Ulster's larger centres dwelt in ethnically-segregated neighbourhoods. In Belfast especially, and also in Derry, some of these ethnic monoliths became sufficiently large to make an important impact on electoral politics, once the parliamentary franchise was extended to include the urban working-class male householder in 1868 and his rural equivalent in 1885. Belfast's characteristic segmented ethnic and electoral boundaries originated in episodes such as the Catholic victory in 'the battle for Leeson Street' during the riots of 1872, when the Falls Road neighbourhood was opened up for Catholic occupation – unlike the other old Catholic neighbourhoods of the inner city, such as the Markets, Short Strand, Dock and, later, Ardoyne areas, which were encircled by Protestant housing.[14] Likewise, in Derry, the walled city centre remained Protestant territory while the Bogside had become a well-established Catholic neighbourhood by the third quarter of the century.[15]

The franchise extensions, and the introduction of democratic local government throughout Ireland in 1898 (1896 in the City of Belfast), interacted with this distinctive social structure to produce a particular style of politics. The democratisation of Irish electoral politics brought about a break between British and Irish party political culture. In the south of Ireland it created what was virtually a one-party system, as the Irish Parliamentary Party, underpinned by a succession of grass-roots organisations, won almost all the seats, the small Protestant elite having insufficient numbers to sustain representation. In Ulster it created a new party-political divide, in which the Catholics ended their subservient alliance with the elite Presbyterian Liberals to become Home Rule Nationalists. At the same time the elite Conservatives swallowed most of the elite Presbyterian Liberals, while embracing plebeian Orangeism with a new enthusiasm. They thus consolidated the 'Protestant vote' and transformed themselves into an Irish Unionist Party which, within a generation had become in essence an *Ulster* Unionist Party.

Electioneering in the north of Ireland also developed a distinctive character. In a first-past-the-post electoral system, with an electorate divided sharply along ethnic lines, issues and ideology were of limited importance. Voting became an ethnic roll-call. Maintenance of the electoral register was by far the most important electioneering activity, both in the positive sense of ensuring that the maximum number of one's own side was registered, and in the negative sense of mounting as many successful legal challenges as possible against those members of the other side who were included in the provisional register. This involved both detailed work in the streets and on doorsteps by registration agents, and legal work at the annual revision sessions by solicitors. The latter were normally paid from party funds for their work. This activity was of crucial importance in what, after 1885, were closely-balanced parliamentary constituencies such as West and North Belfast, Derry City, East Donegal, South Down, North and South Fermanagh, South Londonderry, East, North and South Tyrone. Even in constituencies where the ethnic balance was less closely matched it was necessary to 'maintain the register' lest a seat might be made marginal by the intervention of a third-party candidate. In practice this meant that both sides needed to be on the watch to ensure that the other side's deceased and departed voters were removed from the register, along with ineligible registrants, and all those tenants and ratepayers who for any reason might be portrayed as not being in good standing.[16]

The north of Ireland has been, and still is today, associated with very high turn-outs at elections. Not only urban constituencies such as West Belfast, but also the large and thinly-populated constituencies of Counties Fermanagh and Tyrone regularly recorded voter turn-outs well in excess of 90 per cent throughout the home rule period.[17] Cases of personation, jokes about the dead voting, 'vote early and vote often', and stories of voters arriving at the polling station to find that their votes had already been cast have now been commonplace in Ulster for more than a century. A well-known Unionist cartoon of the pre-1914 period shows 'Joe Gabriel' [i.e. Devlin] blowing his horn over a cemetery to call the dead to the polling booths.[18] To support this stereotype, there are tales of deaths of electors being concealed from opposition canvassers, and of efforts to prevent people from 'the wrong side' – sometimes even, it was alleged, partners in mixed marriages – from getting to the polls.[19]

An examination of the long-running struggle for the representation of the predominantly-Catholic Falls and Smithfield wards on the Belfast City Council (1896–1905) reveals a further dimension to the electoral politics of ethnic demography. The rival groupings were the local representatives of the United Irish League, and the Belfast Catholic Association founded by the eccentric Dr Henry Henry, Bishop of Down & Connor, 1895–1908. Under the Belfast Corporation Act of 1896 women got the vote in local elections more than two decades before they won the parliamentary franchise. The Catholic Association, which wanted to keep nationalist politics out of local government and stood for episcopal authority even in the temporal aspects of public life, controlled the electoral registration procedure in the city's Catholic community until 1904. The CA was believed by the local UIL Nationalists to owe its electoral supremacy to a disproportionate level of support among female voters. The UIL alleged that widowed and other single women tended to be on the electoral register in many cases where an adult son, or other resident male member of the household, might have an equal claim to be recognised as the holder of the tenancy, and therefore of the franchise that went with it. Since the parliamentary register was simply the municipal register without the female electors, it was argued by the Belfast UIL that the CA was pursuing a registration policy which suited it at municipal level but which damaged the nationalist side by excluding potential male voters at parliamentary level.[20]

There has been some controversy over the significance of this ten-year municipal struggle in Catholic Belfast. It is argued here that it reflected a structural change of some significance in Belfast Catholic politics, in essence a shift from a locally-defined, clerically-led Catholic ethnicity which left Ulster 'behind' the rest of Catholic Ireland in its commitment to nationalism in the early 1880s, to an unequivocal identification with an all-Ireland political nationalist movement which was duly confirmed by the dissolution of the Belfast Catholic Association in 1905.[21] Catherine Hirst, on the other hand, suggests that Irish Nationalism in Belfast developed early, and was in no sense behind the rest of Catholic Ireland in this respect. She would regard the struggle of Joe Devlin and a rising Catholic small business class in the 1890s and early 1900s to advance nationalist politics over episcopally-led Catholic politics as simply a blip, occasioned by the dictatorial style of a particular local bishop. Hirst also argues that Irish nationalist manifestations in Belfast preceded any evidence of economic discrimination against Catholics and that this, rather than ethnic competition for jobs and housing, provided the stimulus for Protestant deterrence.[22]

It is probably true that the absence of monster repeal meetings from Belfast in the 1840s had more to do with fear of violence than with any lack of national consciousness; and it may be, as Hirst argues, that organised physical force in west Belfast in the 1860s was more Fenianism than Ribbonism. Certainly Dorrian, who was Bishop of Down & Connor 1865–85 (and effectively in control from 1860), reversed the low-key, conciliatory – and perhaps timid – policies of his predecessor Cornelius Denvir (1836–65). Dorrian was one of the more 'advanced' members of the hierarchy on national and agrarian questions, as well as a strong Cullenite on matters of religion and education. On the other hand he would not allow lay-led organisations like the Catholic Institute and strongly nationalist newspapers such as the *Ulster Observer* to exist outside clerical control. Likewise Hirst demonstrates the early strength of the Home Rule Association in Belfast, which held massive meetings as early as 1872. But although the Belfast Home Rule Association was large and active, its first leaders, Joe Biggar and Revd Isaac Nelson, were in fact Protestants, while the policy of John Duddy and the local leadership of the late 1870s and early 1880s caused Parnell to marginalise the Belfast Association as extremists and land nationalisers.[23] Home Rulers, in fact, won only two of the twenty-nine Ulster seats in the general election of 1874, while winning most of the constituencies in the rest of Ireland.[24]

The so-called 'invasion of Ulster' by the Home Rule movement, begun at the Monaghan by-election of 1883, is appropriately named. Prior to this, Home Rule candidates had appeared in just seven contests in Ulster, of whom only the two in Cavan were successful. Of the six candidates, four were Protestants. From 1871, when Isaac Butt stood unsuccessfully in Armagh, through the general election of 1885, when 21 Ulster seats were contested by Home Rulers, a total of 25 Home Rule candidates tried their luck.[25] Of these three of the five Protestants, but only seven of the 29 Catholics, had any personal connection with Ulster. Whatever the amount of support on the ground, Ulster Catholics played no role in the leadership of the Home Rule movement before the mid-1880s. In rural areas of the north, the Land League was unable to replicate its southern success, nor did the Plan of Campaign operate in Ulster, apart from Donegal and Monaghan.[26] During the decade of the Split, after December 1890, the balance in Ulster between Parnellites and anti-Parnellites differed from that in the rest of Ireland. In the general election of 1892, anti-Parnellites secured 71 per cent of the nationalist vote in the south of Ireland, but 98 per cent in Ulster. A police survey in the same year showed that the ratio in Ulster of anti-Parnellite Irish National Federation members to the Parnellites of the Irish National League was in excess of 30:1. The survey also showed a significantly greater clerical predominance in local political leadership in Ulster than was the case elsewhere.[27]

Thus Catholic support, especially in eastern Ulster, for a lay-led, all-Ireland nationalism remained brittle. Bishop Henry was easily able to thwart the local Nationalist movement for the first ten years of his episcopacy. It is true that there was a whiff of Healyite localism about his activities, and it is also probably true, as one of his detractors wrote, that he 'should never have been allowed outside an infants' school'. But the fact that such a naïve dictatorship could command so much support for so long suggests that the Nationalism of the Catholic electors of West Belfast was less than robust. In 1897, in a straight fight with anti-Parnellite Nationalists, the Catholic Association candidates won all the city council seats in Falls and Smithfield wards with 61 per cent of the vote. They were returned without a contest in 1901, and again in 1904 – four years after the Irish Party reunion – they won all the seats with 56 per cent of the vote. Only after the carefully-timed intervention of John Redmond, in 1905, did Henry agree to wind up his organisation.

Even the endorsement of Michael Davitt could not help the Nationalists. The Cork-born journalist Tim McCarthy wrote to William O'Brien that although Davitt's visit during the 1897 campaign 'seemed to be a huge popular success…the appearance at the booths of the men and women who had votes completely dispelled from my mind the notion that the crowds in the streets [supporting Davitt] represented the poor creatures who were marched into the booths like sheep by the bishop's domineering force of curates. In my experience of elections, I never saw anything so pitiable'. 'I have come to the conclusion', he reported a few weeks later, 'that Belfast nationality, outside a few hundred good men, consists of religious bigotry and an ability to play "The Boys of Wexford"'.[28] Even into the twentieth century a primary allegiance to religious authority in public life, rather than to secular national leadership, predominated both among the upper echelons of the Catholic professional and business elite and among the working masses. The strength of Nationalism lay in the aspiring – and mainly younger – members of the lower middle class: teachers, smaller publicans and bookmakers. This class was larger, better educated, and less deferential towards clerical leadership in secular matters in 1900 than it had been a generation earlier.[29] In 1865 Bishop Dorrian was able, with relatively little difficulty, to close down the lay-controlled Catholic Institute in Belfast, after it had been in existence for six years; in 1905 Joe Devlin's National Club, also six years old, was able to close down Bishop Henry's temporal activities.

To an extent, therefore, the outcome of the conflict between the Belfast Catholic Association and the local UIL suggests the need for some modification of the claims of MacLaughlin and of O'Mahony & Delany that priestly power increased as a result of the Parnell split and the Gaelic revival.[30] Devlin in his local context, supported at national level by John Redmond and John Dillon, effectively redefined and circumscribed the direct role of the priest in political life, so far as the Irish Parliamentary party was concerned. On the other hand, the long struggle also reshaped and constrained Devlin's nationalist vision, for in order to limit overt priestly power he was obliged to modify his own early outlook so as to combat charges of anticlericalism. His weekly paper, the *Northern Star*, began in 1897 under the banner 'Ulster's National and Democratic Weekly'. Its early issues carried regular reports of trade union meetings, and its second editor, the young trainee barrister W.D. Harbinson, was an Ulster Protestant. By 1900 the paper was in financial difficulty and was bailed out by Charles Diamond, the Ulster-born and British-based proprietor of the *Catholic*

Herald group of newspapers, effectively becoming the Belfast edition of Diamond's Glasgow paper. The masthead was changed to 'Ulster's Nationalist Weekly' and most of the later pages of the paper became filled with news, mainly concerning Scotland, of the achievements of Irish Catholics. A couple of years later, on his second fundraising mission to the USA, Devlin encountered the wealth and influence of the Ancient Order of Hibernians of America, and embarked upon the course which was to make his name synonymous with the Order in Ireland as a political organisation and as a symbol of Catholic jobbery.[31] Many priests, most notably Cardinal Michael Logue, disliked the AOH, but others supported it. With the 'Faith and Fatherland' motto which it shared with the Christian Brothers it gave Devlin's politics an unquestionable Catholic flavour, while remaining a body firmly under lay control. These two developments – Diamond's sponsorship of the *Star* and the expansion of the AOH in Ireland – were both products of Devlin's links with the (strongly Catholic Church-based) Irish diaspora and both of them helped to make Devlin's nationalism more overtly and therefore, in the Ulster context, more exclusively Catholic in appeal. Thus he was led down a path which his earlier conduct of Nationalist politics in Belfast before 1900 suggests that he would have wished to avoid.

Another rival – though at that stage a less formidable one – to the Home Rule party for the political leadership of Catholic/Nationalist Belfast and Ulster was that grouping of ideas and attitudes which made up cultural nationalism, republicanism and the separatist movement. Ulster, of course, had been prominent in the uprising of 1798, while Ribbonism and Fenianism had also been relatively strong, at least in Belfast itself. At the beginning of the twentieth century it seemed that northerners were relatively more prominent in the leadership of Ireland's cultural nationalist and separatist movements than was the case in the Home Rule movement. The cultural Nationalist journals, *The Northern Patriot* (1894–95) and *Shan Van Vocht* (1896–99), were powerful, if short-lived, voices for separatism. They were published in Belfast by two energetic young women: the Presbyterian nationalist Alice Milligan (1866–1953), whose father Seaton F. Milligan, was a Belfast businessman and – though Unionist in politics – a respected writer on Irish antiquities; and the Catholic Anna Johnston ('Ethna Carbery', 1866–1902), daughter of the Belfast timber merchant and old Fenian leader Robert Johnston. Milligan continued to be active in cultural matters, but was very much more prominent in the pre-1916 era than later. Both through the cultural nationalism of Belfast's Ulster Literary

Theatre and advanced nationalist groupings such as the Dungannon Clubs, figures such as the Quaker Bulmer Hobson (1883–1969) and the Catholic Denis McCullough (1883–1968) gave the north a prominent position in the separatist movement prior to 1916, playing leading roles in the revitalisation of the Irish Republican Brotherhood [IRB].[32] Another prominent figure in the IRB before 1916 was the Tyrone doctor, Patrick McCartan (1878–1966). Yet he was to write shortly after the Easter Rising that 'the whole business was like a thunderbolt to me'. McCullough was only slightly better-informed about the Rising, and led the Belfast battalion of the Irish Volunteers as far as Tyrone, before turning back. The main planners of the Rising, Tom Clarke (1858–1916) and Sean MacDermott (1884–1916), had been raised in Ulster.[33] They were of course executed, but most of the surviving Ulster leaders of the republican movement disappeared quickly from the headlines of Irish history after 1916. The exceptions were Eoin MacNeill (1867–1945) from the Glens of Antrim, the Lisburn Protestant Ernest Blythe (1889–1975), both ministers in William Cosgrave's governments of the 1920s, and Sean MacEntee (1889–1984), long-serving senior minister in Eamon de Valera's cabinets.[34] MacEntee, in his Dáil speech on the 1921 Treaty, spoke strongly against the partition of Ireland, and opposed the Treaty on those grounds, but with that exception, links with the north after 1921 became the preserve of the intractable minority who continued to support Sinn Féin and the IRA after the Fianna Fáil split in 1926. Ulster was not remembered meaningfully, even by ex-northerners.

A similar pattern is apparent in labour politics. Early trade unionism was primarily craft unionism and therefore, in Ulster, Protestant. The first candidates for political labour in Belfast were affiliated to the Labour party in Britain, and reflected the anti-home rule views of the majority of their local supporters. But in working-class North Belfast the Catholic minority in the electorate was a large one. In 1905, in the first of four fiercely-fought parliamentary contests, the Labour candidate William Walker, to the despair of his election agent (J. Ramsay MacDonald), was manoeuvred by the Belfast Protestant Association into making unequivocal declarations against Home Rule, a Catholic university, and various other Catholic concerns. He thus failed to win the endorsement of the Belfast UIL. He lost to the Unionist, with 47.2 per cent of the vote, though coming even closer in the general election that followed a few months later on a fresh register, with 48.5 per cent.[35] Shortly thereafter, the Belfast labour picture was transformed dramatically by the interventions of Jim Larkin and

James Connolly. Following his failure – foolhardy or heroic, depending on one's point of view – in the Belfast dock strike of 1907, Larkin ended his employment with the Liverpool-based National Union of Dock Labourers and, in 1909, formed the Irish Transport & General Workers' Union [ITGWU]. Although it drew its initial energy from the Belfast dispute, this was a Dublin-based union, which associated itself frankly with radical nationalism. The ITGWU was disliked as much by the Catholic Church as it was by Unionists and Orangemen, but it found a significant base of support among the unskilled working class in the cities of southern Ireland. With the arrival of the socialist writer and organiser Connolly in Belfast in 1911 the ITGWU gained both a theoretician and a new strength in the northern capital. Connolly developed an analysis which linked the national and the social struggles but which also split the labour movement into pro-and anti-nationalist factions, as was happening at the same time in other ethnically-divided regions of Europe.[36] In Belfast he had some industrial success, though little political success, in drawing Catholics into a cohesive labour organisation. Perhaps his most distinctive achievement in the city was to lead a generation of local labour activists of Protestant background to a republican socialist position. Several such individuals made what proved to be a lifetime commitment.[37] But they were notoriously unable to carry a significant number of the Protestant rank and file with them. In later years they either remained in ineffectual opposition in the north or, like Blythe, MacNeill and MacEntee in parliamentary politics, effectively became southerners.

II

Joseph Devlin (1871–1934) was the unquestioned leader of Irish Nationalism in Ulster throughout the period. He had entered Parliament for North Kilkenny at a by-election in 1902, before winning West Belfast from the Unionists by the narrowest of margins in a three-way contest at the general election of 1906.[38] He made an early impression as a parliamentary orator: in 1911 Winston Churchill reported to George V that 'Mr Devlin…is the one new figure of distinction in the Irish party'.[39] To Redmond he was 'the defender of the worker and the poor… an orator, a statesman, a true friend'.[40] Connolly, on the other hand, declared that 'to Brother Devlin and not to Brother Carson is mainly due the progress of the covenanter [i.e. UVF] movement in Ulster'.[41] The main charges laid against Devlin by political opponents are that he introduced sectarianism into the national movement by his reliance for organisational purposes on the Ancient Order of Hibernians, and that he effectively sold the pass on Irish unity by acquiescing – privately in 1914, and publicly in 1916 – in proposals for the exclusion of parts of Ulster from a home rule settlement. The remainder of this chapter will assess these charges.

Devlin was not prominent in the home rule debates during 1912. But once the question of special treatment for Ulster came to the fore in the autumn of 1913 he became a primary focus of interest for both his colleagues and for members of H.H. Asquith's cabinet. Devlin 'is the man who will have the troublesome task', observed Lloyd George.[42] It was after a talk with Lloyd George that the senior Irish Party figure T.P. O'Connor began the process of softening up his younger colleague. He wrote to Devlin on 1 October 1913 that 'it would be well for us to consider some means by which the Orangemen could save their faces, such as complete control of education and religion by the four counties themselves...in the last resort I would suggest a modified form of self-government subject to the Parliament in Dublin'.[43] This was the approach that became known as 'home rule within home rule'. Perhaps relieved at the limited extent of this proposed concession, Devlin promptly declared in public that although they would 'never' agree to the exclusion from home rule of the four Ulster counties, 'Nationalists would gladly go into a conference...to settle the details of a bill that would be acceptable to all sections of Irishmen'.[44] A month later Devlin reiterated to the Liberal chief whip Percy Illingworth, 'on his individual responsibility', that the exclusion of any portion of Ulster 'is outside the realms of compromise'. This appeared to be a new role for Devlin, dealing directly with the Liberals on central questions of policy. But he was careful to copy the letter to Redmond, saying that 'it commits no-one'. He also copied it to John Dillon, his lifelong mentor, adding almost apologetically that 'coming from me I don't think the letter can do any harm'.[45] A few weeks later, however, Devlin made 'a declaration so absolute' against exclusion that O'Connor took him directly to see Lloyd George. When Devlin made clear to the Chancellor of the Exchequer that 'home rule within home rule' was the more palatable option, Lloyd George expressed his own preference for temporary exclusion, but concluded that the decision was 'essentially an Irish question'. O'Connor, the weathercock, now thought that 'with Devlin's view of Irish feeling, and added to that his own strong personal position...exclusion is a policy we should find it difficult *at any time* to acquiesce in'.[46] Dillon also claimed to favour home rule within home rule as the best concession, and thought temporary exclusion might be impossible to sell to their followers. But he considered Lloyd George's idea 'may be right as a tactical move', and wanted to keep himself 'perfectly free'. O'Connor feared that in that situation 'we should lose Devlin and all that he represents'.[47]

The issue came to a head for the first time in February 1914, when Devlin circulated a long memorandum, copies of which are in both Redmond's and Lloyd George's papers. He proposed three concessions: (1) the right of Ulster counties to opt out of home rule after ten years; (2) extra representation for Ulster in the Irish Parliament; and (3) 'such an arrangement of the Senate as would afford them an additional safeguard against unfair treatment'.[48] In a sense it offered the Ulster Unionists less than home rule within home rule, for it retained in Dublin the control of administration; in another sense it offered more, in that it accepted the principle, albeit deferred, of exclusion. Devlin's memo was not as compelling as it might have been, for it devoted too much space to generalised assurances of 'a fair deal' for Protestants, and to denials of the seriousness of the security situation in Ulster. In private negotiation, neither of these arguments was likely to carry weight. The memo elicited a long reply from Lloyd George setting out the tactical case for the alternative proposal of four-county temporary exclusion. Neither Home Rule within Home Rule nor the delayed opt-out plan, he argued, would be accepted by the Unionists in Parliament, thus leaving the government no constitutional alternative but to force the original bill through, using the provisions of the Parliament Act.[49] The first of these concessions would, furthermore, have amounted in Lloyd George's view to a government admission that the unqualified home rule policy offered inadequate safeguards to Ulster Protestants. Lloyd George thus maintained that offering temporary exclusion to four counties immediately would quickly lead to full home rule, and would have the effect of drawing the steam from the boiler of Ulster Unionist resistance.[50] What it really implied was that London, rather than Dublin, would have responsibility for defusing the Ulster Volunteer Force, which may in fact have had attractions for the southern-based Nationalist leaders. Like the boundary commission clause of the 1921 Treaty, it had the characteristic stamp of a Lloyd George negotiation, whereby those on the other side of the table had to meet their part of the bargain first.

At this stage Devlin reverted to his more customary role of organisation man. He now accepted the policy that he has previously resisted so firmly, and took up the challenge of selling it to Catholic Ulster. He first called on three of the Northern Catholic bishops – though leaving his parliamentary colleague Jerry McVeagh to deal with Cardinal Logue, whose disapproval of Devlin's Ancient Order of Hibernians never relented. Devlin also saw 'the principal people' in Belfast, whom he found to be 'reasonable', and he held a private conference in a Belfast hotel 'of all those people whom I thought it advisable to see', a total of 13 priests and 10 laymen. This conference, Devlin reported back to Redmond on 6 March 1914, gave the temporary exclusion proposals 'their fullest and most unqualified support'. Thus Devlin was brought for the first time to swallow the principle of exclusion. The primary reason for his doing so was clearly the pressure that had been put on him by his southern colleagues within the leadership of the Irish Parliamentary party.

Observers outside the movement, conscious of Devlin's force in debate and ruthless efficiency in organisation, constantly predicted that he would revolt. In 1913 some Tories had thought that he was laying the groundwork for a seizure of the Irish Party leadership on an anti-exclusion ticket. The Ulster correspondent of *The Times*, following Devlin's progress round the Ulster dioceses in March 1914, completely misread what was happening: 'few in the inner circles of northern Nationalism will be surprised if it should be found that Mr Devlin believes his nominal chief has gone too far, and is going to say so emphatically'.[51] As we have seen, the opposite was in fact the case. Austen Chamberlain had been closer to the truth when he wrote to Lord Lansdowne on 9 December 1913 that 'Dillon has told Morley that Devlin would stick by Redmond whatever happened'.[52] Ulster Unionist opposition to anything short of permanent exclusion for the entire province brought this phase of the crisis to a halt.

The example of Ulster's effective resistance to home rule between 1911 and 1914 stimulated the emergence of a rival Volunteer movement, IRB-led, in which separatists of Ulster background were prominent. Hobson and MacNeill took the lead in initiating the Irish Volunteer movement in Dublin in November 1913. Although the Home Rule leadership still sought to cling to parliamentary methods alone, and Devlin had firmly resisted any attempt to set up a nationalist paramilitary movement in Belfast, the enormous popularity of volunteering forced the Irish Party leadership to rethink. Accordingly, in June 1914, Redmond demanded a fifty per cent representation on the governing body of the Volunteers for his nominees, by which time almost one-third of the Irish National Volunteer force was based in Ulster.[53] But the prominence of Ulster nationalism in volunteering did not continue into the wartime period: the war in fact played an important part in further widening the difference between Catholic Ulster and the rest of Ireland. The split of October 1914 into the small but determined republican Irish Volunteers, and the larger but less purposeful National Volunteers was everywhere numerically in favour of the latter. In six-county Ulster it was more so, with the Irish Volunteers only amounting to 4.5 per cent of the total, whereas the figure across the rest of the country was 9.9 per cent.[54] Once the war started, Devlin's position as MP for an urban working-class constituency led him to break the precedent of almost a quarter of a century and side with Redmond rather than the more sceptical Dillon in support of British Army recruiting. During the first phase of the war, when most people expected it to be a short one, Redmond and Devlin believed that a policy of shared enterprise with the Unionists in the war effort would provide a context for Nationalist-Unionist reconciliation.[55] No-one was very surprised that Belfast, the Orange citadel, provided proportionately more recruits than anywhere else in Ireland. Far more surprising is that, within the Belfast total, Catholics provide proportionately more of the recruits than did Protestants: in the year 1915, the Catholic 23.1 per cent of the city's male population provided 27.3 per cent of the 14,500 recruits from the city. Elsewhere, counties Antrim and Armagh recruited more than Kildare or Kerry, but Dublin recruited far more than any rural area of Ireland, Protestant or Catholic. Overall Protestants recruited proportionately more heavily than Catholics, but urbanisation levels and socio-economic status were far better predictors of recruiting than was religious denomination. 'A shilling a day' was more important than 'king and country'.[56]

The aftermath of the Easter Rising, together with an improvement in urban wage and employment levels during the later stages of the war, reduced Catholic and Nationalist recruiting to a trickle, only to a slightly lesser degree in Ulster than elsewhere. The Rising of course also presented the Irish Parliamentary Party with the greatest challenge in its half-century of existence. On 23 June 1916, having just a few days previously expressed scepticism as to the possibility of achieving such a thing, Devlin organised a convention of six-county Nationalists, chaired by Redmond, at which the party's proposal to agree to implement home rule at once, with the temporary exclusion of six-county Ulster, was carried by 475 votes to 265. Shortly afterwards the measure was aborted by the Unionists' continued refusal to accept anything short of permanent exclusion. In the eyes of many the damage was done. Dillon later wrote privately that these negotiations 'struck a deadly blow at the Irish party', while Redmond's first biographer and party colleague wrote that 'that day really finished the constitutional party and overthrew Redmond's power'.[57]

Yet, two and a half years later, in the general election of 1918, Devlin was to trounce de Valera and Sinn Féin in the Belfast Falls constituency, winning 72 per cent of the vote in a straight fight. It seems that the negative effect of the June 1916 concession actually had more impact in the south of Ireland where – as will be seen below – concern for Catholic Ulster was no more than skin deep. It is true that the northern Catholic bishops had opposed the concession, as also did the majority of Nationalist activists in west Ulster, who saw no reason why Fermanagh, Tyrone and Derry City should form a part of any concession. The eight-seat general election pact between Nationalists and Sinn Féin in 1918, which embraced all the 'winnable' seats in Ulster that were in danger of being lost to Unionists, makes it impossible to get a perfect measure of Ulster nationalist opinion at this stage. But whereas Sinn Féin won most of the by-elections in Ireland from the beginning of 1917 onwards, it was less successful in Ulster, losing South Armagh and East Tyrone to the Irish Party in the first months of 1918 in straight fights, with only 36 per cent and 40 per cent of the vote respectively.[58] It has been suggested that the Irish Party candidates benefited from some Unionist votes in these cases, but even in the general election which followed (on a greatly extended franchise[59]) an analysis of results in those seats where the pact did not operate suggests that Irish Party candidates performed better than their Sinn Féin opponents in Unionist majority seats, notably Belfast Duncairn and South Londonderry.[60] In East Down, where a rebellion against the pact by the local Devlinites gave the seat to the Unionist minority, the Irish party candidate also performed better than the pact-nominated Sinn Féiner, winning 30 per cent against 27 per cent of the vote.[61] It is true that the pro-Irish Party newspaper, the Belfast-based *Irish News*, continued to be the main source of daily information for Catholics in most parts of Ulster at a time when the Party's Dublin paper, the *Freeman's Journal*, had long since lost its circulation contest with the more hostile *Irish Independent*.[62] But this serves as additional evidence of Catholic Ulster's difference, rather than 'explaining away' the difference to any extent. Claims that the fruitless concessions made by Redmond and Devlin in the abortive 1916 negotiations ended the Irish Party's prospects in the north are therefore less than convincing. 1918, as Marianne Elliott has observed, was a 'false dawn' for Sinn Féin in Ulster.[63]

The electoral balance changed only slightly and temporarily during the following years. Sinn Féin and the Nationalists each won 10 seats on the Belfast City Council in January 1920, but across six-county Ulster as a whole, Devlinite Nationalists won 15 per cent of first preference votes against Sinn Féin's nine per cent. In the first elections to the Parliament of Northern Ireland in May 1921 there was a more significant shift to Sinn Féin: Devlin was the only successful non-unionist candidate in the city, with the Nationalists and Sinn Féin each winning six seats in the province. Sinn Féin did win 11 per cent of total first preference votes in Belfast against the Nationalists' 10 per cent, while province-wide it took almost 21 per cent of the vote against the Nationalists' 12 per cent. But by 1925 Pro-Treaty Sinn Féiners had coalesced with the Devlinite Nationalists to secure complete control of anti-partitionist representation, leaving Anti-Treaty Republicanism as a fringe movement.[64]

During the revolutionary period Devlin was effectively excluded from decision-making and high-level consultation, although his parliamentary interventions did at least secure some public compensation for many of the estimated 10,000 Catholics and trade unionists who were expelled from the Belfast shipyards and other workplaces during the summer of 1920.[65] Sinn Féin, on the other hand, deployed a variety of tactics for Ulster, but had no considered strategy. The 'Belfast Boycott' operated spasmodically in the south against goods from Unionist Ulster between mid-1920 and mid-1922, but it hardened Unionist resolve, while encouraging a shift of Ulster's trade links away from southern Ireland towards Britain. In the Treaty negotiations of Autumn 1921 the Sinn Féin tactic was to attempt – with an eye on international opinion – to 'stage the break on Ulster'.[66] This was not only negative in concept but also ineffective in practice. Finally, Michael Collins's tactics during the first half of 1922 were to provide strong covert support for a revived IRA campaign in the north, alongside his open policy of seeking protection for the oppressed northern Catholics through mediation with the Ulster Unionists and the British.[67] Even this piece of duplicity appears to have had as much to do with his eagerness to prevent the northern IRA from going over to the Anti-Treaty side as it did with his concern for the plight of northern Catholics. Certainly, in Enda Staunton's assessment, 'this was its major result'.[68]

Of course the sufferings of northern Catholics between 1920 and 1922 were very severe, and produced a considerably larger casualty toll than the IRA was able to inflict in the north.[69] But Sinn Féin tactics did nothing to alleviate this suffering, and in fact, along with the southern IRA campaign in general, did a considerable amount to exacerbate it. The murder in Cork City of RIC Commissioner Smyth, a native of

Banbridge, Co. Down, played an important part in provoking the
workplace expulsions and loyalist violence of July 1920. Equally, the
murder of District Inspector Swanzy in his home town of Lisburn in
August of the same year, which provoked a ferocious mob reprisal
against the Catholic minority of that town, was carried out at the insti-
gation of the Cork IRA in revenge for Swanzy's alleged role in the
murder of Cork city's IRA commandant, Lord Mayor Thomas
MacCurtain, earlier that year.[70] In April 1922 the pro-Sinn Féin Bishop
of Down & Connor, Joseph MacRory, urged Collins and the pro-treaty
Defence minister, Richard Mulcahy, to discontinue their campaign of
property destruction in the north, for it would 'only intensify the
slaughter'. In June Seamus Woods, O/C 3rd Northern Division pro-
treaty IRA, who was leading that campaign, reported that 'we are
coaxing the population to a great extent and are daily losing ground'.
By September 1922 a pro-treaty organiser reported that northern
Catholics 'see the futility of our actions in so far as they are concerned'.[71] The old Irish Party strategy of linking the minority in
the north to the political strength of nationalism in the south had
rebounded in an especially cruel way.

III

As distinct from tactics, Sinn Féin had no considered strategy for Ulster.
De Valera told a group of American journalists in February 1921 that
'the so-called Ulster difficulty….has arisen purely as a product of British
party manoeuvring'.[72] Many of the party's more thoughtful activists sincerely believed that the root cause of opposition to Irish independence
on the part of Ulster Protestants was genuine concern about the sleazier
aspects of 'Rome rule' associated, especially, with the sectarianism of
Devlin's Ancient Order of Hibernians. Devlin, regarded as an arch-
opponent of Sinn Féin in any event, was seen by Sinn Féiners as having
confirmed all the prejudices of Protestant Ulster by aligning the
Nationalist movement so overtly with Catholicism and with Catholic
jobbery. Many idealistic Sinn Féiners honestly believed that their brand
of Nationalism, predominantly cultural rather than religious in its
content, was potentially inclusive of Ulster Protestants in a way that the
Nationalism of the Hibernian era was not.[73] But again, recent research
has suggested that this particular point of view may not have been the
predominant one within Sinn Féin. In practice Gaelic cultural nationalism and Gaelic sports did not resonate with Protestants, beyond a very
small circle of enthusiasts and intellectuals. These activities in fact *added*

to the long-ingrained religious barriers that separated Nationalists from Unionists. It has also been suggested that a broader current in Sinn Féin thought may in fact have been *more* strongly – and indeed more bigotedly – Catholic than Devlin and the AOH: the *Sinn Féin* newspaper accused Devlin in November 1914 of forming a secret alliance with the Grand Orient Lodge of Freemasons, while Arthur Griffith's *Nationality* expressed outrage in 1915 when Devlin and other leading members of the Irish Party presented 'the sympathy of the Irish people' to the French socialist premier, Rene Viviani, a supporter of secular education.[74] While the Irish party in the post-1914 era has frequently been characterised as a frock-coated bunch of socially-conservative local notables, in contrast to the progressive young men and women of Sinn Féin, we find the Belfast-based Sinn Féin candidate Dr Russell McNabb telling the electors of east Tyrone in March 1918 that 'the Devlins were nothing more or less than a lot of shop boys, stable boys and bottlewashers'.[75]

In practice Sinn Féin was prepared to accept partition as the price of securing acceptable constitutional arrangements for the south just as, earlier, Arthur Griffith had denounced Redmond for doing.[76] Michael Laffan argues that in 1919–20 Devlin was considerably quicker than Collins to spot that the threat of partition was real and imminent. The Pro-Treaty Sinn Féiner Louis J. Walsh, a Co. Antrim solicitor, also believed that southern Sinn Féiners did not prioritise the situation in the north. In January 1922 he declared that 'Sinn Féin, Nationalist and Labour could ask for no better advocate or more fitting leader than the Nationalist member for West Belfast, Joe Devlin'.[77] Even the Anti-Treaty Republican and later Fianna Fáil leader MacEntee wrote from prison to his wife in Belfast of his 'disgust at the way in which the Republicans [his own party] are using the plight of our people in the north as a propagandist weapon, while in their hearts they care as little about them really as the Treatyites do'. Sinn Féin attitudes towards Ulster, writes Laffan, were characterised by 'ignorance and hypocrisy'.[78]

The differences between Irish nationalism in the north and in the south of Ireland were therefore pervasive and ongoing during the Home Rule and revolutionary periods. The years between 1906 and 1914, when Devlin was a successful Party secretary, running the UIL headquarters in Dublin and injecting AOH organisation and energy into it, is the closest that Ulster nationalism came to an effective and integrated role in the national movement. During the winter of 1913–14 Devlin discovered the limitations on his own position and that of Catholic Ulster. In earlier phases of the home rule conflict, and most especially during the subsequent revolutionary period, northern Catholic circumstances and experience, at the hands of southern nationalists and republicans as well as northern Unionists, were very different. Ex-northerners were little different in that respect from southern Nationalists. Neither the interventions of the Ulster Pro-Treatyites MacNeill and Blythe, nor those of the Ulster Republican MacEntee, brought any amelioration for Ulster Catholics during or after the revolutionary years. If there was a modernising strand to Irish nationalism in this period, Joe Devlin was its most formidable representative.

7

Actions and Views: John Brownlee Lonsdale, Unionist MP, 1900–18 and Party Leader, 1916–18

Brian M. Walker

In the Pantheon of Ulster Unionist leaders, John Brownlee Lonsdale does not feature prominently. Few people today recall his name and most histories of Ulster Unionism largely ignore him.[1] And yet, Lonsdale was a leading figure in Unionism in the first two decades of the twentieth century. A very successful businessman, he was elected Member of Parliament for Mid-Armagh at a contested by-election in 1900, and held the seat unopposed for the next 18 years, a record achieved by no other Unionist in an Ulster rural seat in this period. Lonsdale was secretary and chief whip of the Irish Unionist Parliamentary party, 1903–16, and chairman of the party, 1916–18. He was created a baronet in 1911 and a peer as Lord Armaghdale in 1918. This article will focus not just on his career but also on what he said and how he explained his political position. During the first two decades of the twentieth century, Unionism underwent great change. Political identity for many unionists moved from an Irish to an Ulster perspective. Political activity changed from purely parliamentary means to include non-constitutional means. What can we learn from Lonsdale about these changes? How did Lonsdale operate so successfully at constituency level?

I

John Lonsdale was born at Armagh in 1850. He was the eldest son of James Lonsdale, originally a tenant farmer of some 39 acres near Loughgall,

County Armagh, who built up a successful butter and eggs export business.[2] On the strength of this enterprise, his father acquired in the 1860s an impressive Georgian villa, known as the Pavilion, in the environs of Armagh. He was a keen sportsman and in 1910, three years before his death, his horse Aviator won the Irish Derby. Reflecting a rise in the family economic and social standing, he was appointed county High Sheriff in 1892 and a deputy lieutenant in the early 1900s. John entered the family concern at the age of 16 and, along with his father and brothers, established creameries and butter depots in many parts of Ireland. The firm then decided to withdraw from most of the Irish market, apparently because it suffered boycott from the Land League during the Land War,[3] and to concentrate on trade with the USA and the empire, especially Canada. The enterprise became known as J. & J. Lonsdale and established its headquarters in Manchester, with important centres in London, Liverpool and New York. When the firm was incorporated in 1900, a prospectus claimed that the business was one of the first in England in the import, export and distribution of dairy produce.[4]

After John Lonsdale became M.P. for Mid Armagh in 1900, the press drew attention to his leading role in building up the Lonsdale firm.[5] It was also pointed out that he was chairman of the Manchester Corn and Produce Exchange, a director of the Lancashire and Yorkshire Bank and deputy chairman of the Manchester Ship Canal Company. Following his election he ceased to take an active part in the management of the Lonsdale business, but he did retain some directorships and the non-executive chairmanship of Lonsdale's. In 1887 he had married Florence Rumney, described later as the co-heiress of William Rumney of Stubbins House, Lancashire.[6] Marriage helped the Lonsdales in the local Armagh social and political scene, when in 1891 his brother Thomas married Mary McClintock of Fellows Hall, Co. Armagh, a relative of the leading landed and Orange family in Mid Armagh, the Stronges of Tynan Abbey. John Lonsdale was a member of the Church of Ireland. He was not an Orangeman, unlike most of his contemporary Unionist MPs from Ulster.

By 1900 Lonsdale no longer lived in Armagh, but he retained strong links with the area. The Pavilion, occupied first by his father and then his brother James, until the sale of the property in late 1917, continued to be his base for regular return visits to Armagh, both before and during his time at Westminster. After his election he moved from Manchester to London, where he acquired as his permanent home a prestigious residence in Princes Gardens, S.W. This gave him a good base from which to operate, at a level on par with other Ulster MPs, such as Col. Edward Saunderson, and well above the accommodation of the impecunious William Johnston who had to put up with lodgings on Vauxhall Bridge Road for his London address.[7] He regularly visited the French Riviera, usually over the Christmas period, was a keen golfer and, as befitted the son of a leading member of the Irish turf, rode every morning in London, before attending Parliament.[8] He was a member of a number of London Clubs, including the Carlton. Unlike most other Irish MPs, Lonsdale did not belong to either a Belfast or a Dublin club.

The parliamentary constituency of Mid Armagh was created as a result of the 1884 redistribution act. It was a mainly agricultural area, which included the ecclesiastical capital of Armagh. A parliamentary return for 1884–85 showed that of the population in Mid Armagh 58 per cent were Protestants, of whom 59 per cent were members of the Church of Ireland and 34 per cent were Presbyterians.[9] A Nationalist candidate unsuccessfully stood for Mid Armagh in 1885 and 1886, but thereafter no Nationalist contested the seat, although, from the early 1900s, Nationalists controlled Armagh town council. In 1885, the Mid Armagh Constitutional Association was formed to represent local Unionists and to assume responsibility for selection of the parliamentary candidate and party organisation at election time.[10] The association had a part time agent in the person of Joshua Peel, a local solicitor. In early January 1900, the sitting MP, D.P. Barton, was made a judge, and a by election was called.

On 29 January 1900 a meeting of the Mid Armagh Constitutional Association, chaired by Sir James Stronge, selected John Lonsdale as Unionist candidate, in preference to County Down barrister, John Gordon, QC. This outcome was challenged by Gordon. In the ensuing contest both candidates issued addresses and spoke at meetings. Their main political points were similar.[11] Both supported the government in the war in South Africa, advocated land reform and declared opposition to Home Rule. They backed proposals for a new Kingscourt, Keady and Armagh railway, but Lonsdale had an advantage here because he had promised personal financial support for the railway, while Gordon in his role as a barrister had opposed the scheme on behalf of a rival railway company. Lonsdale won with 3212 votes against Gordon's 1811. Undoubtedly, Lonsdale benefited from his local connections. His stand on the land question was probably helped by the argument put forward, not by himself but by some supporters, that he was the 'son of a farmer, and one of themselves'.[12] At the same time the extent of Gordon's votes revealed considerable dissatisfaction with how Unionist politics were run in Mid Armagh.

II

Over the next 18 years as MP for Mid Armagh, Lonsdale never faced another contest, a record achieved by no other Unionist in a rural Ulster seat. The first part of his career to be examined here runs over the period 1900–6, when there was a Conservative and Unionist government and the challenge for Unionist MPs in Ulster came largely from within Unionist ranks. The relegation of Home Rule to secondary importance for most of this time allowed various internal conflicts to surface. By 1900 a number of the parliamentary associations established in 1885 to involve Unionist electors in party organisation had collapsed, and there was growing resentment at control of parliamentary representation by small groups. Serious unrest also grew in relation to the demand for land purchase, a matter promoted by T.W. Russell, in particular. Populist Orange protest emerged around the person of T.H. Sloan. In a number of constituencies Presbyterian dissatisfaction posed a problem. Lonsdale was able to effectively meet these challenges.

One area which Lonsdale tackled very successfully was that of local issues and patronage. In Parliament over the next six years, he raised many questions about subjects such as the Kingscourt, Keady and Armagh railway. Patronage involved financial gifts to local causes and support for individuals to obtain positions; a role expected of most Irish MPs. Lonsdale received advice about these matters from his agent, Joshua Peel. In February 1900, less than a month after his election, Peel wrote; 'I am afraid that I am giving you a lively time in the matter of patronage but it is one of the penalties of your job'.[13] An early example of this was a request from Peel to urge support for a Thomas Knipe to be appointed to the committee of Armagh Asylum: 'if you can get Mr Knipe appointed it would gratify a large circle of your friends. The Knipes have a large connection and influence'.[14] He was successful and his client proved a useful ally. A few months later, just before the 1900 general election, at a meeting of the Lisadean Tenants 'Association, Knipe proposed a successful resolution in support of Lonsdale.[15] Again, a year later, Peel passed on a warning from Knipe about 'great dissatisfaction' among Mullerton Orangemen over Lonsdale's subscription of three guineas towards the debt on their Orange hall: 'they had heard that you gave larger sums to other places where you did not get so hearty and unanimous support and in fact there was a proposal (nearly adopted) to return the cheque'.[16] Peel urged Lonsdale to send seven guineas.

Party organisation was important for Lonsdale's success. After his first election, the *Northern Whig* criticised the state of Unionist organisation in Mid Armagh, and pointed out that this was a problem to be found in a number of divisions.[17] At least the Mid Armagh Constitutional Association still existed, unlike other associations which had collapsed, and had its own premises.[18] At the same time there were problems, such as the failure to hold recent elections of delegates. On 28 July 1900, Peel reported to Lonsdale a private meeting with his father, James Lonsdale, and leading Armagh Conservative, T.G. Peel, at which they urged a new election of delegates, including reliable friends: 'Your father and he think a successful election of delegates might prevent a contest at the general election...they both came to the conclusion that the present position of the association cannot be defended'.[19] This step seems to have been taken because at the general election later in 1900, there was no sign of internal criticism of Lonsdale. Local involvement was aided by an Armagh borough unionist club. In contrast, lack of broad based party organisations would cause bitter intra Unionist conflict at the 1900 general election and subsequent by elections in other areas, such as Mid and East Down.[20]

Most important of all in Lonsdale's position was his ability to respond positively to his constituents' general concerns. At the October 1900 general election, Lonsdale backed compulsory land purchase, a position not taken by some unionist landlord candidates, but in keeping with his own background.[21] Saunderson in neighbouring North Armagh faced a radical farmers' candidate, James Orr. Lonsdale was unopposed, thanks mainly to his advanced stand on land reform, but also due to family connections. Orr was a distant family relation, while Lonsdale's first cousin, farmer Robert Orr of Ballymagerney near Loughgall, allowed his premises to be used for an anti-Saunderson rally, all of which helped to put Lonsdale in local eyes in the anti landlord camp.[22] At Westminster he strongly supported the Wyndham land act of 1903. This act did not provide compulsory purchase, but it did offer excellent terms to encourage widespread land purchase which Lonsdale and his constituents regarded as sufficient.

While Home Rule was not a major issue in 1900, it had become very important by the general election of six years later. During 1905 and 1906 Lonsdale expounded at length on his objections to Home Rule.[23] He believed that Home Rule would destroy the integrity of the United Kingdom and undermine the union of the Empire: it would result in the suppression of Unionist influence in public affairs in Ireland. In his speeches he referred to 'Irish Unionists', 'Irish

Loyalists' and the interests of Ireland. Within this broad Irish context he also talked of 'Unionists of Ulster'. This perspective was a common one, as we can see from one of the resolutions at a major Unionist rally in Belfast in 1906 which spoke of those present as 'Ulster Irishmen and true lovers of our country'. In 1903 at a public meeting in Armagh Lonsdale declared that since he had been elected he had sought to serve 'the interests of his constituency, of Ireland, and the Empire'.[24] An issue strongly backed by Lonsdale was tariff reform which he believed would cause closer union of the Empire and bring advantages to Ireland and Great Britain.[25] On a rare occasion he referred to the 'British nation'.[26]

Lonsdale spoke regularly on these matters in Mid Armagh, some-times at meetings of his association and sometimes at other events, such as the opening of local Orange halls. At these latter events, Lonsdale was happy to pay tribute to the Orange Order: 'he looked upon the society as one of the strongest bulwarks of the Union'.[27] At the same time he did not become a member or share the enthusiasm of fellow unionist MP, Capt James Craig, who in 1906 called himself an Orangeman first and a Member of Parliament second.[28] The Mid Armagh Constitutional Association had no formal Orange representation, unlike some other associations, but there was a strong overlap between membership of the association and of the Orange Order: Sir James Stronge was both pre-sident of the former and county grand master of the latter. There was no sign of Presbyterian disaffection in the division. Joshua Peel usually ensured that one or more eminent local Presbyterians spoke at election meetings. This sometimes required a little arm twisting. In 1906 he pressed the Revd David Miller, minister of First Armagh congregation, to speak: 'at a time like the present it is surely right for the clergy, the natural leaders...to lead. I feel confident...you will feel a burden laid on you not to keep silence'. He added a P.S.: 'I should say that a short speech of five or ten minutes will be quite enough'.[29]

At Westminster during these years, Lonsdale's role grew. In mid 1903, following the death of William Johnston, he became secretary and chief whip of the Irish Unionist Parliamentary party. A number of sources paid tribute to the business skills which he brought to this posi-tion, in contrast to the less efficient methods of Johnston.[30] Regularly he headed the list of attendances of Irish Unionist members at divisions during parliamentary sessions.[31] He planned debating strategy. Concern grew among Irish Unionists that the Irish administration was unduly sympathetic to Irish Nationalists. This anxiety became greatly height-ened when it emerged during late 1904 that the Irish Under Secretary of State, Sir Anthony MacDonnell, was involved in proposals for Irish devolution. Irish Unionists in Parliament fiercely attacked the government over this and were successful in forcing the resignation of the Irish Chief Secretary, George Wyndham, in March 1905. Contemporaries credited Lonsdale with having devised the effective Unionist campaign against MacDonnell and Wyndham.[32] Lonsdale's leadership at this stage arose in part because the chairman of the party, Saunderson, was unwell and had lost the confidence of some younger and more active Unionist MPs, especially William Moore and C.C. Craig.[33]

In late 1904, during the devolution crisis, a number of meetings were held in Belfast to set up what became the Ulster Unionist Council. This development has been viewed as a response to the devolution crisis:[34] recent interpretations, however, have seen it as more an indirect criticism of the leadership and as a concern among Ulster Unionists to modernise their organisation in face of internal critics.[35] It was Craig and Moore who issued public letters in September, calling for the formation of a new body to respond to the devolution crisis. A special meeting of nine Ulster Unionist MPs, including Lonsdale, Moore and Craig, but not Saunderson, was held in Belfast on 22 October 1904.[36] Lonsdale, as parliamentary party secretary, was directed to summon a meeting of Ulster Unionists to 'discuss the advisability of founding a central Ulster association'. He issued some invitations to this event, but, after he became unwell, the task of organisation fell to Moore and Craig.

At the meeting in Belfast on 2 December 1904, which neither Lonsdale nor Saunderson attended, due to ill health, a resolution was passed in favour of the new organisation and its objectives. The first meeting of the council on 3 March 1905 was attended by Lonsdale but not Saunderson.[37] Given his widely accepted role in the parliamentary party during 1904, it is probable that Lonsdale was an important figure in these developments, although his illness restricted his part. Part of Lonsdale's role may have been to prevent a public rift between Saunderson and younger MPs. At the same time it is possible that Lonsdale had some reservations about the new council. In his apology for missing the December meeting, he gave enthusiastic backing for the council which he believed would be a strong support to the Ulster MP s, but he also said that it would be able to 'declare the mind of the loyalists of Ireland on every important question', perhaps showing concern about the Ulster emphasis of the new body.[38] Subsequently, however, Lonsdale attended regularly council meeting.

III

The years 1906–14 can be treated as a distinct period when Unionists such as Lonsdale found themselves dealing with the new challenge of a Liberal government. The part of his role as an MP which concerned local interests and patronage remained unchanged. He promoted issues such as the matter of a government loan for the building of labourers' cottages in Co. Armagh.[39] Joshua Peel continued to channel to him requests from constituents for support for positions: these included another request from Thomas Knipe, this time for his grand daughter for the job of post master in Armagh. Requests for subscriptions still came his way, such as a letter dated 28 March 1912 about Tandragee Unionist Club: 'a Protestant temperance hall and institute is about to be erected for Tandragee…we heard of your very liberal assistance to one somewhat similar for Armagh'.[40] Unionist constituency party organisation in Mid Armagh grew from 1911 onwards with the establishment of both Unionist clubs and women's Unionist associations.[41]

In late 1906, after the death of Saunderson, there was a possibility that Lonsdale would become leader of the Irish Unionist Parliamentary party.[42] Instead, the position went to Walter Long, former Under Secretary for Ireland, and Unionist MP for South Dublin. From 1906–10, Lonsdale pursued a highly critical stance in Parliament in relation to the Liberal government, particularly the Irish Chief Secretary, Augustine Birrell, with the tabling of many parliamentary questions. In the years, 1906–7, he tabled nearly 700 questions, more than any other MP. Lonsdale was particularly concerned with the power of the United Irish League whom he blamed for boycotting and lawlessness in the west of Ireland.[43] Home Rule surfaced in the form of proposed Council of Ireland. Lonsdale and his fellow Unionists vigorously opposed this proposal which they saw as a first step to Home Rule. He declared that rather than accept changes which would place them under Nationalist domination, 'the Unionists of Ireland are prepared to resort to every means of resistance which may be open to them. This is a matter of life and death to the minority of the Irish people'. He reminded Parliament that Irish Loyalists were not confined to Ulster. If this bill passed, he concluded, it would, 'be fraught with disastrous consequences to the United Kingdom and the Empire'.[44] Eventually the matter was dropped, primarily because Irish Nationalist MPs thought the measure insufficient for their needs. In November 1909 Lonsdale was given a special presentation and dinner by members of the Irish Unionist Parliamentary party in recognition of his services as secretary and chief whip since 1903.[45]

At the two general elections of 1910, Lonsdale was elected unopposed in Mid Armagh. Overall in the United Kingdom the Conservative party increased its number of MPs, but, ironically, this made the liberal government largely dependent on Irish Nationalist MPs to maintain a majority. At the same time, the Liberal party had declared its intention to remove the veto of the House of Lords over legislation. This meant that by late 1910, Irish Unionists faced the strong likelihood of not only a new Irish home rule bill, but also of the loss of their Lords defence. After the January general election, the leader of the Conservative party, Arthur Balfour resigned and was replaced by Andrew Bonar Law. Lonsdale was initially sceptical about this choice.[46] In the event Lonsdale and other Unionists were happy with Bonar Law, partly because of his family connections with Ulster. The Irish Unionist Parliamentary party also required a new leader because after the 1910 January election Long represented an English seat. Following much internal discussion, Lonsdale was deputed to request Sir Edward Carson, MP for Dublin University, to accept the leadership of the Irish Unionist party in Parliament. Carson agreed on 21 February 1910. Lonsdale remained as party secretary and chief whip; in mid 1911 he was created a baronet.

From the start of 1911 until early 1914, Lonsdale was extremely active, both inside and outside Parliament. In response to the King's speech at the opening of Parliament in early February 1911, he opened the case for Irish Unionists to state their fear that changes to the status of the House of Lords would be followed by a new Home Rule bill: he warned that 'any attempt to force Nationalist rule upon Ulster would be met by the most determined resistance'.[47] In the following parliamentary session he joined with other Irish Unionists in an unsuccessful attempt to stop the Parliament act. He took part in late September 1911 in a large Unionist demonstration at Craigavon, Co. Down, where Carson was the lead speaker. In early March 1912 the Home Rule bill was introduced to parliament and over the next 15 months Lonsdale spoke frequently against the bill. As party secretary he had a major responsibility for his party's strategy towards the bill in the Commons. In April he was one of the speakers at a massive unionist demonstration at Balmoral in Belfast, attended by Bonar Law and other leading politicians from Great Britain. In June he presented to Parliament a petition signed by 256,000 Unionist women of Ireland, declaring their opposition to Home Rule. In September, he took a leading part in the arrangements for the signing of the Ulster Covenant in Armagh.[48]

Parliamentary opposition to the Home rule bill continued until June 1913 when the bill passed its second reading. Unionist tactics against the bill, included pushing for exclusion of Ulster as a means of undermining it, failed to work. From June onwards, Lonsdale was engaged closely in two other aspects of Unionist opposition. The first involved numerous meetings, large and small, in Great Britain to gather support for unionist opposition to Home Rule. Lonsdale played a key role in organising these meetings, as well as speaking himself in places such as Aberdeen and Manchester, often with leading English politicians. The second concerned organising additional forms of resistance in Ulster. Lonsdale was a keen supporter of the Ulster Volunteer Force [UVF]: he came forward as one of four businessmen to offer £10,000 in response to an appeal at a meeting of the Ulster Unionist Council on 23 September 1913 for an indemnity fund for the UVF. This September meeting of the council also released the names, including Lonsdale's, of members of a provisional Ulster government, to come into operation on the implementation of the Home Rule bill.[49] At the beginning of 1914, however, Lonsdale became ill and was hospitalised. He was absent from Parliament from late February until November 1914. By this time the Home Rule bill had received the royal assent, but had been suspended with the outbreak of war.

In his speeches Lonsdale elaborated on why he opposed Home Rule and on how he justified the actions of Unionists in this period. He insisted that the Unionists of Ireland were 'loyal subjects of his majesty' and wanted to retain their 'full rights as citizens of the United Kingdom'.[50] His argument against home rule lay basically in three areas: 'the peace and prosperity of Ireland, the integrity of the United Kingdom, and the security of the empire'.[51] As regards the first of these, he believed that Ireland now enjoyed considerable prosperity and would face heavy taxation and grave economic uncertainty under Home Rule. He denied that Unionists sought ascendancy, and claimed that 'under Home Rule they would be treated with constant injustice'.[52] Unlike other contemporaries, Lonsdale rarely used historical arguments to make this last point, or claimed that 'Home Rule would be Rome rule'. Instead, he referred to contemporary examples of United Irish League boycott of individuals, often Protestant or Unionist, in the west and south of Ireland, or the unwillingness of Nationalist county councils to give jobs or the new university scholarships to Protestants and Unionists.[53] In relation to the second area, he asserted that Home Rule for Ireland would not be a final settlement. He argued, often using quotes from Nationalist MPs, that when Nationalists acquired power they would move to Irish independence and therefore the destruction of the United Kingdom.[54] On the third area, Lonsdale regularly asserted that Home Rule 'would be the first step to the disintegration and destruction of the Empire'.[55] If the unity of the United Kingdom was destroyed and the authority of the Imperial Parliament weakened, then the existence of the empire would be seriously threatened.

From Lonsdale's speeches it is clear that both Ireland and Ulster were important to him, in different but complementary ways. During the second reading of the Home Rule bill in May 1912, he made a rare reference to himself as 'an Ulsterman and the representative of an Ulster constituency for many years', in order to justify his claim to understand feelings in Ulster.[56] Three months earlier in Parliament, he had stated that there was not one nation in Ireland, but two, 'sharply divided in race, in religion, and in character'; this statement was made in response to an argument that the Irish nation was exclusively Nationalist.[57] He never made this particular argument again about two nations, although he elsewhere referred to two sections in Ireland – those sympathetic and those hostile to the empire.[58] He retained a strong all Ireland perspective. He continued to refer to himself and his followers as Irish Unionists or Loyalists. He saw Ireland as a partner in the United Kingdom and believed that the country benefited greatly from this link.[59] He continued to speak for both southern and northern Unionists. In part this reflected sympathy for southern Unionists, possibly because of his firm's earlier experience of boycott by the Land League.[60] More importantly, he was concerned with the fate of all of Ireland as vital for the defence of the Union and the integrity of the United Kingdom.

With developments in Ulster from mid 1912 onwards, however, Lonsdale did refer more directly to Ulster Unionists than before and he gave them his strong support, partly because he saw their resistance as the best means to save the union for the whole country. In July 1912 he declared that 'if Ulster held out, Home Rule was impossible', an argument which he repeated again in October 1913.[61] At the same time he denied that he sought an arrangement for a separate Ulster. When he argued for Ulster exclusion in 1912 and 1913, this was a tactic to undermine the Home Rule bill or to force the government to acknowledge the concerns of Unionists in Ulster.[62] The purpose of the provisional government drawn up in September 1913 was, in Lonsdale's words, to be 'a strictly provisional government', and would protect Ulster from a Dublin Home Rule Parliament until 'Ulster resumed unimpaired her citizenship of the United Kingdom'.[63] By 1914, however, after all efforts in Parliament to stop the Home Rule bill had failed, he had come round more to the idea that exclusion of Ulster was a possible compromise to prevent civil war, if the bill went ahead.[64] At the same time he insisted that the exclusion had to be complete and unconditional, and, 'having regard to our covenant', not just for six counties: 'It seems to me that if we accept anything less than the exclusion of the whole of Ulster-nine counties – it will give rise to grave dissatisfaction in Monaghan, Cavan and Donegal'.[65]

Lonsdale defended Unionist non-parliamentary activities in a number of ways. He insisted that Irish Unionists were men of peace who sought to uphold law and order, but because their 'rights and liberties' were now seriously in jeopardy and they faced political tyranny, they had a duty to offer 'stern and unyielding resistance' to the proposals.[66] He believed that giving Home Rule to Ireland was a momentous step for the whole United Kingdom which had not been asked at election time its opinions on the matter. In his view, the Liberal government pushed this Home Rule bill because it was dependent on 'mercenary votes' from Irish Nationalist MPs.[67] He argued that in light of the enormous constitutional consequences of the Home Rule proposals, both for Ireland and Great Britain, the matter had to be put to the electorate. The purpose of the Ulster Unionist measures, in Lonsdale's view, was to show their deep concerns to the public at large and to apply pressure on the government to call a general election. Often Lonsdale stated that: 'the demand of the people of Ulster was that ...they should be given an opportunity of appealing to the people of Great Britain at a general election'.[68] Even as late as July 1914, Lonsdale expressed hope that they could hold up Home Rule until 'the opinion of the people could be ascertained in the constitutional manner'.[69] If this did not happen, and the home rule bill was passed, then the provisional government and the UVF would serve to protect Ulster from Dublin control and civil war. While energetically pushing the constitutional approach, Lonsdale completely endorsed this alternative.

IV

The outbreak of war affected not only Lonsdale's political world, but also his personal one. In November 1914 his 21 year old nephew, Lt James McClintock Lonsdale, died in France from wounds received in action. In 1915, the son of his agent, Joshua Peel, was killed at Gallipoli, while in 1917, the son of the president of his divisional association, Sir James Stronge, was killed in France. These deaths, of course, were only a fraction of the many war losses suffered in Mid Armagh. Lonsdale continued to table parliamentary questions, particularly over army

recruitment in Ireland.[70] In November 1916 in Armagh, he addressed
the annual meeting of his divisional association. He paid special tribute
to the 'gallant charge of the Ulster division' at the Somme. He mentioned briefly the 'deplorable incidents' in Dublin at Easter. He also referred to a special meeting of the Ulster Unionist Council in June 1916
to consider proposals for Ireland brought by Carson from the British
Cabinet. The government's initiative arose partly in response to the
Dublin Rising and partly to encourage greater Irish involvement in the
war effort. At this meeting, attended by Lonsdale, it was agreed by the
council for the first time that they would accept a Home Rule bill
which allowed the permanent exclusion of a six county Ulster. He stated
to his Armagh audience that they had acquiesced in this proposal very
reluctantly and only because they accepted that it was 'in the interests of
national unity' and would 'strengthen the empire and help to win the
war'. Talks between the parties collapsed, however, and the initiative
failed, a matter which Lonsdale did not regret.[71]

At the end of the second week in December 1916, Lonsdale was
elected in London as chairman of the parliamentary party, in place of
Carson, who joined the War Cabinet, as First Sea Lord. Lonsdale retained the position until the beginning of January 1918. On 7 March
1917 he took part in an important debate arising from a Nationalist
resolution from T.P. O'Connor that it was 'essential without further
delay to confer upon Ireland the free institutions long promised to her'.
Speaking from 'the point of view of the Irish Unionists', Lonsdale
denied that Ireland was not already free and asserted the continued
strong opposition of Ulster Unionists to coming under a Home Rule
Parliament. 'Our contention that there are really two Irelands has,
indeed, received striking confirmation' he declared. He believed that
there was one section 'in complete and hearty sympathy with the
empire, ready to share equally all the burdens and sacrifices...'. and
another section 'which makes its offers of service dependent upon the
receipt of political advantage'. He acknowledged the bravery and,
sacrifice of Irish soldiers in the war effort, but claimed that more than
half the new recruits since the start of war had come from Ulster.[72]

This resolution was defeated, but the debate spurred the government
to a new initiative. On 16 May 1917 the Prime Minister addressed a
letter in duplicate to Lonsdale and John Redmond, as heads of the
Unionist and Nationalist parties respectively, to put forward two alternative proposals for the future of Ireland. The first offered Home Rule
with the exclusion of six Ulster counties and the second advocated a
convention in Ireland of the main Irish groups. In the debate which
followed in Parliament on 21 May 1917 Lonsdale rejected the first pro-

posal but agreed to put the second to the Ulster Unionist Council: 'the people of Ulster are a democratic community, and they possess in the Ulster unionist Council a thoroughly representative organisation'.[73] At a meeting of the council on 8 June, attended by Lonsdale but presided over by Carson, it was agreed to accept the convention idea, on the basis of the government's assurance that all proposals would be considered and that no final scheme would be accepted with which the Unionist representatives were not in agreement. Unionist delegates were duly nominated to attend the convention.[74]

The Convention held its first meeting in Dublin in July 1917. Proceedings lasted until April 1918, but while Nationalists and some southern Unionists found common ground, the Ulster Unionists could not agree with the main recommendations of the Convention. Lonsdale seems to have placed little confidence in a successful outcome. In its final days he wrote to one of the delegates, H.B. Armstrong, vice president of the Mid Armagh Constitutional Association: 'The result has been that which we all anticipated-no possibility of agreement'.[75] Meantime, during 1917 Lonsdale continued to speak in Parliament on various issues, some to do with Ireland and others to do with the war effort. He devoted considerable time to the question of the redistribution of parliamentary seats, which was the subject of a parliamentary bill, and obtained an increase in the number of seats for north east Ulster.[76] By December, Lonsdale was again unwell and he consulted Carson and Bonar Law about his intention to give up his seat as MP, and therefore his position as leader of the Irish Unionist Parliamentary party.[77] Following on this, the New Year's honours list carried his name as a new peer. Carson became head of the parliamentary party again in late January 1918.

Subsequently, Lonsdale took the title of Armaghdale, a name compounded of the name of his native county and of his own surname. The seat in Mid Armagh was now filled by his younger brother, James, on 23 January 1918. He was re-elected at the 1918 general election but died suddenly in mid 1921 and was replaced by H.B. Armstrong. Armaghdale retained his interest in politics, although poor health seems to have restricted his public efforts. In May 1918 in a letter to Armstrong, he expressed great surprise when Long was appointed chairman of a Cabinet Committee to draw up a new bill for the government of Ireland: 'I confess that nothing in my whole parliamentary career has surprised me more than that he should have accepted such a position. His zeal for the interests of southern Unionists (Middleton group) appears to have alienated all his sympathies for Ulster'.[78] Again to Armstrong on 10 May 1920 he wrote: 'I am strongly of the opinion that the exclusion of the six counties is far better for us than having the whole of Ulster'. He explained: 'the latter would have set up as much trouble in Ulster as there is now in the south and west of Ireland. I have had a long talk about it with Carson'.[79]

On the evening of 24 Nov. 1920, in his last major parliamentary speech, he spoke in the Lords on the Better Government of Ireland bill.[80] He began by saying that he believed he reflected the views of Ulster unionists. They remained 'firmly convinced that upon the maintenance of the Union depends the peace and prosperity of Ireland and the security of the United Kingdom', and so were opposed to the bill. At the same time they recognised that there had been a change of opinion in Great Britain and they could no longer rely upon a considerable section of the Unionist party which had 'formerly shared our conviction that Home Rule is inconsistent with imperial security', but had now concluded that Home Rule could be granted to Ireland without danger. Accordingly, while they did not accept this view, they would offer no resistance to the proposals. They believed that things had deteriorated with a 'campaign of assassination and outrage'. Nonetheless, from the Ulster viewpoint there was 'no possible alternative' to the bill. He stated that a year ago Unionists had wanted simply the link with Great Britain, but now 'there has been a growing appreciation of the fact that the northern Parliament will be a distinct advantage to us'. He believed that it would enable them to deal swiftly with problems, such as poor schooling in Belfast, and give greater security than just having MPs at Westminster. He stated his confidence that Ulster would respond to this challenge 'with a determination to establish just and efficient government'. He ended with the hope that one day there would be a final settlement 'upon the basis of a United Ireland as a loyal member of a united empire'.

V

John Lonsdale, Lord Armaghdale, died on 8 June 1924. The press acknowledged him as a former chairman of the Irish Unionist Parliamentary party, even though he had held this post for just over a year.[81] Most attention focussed on his role as secretary and chief whip of the parliamentary party for 13 years. An article in the *Northern Whig* stated that he would be better remembered as the 'genial, courteous Ulster gentleman than as the robust Ulster politician', and that 'when it fell to him to speak for the northern cause he did so sincerely, impressively, but always temperately'. Thanks to his business skills and genial personality, he was a very able party secretary. 'His great work for the party', the *Northern Whig* declared, 'was...in the organisation and equipment of the little force for which he was responsible'.[82] He played a strategic role in the party attack on devolution proposals, 1904–5. During the 1911–14 the party fought a rigorous, if only partly successful, parliamentary campaign against the Home Rule bill, and, as secretary and chief whip, Lonsdale played a key part in this. Contemporary accounts of his career also credited him with playing an important role in the campaign within Ulster against Home Rule, in organisations such as the Ulster Unionist Council and the Ulster Volunteer Force. Primarily a parliamentarian, he justified such 'stern and unyielding resistance' as a means to bring about a constitutional solution in the form of a general election on the issue. If this failed he was prepared to justify these other methods to protect 'rights and liberties'. When a general election was called finally in 1918, however, it was too late and things had changed irrevocably both in Ireland and Great Britain.

At the end of his career, Lonsdale gave his backing to the new Parliament of Northern Ireland, but this outcome had not been his goal. His overriding concern in politics had been the United Kingdom and the empire. At the same time it is clear that he retained a strong Irish dimension. He continued to speak for Irish unionists and to argue for union for all of Ireland. For Lonsdale this Irish dimension arose largely because he regarded all of Ireland as an essential part of the United Kingdom and the empire. His case serves as a reminder of the Irish identity which still existed among many northern Unionists. We can see this in others who later became strongly linked to an Ulster identity but who shared an Irish perspective in this period. Ronald McNeill MP, the author of *Ulster's Stand for Union,* published in 1922, with its endorsement of 'the Ulster movement' responded ten years earlier to a question about his self description as an Ulsterman by saying; 'I used the expression "Ulsterman" as a more particular phrase. Of course I regard myself as an Irishman'.[83] Even in January 1916, in a debate in Parliament about conscription for Ireland, James Craig stated that: 'It has always been a pride to a man, no matter what part of Ireland he came from, to say that he was an Irishman'. He went on to declare, however, that if Nationalists opposed conscription 'then I say for my part if this victory is gained, it will be no pleasure to me to call myself an Irishman, and in future it will either have to be a Britisher or an Ulsterman'.[84]

From the perspective that Ireland was vital for the United Kingdom, Lonsdale originally viewed Ulster primarily as the focus to save Ireland for the Union. When he first backed special treatment for Ulster this was to make home rule unworkable. Then his aim became to provide

protection for Ulster until the Union could be restored. By 1914 a
separate deal for a nine county Ulster had become for Lonsdale a possible option, although it would be seven years before the realisation of a
Parliament for six Ulster counties, which he would accept pragmatically
as the only solution. His activities and speeches in the period 1911–14
reveal a growing appreciation, if not complete involvement, in the sense
of community which now grew among Unionists in Ulster. Elements
of an Ulster identity existed before this period, but the shared experience of these events and the impact of dramatic political change led to
important development of this identity. One example was William
Moore, Lonsdale's neighbouring MP for North Armagh, who even in
January 1914 referred to himself and other Belfast Unionists as
Irishmen.[85] At the 1914 July celebrations in Tynan, County Armagh,
however, he stated that 'when people asked Moore was he an Irishman,
he always said he was an Ulsterman' and he believed that 'the word
Ulsterman was coming to have a meaning of its own': he even went so
far as to say that the crisis was 'the final making of Ulster as a nation'.[86]
While for many an Ulster identity became strong, a British dimension
in the form of citizenship of the United Kingdom and membership of
the empire, was also important. In the case of Lonsdale and others,
British identity remained paramount, in spite of their regard for Ulster
Unionism. After 1914 we begin to see new ways of formulating this
British identity. There were more references to the idea of a British or
United Kingdom nation.[87] Some Unionists now called themselves
'Britishers' or 'British', while previously they said they were 'British
subjects' or 'British citizens'.[88]

Armagh and his constituents were also important to Lonsdale. His
success in holding his seat for nearly 18 years without a contest, after his
opposed first election, was unequalled in all other Unionist rural seats in
this period. To some extent his position was helped by his Armagh connections and the assiduous attention he gave to constituents and local
causes. More importantly it was because of his stand on issues such as
the land question. An effective party organisation was another important reason for his constituency success. In spite of some initial weaknesses, his divisional association was well organised, under Joshua Peel,
and was able to give local unionists a strong sense of involvement in
party politics. If he had initial concerns with the Ulster Unionist
Council, his regular attendance at meetings showed that he realised its
importance as a forum for Unionists in Ulster. When he sought to
explain his political position, Lonsdale rarely relied on historical or religious arguments. This may be explained to some extent by the fact that

he lived most of his life, before and after 1900, out of Ireland, and also by his broader concerns for the United Kingdom and the empire, based partly on his experience as a successful businessman. In Parliament in 1913 he stated that 'speaking broadly, the line which divides political parties in Ireland is the religious line, that is to say, in the main, Protestants are Unionists, and Roman Catholics are Nationalists'.[89] While acknowledging the religious division as a fact of life in Irish politics, he rarely adopted a religious argument in political discourse and seldom attacked the Catholic Church, although he did raise issues of discrimination or boycott against Unionists/Protestants.[90] For many of his contemporaries, such as Craig, religious concerns were an important factor in their political stance.[91]

Beside his contribution to Unionism over this period, Lonsdale's career was remarkable in other ways. In the list of Irish and Ulster Unionist leaders, Lonsdale was the only one who was born the son of a farmer: he was also the wealthiest. He built up a flourishing business enterprise. When he died in 1924, his estate was valued for probate at the very considerable sum of just over £300,000: when Lord Craigavon died, his fortune stood at £27,000.[92] Lonsdale's wife was wealthy in her own right. They had no children, but the business was developed by his younger brother and nephews to become an important investment company in the 1930s. By 1960 the firm was partner in the London merchant bank of Kleinwort, Benson and Lonsdale, a £60m.group. In the 1990s the business was taken over by the German Dresdner Bank.[93] Lonsdale was created a peer of the realm in 1918, the culmination of a long social and personal transformation. After his death, T.P. O'Connor MP said of Lonsdale; 'he had the wealth, the appearance, the manners and the ambitions of a man who was bound to end in the peerage'.[94] Lonsdale has been seen as one of a group of business and professional people who took over the direction of the Unionist party from landed members like Saunderson. In many ways this was true. At the same time, Lonsdale had strong social aspirations. His peerage was one crowning achievement of his career. Another came in 1920, when, in succession to the Earl of Gosford, he was appointed his majesty's lieutenant of County Armagh, a post reserved normally for a leading member of the gentry or nobility of the county. Lonsdale's place of burial is of some symbolic importance. While Saunderson was buried in his beloved County Cavan, and Carson in St Anne's Cathedral in Belfast, capital of the new Northern Ireland, John Lonsdale was buried at Putney Vale cemetery, in London, the United Kingdom and imperial capital.

8

Seeking Conciliation: William O'Brien and the Ulster Crisis, 1911–14

Sally Warwick-Haller

> Now, I mention these few suggestions of my own merely to remind you how far from impossible it would be to placate every rational Protestant in Ulster if once we could only get the best men of all parties – English and Irish – together round a friendly council board.

Introduction

The words above were delivered by William O'Brien, MP for Cork, on 1 March 1913 at a meeting of the All-for-Ireland League. The theme of this occasion was 'conference and compromise' and 'mutual concession', and for O'Brien there was no sacrifice he was not prepared to make to allay Ulster's fears of Home Rule, short of the 'impossible and unthinkable' notion of partition, over which there could be no compromise.[1] O'Brien had been one of Ireland's foremost politicians: he was most famed as a radical agrarian, veteran of the Land War and responsible for launching the Plan of Campaign and the United Irish League. Between the 1880s and 1903 he had received much popular acclaim, and few Irish Nationalists could make decisions without considering O'Brien's position. By the early 20th century, in contrast, he had slipped to the fringes of Irish politics (with the exception of Cork), but his views during the passage of the third Home Rule bill and the crisis over Ulster are still of considerable interest and significance.

O'Brien's proposals for conciliation will be examined and compared with similar schemes, though the question of how much his ideas could have won the support of Irish Unionists must also be addressed.

O'Brien was a committed Nationalist, but his nationalism, unlike the vast majority of his fellow-Nationalists, was not founded on recognising a separate ethnic identity for Catholic Ireland. His nationalism, transcending ethnic boundaries, had been inspired (as O'Brien himself acknowledged) by Thomas Davis's vision of an Irish nation that brought together all classes and creeds. O'Brien's nationalism was based on a strong sense of place, that of the whole island – a single state, but one that must make significant concessions towards minority interests.

'Conference and Conciliation'

Between 1911 and 1914 O'Brien stressed the importance of concessions to meet Unionist fears: privately in correspondence with, for example, H.H. Asquith and Chief Secretary Augustine Birrell, and publicly in his parliamentary speeches, letters to *The Times*, through his newspaper, the *Cork Free Press*, and in addresses to meetings of the All-for-Ireland League. He was convinced that moderate Unionists could be detached from the extremists, whom he maintained formed only a small minority of the Irish Protestant community; proposals to Ulster, as long as they were reasonable, would greatly undermine the entrenched Unionists' opposition to Home Rule.

Such a stance was very much in line with the attitude O'Brien had taken since his dramatic conversion to the policy of 'conference and conciliation' of different classes and creeds after participating in the 1902 Land Conference. O'Brien's 'new' nationalism rejected the more populist form of the United Irish League; now he sought to embrace those elements of the Anglo-Irish ascendancy who extended a hand towards a 'new' Ireland where all could live in good will and peace. O'Brien now preached his new theme of conciliation with as much conviction as he had fought landlordism in the Land Wars of the previous century. However, this approach alienated him from his former colleagues in the land agitation and the Irish Parliamentary Party (IPP), who increasingly regarded O'Brien's mind as 'unhinged'.[2]

After the Land Conference relations between him and other leading Nationalists, especially John Dillon and John Redmond, had become steadily more acrimonious, culminating in November 1903 with O'Brien's dramatic resignation from the Irish party and the United Irish League. Full of bitterness, and portraying himself as a martyred figure, betrayed and driven out by his enemies in the movement, he continued to denounce his critics who had not shared his enthusiasm for the Land Conference and ensuing Land Act.

His resignation in 1903 had some important consequences. First, despite a temporary and brief return to the party, followed in 1910 by the founding of his alternative movement, the All-for-Ireland League, O'Brien's action in 1903 had detached him permanently from the mainstream of Irish politics. Second, it had also brought him closer to the Earl of Dunraven, who had chaired the Land Conference; they now corresponded regularly up to 1917. Dunraven, like O'Brien, supported a policy of co-operation and conciliation between Unionists and Nationalists, and he was the main inspiration for O'Brien's belief that Irish Unionism could indeed be reconciled to Nationalism if the latter could agree to crucial concessions. However, Dunraven, a Southern Unionist, did not speak for the majority of his class. In 1904, he and a few other progressive landlords had launched the Irish Reform Association to put into practice the view that conference and concilia-tion could be applied to other problems in Ireland, and they came to focus on 'Devolution'. While O'Brien had remained publicly detached from Dunraven's organisation, he was privately sympathetic, but at this stage public support would have precluded any possible return to the IPP, which also denounced the Devolution ideas.

Further consequences of his 1903 action were the rapprochement between O'Brien and another political outcast, Tim Healy, and the launching in 1910 of the All-for-Ireland League, which secured Healy's support. The occasion which precipitated this development was the celebrated 'Baton Convention', where O'Brien's opposition to Birrell's Land Bill of 1909 was shouted down, and he was publicly humiliated. Anti-semitic feelings had been loudly voiced at this meeting, and were aimed directly at O'Brien's wife, Sophie, a Russian Jewess who had converted to Catholicism and whose fortune had financed many of O'Brien's ventures. From now on O'Brien railed unrestrainedly against the IPP, which he declared had come under the influence of the Nationalist MP Joseph Devlin and, as a result, was being dominated by the sectarian, Belfast-based Board of Erin of the Ancient Order of Hibernians. He blamed Devlin and this organisation for his treatment at the Baton Convention, and the passing of time served only to increase his bitterness; when he later reflected on the turn of events and who was responsible for partition, he wrote

The Board of Erin Hibernians, who became thenceforth the real dispenser of all power and offices and titles...had every demerit that could inflame sectarian passion in Ulster…Into this sinister fraternity, now the undisputed masters and wirepullers of the public movement, no Protestant Irishmen, were he the most illustrious in the history of the nation, was permitted to enter. The new disability and its Sacramental Test debased the National Ideal from the aim of Wolfe Tone – which was 'to unite the whole people of Ireland, to abolish the memory of all past dissensions'… – to the level of a Catholic Orangeism in green paint, deformed by the same vices of monopoly and intolerance which had made Protestant Orangeism a National scourge. The results were catastrophic…the Irish Party ceased to exist as the National Party of Parnell, and became the sham-Catholic Hibernian Party.[3]

These words expressed O'Brien's vindictiveness towards the IPP, though his criticisms were not without some foundation. Moreover, his sentiments do help to explain his sympathetic understanding of Ulster Protestant fears that a Home Rule Parliament in Dublin would be modelled on 'Tammany Hall-style' politics and be a breeding-ground for corruption and sectarianism.

The All-for-Ireland League drew heavily on the support the county and city of Cork gave to O'Brien. The declared purpose of this new League was to pursue a policy of conciliation – and, in O'Brien's words: it would promote self-government and above all, 'a combination of all the elements of the Irish population in a spirit of mutual tolerance and patriotic good will, such as will guarantee to the Protestant minority of our fellow-countrymen inviolable security for all their rights and liberties'.[4]

To what extent could the All-for-Ireland League live up to its declared aims? Though it did win the support of some progressive landlords, including two members of the 1902 Land Conference – Dunraven and Colonel Hutcheson-Poe, it would never win the backing of that many Protestants; very few Unionists responded to O'Brien's invitation to attend a key meeting in Cork in 1913 on the Ulster crisis, a meeting designed to promote his policy of conference and conciliation. Many Southern Unionists even admired Ulster's resistance to Home Rule, and hoped that this would be a means of destroying the bill.[5] O'Brien's aim to attract '*all* the elements' of the Irish people in a spirit of tolerance was flawed from the start, for his invective against the IPP continued unabated. To be all-embracing the League should also have established a working arrangement with Sinn Féin, who represented another 'element'. Though O'Brien did have some contact with Arthur Griffith, Sinn Féin's commitment to abstention from Westminster proved a major stumbling block, despite the fact Griffith admired O'Brien for his efforts to stop partition and his denunciation of the IPP.[6] The League never fulfilled O'Brien's hopes. The Ulster crisis, far from giving it a special role to play in Irish and English politics, placed it under considerable strain, and many of O'Brien's Nationalist supporters felt he was making too many concessions to Ulster in his attempt to meet Unionist fears.

O'Brien's links with Unionists had surfaced not only in his private backing for Dunraven's Irish Reform Association, but also in his support for federalist ideas, or 'Home Rule all round', which had been gaining ground in Unionist circles since 1909. Dunraven's interest in federalism would have helped to make it acceptable to O'Brien. Moreover, there were financial rewards for some of the federalist funds collected in North America were passed to O'Brien as much-needed help for his new League, the two general election campaigns of 1910 having placed a severe strain on his finances. The motives of some of the federalists, particularly those of the maverick Moreton Frewen, are questionable as far as helping O'Brien was concerned, for Frewen saw federalism as a way of bolstering the *status quo* in Ireland and undermining Redmond's IPP and the Liberal-Nationalist alliance, and he viewed O'Brien's League as a crucial pawn in the struggle against Redmondism.[7]

Proposals for the Third Home Rule bill

Frewen had greatly overestimated the support O'Brien could muster, for after 1910 O'Brien commanded little notice (outside Cork) in Nationalist and Liberal Government circles. His often-proclaimed proposals would not have been taken that seriously. This should not, however, belittle his attempts. In March 1914, in words that sounded prophetically ominous, O'Brien ended an impassioned speech in the House of Commons in which he gave vent to his deepest misgivings over Asquith's proposed amendment to the Home Rule bill and the prospect of even temporary partition: it 'will mean cleavage that will go down to the very roots of Irish nationality such as we have known it with consequences that even the least thoughtful amongst us may well recoil from contemplating'.[8]

O'Brien's plan had been to forestall objections to the Third Home Rule bill by ensuring that when it was published it contained protection for the Protestant community. Thus five months before Asquith introduced the bill, he wrote at length to the Prime Minister outlining his ideas. The arguments in the letter were presented in a calm, considered and, largely, logical manner. He began by stressing that he would prefer a bill modelled on Canada, in effect Dominion Status, but he recognised the difference between the ideal and what was practical. Thus he stressed the need for Asquith to ascertain what guarantees would meet Irish Protestant fears. However, and this is a point that would under-mine his perception in 1911 of the problem, he was thinking of the more moderate elements in Irish Unionism, more specifically, 'the bulk of the Protestant landlords and farmers in Ireland'. This was simply a reflection of his experience of the Land Conference. Thus he pro-ceeded to state that such 'sober-minded men' could be consulted in an event modelled on the 1902 Conference. Here O'Brien was not facing up to the urban resistance that was already being marshalled in Ulster.

The next stage in the scheme he outlined to Asquith was to consider the principles that were most likely to be acceptable, and the choice was between two routes. First, there was the idea of 'a general Federal scheme, applicable (even if not immediately applied) to England, Scotland and Wales', or 'Home Rule all round', a scheme that O'Brien clearly still supported, but he suspected that it would be thought unsafe for such a solution at this point.[9] There were divisions within the feder-alist camp between Ireland as a nation, on the Canadian model (which O'Brien favoured) or with a 'provincial status', similar to that of an American state within US federalism – the Unionist interpretation (an avenue Redmond and T.P. O'Connor had briefly explored and rejected the previous year).[10]

The second alternative was O'Brien's preferred option, 'experimental Home Rule' (a five-year experiment was what he had in mind). He outlined to Asquith merely the general principles, and was somewhat imprecise on the detail of how his scheme would work; the only real suggestion at this stage was removing the 'sectarian' Board of Erin from its dominant position in the IPP. Later, as the Home Rule crisis grew, O'Brien became clearer as to exactly how his policy could be imple-mented. The advantages of an experimental approach would be two-fold: O'Brien was, naively, optimistic that 'the good sense' of the Irish people would prevail and would 'indeed, compel the Irish leaders to remove any danger of the rejection of the bill'. He also argued that the difficulties over such issues as the police and judiciary, matters that caused considerable concern to Ulster Protestants, would be resolved.

A final part of his plan, and one that was presented in a less con-vincing way, was the suggestion of a conference once the bill was in-troduced – or after it had been passed by the House of Commons. O'Brien certainly saw 'conferences' as the panacea for all problems, though he was rather imprecise on what he expected such a confer-ence to achieve, except that it might act in an amending capacity and turn the bill into a measure to which all participating in such an event could give their consent. He added the proviso that the Unionists might be promised a general election, in 'the very unlikely event' of their being forced to oppose the third reading of a bill based on the principles of self-government agreed to by such a conference.

O'Brien concluded his letter on a more ominous note, stressing again the need to soften Irish Protestants' hostility to Home Rule: 'since, little as the threats of actual civil war need to be regarded, it is only too certain that discontent and exasperation in the North Eastern counties of Ulster would be a most grievous addition to the difficulties of an infant Irish legislature'.[11] Though O'Brien was playing down the thought of a severely violent response from Ulster Unionists, he did stress that their discontent must be taken seriously – a theme to which he would often return: in his Cork paper in January 1913 he declared 'the opposition of Ulster must be treated with all respect. Doubtless it is a genuine and sincere expression of the fixed determination of determined men'.[12] He rejected Redmond's line that Ulster was bluffing. O'Brien would, indeed, become very critical of the Liberal Government for their attitude to Ulster; 'we ought', he wrote to Augustine Birrell in November 1913, 'to do all that men can do to satisfy those who are after all *one fourth of the population*, and up to this [time] nothing whatever (beyond smooth words) has been done or even suggested by the Government'.[13]

As the crisis over Ulster unfolded O'Brien began to sketch out his suggested amendments to the bill for meeting Irish Unionists' fears. Under his plan of an experimental period of five years, the Irish Unionist MPs at Westminster (ten for Ulster and two for Trinity College Dublin and Rathmines, representing Southern Unionists) should have two rights. They should have the right of 'suspensary veto' on any bill passed by an Irish Parliament, and this would allow the bill to be offered to Westminster for approval or rejection, but action by the British Parliament had to be taken within a month of the veto being exercised. Second, the Irish Unionist MPs should be able to demand (in a written supplication) that the House of Commons debate any administrative act of the Irish executive. O'Brien had in mind here three issues that were of particular concern to Unionists, especially in Ulster: education, justice, and the police. O'Brien justified these proposals on the grounds that an infant Dublin Parliament would thus be encouraged to act with restraint in its first years, and would hesitate to introduce a bill which would cause Irish Unionist MPs at Westminster to exercise their right of veto, and Westminster to reject an Irish bill. The exercise of such a veto would be 'a grievous humiliation and intolerable', and could only be stomached as a temporary procedure, he argued. O'Brien, optimistically, believed that five years of a Dublin Parliament behaving sympathetically and responsibly towards Unionists would be sufficient to allay many of the latter's fears of 'Dublin rule'.

To assuage apprehensions still further, he had a number of additional important proposals. He advocated a form of Proportional Representation [PR] in order to increase considerably the percentage of Ulster Protestant representation in the lower house of a Dublin Parliament. O'Brien presented somewhat contradictory arguments over this: in one place he claimed that this would give Unionists 'a representation proportioned to their numbers', while in another, in his speech to the House on the bill's second reading, he admitted that there could be no arithmetical justification for his proposals. Yet, on both occasions he was consistent about his aims: 'Here you would have established a body which could not possibly be put down by oppressive means'; moreover, with the co-operation of some thirty Catholic Nationalists it could even have sufficient numbers to form a governing majority committed to 'a National Peace Programme which would efface all the old distinctions'. This suggestion of doubling the number of Ulster Protestant representatives did not, predictably, meet with approval from mainstream Nationalist circles.

Another proposal focussed on the Senate, which was initially presented in the bill as a nominated one – an attempt to protect minority interests. O'Brien denounced this on the grounds that it would be packed with IPP placemen (an argument also used by Craig). His alternative was for the upper house to be chosen through indirect elections, with county councils, chambers of commerce and city corporations assuming the function of an 'electoral college', and that Senators should include Chairmen of County Councils and the Lord Mayors of Dublin, Belfast, Cork and Londonderry. However, when O'Brien drew an analogy with the United States Constitution, with State governments selecting the Senate, he undermined his argument, for by this time America was moving speedily towards a more democratic system of direct elections for the Senate. There was, in fact, superficial agreement over the selection of Senators between the IPP and O'Brien. Both opposed the idea of a nominated Senate, but for different reasons; the former objected to the requirement that members would be chosen initially by Westminster for an eight-year term of office. The Senate clause was subsequently amended to allow it to be elected under PR.

A further suggestion reflected O'Brien's comprehension of Ulster Protestants' fears (which he shared) of corruption and domination by

Catholic sectarian influences. He proposed delegating local powers to Ulster over justice, education and the police; county court judges, inspectors of education and county inspectors of police could be appointed by panels set up by Ulster county councils. In addition, he demanded adequate safeguards against a 'spoils system' developing under a Catholic Dublin government. Sectarianism could be avoided by having a carefully selected group of Irish civil service commissioners, who would be responsible for most appointments. A merit system must be instituted so that all candidates could apply on equal terms for positions.

To sum up his recommended changes, O'Brien argued that, in practice, in many respects control from Westminster would continue for a number of years and would 'enable Carson to brag that he had not fought in vain'. As he explained in a letter to Birrell in November 1913, he was confident that Carson would accept his ideas, but should he oppose them, the Ulster leader would isolate himself from most Protestants, and in the event of rejection by Carson, a referendum on these proposals should decide their fate. With his habitual belief in the supreme value of such events, O'Brien advocated that his ideas should be submitted to a conference for consideration and to form the basis of a compromise.[14]

While the main focus of compromise would be on Lloyd George's county option plan, there were others who, like O'Brien, sought for ways of avoiding partition, and there were some similarities with O'Brien's ideas. Sir Horace Plunkett argued for the temporary inclusion of Ulster in a Home Rule Parliament for a fixed time-period, at the end of which the province could choose whether to stay or leave. He too favoured the conference approach, with representative Irishmen discussing amendments to the bill. On the other hand, Plunkett dismissed two key elements of O'Brien's scheme. He viewed the idea of administrative autonomy for Ulster, or part of it, as undemocratic and conducive to sectarianism and patronage, while the concession of more power being given to the Protestant minority, whether through the right of veto on legislation or through increased representation in an Irish Parliament, was 'a thoroughly bad class of solution, undemocratic and tending to stereotype existing divisions'. He did consider in a more positive light the notion of Ulster representatives having a veto on legislation that would only operate in their own area.[15] Although some exchange of views between O'Brien and Plunkett in this period might have been expected, there is no evidence of this having occurred, or of any contact between them. One possible explanation is that Plunkett bore a strong personal dislike of two men with whom O'Brien had close contact: Moreton Frewen and Dunraven, and he had also been critical of the 1902 Land Conference.[16]

Another compromise scheme, proposed by the radical Ulster Protestant, Alec Wilson, had grown out of a meeting in the autumn of 1913 of Northern Protestants unhappy with Carsonism, at Ballymoney, County Antrim. Like O'Brien, he favoured a form of PR for the lower house of a Dublin Parliament so that Ulster could have a bigger presence, but Wilson added a further protection: the Senate should be given increased numbers and powers. There is another echo of O'Brien in that Wilson and his colleagues also advocated the right of appeal to Westminster on any bill considered to be unjust, should a third or a quarter of the Irish elected representatives request it. Unlike O'Brien this right was not seen as only a temporary measure.[17]

A third scheme came from Sir Edward Grey, 'Home Rule within Home Rule', which would have involved some administrative devolution to North East Ulster, a plan which recognised – as O'Brien had done – Ulster Protestants' fears. In late 1913 Asquith himself seriously flirted with these proposals, in the form of his 'Suggestions'. However, unlike O'Brien, this formula did not involve an experimental period. This conciliation plan was short-lived, given the Opposition's refusal to consider it, and as Patricia Jalland surmises, the 'Suggestions' were very much a tactical move on the Prime Minister's part to buy time as a negotiating lever with the Nationalists, and to soften their attitude to the notion of major concessions to Ulster like county option.[18] O'Brien, though, viewed Asquith's proposals as a recognition of his own arguments. On 1 April 1914, after the Curragh Mutiny, he delivered a hard-hitting attack on the Government, accusing it of 'drifting' for the past two years, while Asquith's 'Suggestions' were really his own, with the only difference being that 'Home Rule within Home Rule' applied solely to Ulster, while O'Brien had also been concerned about the Protestant minority in other parts of Ireland – a crucial distinction.[19]

A final proposal that should be mentioned, and one which O'Brien greatly welcomed as reflecting a kindred spirit, was suggested in the celebrated letter to *The Times* in September 1913 from Lord Loreburn, the Liberal Lord Chancellor, who called for a conference (and also implied that he favoured a system of devolution for the United Kingdom as a whole). Prior to this publication, Loreburn had been in contact with O'Brien, who had been putting pressure on conservative federalist Liberals like Loreburn, who declined an invitation in July 1913 to attend an O'Brienite meeting in Cork.[20] In their correspondence, however, Loreburn seemed to approve of O'Brien's approach. On 12 August 1913 he had stressed in a letter to him how much he agreed with O'Brien's view that a settlement by consent had to be encouraged. While, he did not explicitly endorse the details of O'Brien's proposals, he did indicate in a further letter of 19 November that they were very acceptable; though once Home Rule was up and running in Ireland, the experience would highlight 'the futility of perpetuating unnecessary precautions', but he saw their value in allaying inevitable apprehensions in the transition period. Loreburn also gently lectured O'Brien on the importance of calming down his attacks on Redmond and the IPP for these were not conducive to producing a mood of conciliation and all-round agreement, since the success of any suggestion was dependent on securing the consent of Redmond, who, in the present climate, could hardly be expected to accept proposals that could be construed as a triumph for O'Brien's side.[21] O'Brien, though, did not heed the wisdom of this advice. He and the IPP were such worlds apart that his public enthusiastic response to Loreburn's letter was greeted with dismay by the party on the grounds that if Nationalists were involved with people like Loreburn it would give succour to the Unionists and also undermine the Liberals' stand on Ireland.[22]

Did O'Brien's ideas have any chance of acceptance by Irish Unionists?

As far as Southern Unionists were concerned, the evidence would suggest a far from clear response. Correspondence and memoranda in the Bonar Law and Balfour Papers indicated a growing anxiety among Southern Unionists as the discussions increasingly focussed on the exclusion of Ulster, for Home Rule with partition would be seen by many Unionists as the worst case scenario.[23] Andrew Bonar Law acknowledged that there was a marked change of attitude by Southern Unionists compared with 20 years previously, for now there was evidence that they would not take open action against Home Rule, which they saw as inevitable.[24] Walter Long, in a 'Very Secret Report' on the state of affairs in the South and West of Ireland, also referred to this spirit of resignation: the wealthier merchants and urban professional classes did not want Home Rule, but some Unionist merchants, for instance, did make the comment that in the light of their experiences of the Liberal Government for the past six years or so, with little protection for property rights and weak administration of the law, the state of affairs could not be much worse under a Home Rule Parliament. As for the prospect of the exclusion of Ulster, he observed that some Loyalists in the South and West had seen this as betrayal, but this was not the view of 'intelligent and sensible' Unionists, who saw Home Rule with Ulster excluded as a preferable option to full Home Rule. The reason he gave was that, despite the fear of sectarian politics being adopted, a Redmondite government, in the pursuit of including Ulster at a later stage, would be tolerant and fair towards Southern Unionists.[25]

In September 1912 Dunraven, in a letter to Bonar Law took a fairly positive view of the prospects for Home Rule among Southern Unionists:

> A great number of former Unionists – the younger among the landed gentry and commercial classes, sharing these views are in favour of domestic self-government and want to have a hand in it. Other Unionists though not liking Home Rule, believe it to be inevitable and desire to make the best of it; and others detesting Home Rule detest still more the violence of Carsonism. That is the condition of public opinion here, though it does not show itself publicly it looks for some compromise.

Such a compromise had to ensure the completion of land purchase on the lines of the 1903 Land Act, and was one with which O'Brien fully agreed.[26] O'Brien's correspondence with Dunraven echoes these sentiments, that moderate Unionists secretly wished for compromise.[27]

Given the relationship between Dunraven and O'Brien, the latter's optimism must to a large extent have been influenced by the views of progressive landlords who supported the All-for-Ireland League and O'Brien's conciliatory approach. Dunraven and O'Brien both believed that moderate opinion in Ireland was silent in the face of the violent stance on each side held by the 'Molly Maguires' and 'Carsonism'.[28] The basic flaw in O'Brien's argument that nine-tenths of Unionists would support his plan was that he viewed the situation too much from a Southern perspective, and even here little evidence exists of enthusiasm for his schemes from Southern Unionists. In January 1918, with the growing rapprochement between Redmond and the Southern Unionists in Lloyd George's Irish Convention of 1917–18, O'Brien remarked, somewhat bitterly, to Moreton Frewen how things could have turned out so differently if only Southern Unionists had given him a small part of the support they were now giving to Redmond – now when it was too late.[29]

Lord Hythe, an active Unionist-federalist had, in early 1914, pointed out to Bonar Law that there was a lot to be said for O'Brien's proposals,

for 'he and his party stand for purity of administration. What the
Ulstermen most fear is that under Home Rule, the administration of
the country will fall into the hands of Devlin's Tammany Hall organisation, which is the cause of the whole situation as far as Ireland is concerned'.[30] These words reinforce the fact that O'Brien understood Irish
Unionist fears, and had tried to meet their apprehensions.

What evidence is there that O'Brien's plans would have found any
support among Ulster Protestants? Carson, in his speech during the
Committee stage of the Home Rule bill in June 1912 commended
O'Brien and his movement for its emphasis on conciliation, and especially for his efforts to reconcile Protestants from Ulster as well as elsewhere in Ireland. O'Brien and his colleagues had made speeches which

> if they had been made by the majority of them [Nationalists] for the last
> 20 years might, I admit, possibly have had some effect on some of the
> Unionists in Ireland. Their idea was certainly a worthy idea, nobody can
> deny that, of bringing about a reconciliation and better feeling, and the
> moment they do that they are denounced, and they are boycotted, and they
> are persecuted, and they can hardly hold an election in Ireland.[31]

The clear inference in Carson's words was that it was too late for any
accommodation with Irish Nationalists. His subsequent refusal even to
countenance the idea of 'Home Rule within Home Rule', which
would have offered permanent protection for Ulster, would make it
extremely unlikely that O'Brien's plans, involving as they did only
temporary arrangements, would have had any influence on Carson.

What were the views of the 'silent majority' among Ulster Protestants? Loreburn in his letter to O'Brien of August 1913 had given
him some encouraging words:

> I read your speech in the paper you were good enough to send me and the
> same day it came oddly enough [sic] a Tory gentleman called here. He told
> me that an Orangeman had read your speech and said to him that if Home
> Rule meant what you described and the spirit of it he would become a
> Home Ruler himself.[32]

In O'Brien's papers there is a little evidence of contact with Ulster
Protestants opposed to Carson's tactics, but not sufficient to produce
the argument that his ideas would indeed have separated moderate
Unionists from the more extreme elements. The scanty evidence that
exists is focussed on developments in Ballymoney (County Antrim), a
place known for having a radical tradition, and where a meeting of

Liberal Protestants was held in October 1913 to protest against 'Carsonism' and to emphasise that not all Ulster Protestants were against Home Rule. A leading organiser of this meeting had been keen to impress O'Brien in the weeks before the event:

> That there are thousands of Unionists (or at least of Protestants with an open mind about the advantages, or disadvantages of Home Rule) who are sick and tired of Carson's campaign. In at least one place I have got a promise of public expression of this feeling should I ask for it. I have been to Belfast and met a group in the offices of the Ulster Guardians. They seemed to think there was a chance of a successful meeting in Ulster Hall, should we choose our chairman and speakers with sufficient tact. They were unanimous in voicing the opinion, and the echo of yours, that it would be a great pity to let any demonstration be under the auspices of the Ulster Liberals, tho[ugh] all present belong, I believe to this category.

The writer went on to stress that the 'splendid class of farmers' offered the best hope. He, and O'Brien too, were thus failing to see the importance of urban Ulster. Above all, however, the note conveyed to O'Brien by this correspondent was one of optimism: 'from what I have seen of its [a Protestant Home Rule movement's] strengths under the surface, I certainly expect surprising developments if here and there it can successfully and enthusiastically face the daylight'.[33]

This evidence must, though, be treated with caution, as the main organiser of this Ballymoney meeting and the author of the above words was Captain Jack White who was not in any way characteristic of Ulster Protestantism. He had on the face of it a good Ulster Protestant/Unionist pedigree: the son of a Field Marshall (he had openly admitted to O'Brien that he was relying on his father's name to build up support), and himself a former army officer with the Gordon Highlanders and a hero of the Boer War. But, White had already been attracted to socialism, and by 1913 was working with the advanced Nationalist, Roger Casement, a fellow-organiser of the Ballymoney meeting. White had already – by his own admission to O'Brien – recently shown considerable interest in the Gaelic Revival, and would very shortly be involved with James Connolly and the ITGWU, helping to found and train the Irish Citizen Army.[34]

The Ballymoney meeting was also addressed by the radical Ulster Protestant Alec Wilson, who, when he sent Asquith the proposals for a solution that had come out of the meeting (proposals that reflect some links with O'Brien's suggestions), wrote in his covering note: 'It is the hope of a considerable and growing body of Ulster Protestants that the recent meeting of Ballymoney may be followed by a series of other meetings, out of which may come an Ulster movement in favour of peaceful acceptance of the new order'. Wilson added that, though none of the points were new ones, each of them 'is designed to remove some of the fears of actual Carsonites. That is to say, that I have discussed each of the suggestions with men who have signed the 'Covenant' and when they were in a frame of mind to discuss anything at all, these points have met with their approval'.[35] The meeting had not met with the success that White had hoped, the local minister of the Presbyterian Church, J.B. Armour and a Liberal Home Ruler, did not attend, the press coverage tended to be unfavourable, and the series of follow-up meetings did not materialise.

The views of White and this event at Ballymoney must have had some influence over O'Brien, and provided some of the basis for his ex-aggerated claims for potential Ulster Protestant support for his ideas. However, O'Brien and White did not see eye to eye. O'Brien suggested, as an alternative to open meetings, a private memorial of sympathisers who might be afraid to come out into the open – perhaps a more realistic plan for gathering support; but this notion was dismissed by White in no uncertain terms as one he could not possibly pursue. A solicitor from Ballycastle, L. Walsh, whom White had visited, and who thought O'Brien's idea 'most effective', explained the Captain's response to O'Brien: White was too enthusiastic to 'do the spade work of the humdrum politician'; he was not diplomatic enough and had little patience for those who did not have the courage to voice their opinions openly.[36]

There are a couple of other snippets of evidence in O'Brien's papers, which must have offered a little comfort and hope. For instance in May 1914, when almost total deadlock over Ulster had been reached, O'Brien received a letter from H.C. Smith of Belfast, a declared Protestant Unionist and member of the UVF. This letter conveyed a sincere appreciation for the conciliatory efforts he was making: 'if the Nationalist party as a whole were as reasonable as you are I think a way out of the present difficulty could easily be found'. Smith then proceeded to stress what he saw as the main cause of concern to Ulster Protestants, that 'the huge commercial interests of Ulster would be at the mercy of the agricultural vote in the South and West'. This correspondent's solution was for Ulster Protestants to have a majority in the Senate; a mere veto over legislation affecting Ulster (as O'Brien recommended) would not be sufficient, while effective control in the Senate would certainly allay the fears of reasonable Unionists in Ulster and would also protect Southern Unionists, 'and be far better for them than if Ulster were excluded'. Smith concluded his letter with a request that O'Brien call a Nationalist conference (or preferably an Irish conference) to discuss these suggestions, and such a gathering would receive a lot of support from the moderates 'and completely dish the extremist faction.' O'Brien, naturally, warmed to the idea of a conference, while seeing this letter 'as a proof' of 'how easily peace might even yet be made', but he did not, however, agree with the idea of Unionists really controlling the Senate. O'Brien's argument was that action by the members of an upper house would lay themselves open to 'cheap claptrap against a privileged order'. He very much preferred his own solution of the Protestant minority having 'a commanding power' in the Senate. Nevertheless, he left the door open for Smith's notion – if there was proof 'your much more moderate suggestion would satisfy our country-men in Ulster', there would be no problem in putting it to an Irish conference.[37]

Two political allies

O'Brien shared many of his schemes with his fellow-conciliationist Dunraven, to whom he showed drafts of letters and discussed tactics. Their correspondence was frequent, until their differences over Lloyd George's 1917–18 Irish Convention led to a significant cooling-off in their letters and friendship. Dunraven had, until then, been very supportive, while still following his own agenda of seeing a federal solution as the main way forward. Though he, like O'Brien, deplored the idea of partition, he argued that, as it may be forced on them, the larger the area to be excluded, the better, on the assumption of it leading to a scheme on federal lines.[38] O'Brien's response highlighted their differences: while excluding the whole of Ulster would be the better of two bad alternatives, he was very clear that any exclusion of Ulster: 'in whole or part as a *fait accompli* preliminary to a federal scheme, would be for me under any conditions impossible'.[39] O'Brien was never a total convert to federalism.

In their correspondence there is evidence that Dunraven did attempt to act as a restraint on O'Brien: 'It would be politic to avoid personali-ties as much as possible at present' he wrote to him in the autumn of 1912, though he shared O'Brien's views on the 'Molly Maguires' element of the IPP, he advised O'Brien to tone down his criticism of the Nationalist party.[40] Dunraven openly supported O'Brien in his call for 'conference and conciliation', and attended and addressed meetings of the All-for-Ireland League – as he said in a letter to O'Brien in early 1913, he was keen to 'keep publicly close in touch with you and the-all-for Ireland policy'.[41]

Dunraven also acted as the pessimist, or realist, in their relationship. In a typical example, when O'Brien's hopes had been once again raised by H.C. Smith's suggestion in May 1914 that O'Brien call a conference, Dunraven, on reading Smith's letter left no doubt about his views on any prospects for success for the conference approach at this late stage of the Ulster crisis: 'But to tell you the truth I do not see much chance of a conference of any kind just at present. It is too late. We are sitting on the very edge of a volcano and unless something occurs pretty soon to avoid an immediate catastrophe I do not see what chance a conference has'.[42]

O'Brien's other main political ally, Healy, though publicly in agreement with him, in private was clearly sceptical of his colleague's ideas. In the autumn of 1911 he warned him of the dangers of proposing a conference too early; when O'Brien responded enthusiastically to Loreburn's intervention and call for a conference, Healy again expressed his strong reservations. Only Ulster Unionists would benefit from conferences, he declared. He argued that O'Brien's suggested concessions to Unionists would not work, and he discounted the influence of the sectarian Ancient Order of Hibernians on the IPP as a factor working on Unionist opinions. In Healy's view, O'Brien's proposals would undermine the Home Rule bill and produce some form of partition. Healy was really closer to the IPP position than he was to O'Brien: like the former he was deeply suspicious of conferences, and, like Redmond and unlike O'Brien, he felt that the resistance of Ulster Unionists and their demand for exclusion was a matter of bluff, a claim he maintained for some time.[43]

Conclusion

After May 1914 O'Brien would continue to call for conferences with Unionists, but rather half-heartedly, as he did at the outbreak of the Great War. One reason he supported the recruiting campaign was the hope that it would lead to co-operation between Unionists and Nationalists, and for a while he threw his full weight behind federalism, as his correspondence with Frewen underlined.[44] Still, two government initiatives to hold conferences did not receive O'Brien's backing. In July 1914 he denounced the Buckingham Palace Conference because of its composition and terms of reference, since it was focussing on defining the area to be excluded.[45] He subsequently declined Lloyd George's personal invitation to join the Convention of 1917–18, despite pressure from Dunraven and the fact that Lloyd George had come considerably closer to O'Brien's ideas. If O'Brien had had his way it would have been a much smaller conference and it would have accepted that recommendations it might make should be put to a referendum – these he gave as some of his reasons for refusing to participate. But, his main reason was that it was doomed to failure, for it 'is out of touch with the public opinion of Ireland and will be bitterly resented as an attempt by governmental influence to rehabilitate a party of politicians whom the country has tried with the most amazing patience [sic] and has found woefully wanting'.[46] O'Brien was very conscious of the changes that had engulfed Ireland after '1916'; he and Healy abandoned federalism, and his correspondence reflected his awareness of his complete powerlessness to have any influence at all.[47]

To the end of his life O'Brien deeply mourned partition, and this caused him to denounce the 1921 Treaty and to support Eamon de Valera and the anti-Treaty forces. In August 1914 he had declared in an address to all MPs that partition must fail, 'because the splitting of Ireland into two irreconcilable sectarian camps will be an intolerable national wrong, the consequences of which I shrink from putting into words'.[48] Even though O'Brien had, since 1910, operated on the margins of Irish political life, and his political influence had been but a shadow of his role in the Land War, his efforts as a conciliationist over the 1911–14 Ulster crisis should be acknowledged. He had recognised the bitter sectarian feelings that were gathering force in North East Ulster. He always maintained that his plans could have had a chance, and would have been acceptable to 90 per cent of Irish Protestants. No one escaped the blame for the failure of his plans and for the ensuing divisions between Ulster and the rest of Ireland: Orange politicians, aided by Conservative party members were partly responsible, but the main culprits were Redmond and the sectarian Ancient Order of Hibernians within the IPP: 'But the man would either be a knave or a fool who ought not to have foreseen that the moment you raise the loathsome cry of "Up the Mollies" from the Falls Road, that it would be answered by the still more loathsome and idiotic cry of "To Hell with the Pope" from the Shankill Road'.[49]

O'Brien's nationalism cannot be categorised; it did not preach primordial or modernist theories, but he did lean towards modernism in that he argued that the Irish nation could be constructed and that a 'new' nationalism embracing all classes and creeds could be forged.[50] At

the same time he recognised the ethnic identity of Unionists, but did
not see this in terms of seeking to remain with Britain; he sincerely believed that most Unionists could be persuaded to feel more Irish than
British as long as Unionist opposition could be forestalled and
Protestant fears allayed before they were aroused – a point reiterated by
Jalland, who argues that an early concession over Ulster, incorporated
into the original bill, would have seriously undermined the Unionist
case.[51]

Attractive as this argument is, it is difficult to find sufficient evidence
to justify O'Brien and Jalland's claim. Moreover, fellow-Nationalists had
not shared O'Brien's approach. It is possible that O'Brien's close Jewish
and French connections through his wife's family helped to separate
him from his contemporaries' view of Ireland and to give him a more
outward-looking attitude. Redmond and the IPP as a whole abhorred
the idea of conferences (as did Healy), and the party's tactics, once the
bill was published was to stave off amendments (with the exception of
the issues of land, finance and the Senate). O'Brien had been too inspired, and indeed misled, by the Land Conference. He had rather
naively believed that the experience could successfully be repeated to
resolve the Ulster question. He had not fully grasped the differences
between Southern and Ulster Unionists; nor, despite his best efforts,
had he appreciated the complexities of the Ulster question, which were
far more intractable than the relatively straightforward land question.
Nevertheless, in February 1927, a year before his death, some still
looked to O'Brien to heal the rifts in Irish society, and though the
words of one correspondent really applied to the divisions in the South,
they are also testimony to his efforts as a conciliationist: 'I honestly and
sincerely think you are the only man in Ireland today who could, and
who is willing to unite our disjointed national forces, and give a lead to
the country. What a glorious sunset it would be to your great career in
Ireland's service'.[52]

9

'Not a Historical But a Prospective Application'?[1] The 1798 Rising as Recalled in the Irish Popular Press of 1898

Marc Mulholland

The construction of a memory of the 1798 Rebellion has been discussed in terms of its sustained treatment in books and pamphlets and its emotive celebration in public commemorative acts.[2] Here its recall in a selection of the Irish press on the occasion of the centenary in 1898 is analysed. These journalistic pieces provide the most condensed and presumably widely read commentaries. They shed some light on the diffusion of memory to wide and variegated social groups.

Newspapers have generally been thought of in two ways in media theory. Structuralists argue that the interests of a socio-economic elite delineate the bounds of acceptable news reporting and colours its tone. Protestations of neutrality or even subversive intent mask an acceptance of societal norms as interpreted by a hegemonic governing interest.[3] A less top-down version of the same approach suggests that news media reflect and reinforce culture, rather than generating it.[4] Historians of particular newspapers or other discrete media organs are more inclined to highlight the particular proclivities of individual journalists, or schools of journalism, or editors, or proprietors.[5] There have been productive attempts to combine this genre, with news output being analysed as a product of tension between individual reporters, newspaper businesses, and the pressures of social environment.[6] More recently, the idea of multi-culturalism has focussed attention on the fracturing of homogenous national audiences in an era of globalisation. This, it is argued, has given rise to numerous media forms that address subaltern niche-markets.[7]

This latter perspective invites consideration of places and periods in which nation-states were yet in the process of formation. Ireland and particularly Ulster, in the run up to partition, might be considered analogous. Benedict Anderson, prominent amongst theorists of nationalism, has asserted the role of print culture in unifying audiences around a common language, set of cultural reference points and, often, a map image of the nation.[8] Ernest Gellner emphasises the generation of vertically bonded societies on the basis of homogenising markets.[9] Such processes are taken to have spontaneously spread national consciousness from an intellectual minority to, by the Great War, the mass of European populations. Recently Jim Mac Laughlin has tested such theories in the context of Ireland. He argues that Irish Nationalist and Ulster Unionist traditions should be understood as rational expressions of regional interests rather than as merely irrational manifestations of social forces driven blindly by literacy, print culture and the market.[10] In stressing regionalism in his explanation of the formation of identities, Mc Loughlin pays particular attention to the provincial press of Ulster.[11]

While Mac Loughlin is justified in paying close attention to the provincial press, it is the case that, if anything, provincial publishing declined in the 50 years or so after the mid-nineteenth century, as the development of railways meant that periodicals and such were readily available from metropolitan centres. The provincial press relied upon news syndicated from Dublin and London, and their readers were very aware of 'national' discussions. Ulster's press did not publish in a vacuum. The focus of the following discussion is on the commemoration of a common history, a rebellion of the basic narrative of which was not substantially in dispute from region to region, and thereby to analyse the filtering of 'national' knowledge through provincial papers.[12]

Moreover, the newspapers dealt with here did not simply address regional audiences but also class-based niche markets. While taking on board Mac Loughlin's point about Unionism and Nationalism being rational political interests in specific geographical settings, the discussion below points out significant variations of interest within these blocs. The uses made by the Ulster press of an event commonly acknowledged across all of Ireland – the 1798 rebellion – but variously received by region, religion, political persuasion and class, should be able to shed light on the reproduction of two polarised and antagonistic identities, Nationalist and Unionist, that clashed in the 'Ulster Crisis'.

Ireland, as the *Belfast Telegraph* recognised,[13] was already split into two by 1889, though still primarily in a political sense, between loyal and disloyal, rather than territorially, between north and south. Newspapers here analysed can consequently be grouped into schools. The *Freeman's Journal* and the *Irish News* are clearly Nationalist; the *Belfast Telegraph*, *News-Letter*, *Northern Whig* and *Irish Times* Unionist.[14] Sub-divisions within these broad categories, and indeed polarities cutting across them, further individualise each publication. Both the *Freeman's Journal* and the *Irish Times* were national papers with a clearly southern focus, as opposed to the Ulster ambit of the others. Differing outlooks, format and price indicate where in the class spectrum the papers expect to find their audience. The Ascendancy, liberal unionism of the *Irish Times* contrasted to the militant and sectarian loyalism of the *Belfast Telegraph*. Healyite [for T.M. Healy] clericalism characterised the Nationalism of the *Irish News* while the *Freeman's Journal* offered a more mainstream blend of Dillonite [for John Dillon] politics with a twist of William O'Brien style aspirations for Nationalist unity.

Every newspaper looked at here refracted the events and legacy of 1798 through a particular prism. They all shared a broad bedrock of agreed data on 1798, as it was then understood. For example, Presbyterian and Catholic leadership of the United Irishmen was admitted while the role of Church of Ireland leaders was underplayed, the turning point of the Wexford Rising was seen to be New Ross rather than Vinegar Hill, and so on. What the papers do reveal is an interpretation of the 'facts' thought suitable for and acceptable to their target audiences.

An 'establishment' survey history of Ireland published, first published as part of the *Cambridge Historical Series*, in 1896 (and reprinted in 1898), sets out the 'objective' circumstances of the Rebellion as then generally understood. The French Revolution 'came like a tempest' inflaming 'the most daring and enthusiastic in Presbyterian Ireland.' Theobald Wolfe Tone, a man of 'no common powers' and 'infinitely the first of the rebel leaders', founded the United Irishmen in 1791 with the aim of linking advanced Presbyterians with the befuddled but stirring catholic masses. The fall of Lord Fitzwilliam as Lord Lieutenant, a champion of reform and catholic rights, imparted from 1795 an 'enormous impulse' to revolutionary currents. Even yet, 'the United Irishmen, except in Ulster, were hardly organised; and the Catholic peasantry were still a chaotic mess'. The Orange Order, established in 1795, mobilised the 'Established Church in the lower ranks of life' in a 'kind of Holy War against the Catholic population in parts of Ulster'. The United Irishmen latched onto the rising wave of sectarian violence to enrol Catholics in their tens of thousands. An attempted French invasion in December 1796 failed; nevertheless 'Ulster ... and other parts of Ireland, were in a state of hardly suppressed rebellion' while 'the feud of the Orangemen and the [Catholic] Defenders grew more desperate'. In response, 'anarchic government acquired despotic powers by means of a system of terror' and its counter-revolutionary excesses were 'widespread and revolting.' This succeeded in breaking the 'head of the rebellion'. To crush the rank and file, elements of the government 'deliberately resolved to force in-surrection into premature being, and to stifle it in blood before it could obtain help from abroad.' Whipped in desperation by reckless repression, various parts of Ireland broke into 'sanguinary rebellion' in 1798. Only in Wicklow and Wexford, southern Ireland, was the rising general: 'from the first ... a savage war of religion', with cruelties but also heroism on either side. With few British soldiers involved, the civil war of 1798 'called out high Irish qualities, if it was full of horror.' The rebellion in Ulster took the form of isolated skirmishes, as here the United Irishmen 'stood aloof from a purely Protestant and Catholic conflict, which ran counter to their hopes and sympathies'. The Rebellion was smashed, and Ireland divided and crushed was ripe for the Act of Union, which still dominated Irish politics nearly a hundred years later. The principle concentration is on the Ulster newspapers, but the Dublin produced *Freeman Journal's* (est. 1763) and *Irish Times* (est. 1859) are considered as 'controls' in that they represent, respectively, quasi-official all-Ireland Nationalism and Unionism, against which the Ulster variants may be compared.

I

Turning first to the *Freeman's Journal,* it is important to note the context in which it was publishing. Since the split of the Irish Parliamentary party [IPP] in 1890/1, Nationalists had not only been bifurcated between Parnellites (led by John Redmond) and anti-Parnellites (led first by Justin McCarthy and from 1896, John Dillon), but the latter majority faction itself suffered internal tensions with Tim Healy leading a clericalist wing and William O'Brien branching out into re-involvement with militant agrarian agitation. The *Freeman's Journal* echoed the increasingly common opinion of the late 1890s, that such dissension had only brought 'dark days' to the Irish cause.[15] Commemorating the 1798 rising, it hoped, would rejuvenate the movement, kindling anew fiery *élan*. To this end, it filled its pages with direct admonitions for the present generation to emulate the steadfast coherence of the United Irishmen: 'faction, by whatever colour, is rebuked by the graves of these men'.[16] Divisions and treachery within the ranks of the '98 insurgents were generally ignored – such was not the role model that the paper wished to project. An appeal, too, was made to the unquenchable sprit of the rebels. At times this was posed in terms of the blood sacrifice: 'They had not a chance, but they knew how to die, and dying to teach their conquerors a lesson that will never be forgotten'.[17] Similar sentiments contributed to the inspiration for insurrectionary action in 1916.

The *Freeman's Journal* actively drew upon the '98 celebrations to encourage pan-Nationalist unity. O'Brien had established the United Irish League [UIL] in the west, and the paper put great store by it, hoping that, as with the Land League, it would 'eventually unite the people in a compact organisation'.[18] It not only reported on the '98 centenary celebrations, therefore, but also actively organised and moulded them. Every edition carried an extensive '98' column and regular editorial comment. A special edition of the *Freeman's Journal* was planned for 18 June 1898, which invited the public to contend for prizes in writing articles on the theme, while a 3d '98 Almanac was on sale the year round. It was certainly successful in raising the profile of the issue. With satisfaction it noted, 'no meeting is complete in the present year…without an allusion to the gallant men of '98'.[19]

Celebrating '98 was in practise an opportunity for rival Nationalist factions to compete for legitimacy and influence. Republicans, in particular, hoped to claim the mantle of the United Irishmen.[20] The *Freeman's* saw in this an opportunity rather than a problem. The '98 centenary could be used to incorporate the republican fringe, few in number but rich in *élan* and energy. When it noted that at a demonstration in Mallow, 'Nationalists and Parnellites were supported by men who have no faith in any form of constitutional action' there was an implied hierarchy but no hint of exclusion.[21] Separatists were acceptable as a branch of the Nationalist family.

The *Freeman* slotted the '98 Rebellion into a fused calendar of revolutionary and constitutional struggle. The succession of highlights included Daniel O'Connell's movement, the 1848 Young Ireland rising, the Fenians and 1867, the Land League, and the Nationalist movement. Of course, the IPP saw the way forward as purely legal and limited in aspiration. Nevertheless, the inference was that such constitutionalism was tactical rather than principled in origin. As Sir Thomas Esmonde, MP, put it at a 30 May speech on Vinegar Hill, Enniscorthy, 'we are rebels in sentiment, and should occasion offer we be rebels in act and deed'.[22]

Politically, the campaign waged by the *Freeman's Journal* met with considerable success. Nationalist unity (though not including republicans) was achieved in 1900. As F.S.L. Lyons notes: 'Reunion came partly because even the most purblind politicians could not but be aware that their internal struggles looked cheap and trivial in the context of the centenary of the 1798 rebellion'.[23] Political considerations inevitably coloured *Freeman's* treatment of the 1790s as an historic era. First it must be said that there was virtually no mention of the north of Ireland, nor, more strikingly, any attention brought to the fact that that Catholics and Protestants had united in common cause. This was presumably considered extraneous to the real lesson of pan-Nationalist unity that the *Journal* wished to draw. Henry Grattan and the opposition orators of the Irish Parliament were lauded,[24] but the distance between them and the revolutionaries was not indicated. It is true that at one point that Wolfe Tone was favourably contrasted to Grattan, but not for being a revolutionary or a republican, but for abandoning illusions:

> Irish Catholics owe scarcely less to him [Tone] than O'Connell...it was the spirit that Tone breathed into the Catholic Committee that won the Emancipation Act of 1793. He taught them the policy, which it took O'Connell, as his letters show, ten long years of unavailing effort to discover, of relying on strong popular agitation and uncompromising public action, rather than on prayers and pleading of public peers and 'the classes' to secure their rights. Nor can it be doubted that in his attitude to the corruption and subservience of the Irish Parliament he was wiser than Grattan.[25]

This extract showed O'Connell still marginally higher than Tone in the pantheon – he was to plummet precipitously in the twentieth century. Tone's contribution was deemed to be to the mobilisation of the *Catholic democracy*. He foreshadowed the Emancipation campaign of the 1820s, the Repeal movement of the 1840s and, most pregnant, the Land War/ National movement of the 1880s. The article went on to attribute to Wolfe Tone the 'invention' of non-sectarian Nationalism and the internationalisation of Irish Nationalism. Tone's revolutionary politics were discussed last: 'Like Burke in politics, and Shakespeare in literature, Tone was too big to belong to any school; and so it is that he is claimed by all. The truth is that, uncompromising in principle, Tone was a great opportunist in policy, like every great statesman that hopes to harvest some of his own seed sowing'.[26] The 'semi-constitutional' inference here looked back to the days of the New Departure and forward to the unified Sinn Féin of 1917–19. '98 served as the canopy of a Big Tent, fit for celebration '"by all sections of nationalists"...worthy of united commemoration'.[27]

The contention that the Wexford rising was largely unplanned and provoked only by military repression was commonly rehearsed in the pages of
Freeman's. This, of course, was the standard line at the time. R.R. Madden
wrote, for example: 'The admitted policy of Lord Castlereagh was to accel-
erate the explosion of the insurrection in order to confound the plans of its
leaders. For this purpose it was necessary to drive the people mad with
terror'.[28] It was also generally accepted by the Unionist press.[29] But there
was an additional political reason for the *Freeman's Journal* to emphasise this
aspect of the historiography. If Wexford, and indeed elsewhere, was provoked by extreme repression, then the rising could be justified, indeed seen
as 'a solemn and sacred duty',[30] by these peculiar circumstances. Then it
became legitimate to praise revolution in the 1790s and practice constitutionalism in the 1890s, without needing to rationalise this shift in strategy
by admitting the solution of core grievances.

Most emphasis was put on examples of 'English barbarity'. The
Freeman's Journal recalled that: 'The skies ever reflected the glare of
burning cabins and chapels; the air was ever filled with the agonising cries
of the victims of military brutality – strong men and women and children
were murdered and outraged and tortured day after day'.[31] This was partially motivated by a desire to identify the common enemy against whom
all shades of Nationalist opinion could unite. By demonising Britain it
was hoped that 'petty jealousies' could be overcome.[32] For the *Freeman's
Journal,* the movement of the 1790s was potentially constitutional, provoked into revolution by savage repression. The ideology of republicanism was sharply downplayed. Wolfe Tone's thinking was blurred into that
of Home Rule politics. The rising itself was portrayed not so much as
due to a consciously republican conspiracy, more as an 'Irish peasants
War'.[33] Certainly no serious attempt was made by the paper to define the
distinctiveness of United Irishmen outlook. For the same reason, the issue
of Protestant involvement, and the entire northern revolt, was ignored.
Historical analysis was harnessed to the aim of building pan-Nationalist,
Catholic unity in the 1890s.

II

The *Irish News,* a specifically Ulster paper, was in the Healyite tradition. It
had been established in 1891, mainly on the initiative of the local Catholic
hierarchy, to counter the Parnellite *Morning News.* This it successfully did,
and the rival title was soon swallowed up, leaving the *Irish News* as the pre-
eminent voice of Ulster Nationalism. Though increasingly challenged, in
particular by the young Dillonite, Joe Devlin, the clerical bent of the paper
was still apparent in 1898. The slogan over the editorial, *Pro Fide Et Patrie,*

accurately reflected its priorities.[34] Naturally the *Freeman's Journal* had
carried approving references to the Catholic Church in connection with
1798,[35] but in the *Irish News* they were much more frequent and a good bit
stronger – 'the priesthood do not fear to speak of '98' it proudly stated.[36]
Indeed, at times the rebellion was posed as being for Catholicism before
nation: ''98 insurgents 'fought and died with Spartan heroism for faith and
country'.[37] Nor was interest in the Church limited to issues concerning the
rising. The dedication of the new St Vincent de Paul church in Ligoniel received much attention,[38] and in discussing the Spanish/American conflict
the diplomatic role of the Papacy was prominent.[39]

The *Irish News* was little concerned with building Nationalist unity. It
was positioned on the margin of national politics and moreover suspicious
of rival secular trends. Its political interests were firmly localised. 'The
'98 centenary celebrations', it warned its readers, 'so far as the North is
concerned, appear to have exercised a similar influence on the Orange in-
tolerants to that which the red rag does in the bull-ring'.[40] Sectarian
tension, leading to riots in Belfast over Monday 6 and Tuesday 7 June, absorbed much of its attention. Beforehand it criticised Unionist editorials
for stirring up trouble.[41] Indeed, trouble was forthcoming. Devlin organised a '98 commemoration at Hannahstown on Monday 6 June. As
Nationalists returned to Belfast, they were attacked at Broadway by a loyalist crowd from the Sandy Row. The military intervened, but rioting
spread the following day. For a period, Belfast was under military control
as the Royal Irish Constabulary, who suffered 100 casualties, went off
duty. Around 700 Catholics were driven from their workplaces and, as
usual, shipyard workers were prominent in the violence.[42] The *Irish News*
in the aftermath lashed the Orange rioters as 'treacherous', 'cruel', 'cowardly', 'savage', 'wicked', 'dastardly' and 'devilish'.[43]

Protestant politics fared somewhat better when the '98 rebellion was
being discussed. True, there was surprisingly little specific reference to
the northern uprising. Much of the general material, referring to the
leadership of priests and government provocation, seemed to apply
better to events in the south.[44] As with *Freeman's*, '98 material in the
Irish News borrowed heavily from Fr Kavanagh's history of the insurrection, infused with Catholic piety and heavily weighted to events in
Wexford and Conaught, rather than Ulster.[45] However, paeans to unity
across the religious divide, absent from the *Freeman's Journal*, do appear:
'when North and South, Orange and Green, were united by a bond of
brotherhood and patriotism in an endeavour to have the wrongs of
their motherland put to right'.[46] In the wake of the riots, it was argued
that the 'mad ignorance of the rioters lies in the fact that the movement of '98 was essentially unsectarian'.[47] Yet these invocations of

toleration and inclusiveness lacked conviction and force. The *Irish News* clearly, and perhaps naturally, preferred fulminating against Protestant bigotry, violence and expulsions.

As with the *Freeman's Journal*, there was little discussion of United Irishmen ideology. However, while fulsome praise for William Gladstone at the time of his death pays testimony to the paper's political constitutionalism,[48] the *Irish News* was at times more prepared to validate the revolutionary spirit. Complaining about English historiographical smearing of '98 it asked rhetorically, 'why should Irish rebels and their insurrectionary strategy be singled out for redundant reprobation? Englishmen have often fought for freedom. Our throne and Parliament are both revolutionary'.[49] There is here an attempt to deny the distance between Whiggish notions of Glorious Revolution and republican rebellion. The *Irish News* invokes pride in revolution, only to neuter it by reference to the primacy of gradualism and continuity. 'Fighting for freedom' here refers to the campaign for Home Rule, Ireland's own anticipated 'Glorious Revolution', rather than to republicanism.

III

Generally, as regards the Nationalist press, there was surprisingly little on the actual history of the '98 rising. Amongst the Catholic activists, or at least amongst those involved in politics to some degree, there was, however, knowledge of what had happened one hundred years ago. The practice of naming local clubs after United Irishmen leaders – William Orr, Fr Murphy, Thomas Russell, Samuel Neilson, Lord Edward, Michael Dwyer, Betsy Gray and so on – indicated reasonably detailed knowledge of their lives and time. No doubt Madden's work was important in propagating this emphasis on heroic biography.[50] There was evidence that Ulster Nationalists were not lacking in this biographical enthusiasm. The Revd William Thomas Latimer had in 1897 published *Ulster Biographies Relating Chiefly to the Rebellion of 1798*, and at least one club was knowledgeable enough to raise questions over, and debate the legitimacy of, its adopted patron. Newbridge '98 Club agonised over whether Roddy McCorley was a 'patriot of the first order' as 'his good reputation had not been historically confirmed'. With reservations, they found in his favour.[51] The provision of synopsises of the events and history of '98 by Nationalist newspapers was evidently considered superfluous. Instead, books were recommended[52] and historical material was relegated to supplements and monthly magazines.[53]

Both the *Freeman's Journal* and the *Irish News* carried a political analysis informed by a reasonable understanding of dedicated historiography as it stood in the late nineteenth century. '98 was characterised as an episode in a protracted national struggle. Its association with republicanism and separatism was attributed to contingent, inessential factors, notably British repression. Essential features – anti-sectarianism, assertive extra-parliamentary action, democracy and popular piety – were absorbed into subsequent constitutional phases of struggle. As such, then, the United Irishmen tradition was part of the weave of nationalist campaigning, rather than a militant counter-culture.

IV

In the Unionist press attitudes to the '98 centenary ranged from condescension to contempt.[54] The Dublin based *Irish Times* can be taken as the epitome of respectable, all-Ireland Unionism. This catered primarily for the professional and landed southern Unionist elite, as reflected by the prominence given to the activities, for example, of the Primrose League[55] or the Landowners' Convention.[56] Undoubtedly this paper, as it could afford, was the most broadminded of all the publications here looked at that. When discussing Thomas Davis, it was able to praise 'the charm of his manners, the purity of his motive, and the breadth of his sentiment'.[57] The Wexford rebels, without fail vilified by the rest of the Unionist press, 'exhibited courage', according to its liberal opinion.[58] New objectivity in historical research was embraced by the paper. The historian, J.T. Gilbert's death, 24 May, occasioned an editorial and an obituary fulsome in its praise: 'The literary legacy that he has left represents the makings of history – of history that has yet to be written with a broader, freer sweep of the pen, a wider range of positive opinion than that which has heretofore been rendered possible'.[59] This would have found approval amongst the members of the Royal Irish Academy, most of who would have subscribed to the *Irish Times*. As regards 1798 itself, the paper mainly ignored the matter. Its few comments on the centenary are illuminating however. Rather than condemn it for raising party passions, admittedly less of a pressing problem outside the north-east, it argued that centenaries are generally positive events, as they raise historical awareness and interest: 'most produce a residuum, at least, of true facts, however adorned, or rather disfigured, by party sentiment'.[60] To avoid political controversy itself, what little attention the *Irish Times* devoted to the history of the period, was on military and logistical aspects.[61] Events were usefully contextualised within the wider European scene at the time. This, however, did tend to empty the analysis of any sense of internal dynamic within Ireland itself. Combined with a somewhat lofty dismissal of United Irishmen ideology as utopian,[62] this leads to suspecion that a political rationale did in fact lie behind the paper's attempt to characterise 1798 as wholly conjunctural and accidental. The rising itself is described not as a purposeful revolt but as the 'backwash of the subsiding agitation'.[63] It aloofly identified United Irishman ideology as a foreign enthusiasm, with no relevance to Ireland's real problems. The '98 Rising was the death spasm of an idealism utterly ill suited to native conditions. The treatment of the era by the *Irish Times*, while hardly ambitious in scope, stands much closer to modern historical standards than anything even attempted by the other papers.

V

The *Northern Whig* (est. 1824) though firmly on the moderate wing of Unionism still addressed itself to the particular concerns of its Ulster audience. The paper's tone was one of reasonableness and deference to law and order; it was strongly pro-state.[64] Towards the centenary celebrations the *Whig* adopted an attitude of extreme disdain, disparaging Nationalist marchers as 'irresponsible residuum' looked upon with distaste even by responsible Catholics.[65] The newspaper was loath to mention '98, and firmly fixed its gaze on more elevated topics. At times this was almost bizarre: 'When we hear so much of a Ninety-Eight celebration devised by those who wish to promote division and strife amongst Irishmen and the people of the United Kingdom generally, it is delightful to see the birthday of one great Englishman being celebrated year after year...Shakespeare'.[66] As suggested in this quote, the *Northern Whig* opposed raking the issue of 1798 up for fear of causing trouble. As befitted such a patrician paper it had virtually an obsessive (if merited) fear of a resurgence of sectarian violence along the pattern of 1864, 1872 and 1886.[67] Belfast it believed to be a 'combustible city',[68] so it is not surprising that it had little time for Protestant extremists either, indeed, even the Orange Order itself,[69] though the paper did differentiate between Nationalist commemoration of the rising and the Twelfth July marches which, it argued, were 'not intended to lead to other battles'.[70] It took pride, throughout, in its own moderation, and that of the state. Only in the United Kingdom, it boasted, could demonstrations such as those in memory of '98 be tolerated.[71] For these demonstrations were considered by the *Northern Whig* to be of a 'thoroughly seditious character'.[72] The rising itself was a 'treasonable conspiracy and a disastrous outbreak in arms'.[73] Unlike the Nationalist press, the *Northern Whig* was keen to highlight the republicanism, based on French principles, of the United Irishmen; not so as to praise them, but to condemn: 'The Rebellion of Ninety-Eight, as promoted by Wolfe Tone and his confederates, was avowedly to set up the independent Irish Republic by French arms. France at that time might still be nominally considered a republic, but a republic

just changing into a military despotism...'.[74] From here it went on to tar
the contemporary Nationalists with the same brush: 'The Irish movement
is no longer for Home Rule...but for pure and absolute separation, and
separation even by foreign arms. This is what is meant by the '98 celebrations. They can have no other meaning whatever'.[75] And later, 'the demonstration was well understood to have, we repeat, not a historical but a
prospective application'.[76] The *Whig* had no hesitation in interpreting the
ambiguity of the Nationalist movement on '98.

The *Northern Whig* could see virtually nothing laudable in the aims of
the United Irishmen. Admittedly it talked at times of any just causation
of revolt since having vanished, implying that they were extant in 1798,
but such vagueness can be countered by many emphatic declarations.[77]
For example, 'There was never a rebellion with so little justification'.[78]
However, 'mingled motives' are at least acknowledged,[79] and a parallel
was made between the United Irishmen and modern Nationalists, to
the latter's detriment: 'However the men of Ninety-Eight must be
condemned, they at least risked and suffered something openly'.[80]

France's experience, however, was held up as the only possible model
for the aftermath of a rebel victory.[81] The historical lesson of '98 was
that it showed the necessity of Union – Grattan's Parliament, indeed
any independent legislature in Ireland, must eventually lead to secession.[82] Union, it argued, was shown by '98 to be the only viable alternative to anarchy.[83] The contemporary political implications of this
would have been obvious. Overall, the *Northern Whig* looked back on
1798 in pity rather than anger. It articulated a variety of cerebral
Unionism, seeing no merit in United Irishmen ideology whether origi-
nating from Catholic or Protestant. In fact, there was virtually no dif-
ferentiation attempted between the two blocs in the revolutionary
movement. When it condemned foolishness, or acknowledged courage,
it did so indiscriminately. The '98 rebellion, for this paper, served only
to strengthen the argument for Union. It believed an objective analysis
of the era undermined Nationalists from both sides. If Nationalists, as
they professed, aimed only to achieve a limited Home Rule legislature,
then the fate of Grattan's Parliament, destroyed by the forces it helped
to unleash, proved this to be a dangerous pipe-dream. But in reality, as
the United Irishmen were clearly republican and separatist, then the
Nationalist celebration of the centenary exposed their true intent.

In its discussion of the history of the 1790s, the *Whig* emphasised
the European maelstrom as Ireland's context. In doing so it stripped the
United Irishmen of Hibernian innocence claimed for them by contemporary nationalist writers. For the *Whig*, the United Irishmen were a
parochial symptom of the disease of European revolutionary excess,

rather than the expression of an irrepressible national spirit of resistance. The Union, thus, was depicted not as an anti-national and reactionary scam, but as the corollary of the emergence of a liberal United Kingdom, vanquishing Bonaparte and winning the leadership of progressive international statesmanship. At the turn of the centenary, liberal unionism in the north looked to the UK's beneficent international power rather than the revolutionary ideals of the United Irishmen.

V

In common with the *Northern Whig*, little enough was written about '98 in the *Belfast News-Letter* (est. 1737), a Conservative rather than Liberal Unionist newspaper. Neither the commemoration nor the event itself was much considered. At times this was excused by a dismissal of its historic significance: 'the rebels in that year were guilty of many cruel deeds, and they had no leaders whose names are worthy of remembrance'.[84] Nevertheless, the reason for reticence on the matter was more tellingly told by a plethora of comments indicating shame at the events of '98. This is summed up well by the terse declaration: 'Ulster wants to forget it all, because Ulster is not proud of the rebellion, and Ulster is loyal'.[85]

Such embarrassment was clearly due to Ulster Protestant involvement in the rising. Unlike the *Northern Whig*, this fact was clearly acknowledged, if only to quickly explain such a lapse. Excuses were located in the 'purity' of motive of Protestant United Irishmen,[86] an argument provided by Dr Kane, Grandmaster of the Orange Order and something of an authority for both the *News-Letter* and the *Belfast Telegraph*. This 'purity' stands in contrast to the *Northern Whig*'s 'mingled motives'.

Likewise dissimilar to the *Whig*, the *News-Letter* differentiated between the Catholic and Protestant wings of the United Irishmen. In their depiction, the southern rising was characterised by a priest-led and sectarian movement, which even then alienated the northern Protestants, helping to stifle the revolt in Ulster. Protestant involvement in this southern morass was consciously downplayed, and those who did get directly involved were condemned as renegades: 'these men, as typified by Wolfe Tone, had given themselves body and soul to the spirit of Atheism and of revolution as it had arisen in France'.[87]

All this contrasted to a grudging recognition of the justice of demands raised by the Ulster insurgents. The *News-Letter* argued that: 'Short of a Republican form of government, the reforms they demanded were just and reasonable'.[88] No such concession was offered to the southern Catholic rebels. The crime of Wolfe Tone amongst others, presumably, was to get mixed up with Catholics.

For the *News-Letter*, the whole episode of '98 was a sad mistake, but one in which the barbarity of the Catholic rebels must be demarcated from the simple delusion of northern Protestants. While they accepted some basis for Protestant grievance, they nevertheless considered that they had been duped. For this reason, 1798 contained nothing, which Unionists could look back upon favourably. 'There was nothing in the rebellion that Irishmen of to-day have any real reason to be proud of', they concluded.[89] So while the *News-Letter* did take up the Nationalist argument that the government provoked the uprising, disposing of the issue by noting that, of course, the United Irishmen wanted revolution, so they must be held culpable,[90] it was generally content to let the uncomfortable subject be. Its attitude was well encapsulated by a poem printed in the wake of the riots:

> Turn Down the pages of the story,
> Blot out its blood with tears,
> May its rancour be all forgotten,
> In the peace of the coming years.[91]

The *News-Letter*, like the *Whig*, noted the essentially foreign (French) ideology of the United Irishmen, but was more keenly aware of its local resonance in its own heartland of Protestant Antrim and Down.[92] It resented this, but with a mingling of sympathy for misguided rebels.

VI

The *Belfast Telegraph* was more orientated to the Protestant working classes than the others here discussed. At half a penny, it was the cheapest of the lot, and its small articles were obviously tailored for a less-educated readership. Its populism can be seen in the titles of its regular columns – 'The World of Sport', 'Women's World' and so on. News articles tended towards the coverage of the scandalous and sensational – crime, assault, murder, suicide, war etc. Quite often it would carry up to six or seven pictures.

The *Belfast Telegraph*'s politics were similarly populist. It was strongly Orange, carrying regular reports from lodge meetings. As might be expected, anti-Catholicism, especially sniping at the papacy, formed a staple of its content.[93] This was matched by a firm anti-Nationalist stance. It called for a complete ban on the '98 commemoration march in Belfast.[94] The logic was that, as a minority, Catholics should expect less than standard civil privileges and protection,[95] especially as 'rebel processionists' had 'absolutely no stake in the city'.[96] Indeed, when discussing the Catholic masses, the paper was virulent. It argued that 'the ignorance that prevails and the impressionableness of the Celtic nature provide the professional agitator with the very material he requires'.[97] While it did not support the Protestant mobs during the June rioting, it certainly offered only lukewarm and ambiguous support to the unpopular RIC, criticising them simultaneously for slackness and provocation. Out of all the Unionist papers here discussed, the voice of the *Belfast Telegraph* resonated most closely with that of ordinary Protestant workers.

On the topic of 1798, it found much common ground with other Unionist publications. It agreed that the defeat of the rebellion was positive,[98] argued that there was no excuse for it,[99] and quoted Dickey's disavowal of protestant involvement in the rising, prior to his execution: 'the Presbyterians of the North perceived too late that, if they succeeded in subverting the Constitution, they would ultimately have to contend with the Roman Catholics'.[100] Nevertheless, though by no means copious, there were an unusually high number of articles carried on 1798 as history. More, indeed, than in the *Freeman's Journal* or the *Irish News*. Perhaps this is to be explained by a less educated and poorer readership that lacked access to historical books. Another factor, though, must have been the tension within the popular Protestant mentality; between folklore of ancestors who had 'turned-out' and intransigent resistance to contemporary Nationalism.

This may account for the unusual lengths to which the *Belfast Telegraph* went to counter Nationalist historiography. As with the *News-Letter*, though in somewhat more detail, it refuted the argument that Britain forced the insurrection.[101] William Pitt the Younger was rehabilitated from the demon caricature of Nationalist history, to man of 'great shrewdness and foresight...one of the greatest British statesmen'.[102] Considerable effort was expended to establish the savagery of the rebels. An article to this effect was ironically entitled, 'The "Glories" of '98', and subtitled, 'Record of Rebel Atrocities'. As the introduction noted, the aim was explicitly to expose 'Nationalist propaganda'.[103] To this end some grisly images were painted, particularly surrounding the 5 June 1798 Scullabogue massacre in Wexford: 'As [victims trying to escape]...fell, the insurgents dipped their pikes in their gore and licked them'.[104] The southern revolt was portrayed as a sectarian war of extirpation, Fr Murphy as a superstitious mystic and his followers as deranged fanatics. M.W.S., standing for Murder Without Shame, was described as emblazoning the rebel banner. In accounts of military encounters, rebel fighters were invariably depicted as cowardly and incompetent, whilst state troopers and yeomen were heroic and resourceful.

Elsewhere, an article written by John Redmond for the journal, *Nineteenth Century* (which seems to be the same, or very similar to, a speech he made in the Rotunda 22 November 1897, published in *Historical and*

Political Addresses, 1898; a quote carried by the *Belfast Telegraph*, 4 April, matches exactly a passage carried in Redmond's book, pp. 174–75) was editorially rebutted by the *Belfast Telegraph*.[105] The contrast between the two accounts was marked. To take one example, the *Belfast Telegraph* stated that one hundred plus 'loyalists' died in the Scullabogue massacre.[106] In Redmond's account, this was reduced to between 50 and 50 'English prisoners' being murdered, against orders.[107]

The *Belfast Telegraph* painted a sorry picture of southern anarchy and murder during the 1798 rebellion. From this it concluded that to celebrate '98 was equal to celebrating sectarian slaughter.[108] How the northern rebellion was depicted was very different. The article entitled, 'The Rebellion of '98. The Outbreak in the North', contained nothing like the bloodcurdling anecdotes of the earlier piece.[109] The paper agreed with Kane that the Presbyterian United Irishmen were 'morally good',[110] and argued that they rose less due to a separatist intent, but to protest at 'tithes, taxes and rent'.[111] Their principled republicanism was contrasted to the Home Rule demand of contemporary Nationalists: 'The United Irishmen no doubt dreamt of an Irish Republic in which there would be no distinction of race or creed, but they did not seek the establishment of an Irish Parliament, for they had that already'.[112] Genuine grievances were admitted to exist but, of course, by 1898, they were said to be all resolved. The real difference from the *News-Letter* came with an exposition of the 'gallantry' of the northern rebels.[113] 'They fought honourably, unlike the rebels of the south, and they took their beating with good grace'.[114] The paper contended that it was not the Nationalists who were the inheritors of the '98 mantle, but rather the loyalists: 'The descendants of the men who rose in those days are among the most loyal in the British empire, and the parties who to-day assembled in Smithfield Square were neither their political nor their lineal descendants'.[115]

For the *Belfast Telegraph*, '98 was still an aberration mercifully scuppered by sectarianism,[116] but while the southern rebellion was thoroughly infused with, and based upon, sectarianism, that in the north was guided by purer 'Republican and Socialistic' tendencies.[117] It seems that a grudging pride was taken in this, reflecting a general protestant working-class sympathy for those who 'turned-out', largely incomprehensible to middle-class Unionists. The *Belfast Telegraph* tentatively moved towards at least partially claiming the heritage of 1798. It engaged in a limited historiographical struggle in which it found itself torn between blackening and claiming the event under consideration. It should not be thought that this paper carried any great abundance of historical material on 1798. But it did so somewhat more than any other paper here looked at, and the ambiguity of its approach makes it among the most interesting. The paper hovered on the edge of lauding not merely the courage of the United Irishmen, but their republican, egalitarian ideals. There was a hint that such idealism, 'Republican and socialistic tendencies', retained a contemporary relevance for local and United Kingdom-wide, if not Irish national, politics.

VII

Most of the newspapers of the time made some nod towards objectivity by at least reproducing original, often military, sources.[118] Few, however, adhered to its spirit. The Nationalist press, especially the *Freeman's Journal,* took the most explicitedly anti-historicist approach. Even in his obituary, *Freeman's* condemned Gilbert as 'dry in style and wanting in perspective'.[119] W.H.E. Lecky, for his part, was criticised as 'pedestrian'.[120] Encouraged, as reading material on 1798 in their stead were the works of John Mitchel, Thomas D'Arcy Magee and Charles Teeling, all regulars from the Young Ireland stable, fit to edify the nationalist mind.[121]

In general, the Unionist press discussed the issue of 1798 less, but when they did made more claims of impartiality. Nationalist 'propaganda', for example, was rigorously berated.[122] The historians they drew upon, however, were those like W.H. Maxwell, (1792–1850), a novelist who wrote his *History of the Rebellion in 1798,* specifically to counter Madden's work.[123] All the Unionist papers, with the partial exception of the *Irish Times,* followed the Nationalist press in deploying the commemoration to reinforce political comment.

It is true that the press at this time had other things on its mind, including the Spanish/American war, Gladstone's death, the Local Government act, war in Sudan and the Irish Trade Unions Congress conference in Belfast. Nevertheless, the centenary was a major event. The *Freeman's Journal* hoped to engineer Nationalist unity and harness separatist energy. It presented '98 was an expression of seamless Nationalist aspiration, not a strategic alternative to constitutionalism. Under pressure from the Dillonite Devlin, who took the lead in Belfast's '98 commemoration, the *Irish News* emphasised the clerical heroism of '98, and berated Orange opponents. The *Irish Times* denied the era's revolutionary nationalism had relevance to Ireland at the turn of the century. The *Northern Whig* refused to recognise any practical progressive content in the United Irishmen movement. Aware of heavy Presbyterian involvement in '98, the *News-Letter* leavened strident condemnation with sneaking respect. The *Belfast Telegraph* found something to admire in the republican idealism of the Protestant insurgents. Ulster, just as it had its own experience of 1798, constructed its own memory of that Rebellion.

10

'Ireland is Out for Blood and Murder':[1] Nationalist Opinion and the Ulster Crisis in Provincial Ireland, 1913–1914[2]

Michael Wheatley

In the middle and west of Ireland, the Ulster crisis came to dominate local political life only from the autumn of 1913 – before that time, the paramilitary Ulster campaign against Home Rule was not seen as a looming and ever-growing physical threat, but primarily as a political and propaganda campaign, 'a bluff' to undermine British support for the Home Rule bill before it could pass.[3] For a long time, Nationalists' confidence in their ability to defeat Ulster's political challenge remained intact. Complacent apathy was a far more typical response to events than either wild enthusiasm or paranoia. It was only in the autumn of 1913, when Ulster's 'bluff' of England seemed suddenly to be working, undermining the resolve of Liberal politicians and making Ulster exclusion a serious prospect, that the Ulster crisis in provincial, Nationalist Ireland become a reality.

When the Ulster crisis did break in provincial Ireland, it transformed local politics. 'Parish pump' rivalries and considerations were subsumed into the pervasive, national issue of whether the Home Rule bill would fail. Large numbers of people, formerly quiescent, were mobilised into political and paramilitary activity through their participation in the Irish Volunteers. In the words of the Nationalist scholar and politician Tom Kettle: 'From time to time a great wave of emotion and action sweeps through the life of a people, stirring it all, shallows and depth. Such is volunteering'.[4]

The response of the Irish party to this new movement was wholly ambiguous. On the one hand, its national leadership was hostile to mass paramilitary activity and attempted to hold it back. On the other, local party support remained essential, and was sometimes soon forthcoming, for those local companies that were formed. The change of official party policy at the end of April 1914, to encouragement and participation, triggered a rush of new companies, but not the commonly supposed 'vampirisation' of the movement by the party. The Volunteers in mid-1914 were not just the Irish party dressed up in slouch hats and bandoliers. As a public manifestation of intense political activity, they represented a rather large tiger which the party's leadership held, just barely, by the tail.

The present assessment is based upon an analysis of 18 weekly newspapers, from the autumn of 1913 until the outbreak of war in August 1914, published in five politically-linked counties in the Irish midlands and East Connacht – Leitrim, Longford, Roscommon, Sligo and Westmeath. Such newspapers remained the most important forum for the dissemination of opinions among the intertwined commercial, professional and political elites of 'small town' Ireland. Political affiliations were clearly flagged – 12 of the newspapers were Nationalist, two independent and four Unionist.[5] Of the Nationalist papers, 10 were consistent supporters of John Redmond and the Irish Parliamentary party and two, owned by the 'factionalist' brothers Jasper and George W. Tully, were bitter opponents. Competition was intense, with the costs of entry for new titles low and Dublin dailies (particularly the *Irish Independent*) making inroads. This meant that while local owners and editors still saw themselves as the vanguard of opinion, they could never move so far ahead as to risk losing circulation, printing contracts and advertisers. The provincial press may have remained the crucial communications medium for nation building in Nationalist Ireland,[6] but it was just as much the mirror as the leader of local opinion.

The crisis breaks: September–November 1913

By November 1913, a new mood of alarm and bellicosity permeated provincial Ireland. It was summed up by a late-November leading article in the *Sligo Champion*, the mouthpiece of Sligo's bourgeois, Catholic establishment. The paper called, as it had for several weeks, for an Irish Volunteer corps to form, to protect the people's rights and enforce their will. Force had been substituted for the ballot box. The demands of four Ulster counties were being heeded because they had taken up arms. Ireland had to show that she was prepared to defend her rights by weapons which were the only methods her opponents would respect. 'Our rights as men are threatened, our national interests disregarded, our votes are to be of no avail'.[7]

It was not, however, the development of 'Carson's army' in Ulster which had triggered this new mood. Indeed, only one contemporary Ulster event, the formation of the 'Provisional Government' in Belfast at the end of September, attracted significant coverage in the local press. Nationalist papers dismissed this as another publicity stunt. The *Sligo Champion* wrote of Carson's martial publicity that it only embarrassed his fellow Unionists.[8] For the *Sligo Nationalist*, 'vicarious revolution of this kind is going to frighten no one'.[9] Jasper Tully opined in the *Roscommon Herald* that Carson was 'making civil war with his tongue' and that as a lawyer he was always keen to 'keep on the windy side of the law'.[10] Thereafter, there was virtually no other coverage of Ulster events before December, in any local paper.[11]

There was another news story which increased tension among provincial Nationalists at this time, but it originated not in Ulster but in Dublin. The 'great lockout', 'Larkinite' strikes, 'deportations' of Catholic children and street violence were deplored right across the local press, which lamented the damage done to Irish trade and industry. Parallels were drawn to Ulster events: the *Longford Leader* and *Westmeath Independent* compared events in Dublin (violent police treatment of demonstrators) to those in Belfast (free rein given to Carson's followers).[12] As the strikes continued, some began to see more sinister plots against Home Rule. The *Roscommon Messenger*, owned by Redmond's friend John Hayden MP, condemned the Dublin workers as 'innocent pawns' of men allied to Tories. Ireland's religion was reviled and its nationality mocked. The strikers were acting to 'strike the cup of victory from our lips'.[13] The Tully brothers seized the opportunity to denounce a conspiracy – James Larkin, the 'Englishman', was working hand in glove with Dublin Castle against Home Rule.[14] A *Midland Reporter* leading article, 'English Over All', linked the Dublin strike leaders to 'the lowest forms of English socialism', tainted by English ideas and English money. Home Rule could become impossible, with both Larkin and Carson installed as 'dictators' in Dublin and Belfast respectively.[15]

However, the events that most triggered Nationalist alarm occurred in Britain where, for the first time, Home Rule appeared to be seriously endangered. Starting in September, a succession of initiatives by Liberal politicians indicated a failure of government resolve and a risk that Home Rule would be at best mutilated and at worst lost. This began with a letter to the [London] *Times* from the former Liberal Lord Chancellor, Lord Loreburn, published on 11 September and calling for an all-party conference and compromise with the Unionists. Locally, the danger posed by Loreburn's letter was immediately identified by John Hayden, who declared that for all the talk of compromises and conferences it was inconceivable that the government could 'destroy' their work of the last several years. Hayden's newspapers, however, feared that Ulster's bluff had now worked.[16] Coverage across the local press was comprehensive, with almost every Nationalist commentator opposing Loreburn who, it was argued, did not speak for the government.

Thereafter, press speculation persisted right to the end of the year that Loreburn's key proposal, for a conference, would be taken up by the English parties. Sometimes almost daily, the Dublin papers carried such stories and the local press was peppered with rumours of 'conversations'.[17] The next major development, moreover, was the initiative not of an ex-minister but of a serving one. Winston Churchill, in a speech in Dundee on 8 October, stated that there would have to be a general election before Home Rule could come into operation. In addition, Churchill supported special treatment for North-East Ulster. This was a major news story locally and aroused strong and polarised opinions. Some, like the *Western Nationalist*, described Churchill's speech as a ploy to wrong-foot unreasonable, rejectionist Unionists.[18] Several were far uneasier, lamenting Churchill's 'ambiguity' and 'hazy attitudes.' The *Sligo Champion* flip-flopped between the two stances, first praising Churchill's 'able and conciliatory' speech, but then, in a leading article 'No Partition of Ireland', calling it 'strange and ambiguous at the time'.[19] There was, however, no ambiguity for the factionist Jasper Tully. Churchill's speech was 'A Stab in the Back', part of a deep intrigue against Ireland.[20] Such hostility was not confined to dissident Nationalists. For J.P. Farrell, MP for North Longford and owner of the *Longford Leader*, Churchill was now a 'shuffler'. Any minister who betrayed Ireland would have on his tombstone the undying hatred of the Irish race.[21] Nor was the speech's significance lost on the Unionist press, which wrote of government retreat and Ulster exclusion.[22] The political mood had clearly changed. Home Rule was now, according to the *Roscommon Messenger*, 'the chief and almost only topic of discussion' in Ireland and Great Britain.[23]

Tension was intensified by a succession of speeches, reported locally, by Irish and British politicians. Redmond was moved to make explicit rebuttals of first Loreburn (at Cahirciveen, Co. Kerry on 29 September) and then Churchill (at Limerick on 12 October, where he famously declared that the 'Two Nations' theory of Ireland was 'an abomination and a blasphemy'). These two speeches were reported in detail and hailed at the time for their removal of 'fear and doubt'. They formed, however, only part of a process of oratorical ping-pong in which Liberal speakers such as Sir Edward Grey, R.B. Haldane, Churchill and Asquith created new fears. These public utterances provided a confusing mixture of robustness, compromise, kite flying (notably proposals for 'Home Rule within Home Rule') and evasiveness. Churchill at Manchester on 18 October repeated his sins of Dundee and went further, saying that 'the genuine needs and legitimate aspirations' of Ulster had to be met. In a coded advocacy of temporary Ulster exclusion, he went on to say that there could be no solution 'destructive of the permanent unity of Ireland'. Commenting on this, the *Sligo Champion* noted that 'he has a way of saying things that are perplexing and ambiguous'.[24]

The master of ambiguity cloaked in apparent precision was, however, the Prime Minister, and Asquith's speech at Ladybank on 25 October seen as both reassuring and alarming. At one level, Asquith firmly rejected the notion of a 'conference' and proclaimed that there would be no betrayal. For the *Westmeath Independent* this meant that Home Rule was again, in the words of Redmond, 'full steam ahead'.[25] The Unionist *Sligo Independent* lamented that Asquith had missed the chance to be conciliatory.[26] However, Asquith's speech also stressed that the government would look at any reasonable proposal for peace and used similar weasel words to Churchill's at Manchester: that 'nothing is to be done which will erect a permanent or insuperable bar in the way of Irish unity'. For Jasper Tully, Asquith's use of the word 'permanent' clearly indicated an intention to kill Home Rule by exclusion.[27] The *Western Nationalist*, a supporter of the speech, nevertheless noted the volume of press speculation across Ireland and Britain that provision would have to be made for Ulster exclusion, 'for a time'.[28] The *Leitrim Advertiser*, *Longford Journal*, *Midland Reporter* and *Roscommon Herald* all went on to report new predictions of a conference, or 'interchange of views', between the British parties.[29]

The result of all this, in the language of the *Westmeath Independent*, was that the public mind was 'disturbed' and that 'for some little time back we rather felt in a somewhat querulous position'.[30] On 16 October, the dissident Lawrence Ginnell, MP for North Westmeath,

addressed his Westmeath Nationalist Executive and made an unequivocal call to arms. He still believed, he said, that Carson's followers would
not fight, but they had 'succeeded in alarming a number of timid
Englishmen'. It was now 'common prudence' he said, 'for us to be
ready if they do renege…it will be for us the Nationalists to adopt and
put into practice those rights of rebellion and their rights which
Sir Edward Carson has been loudly preaching in Ulster with
impunity'.[31]

The volunteers form

During November, stories on volunteering became increasingly common in the local press. The inaugural meeting of the Irish Volunteers at
the Dublin Rotunda, at the end of November, was of major importance
to local editors and writers. In Athlone, however, volunteering pre-
dated events in Dublin. Indeed the formation of Athlone's 'Midland
Volunteers', in mid-October, seems to have acted as a spur to Dublin
Nationalists rather than the other way around.[32] Though by later standards a pathetically small number, who seem only to have drilled twice
and then given up (according to the police, 54 men drilled on
22 October; 24 on 29 October),[33] the Midland Volunteers were nevertheless the first to drill publicly in Nationalist Ireland and were hailed as
such. The *Westmeath Independent*, however, hugely exaggerated their
impact. In what was effectively a fantasy, the paper reported that over
5,000 men were parading, with buglers, drums and cavalry, formed into
20 companies.[34] It was this myth which was reproduced in the press
locally as well as in Dublin.[35]

One local Irish party figure who took Athlone events seriously –
whether real or fantastic – was Farrell, who in a series of Longford
speeches cited Athlone as an example to be followed. On 26 October,
he advocated what he called Redmond's policy of 'no conciliation or
compromise' with Orangemen:

> We hear they began to drill over in Athlone last week, and you would find
> we could get a few drillmasters around Longford too. I am not too sure it
> would not be a very good thing to learn the 'goose step' on a bit of an
> evening and show these 'patriots' or rather Loyalists in the North of Ireland
> that they are not going to have it their own way (cheers).[36]

He did go on to add, 'but we are gaining it [Home Rule] without that,
gentlemen', but the message was repeated at another Longford public

meeting on 24 November. Here he noted that the efforts of the English democracy were being undone by the 'wooden guns' of Ulster 'patriots', but was glad that a movement had grown up among younger men to counter this. 'I think, boys, we may give it a turn in Longford too (cheers).' The government, which was now conniving in a plan to carve out Ulster, would not dare stop Irishmen if they emulated Carson. 'I hope that when we open a recruiting station you will all turn up and drill'.[37]

Farrell's calls for drilling were echoed locally. The political rationale was that the example of 'Carson's army' had to be copied and the effect of Ulster's volunteering on 'English' opinion emulated. According to Jasper Tully, Carson had unwittingly taught Nationalist Ireland that it was possible to arm and drill. The three other provinces of Ireland could surely raise treble the 80,000 men raised by the Ulster Volunteers.[38] 'A man with a rifle always commands respect from the rulers of a country'.[39] As the *Western Nationalist* put it, Orangemen now believed that their threats would work. An Irish 'enlistment' would be a powerful antidote.[40]

However, the Volunteers were now also seen to have an explicit military purpose. The *Sligo Champion's* advocacy of the use of weapons, 'the only methods our opponents say they will respect' has already been noted. For the *Westmeath Independent* the upsurge of volunteering was seen by many as evidence that Nationalists were taking Ulster's threat of war seriously.[41] A constant refrain was that local Nationalists had to be defended against an attack on the south of Ireland, whether in the form of 'Carson's march south', an 'Ulster onslaught' or even a 'looting expedition'.[42] Admittedly, this military role was seen as defensive; there was no reference to any offensive role away from home, whether to aid Ulster's Nationalists or to enforce Home Rule across Ireland. The *Sligo Champion* could say that the Volunteers' role was to 'take such steps as are necessary to enforce the rights of the people by law and equity', but they were not embodied to suppress Carson, but as a 'protective and defensive force'.[43]

Despite support from much of the press and a number of more junior politicians, Farrell was, apart from the independent Ginnell, the only local MP publicly to advocate volunteering in 1913. The Irish party's leadership were alarmed at the launch of the Volunteers in Dublin and enforced a policy of restraint on their followers. In December 1913, John Dillon's associate John Muldoon MP wrote to the Cork party man J.J. Horgan that 'Redmond does not like this thing, neither does Devlin, but they are loath to move at present...Dillon is much more against it.'[44] According to Stephen Gwynn MP (at the time the head of the party's Irish Press Agency), the Volunteers were 'a development which Redmond on his part neither willed nor approved'.[45] Though public attacks by the party on the Volunteers were rare, amounting to little more than a condemnatory letter to the Dublin *Freeman's Journal* by the MP Richard Hazleton, the leadership's distrust of the Volunteers undoubtedly checked their early growth. The spirit of the Volunteers did not yet match its later depiction by the MP Arthur Lynch, as being like 'setting the prairie on fire'.[46] As of 28 March 1914 they still, according to the Irish Chief Secretary, Augustine Birrell, numbered only 10,489 members, enrolled in 57 companies.[47]

In the five counties there were no open attacks on volunteering from public figures, but the advocacy of drilling and the use of arms did abate. The net result was that the initial wave of support for volunteering was not often translated into the formation of Volunteer companies. In Longford, Farrell ceased publicly to advocate volunteering and no company was formed until May 1914. Even in Mullingar, where Ginnell's followers were not bound by party loyalty, a corps was not started until April. When they did publicly address the subjects of Ulster and Home Rule, party spokesmen provided a diet of constant reassurance: the government was firm, the inter-party conference would not happen, the whole bill would pass. The Unionist leader Bonar Law's confirmation at Bristol on 15 January 1914, that there had indeed been British inter-party talks and that they were over, was then presented as a victory.[48] The message of Redmond, speaking at Waterford on 25 January, was that 'we have fought and we have won'.[49] At the end of January, the party nationally announced that its Home Rule Fund would close. As the Roscommon party boss and Mayo MP John Fitzgibbon put it, 'we must be very confident the battle is over when we are not appealing for fresh ammunition'.[50] However, despite all this confidence and restraint, four Irish Volunteer corps did form locally in early 1914, in the towns of Athlone, Granard, Boyle and Sligo.

Athlone

There was in Athlone a core of advanced Nationalist support independent of the Irish party and dating back several years. Advanced views in the town became centred on the Athlone Pipers' Club and, from 1911, the only Fianna company in the five counties. In November 1913, though the town's Midland Volunteers were no longer drilling, there was sufficient advanced Nationalist support for there to be an anti-recruiting demonstration against the band of the Leinster regiment.[51] For all their hostility to recruiting, the town's advanced Nationalists had in October joined with a number of army reservists and Irish party activists to inspire the original Midland Volunteers.[52] At the end of the year, they met to reform and affiliate to the national Volunteer movement.

However, the support of Irish party figures began to drop away. When, at the end of January 1914, the Pipers' Band refused to play at a nearby party rally, the *Westmeath Independent* duly attacked them.[53] Without party support the town's Volunteers made little headway. According to a Cabinet paper prepared by Augustine Birrell in April 1914, there were in Athlone only 40 Volunteers.[54] Even by June there were still only 75.[55] Though the original plan was to drill twice a week with the Pipers' Band,[56] there were no police reports of drilling after March.

Granard

In Granard, in north Longford, the Volunteers were far more vigorous, even though the core of their leadership was also independent of, and indeed hostile to, the Irish party. Their leader was John Cawley, creamery manager and former Sinn Féin supporter, who according to the later IRA man Seán MacEoin, was the 'centre' who recruited him to the Irish Republican Brotherhood in 1914.[57] However, unlike in Athlone, the new corps retained the support and encouragement of Irish party figures throughout. Its activities were regularly reported in Farrell's *Longford Leader* and its formation was first mooted in November 1913, when Farrell was still active publicly in promoting the Volunteers. Granard's Urban District Council – well stocked with party figures – gave permission for the Town Hall to be used to form the first company.[58] The corps flourished from the start and the town, with a population of 1,531 in 1911, saw 100 men enrol at the inaugural meeting.[59] By February the *Longford Leader* reported that some 200 men had enrolled and that they had paraded with pikes at a county Ancient Order of Hibernians [AOH] rally addressed by Joe Devlin.[60] Nevertheless, political friction between Cawley and the Irish party was always close to the surface and from late April he was in open dispute with the party (and was later taken to court) when supporters tried to engineer his co-option to Granard UDC.[61] Such tensions did not, however, stop 150 Volunteers parading through the town to celebrate the progress of the Home Rule bill in May.[62] Locally they were backed by a broad coalition of Nationalist support, drilling actively throughout early 1914.

Boyle

Moves to establish the Volunteers came later in Boyle, in the north of Co. Roscommon, with the first formation meeting held at the beginning of February. Unlike the companies in Granard and Athlone, the Boyle Volunteers were led from the start by Irish party stalwarts, notably the leading Boyle merchant and long-standing enemy of Jasper Tully, T.J. Devine.[63] Indeed Devine's role was so prominent that Tully's *Roscommon Herald*, despite advocating volunteering for months, refused to publish any report of the Boyle corps until May. With that exception, there was a broad coalition of support for the new corps. The inaugural meeting in February was led by Devine, attended by the local clergy, Hibernians, Gaelic Leaguers and Gaelic athletes.[64] The *Western Nationalist* claimed the enrolment of 800 men at the first public meeting of the corps on 8 March, reporting Devine's call for Hibernians across Ireland to be in the vanguard of the Volunteers.[65] Later that month, the paper reported that the town companies were drilling three times a week.[66] If the initial membership of 800 proclaimed by the *Western Nationalist* seems fanciful, the lower numbers reported by the police were still high for a town with a 1911 population of 2,691. Their estimate was that 700, of whom 400 enrolled, attended the 8 March meeting. Some 300 were present at each of several parades in April.[67]

Sligo

At the end of 1913, Sligo's politics became focused on the issue of the Home Rule bill. At this time, tensions were running sufficiently high for local Nationalists to organise a boycott of twenty-seven Unionist town merchants, who had signed a public address from the county to Bonar Law. The boycott, to the dismay of the Unionist *Sligo Times* and *Sligo Independent*, was connived at by the *Sligo Champion*, which published the names of all the signatories.[68] The town's mayor, John Jinks, denounced traders who had pretended friendship with their Catholic customers. If Catholics confined trade to 'their own', the minority could not live for 24 hours in Sligo.[69]

In January 1914, Jinks enhanced his leadership of the town's politics when the Corporation, on his initiative and that of his fellow alderman and Transport Workers' boss John Lynch, agreed to promote the Volunteers.[70] As in Boyle, the leadership of the Sligo Volunteers came from party men, notably Jinks, Henry Monson (a leading Hibernian) and Edward Foley (alderman and UIL man). Though a broad coalition supported the Volunteers, their early membership seems to have been derived from those Hibernians and Transport Workers who had, in political alliance, dominated elections to Sligo Corporation for over two years. This class bias was noted in the Royal Irish Constabulary [RIC] county inspector's report that there was 'great apprehension [about the Volunteers] among the better classes of both sides of politics'.[71] However, Jinks, Monson and Foley were all successful businessmen and Foley, who owned the town's brewery, was one of Sligo's richest men. The spread of support for the Volunteers under Jinks was broad. It certainly embraced the *Sligo Champion* and its rival the *Sligo Nationalist*. At the inaugural Volunteer meeting at the beginning of February it also encompassed language enthusiasts, former IRB men, Gaelic athletes and the clergy. Over 460 men enrolled at that first public meeting.[72] Birrell's Cabinet paper of April 1914 estimated that there were 530 members, drawn primarily from the Hibernians, Gaelic Athletic Association and Irish National Foresters.[73] By late-February, the corps was organised into five companies, under eight ex-army drill instructors, with one company drilling each weekday night and the whole corps parading on Sundays.[74] It was one of the largest and most active Irish Volunteer corps in the country.

The varying progress of these four corps demonstrated that they could not flourish without the encouragement of 'leading' men and local Irish party figures. With the exception of Athlone, large numbers of men mobilised for regular drills, lessons, route marches and parades. The numbers of participants and the level of activity implied a new, heightened level of political mobilisation, but only where there was local party support. The contrast between the movement's stagnation in Athlone and its blossoming in Sligo was stark. Advanced Nationalists, and even outright opponents of the Irish party, could flourish in the Volunteers in early 1914, but only where local party leaders took their feet off the brakes.

Restraints removed – the volunteers take off

Though the first wave of volunteering was limited, the sense of political crisis remained pervasive in the local press and intensified during 1914. News reports and leading articles, speeches and public resolutions focused on the events – the climb-downs, parliamentary manoeuvres, army mutiny, gun-running, all-party conference and finally bloodshed – which weakened the case of those who argued that Home Rule could be won in Parliament. Specifically the events (all of them setbacks) which triggered detailed coverage were:

- Asquith's announcement on 9 February that an offer to Ulster's Unionists would be forthcoming,
- Asquith's announcement on 9 March of that offer (of 'temporary', county-by-county exclusion) and the Irish party leadership's reluctant agreement to it,
- the Curragh mutiny of 18–20 March, seen as risking the collapse of the government and making government coercion of 'Ulster' next to impossible,
- the Larne gun-running of 24–25 April, seen as a major accession of strength to the Ulster Volunteers and as, at best, colossal negligence by the government,
- the government's announcement on 18 May that there would be an Amending bill for Ulster's exclusion (tabled subsequent to the Commons passage of the Home Rule bill), followed by two months of rumour and speculation,
- the Buckingham Palace all-party conference of 21–24 July, the announcement of which, though it quickly failed, was greeted with alarm,
- the Irish Volunteers' gun-running at Howth, Co. Dublin, on 26 July, and
- the Bachelor's Walk killings on the same day, when men of the King's Own Scottish Borderers killed three Dubliners.[75]

All of these were major news stories for the local press, the editorial response of which became more polarised. At one extreme the Tully brothers continued to denounce what they saw as a succession of betrayals and plots by a corrupt government, while at the other, John Hayden's newspapers regularly voiced whatever rationale was being advanced by the Irish party leadership to justify its latest reverse. Meanwhile the *Westmeath Independent* oscillated wildly in its views, between a January prediction that anyone proposing the division of Ireland would be regarded as a traitor and a March paean of praise for Asquith ('The Occasion – The Man'), who was now proposing just such a division.[76]

The other Nationalist papers, while all still professing loyalty to the party, gloomily charted the reverses that it suffered. Sometimes they put a brave face on them, but they just as often gave expression to outbursts of despair or disgust. Thus, for the *Leitrim Observer*, the March county opt-out proposal was 'gall and wormwood to the mind of every patriot…bitterly humiliating' and it was bad 'that we must parley with plunderers'.[77] The *Western Nationalist* after the Curragh reported a belief that a government so lacking in backbone could only last a short time.[78] The gunrunning at Larne, for the *Strokestown Democrat*, confirmed 'the majority of discerning Nationalists in their suspicions of the government'. It had sought permanent Ulster exclusion and the Curragh bungle was 'permitted or contrived'. Irish Nationalists had to realise that 'they are being sold'.[79] By June, even Hayden's papers adopted a tone of rising alarm. His *Westmeath Examiner* predicted that 'the people are in earnest and will secure freedom at any cost'.[80] These outbursts were best exemplified by the despair of Farrell's *Longford Leader* in March. It believed that Ireland, a Catholic and Nationalist nation, was hated by the whole ascendancy class of Great Britain. Its Catholic religion was the obstacle to its freedom and now Asquith's government had succumbed to this feeling. Though the Irish party had with the 'deepest reluctance' accepted the county opt-out proposal, 'it is moments like these that try men's souls'.[81]

Against this background, more Volunteer companies were formed across all of the five counties during March and April. At the end of April there were 17, most of which were satellites of three of the corps (Boyle, Granard and Sligo) formed earlier in the year. The most significant event, though, was the formation of a corps in Mullingar, Co. Westmeath in mid-April. Supporters of both Ginnell and the Irish party participated in forming the corps. Again, it drew upon the full range of Nationalists in the town and by early May had around 400 enrolled members.[82]

Given the pressure of events, successive setbacks to Home Rule and a steady accrual of Volunteer members and companies, a change in the party leadership's policy was only a matter of time. Writing of his friend Dillon, the English radical Wilfrid Scawen Blunt stated that 'it was the Curragh incident that convinced him that the National Volunteer movement should be openly supported'.[83] Locally, an AOH memorandum in favour of the Volunteers was said to be circulating in Longford from mid-April.[84] Elsewhere, the first signs of an overt change in policy came after Larne, at the end of that month. In Roscommon, Hibernian divisions from 27 April received a circular from the national secretary, J.D. Nugent, calling on them to make themselves available for Volunteer drill.[85] On 11 May, Redmond's brother William went public in a letter to the *Westminster Gazette*, lauding the Volunteers and predicting results 'quite as unfortunate as anything which might conceivably happen in Ulster' should Home Rule fail.[86] The party was now placing itself in the vanguard.

The net result was that in May and June the pace of what the police called 'branch' formation accelerated rapidly. By the end of June there were 26 'branches' in Leitrim; 15 in Longford; 20 in Roscommon; 15 in Sligo and 20 in Westmeath, making 96 in all.[87] The grand formation meeting in Longford town, led by Farrell, was on 27 May; Roscommon town's with Hayden was on 1 June. Both mirrored the meetings that had taken place before in other towns. The full gamut of Nationalist society was present – in Roscommon town leading figures of the UIL, town tenants, Gaelic Club, clergy and town commissioners all played their part. Speaking with Hayden was the Gaelic Leaguer and former member of the Sinn Féin national executive, Father Michael O'Flanagan. The crowd watched a Roscommon-Athlone football match and were played to by the Athlone Pipers' Band. It was reported that 250 men attended the corps' first parade.[88]

Vampirisation?

Volunteering undoubtedly became a mass movement in the five counties during the summer of 1914. In July and August, the total of local police-recorded 'branches' ballooned from 96 to 208, with an estimated membership of approximately 20,000.[89] To put the scale of this mobilisation in context, the total male population of all five counties in the 1911 census was just under 176,000. Substantially fewer than half of these would have been of an appropriate age to volunteer. It is clear that the Volunteers mobilised anything between 25% and 35% of local young and middle-aged men. Moreover, unlike the local UIL, which also had a (nominal) membership of some 20,000, the Volunteers were active, not only enrolling but drilling and parading week after week. There is no doubt that the change of party policy towards the Volunteers spurred this mushrooming growth, but it remains unclear just how far the party controlled the movement, let alone absorbed it.

David Fitzpatrick maintains that 'the party vampire' was at 'its most incisive' when it took control of the Volunteers in mid-1914.[90] Already by mid-April Tom Kettle had written to Stephen Gwynn that party supporters 'have already come into the movement so heavily that there is a danger of their swamping the ship.'[91] According to Fitzpatrick, when Redmond publicly forced the Dublin-based provisional committee of the Volunteers to accept 25 Irish party nominees, this reflected a fait accompli in the countryside.[92] In the five counties, party stalwarts were nearly always prominent in the wave of new companies. Redmond's June take-over generated barely a local murmur. Out of nearly a hundred local corps at the time of the takeover, resistance to his demands was mooted in only three. The local Nationalist press universally backed Redmond. The *Leitrim Observer* hailed 'Redmond, the Leader, the real general'.[93]

In Athlone, the process of party take-over was plain to all. At the end of May, O.J. Dolan (grocer, publican, auctioneer, town councillor and Chief Ranger of the Foresters) put his name to a circular calling for the town's corps to be put 'on a sound footing' at a public meeting. When held in June, it was attended by over 700 with, according to the *Westmeath Independent*, 50 to 60 of the 'Sinn Féin element' interspersed. Conn O'Frighil, the current president of the town corps, stated that though he opposed Redmond's takeover of the Dublin 'provisional committee' he was prepared to hand local leadership to 'more influential people'.[94]

However, Athlone was one of only two instances locally in which there was an actual change of leadership. There was no general purge. The Granard corps remained firmly under Cawley. In Co. Roscommon, Jasper Tully had finally pitched in as an active reporter and supporter of the Boyle corps.[95] In newer corps such as Roscommon town, Longford and Mullingar, the leadership remained just as broadly based. The Sligo town corps continued to be a very broad church of all Nationalists and Alex McCabe, one of a handful of IRB men in Co. Sligo at this time, became a leading Volunteer organiser across the county as company after company was formed. Not only did Sinn Féin supporters and other advanced Nationalists remain, or become, prominent in the Volunteers, but a significant number of men emerged who had played no local political role in the past. The sheer numbers parading, drilling, being lectured and raising funds were on a scale not seen in recent years. In terms of organised commitment, week after week, they exceeded any popular mobilisation since the height of the Land War at the beginning of the 1880s.

There are also some indications that 'vampirisation' worked in reverse – it was the Irish party rather than the Volunteers who were losing blood. This was particularly apparent in the party's main local organisation, the UIL, whose historic stimulus to activity from land disputes and agitation had largely receded. The party's termination of the Home Rule fund early in 1914 removed another major prop –

fund-raising – to branch activity. RIC 'Crime Special Branch' reports of UIL fund-raising indicated that the effect was dramatic, as shown in Table 10.1:

Table 10.1   *Funds raised by the UIL by county, Sept. 1913–Sept. 1914 ($£s$)*[96]

	Leitrim	Longford	Roscommon	Sligo	Westmeath
Q4 1913	87	186	120	227	68
Q1 1914	96	52	106	124	128
Q2	17	21	48	18	19
Q3	8	10	32	39	2

Though the series was erratic from quarter to quarter, the change of trend was consistent across all five counties. The decisive downturn in fund-raising came in the second quarter of 1914, after the closure of the Home Rule fund and during the 'lift-off' of local volunteering. There are no equivalent police records of Volunteer funds raised, but it seems almost certain that some funds not raised by the UIL went instead to the Volunteers.

The UIL's future role after Home Rule had in any case been in doubt. Annual branch 'reorganisation' meetings (i.e. AGMs) were punctuated by comments that they would be the last held. When the South Westmeath executive reorganised in January 1914, 'many realised that they were meeting for the last time for reorganisation'. Farrell expressed the same sentiments to the North Longford executive at the same time.[97] Fitzgibbon predicted that the UIL would soon have done its work and that the Gaelic League would take its place.[98] However, as the future of Home Rule became progressively less secure during 1914, the message was instead put out that the UIL would have to keep up the struggle. As Farrell expressed it in May, the party would keep the government in office for the necessary time and the UIL would keep going until there was a parliament on College Green. However, Farrell then told his audience that they now also had the chance of an Irish army, which they must take. They should be doubly armed, 'first by the vote and then by our guns'.[99]

Physically, the sheer proliferation of Volunteer drills and meetings pushed the more humdrum work of the UIL out of the limelight, clashing with the routine of branch committees and resolution passing. With little land agitation, minimal fund-raising and the completion of the county council elections at the beginning of June 1914, there was very little for UIL branches to do. The level of activity of the UIL branch organisations can be gauged from the frequency of reports of meetings in the *Longford Leader, Roscommon Messenger, Roscommon Herald, Sligo Champion* and *Western Nationalist* (Table 10.2):[100]

Table 10.2   *UIL reports in local newspapers, Jan.–Sept. 1914*

	Jan.	Feb.	Mar.	Apr.	May	Jun.	Jul.	Aug.	Sept.
Longford Leader	16	3	12	13	13	7	9	5	5
Roscommon Herald	14	17	20	11	25	11	6	9	2
Roscommon Messenger	7	5	11	8	3	6	2	4	5
Sligo Champion	55	31	46	36	48	21	25	23	16
Western Nationalist	13	5	6	3	8	2	3	1	3

Though the UIL's affiliate, the AOH, saw a much smaller fall, a clear shift to lower levels of party activity occurred in the third quarter of 1914, the period of maximum Volunteer activity. Nor was this shift triggered by the outbreak of war in August. The fall in branch activity preceded the war, in the two months of June and July, which witnessed the climax of the Home Rule crisis and the most rapid rate of Volunteer company formation. Reporting of the Volunteers in the press also dwarfed that of the UIL. Over the third quarter there were 85, 170 and 133 Volunteer company reports in the *Longford Leader, Roscommon Herald* and *Sligo Champion* respectively, against 19, 17 and 64 UIL reports.

In February 1915, the UIL National Directory reported, and had to justify, a nationwide collapse in the number of branches sending in sub-scription fees. (For the five counties only 65 branches were paid-up against 121 in the year before.) The Directory's rationalisation was that: 'In order to give an opportunity to the better organising of the National Volunteers, the work of organisation in connection with the United Irish League was not pressed during the year...'.[101] It seems clear that the Irish party did not 'vampirise' the Irish Volunteers at the local level in the summer of 1914.[102] Though the party's change of policy towards the Volunteers greatly accelerated their formation, and though party men took a prominent role in nearly all companies, the movement mobilised thousands of members who had not recently been politically active. Its leadership continued to be drawn from all local Nationalist societies and organisations. If any one movement weakened from loss of 'blood', it was the Irish party (in particular the UIL), not the Volunteers.

'Playing with fire'

Dillon, though he now called himself 'strongly in favour' of them, described the Volunteer movement as 'playing with fire' in a letter to his friend Blunt at the end of May. He continued: 'And unless it is kept under reliable control – it might at any moment utterly ruin the National movement – and repeat the disasters of 1798'.[103] According to a series of reports, 'The State of Ireland', prepared for Dublin Castle by district magistrates in the summer of 1914, the 'reliable control' desired by Dillon was lacking. Though the magistrates considered their localities relatively crime-free and relations between police and public to be good, the ballooning Volunteer companies had, according to Capt Owen in Roscommon, 'no responsible leaders' and if armed were 'a menace to the public peace'. There might also be retaliation against local Protestants if Ulster Catholics were attacked.[104] Elsewhere, the Volunteers were consistently seen as dangerous:

> The National Volunteer force may in time become a source of danger to the public peace. In its ranks are many undesirables. (Castlerea),
> The Volunteer movement is popular with young men, but it is doubtful if it will last. As there are no responsible leaders there is a danger that the men might easily get out of hand. (Mullingar),
> National Volunteers disloyal, and if they become roused, would get out of hand and become a dangerous rabble. (Sligo).[105]

In Roscommon the RIC county inspector, after 'moving quietly about' during June, believed that the UIL and AOH were the chief organisers of the county's Volunteers, but went on:

> The corps have no proper leaders and are under no proper control....These bands of young men coming together are beginning to feel their strength and when they get arms their existence looks like being a serious menace to the peace of the county and to the liberty and security of the minority who hold different political views.[106]

The rhetoric fed to these 'bands of young men' had moved on from the political role, and even the locally defensive military role, advocated for them in the autumn of 1913. Again and again the justification was now for 'Ireland's army', the purpose of which was to ensure the arrival of Home Rule and its subsequent enforcement. Though references to more separatist goals than 'Home Rule' remained infrequent,[107] the language used was significantly violent and bellicose. Volunteers at Streamstown, Co. Westmeath, were told that Ulster had declared for the 'arbitrament of the sword'. Orange fanatics sought for the blood and murder of Catholics. The only choice for those who 'believed in constitutional government' was to meet force by force.[108] The Boyle Volunteers heard that the Home Rule bill had been too dearly bought to be trifled with – 'they had the men, and they would get the guns to shoot down every man who opposed them (renewed cheers)'.[109] The diligent Irish party organiser, the co-regional director of the AOH John Keaveny, could only 'hope' that the soon-to-be Lady Carson would not be left a widow, her husband shot by 'Nationalist troops'.[110]

The bellicosity of Nationalist rhetoric climaxed at the end of July in response to the killings at Bachelor's Walk in Dublin. There were, of course, still some instances of relative restraint, but the tone of Farrell's *Longford Leader* was widely echoed. Dublin Castle and the 'ascendancy gang' were 'the enemy at every turn of Irish race and sentiment'. The bloodshed would 'cry to heaven for vengeance on the heads of our national enemies, and will not cry in vain'.[111] In almost every local town the Volunteers led marches to rallies to hear denunciations of the killings. In Roscommon town they heard a denunciation of 'the dirty hacks of the English government', cowards and murderers. After 'the English' (i.e. the King's Own Scottish Borderers) were beaten, all they could do was shoot women and children. An English visitor to the town was threatened by a Volunteer.[112] Elphin in Co. Roscommon was said to be 'panic stricken' and nearby Strokestown showed 'a grim determination of revenge'.[113] At the Sligo meeting, organised by John Jinks and led by 300 Volunteers and the Hibernian band, one speaker denounced the blood shed by the 'cursed dogs of England' (and the 'cursed Scottish hounds') and said that if the government did not act then Ireland must take it into her hands to punish them. Ireland must have Home Rule, and 'if any English party tries to stop us then the rifle must speak at last (cheers)'. For Henry Monson at the same meeting, the blood of the victims cried for vengeance and the killings showed that Ireland could depend only on her right arm – the Volunteers. If there were to be a war, said Jinks, the men and women of Sligo would be at the front.[114] Jinks, that pillar of Sligo's bourgeoisie and machine politics, later declaimed to the Sligo Guardians: 'Ireland has been governed by the heel and the boot, but I will say here publicly, in the presence of the press, that Ireland is out for blood and murder – if murder is required. We will not stand any nonsense in the future...if a shot is fired at our people in the North we are prepared to meet them'.[115]

The eve of the World War, therefore, saw provincial Nationalist opinion almost totally absorbed in the Home Rule crisis, experiencing a mass political mobilisation, militarism and a bellicosity of language unseen in recent times. For the *Sligo Champion,* Volunteering was 'the healthiest and most significant manifestation of the National spirit that has been seen in Ireland in the lifetime of most of us'.[116] For the *Roscommon Herald,* it was the spirit of men with guns 'which counts today in Ireland'.[117] The Irish party, erratically and inconsistently, had on balance gone along with Kettle's 'great wave of emotion and action'. However, though the goal of the Volunteer movement was still Home Rule, the Irish party did not create the Volunteers, was marginalised by them and certainly could not be said to control them. Faced with such a 'great wave' the Irish party was swept along, if not yet, as after Easter 1916, swept away.

11

The *Irish Independent* and the Ulster Crisis, 1912–21[*]

Patrick Maume

Introduction

The *Irish Daily Independent* was founded in December 1891 as the official daily of the Parnellite faction which emerged from the split in the Irish Parliamentary party in December 1890. In 1900 the business magnate William Martin Murphy acquired the newspaper from its insolvent holding company and merged it with his *Daily Nation* – which reflected the views of T.M. Healy, Parnell's bitterest critic, who had quarrelled with the majority of Anti-Parnellites (led by John Dillon) and led a clericalist splinter group. The merged newspaper was edited by the pietistic and imperialistic founder of the *Irish Catholic*, William Francis Dennehy. For the next four years the *Independent and Nation* operated as a mouthpiece for Healyite conservative Nationalism, losing Murphy £20,000.

By 1904, with Healy politically marginalised, Murphy decided to dispose of the paper.

However, a survey commissioned by Murphy for the benefit of potential buyers reported in July 1904 that there was a gap in the Irish market for a cheap, popular daily modelled on the Northcliffe papers in London. Murphy decided to undertake this enterprise himself. He bought out minority shareholders, formed a private company, and invested heavily in new printing machinery and a specially redesigned building at 111 Abbey Street. (The paper previously operated from leased premises in Trinity Street, near College Green.) A new editor,

T.R. Harrington (formerly chief reporter) was appointed in mid-1904 and sent with other senior journalists to London to study the techniques of the British popular press. Until retirement in 1931 Harrington, with fierce attention to detail, ruled the *Independent* office. When the new paper appeared on 2 January 1905, Murphy had already spent £50,000.

The *Independent* made extensive use of compressed news items. A vigorous marketing drive, coupled with early provincial rail delivery, made it the first Dublin daily to build a nationwide mass audience. From 1908 the advertising manager, T.A. Grehan, systematically pursued customers and adopted London advertising techniques to a degree previously unknown in the Irish market (despite advertisers' initial suspicions that readers of a cheap newspaper were not worth cultivating). In November 1909 the *Independent* became the first Irish newspaper to publish audited circulation figures.

The previously dominant *Freeman's Journal*, controlled by the Irish Parliamentary party, was slow to respond (especially since the IPP leaders were on bad terms with Thomas Sexton, the clever but neurotic chairman of the *Freeman* board). It continued to print party leaders' speeches in full; its reaction to events was hindered by the need for party approval. Sexton's long-term policy of cutting investment to maintain dividends starved the paper of capital; from 1910 it reported losses, while the *Independent* grew in size and increased circulation. The growth of the *Independent* indicated the Irish party's waning ability to impose its dominance on Nationalist civil society, and the potential for a consumer-driven commercial press to displace more explicitly political party-related newspapers. This did not, however, mean that the *Independent* could advance an agenda of its own. Murphy and (especially) Harrington knew that outright opposition to the IPP could trigger a damaging boycott by party loyalist readers and advertisers.

Murphy attributed this success to Harrington's professionalism, and trusted the editor's judgment on most matters concerning the paper. Harrington in turn moderated Murphy's hostility to the Irish party leadership, to the annoyance of Healy and his political allies, who complained the paper did not report them on the same scale that the *Freeman* reported their rivals. Harrington could be startlingly outspoken to Murphy when he considered it necessary 'to defend your property against yourself'.

Murphy and Harrington saw the *Independent* as a 'business proposition' tapping a growing consumer market, but its business ethos influenced its veiled hostility to the Irish party. Murphy saw himself as a

deserving outsider who had clawed his way into the business establishment by sheer talent; though he saw links to a wider imperial market as
benefiting Ireland he resented the complacent Protestant/Unionist elite
who traditionally dominated the Dublin Chamber of Commerce. At
the same time he shared the suspicion (widespread among middle-class
Nationalists as well as Unionists) that the Irish party leadership were
not competent to secure Home Rule or govern Ireland if they did.
While the *Independent* refrained from open attacks on the Irish party
leadership it highlighted widespread hostility to Catholicism among
British Liberals, denounced the abortive 1907 Irish Council bill,
and complained that Lloyd George's 1909 People's Budget increased
Ireland's tax burden, which it complained was already excessive.
Dissident Nationalists led by Healy and William O'Brien exploited
these issues to make a relatively strong showing at the January 1910
election.

These mutterings abated when the January 1910 general election
gave the Irish party the ability to bring down the Asquith government
and the Liberals committed themselves to introduce a new Home Rule
bill after the abolition of the Lords' veto. The *Independent* distanced
itself from the dissidents, who were driven back into O'Brien's Co.
Cork electoral stronghold. Public interest in the political crises of the
coming years would greatly increase Irish newspaper readership, with
the cheap *Independent* as principal beneficiary; meanwhile widespread
Nationalist resentment towards Britain and the Unionists, combined
with suspicions about the competence of the Irish party leadership,
shaped and was channelled by the *Independent's* political coverage in the
last years of the Union.

Naming terms

The introduction of the Home Rule Bill was delayed until February
1912 by the need to pass the Parliament act and Lloyd George's 1911
Insurance act. In the meantime, the Irish party leaders tried to restrain
speculation on its likely terms. They believed the important thing was
to get an Irish Parliament established as the basis from which further
concessions could be demanded. Nonetheless, dissident groups and
journals outside the party's control discussed the prospects for the bill
and often suggested the party would be fobbed off with provisions so
restricted as to be unworkable.

From October 1911 the *Independent* called for the Home Rule bill to
include control of customs and excise, and attacked John Dillon and

T.M. Kettle for their willingness to abandon this claim.[1] It endorsed Erskine Childers' argument that only fiscal autonomy and Dominion status could provide a lasting settlement – 'Ireland cannot be made self-reliant and self-respecting through doles and subsidies'.[2] The *Independent* lauded Childers' book *The Framework of Home Rule*,[3] and called for fiscal autonomy as advocated by a preliminary committee set up to report on the financial arrangements for Home Rule. (This advice was not followed in the bill).

The eventual bill was welcomed as justifying the rejection of the (less expansive) Irish Council bill. However, the *Independent* thought it could benefit from 'useful amendments'; the complicated financial machinery of the draft Home Rule bill would breed fiscal irresponsibility and incessant Anglo-Irish disputes.[4] Murphy also feared reduced Irish representation at Westminster would weaken Irish ability to influence fiscal measures outside the competence of the Irish Parliament.

The paper complained that Unionists, instead of offering serious amendments, devoted themselves to 'worthless and farcical' wrecking proposals. Unionist speeches on the third reading were dismissed as 'ridiculous and intolerant' and the *Independent* made the standard Nationalist point that the Dominions showed self-government did not lead to anarchy and separation.[5]

Wooden guns

As soon as the result of the 1910 general election became known, Ulster Unionists threatened to resist Home Rule by force and began locally organised drilling. Nationalists dismissed this as a stunt got up for the benefit of the London Unionist press, like similar manoeuvres in 1886 and 1892–93. The idea that figures like Sir Edward Carson, who had prosecuted so many Nationalists for threatening behaviour, might take up arms against Parliament was seen as too ridiculous to discuss seriously. The military deficiencies of the centrally-organised Ulster Volunteer Force [UVF] (founded early in 1912) were similarly mocked; occasional arms seizures by Customs were dismissed as the UVF playing to the press gallery

The *Independent*, like most Nationalist papers, initially mocked the martial rhetoric of Ulster Unionists as a 'bogey'.[6] A *Weekly Independent* cartoon of unmartial Ulster Volunteers drilling with wooden rifles (accompanying a reprint of a *Westminster Gazette* article dismissing 'the Ulster Will Fight Comedy' as a bluff, a disavowal of violence by the Church of Ireland Bishop of Kilmore, and a statement by the Unionist

Saturday Review that an Ulster Parliament was unthinkable),[7] inspired a 'Poets' Corner' contributor to travesty a popular Nationalist ballad:

> *'The Risin' O' the Moon – Up-to-Date'*
> 'Och, then tell me George McGregor, whaur the bloody fray's to be?'
> 'In the ould spot by the "public" right well known to you an' me.
> An' we'll batther with our drumsticks a right loyal marchin' tune,
> With our German rifles glintin' by the Risin' o' the Moon'.
>
> Out from many a well-filled tap room eyes were watching thro' the night
> Many's the eager pressman's pencil waited, ready for the sight,
> Sounds re-echoed thro' the byways like the warblin' of a coon
> But the German rifles cracked not by the Risin' o' the Moon.
>
> Well they fought upon their carpets, well they warred in Press and pub,
> Well the daring, dauntless drummers pounded forth their rub-a-dub.
> But, thank God, the day is coming when we'll find no silly loon
> Who will dream of German rifles at the Rise of Freedom's Moon.[8]

Considerable attention was given to Protestants who denied the existence of Irish Catholic intolerance and to exposures of Unionist press misrepresentations (such as the Catholic Bishop of Cloyne's successful libel suit against the *Dundee Courier*, which claimed Cobh priests ordered Catholic shopkeepers to dismiss Protestant employees).[9] Andrew Bonar Law's declaration that Ulster showed there was no Irish national desire for Home Rule was described as surveying a fragment and presenting it as the whole country. His 'intoxicated' speech at Blenheim was juxtaposed with 'Orange outrages and intolerance' in Belfast; his subsequent qualifications were headlined 'Bonar Law Eats His Treason'.[10]

The appearance of the Ulster Volunteer Force [UVF] initially did little to check this ridicule:

> They have handsome wooden guns
> Made in Italy, for fun.
> They'll be lighter for the run
> Says the Shan Van Vocht.[11]

The Ulster Covenant was described as 'Orange Bluff – Terms of the Great "Covenant" – Farcical Document'.[12] *Independent* reporters gave the mass signing ceremonies slightly more respect. They found 'a curious blend of religion and politics', with 'nicely arranged perfor-

DUBLIN, SATURDAY, JANUARY 14, 1911.

ORANGE FIREBRANDS AT "DRILL."

Source: Courtesy of the National Library of Ireland

mances', noting that the ceremonial surrounding Carson was a 'travesty' of those accorded to royalty.[13] The Newry *Frontier Sentinel* was more forthright in declaring that the 'notoriously wicked' Covenant presented Irish Catholics as 'the spawn of the Devil' whose greatest delight was to persecute their Protestant fellow-countrymen; it was promptly sued for libel by several Newry signatories. The jury could not agree on a verdict.[14]

The *Independent* initially treated partition proposals as just one more wrecking tactic. The paper noted the *Irish Times* denunciation in September 1911 of partitionist views expressed by Anthony Traill, the Antrim-born Provost of Trinity College.[15] The *Independent* dismissed the amendment for the exclusion of the four Protestant-majority Ulster counties proposed by the dissident Liberal MP Thomas Agar-Robartes in June 1911 as a 'travesty'. It was astonished that any Liberals supported it,[16] and noted John Dillon's statement that he would not accept Home Rule with partition.[17]

Riots

The UVF was created as much to control its members as to prepare for effective resistance; both previous Home Rule Bills were accompanied by sectarian riots in Belfast, and the Ulster Unionist leaders feared spontaneous violence would allow their movement to be suppressed under pretext of police action. In February 1912 a proposed Home Rule meeting to be addressed by Winston Churchill had to be moved from the centrally located Ulster Hall to Celtic Park in Nationalist West Belfast, and Churchill narrowly escaped injury when his car was attacked by Unionist rioters. At the beginning of July 1912 drunken members of the Ancient Order of Hibernians [AOH], returning from a locally organised Nationalist rally (intended as a riposte to the Agar-Robartes proposal) attacked a Protestant Sunday School excursion at Castledawson, Co. Londonderry. This led to widespread rioting in Belfast, with many Catholics expelled from their workplaces; some southern Nationalists advocated a boycott of Belfast businesses, but this was discouraged by the IPP leadership.

As sectarian violence revived in the North, menacing notes intruded into the *Independent's* coverage. The use of threats to prevent Winston Churchill speaking in the Ulster Hall was presented as proving the hypocrisy of Unionist claims that free speech and personal liberty could only be preserved under the Union[18] The pelting of Lord and Lady Pirrie (involved with the Churchill meeting) at Larne with the apparent approval of the Unionist MP W.J. McGeagh McCaw was sarcastically attributed to 'the gentlemen who want safeguards'.[19] It accused Unionist leaders of direct complicity in the 1912 Belfast riots – an issue which recurred in the paper's coverage over the next ten years, involving far more extensive and deadly riots than the relatively limited disturbances of 1912.[20]

Even as it focussed its attention on James Larkin, who often cited Carson's activities as a precedent, the paper treated Carson with increas-

The attack on the Pirries: Cartoon by Charles A. Mills
Source: Courtesy of the National Library of Ireland

ing seriousness. In July 1913 it noted incidents ranging from riots in
Newry and Derry[21] to the beating up of a *Dundalk Democrat* reporter at
the Castlecaulfield 12th July demonstration.[22] The *Independent* complained that while the Castledawson incident has received extensive
publicity, the July 1913 wrecking of Castledawson AOH hall and several
Catholic homes by Belfast Orange followers of the street-preacher
Arthur Trew attracted little coverage.[23]

In September 1913 the paper echoed Devlin's accusation that Carson was provoking civil war and called him a reckless fool playing with gunpowder. The idea of Unionist bluff had not wholly disappeared; the London correspondent ridiculed Ulster Volunteers for setting up an insurance scheme to safeguard against the consequences of their own proposed rebellion, and quoted legal advice that such insurance policies were self-invalidating.[24]

Partition in prospect

The Irish party's central dilemma was that if the Liberal government depended on its support, it also was dependent on the Liberals. As early as the drafting of the bill, a section of the Cabinet (led by Lloyd George and Churchill) favoured a partition-based compromise; in late 1913 clandestine contacts between Liberals and Conservatives revived the possibility.[25]

Resistance to partition was so central to the *Independent*'s editorial politics in the following years that it is important to consider why the issue provoked Murphy so fiercely. Murphy's suspicion that the Irish party leaders were mediocrities, incapable of obtaining Home Rule or making it work if they got it, was not merely the product of personal bitterness at the defeat of Healyism and the Irish party's long-running suspicion of his influence; it reflected the long history of post-Parnellite factionalism and the mixed record of local government (not to mention Redmond's disastrous management of the Parnellite *Independent* in the 1890s) and was widely shared by middle-class Nationalists as well as Unionists.

Many commentators, with the benefit of hindsight, point out how such critiques of partition as those in the *Independent* play down the independent agency of Ulster Unionists, exaggerate the malevolence of British statesmen, and give relatively little attention to the central defect of partition – the position of Northern Nationalists. Such commentators point out that many – including the *Independent* – who criticised Redmond for accepting partition, in practice treated partition as secondary to sovereignty. In fact, the *Independent* did not separate the two issues; it complained that by forcing Nationalists to accept partition the Unionists and the British showed that even under Home Rule Nationalists would remain second-class citizens, subordinated to British political requirements. This also explains why the *Independent* refused to suggest any compromise proposals to conciliate Ulster Unionists (apart from those which fitted its own views about the need to safeguard business interests under Home Rule). For most Nationalists in 1914 compromise to avoid partition seemed blackmail extorted by an arrogant Ascendancy rather than an attempt to accommodate the fears of a vulnerable minority; both views possess legitimacy.

By October 1913 the *Independent* grew increasingly concerned at official hints, especially from Churchill, that the government might raise 'an Offa's Dyke between the North-East corner and the rest of this country'.[26] 'We see no valid reason whatever why this little country should have two Parliaments within its shores'.[27] The *Independent* denounced Churchill and recalled old suspicions that Nationalists could not rely on Asquith. (These dated back to Asquith's 'Cromwellian' refusal to release imprisoned Irish dynamiters as Home Secretary in 1892–95, and his involvement in 1900–1 with Lord Rosebery's 'Liberal Imperialist' faction which supported the Boer War and denounced Home Rule as a political liability.) It covered a series of meetings addressed by Redmond in Ireland (culminating in his 12 October 1913 Limerick declaration that Nationalists repudiated partition as 'an abomination and a blasphemy') as proof that support for Home Rule remained undiminished.[28] The *Independent* suggested Carson's bluster about civil war might cause his arrest; but in November it reported rumours that the Cabinet favoured the exclusion of four counties. As expectations of possible concession built up in January and February 1914, the paper declared itself opposed to even temporary exclusion.

When Asquith announced on 9 March 1914 that he would introduce an Amending bill allowing Ulster counties with Unionist majorities to vote themselves out of Home Rule for six years, Murphy told Healy he was so shocked by Redmond's acquiescence that he could not sleep, though he never missed a night's sleep during the struggle against Larkin. Murphy went into the *Independent* office for the next four nights to ensure the paper kept opposing the proposal.[29] The Unionists' failure to respond with immediate concessions led the *Independent* to demand that the government withdraw its offer. When the Liberals introduced the Amending bill, the *Independent* excoriated the 'timid and weak-kneed government' and declared 'we hope the agitation throughout this country may be strong enough to avert such a calamity'.[30] Anger at the prospect of partition led the *Independent* to encourage the nascent Irish Volunteers when the *Freeman* and the Irish party leadership were trying to discourage them.[31]

The spectre of civil war

Asquith's proposals were followed by a period when Britain seemed on the brink of civil war. The 'Curragh mutiny' in March, when Army officers chose to resign rather than act against the UVF, was followed by the landing of a shipload of UVF rifles at Larne in April. Redmond asserted his control over the rapidly spreading Irish Volunteers, but their

Source: Courtesy of the National Library of Ireland

original separatist-oriented leadership continued to operate independently. As the government pressurised the IPP leadership to agree to further concessions to the Ulster Unionists, fears were expressed that local UVF and Irish Volunteer units might collide and embroil the whole country. The Buckingham Palace Conference of 21–24 July, called by the King in person, broke down over disagreements about the area to be excluded. The landing of arms at Howth on 26 July by the separatist Irish Volunteer faction, followed by the deaths of three people and the wounding of many others when British troops fired on a jeering crowd at Bachelors' Walk, provoked Nationalist outrage. Though the government and IPP defused the situation by blaming the officials on the scene while exculpating their superiors, the possibility of civil war distracted attention from the European crisis until the actual outbreak of war on 1–4 August.

Just before the Curragh Mutiny, the *Independent* praised a speech by the General Officer in Command in Ireland, General Sir Arthur Paget declaring that if ordered north the Army would act without question.[32] The Curragh Mutiny provoked angry complaints that the Conservatives substituted an 'Army Veto' for the Lords' veto. 'The Sword Rules Parliament Once More' declared the headline-writers. 'Home Rule Prospects Fading…Effects of the Wait and See Policy…British Mutiny Condoned…Disgusting Exhibition of Government Weakness – Banal Excuses and Explanations'. An angry editorial proclaimed this was worse even than partition; the government yielded to General Gough like a 'debilitated old man' before a 'robust prize- fighter'.[33]

After the Larne gunrunning ('Ulster Filibusters' Coup – Law Set at Defiance by Unionists – Wild Stories of Piracy and Gunrunning Under Arms') the *Independent* called for the UVF leaders to be prosecuted, declaring that the 'cowardly and ludicrous' government encouraged Carsonite aggression.[34] It repeatedly denounced the prospect of conciliating the Unionists by whittling down Home Rule through permanent partition and the exclusion of customs and the post office from the Dublin Parliament's authority. The *Independent* protested that too many sacrifices had been made; they only emboldened Unionists to demand more concessions.[35] Still assuming that calls for partition represented a Unionist attempt to wreck all-Ireland Home Rule rather than Ulster Unionist desire to save themselves at the expense of their southern allies, the *Independent* declared that since British Unionist leaders accepted the principle of Home Rule Irish Unionists should drop partition and join Nationalists in securing workable financial arrangements.[36] It suggested Ulster might get additional seats as a quid pro quo.

As Parliament debated further concessions to the Ulster Unionists, the *Independent* recalled how often the Irish people had been told Carson was bluffing; now, it complained, he held the government in the hollow of his hand. 'King Carson and King George...Dictating to His Majesty on Home Rule bill; the Irish People as "Traditional Enemies"; No Amending "Tomfoolery" for Him'.[37] It shared Childers' fear that the bill might be turned into a strictly federalist measure, specifically precluding future dominion status.[38] The crowning danger, the editorial writer thought, was that from their new position of strength the Unionists would accept Asquith's offer of partition, leaving Irish services fragmented and the country worse off than before.[39] 'We hope the agitation throughout this country may be strong enough to avert such a calamity'.[40]

There was, however, a limit to how far opposition to partition could be taken. The *Freeman* suggested that the *Independent's* denunciation of 'the worst arrangement that could be devised' meant the IPP should bring down government and Home Rule bill rather than accept partition. The *Independent* repudiated this suggestion, and attacked the adoption of such a position by William O'Brien as 'illogical and senseless'.[41] When George V called the Buckingham Palace conference it combined calls for Redmond to stand firm with angry predictions that the Irish party would 'go on surrendering so long as Sir Edward Carson insists on making demands', accused the 'cowardly' Liberals of using the King to conceal their own responsibility for 'the dismemberment conference' and insinuated that they had colluded with Carson.[42] It paused only to note an 'Austrian tragedy', the assassination of Archduke Franz Ferdinand, as a long-term threat to the peace of Europe since the new heir would find it difficult to hold the Hapsburg Empire together after Franz Josef's death.[43]

The Bachelor's Walk shootings (stray bullets struck the *Independent's* auxiliary offices across the river at Carlisle Buildings) were denounced as further proof of official favouritism. The breakdown of the Buckingham Palace conference was welcomed: 'There is enough vitality in the country to resist any further mutilation. Ireland can no longer be treated as a corpse on the dissecting table'.[44] Within a few days the *Independent* called for Ulster and Irish Volunteers to join forces against Germany.[45]

Between war and rising

The outbreak of war seemed to place the Home Rule question on an entirely new basis. Some commentators even thought Carson would be left politically isolated by the Conservative and Unionist protests against the passage (and suspension) of the Home Rule bill in September 1914 after Redmond's dramatic declaration of support for the Allied war effort. There were predictions that the war would bring Unionists and Nationalists together; at the same time many on both sides justified participation as strengthening their postwar position vis-à-vis their rivals. The war was expected to be short; as it continued pre-war fears and discontent re-emerged. Nationalists were particularly disturbed by the formation of a Liberal-Conservative coalition in May 1915, in which Carson held office.

The *Independent* reacted to the war with a vigorous pro-recruiting line, presented partly as a means of avoiding partition:

> If the Ulster Orangemen can with truth charge us with hanging back when our help would be of value while they send their thousands to the front there will be no answer to their claim for the partition of Ireland. If the volunteers of the South would follow the example of the National Volunteers from Belfast, Mr Redmond would be able to redeem his pledges and avert the calamity.[46]

This did not make it less suspicious of the Asquith government. In August 1914 it backed Redmond's demand that the Home Rule act should be put on the statute book immediately rather than waiting until the end of what was expected to be a brief war. At first it hoped Carson's intransigence would leave him isolated.[47] When the act was passed amidst Unionist protests (and immediately suspended) it complained the government were 'prepared to surrender entirely too much'. The promise of an Amending bill gave Unionists every incentive to persevere with audacious and mischievous bluster; the Lords' Veto had been replaced with an Ulster veto.[48] The cartoonist Gordon Brewster showed Lloyd George as a tailor, fitting a suspicious 'Pat' with his new Home Rule suit.[49]

In the early stages of the war, the paper's principal concerns were the growing tax burden and the Irish party's intolerance of criticism. Murphy's belief that Harrington was chiefly responsible for the *Independent's* sales, which shot up with the demand for war news, allowed the editor to exert a restraining influence over the proprietor's demand for more criticism of the IPP. The *Independent* accepted the formation of a coalition government in May 1915 as inevitable, but warned that Irish Nationalists required extra vigilance. Carson's appointment to the Cabinet aroused particular concern. An editorial writer thought it bizarre that he might now prosecute those who made seditious speeches.[50]

DUBLIN, SATURDAY, JUNE 10, 1916.

SPOILING THE FIT.

"IN A TRAP"

Court Martial on Co. Surveyor

aware that the paper "Nationality" was circulated through the country.

Mr. Hanna read an extract from the MS. found in accused's house as follows:—

It is not possible to find a reason for the people deserting the wholesome food of native production and taking to white bread

AMOROUS MASON

Wooed and Jilted a Cook

Source: Courtesy of the National Library of Ireland

    The *Independent* reported the trial of Sean MacDiarmada for a speech 'calculated to discourage recruiting', which incorporated extensive quotations from Carson's advocacy of rebellion and exhortations to imitate that distinguished statesman. Healy, defence counsel, reminded the judge his client might become a Cabinet Minister.[51] Carson resigned a few months later and joined Lord Northcliffe in accusing the government of mismanaging the war. The *Independent* attacked Carson's 'irresponsible' criticism and demanded that Northcliffe's papers should be closed under the Defence of the Realm Act. (Several Irish separatist papers had been suppressed in the first months of the war).[52] By the end of the year it feared Unionist Ministers would dilute the Home Rule act.[53]

Sea-green incorruptible?

The 1916 Rising triggered the conflicting expectations which had been frozen at the outbreak of war. Lloyd George undertook an initiative aimed at bringing about immediate Home Rule on the basis of six-county partition (to be renegotiated after the war). The *Independent's* role as a focus for Nationalist opposition when most advanced Nationalists were imprisoned or disorganised represents its most important direct intervention in the Ulster Crisis.

The *Independent* initially presented the 1916 Rising as inspired by Carson's example. At Murphy's direction, this became a wider attack on the Liberals and IPP. On 1 May Murphy composed a long memorandum for Harrington's guidance. Murphy spilled out his political frustration, declaring that the principal blame for the Rising lay, not with Carson and his followers,[54] but with the Liberal Government 'who permitted them to form an armed body of men for the avowed purpose of rebellion. This example was not lost on the rest of Ireland and the whole country became an armed camp of irresponsible bodies of men while the government looked on approvingly'. Sections of Murphy's memorandum were reproduced in *Independent* editorials as the paper accused the Irish party of encouraging Liberal reluctance to take firm action against Carson, of first dismissing the UVF as trivial bluffers and then falling into a panic; Liberal and IPP reluctance to repress Carson was equated with their reluctance to take action against Larkinism.[55]

As early as the evening of 5 May, when only seven executions had taken place, the paper's London correspondent distinguished between physical-force separatists provoked by Carson, who deserved leniency, and the 'anarchical syndicalism' of Liberty Hall.[56] At Murphy's prompting, the paper declared the Liberals' 1906 repeal of the Arms act at Redmond's request to be one of their greatest blunders, and demanded the disarming of all Volunteer forces.[57] The *Independent* noted that the *Freeman* devoted more space to blaming the *Independent* for the Rising (because of its criticisms of the Liberals and the IPP, its encouragement for the Irish Volunteers in 1914 and its publication at the outbreak of the war of suggestions that the Militia Ballot act could be used to implement

conscription) than attacking Carson. The *Independent* called the accusations deliberate untruths 'inspired by malice engendered by its own
failure and envy of the success which has been attained by this journal',
accused the *Freeman* of opportunistically supporting Connolly and
Larkin in 1913, and suggested it wanted the *Independent* suppressed so
Freeman staff could jobhunt in peace.

The *Independent* feared removal of Sinn Féiners from the civil service
might become a purge of Catholics and Nationalists. It pointed out that
no attempt was made to remove civil servants who supported UVF
threats of armed resistance,[58] and claimed that Eoin MacNeill and other
arrested Volunteer activists who had not joined the Rising were no
more treasonable than the unarrested UVF.[59] The *Independent* noted
with increasing disquiet suggestions by British Conservative newspapers
that Home Rule with partition might come into immediate effect and
reports that Lloyd George had offered six-county exclusion to the
Ulster Unionists. 'Too many concessions have been made [to Ulster]
already. Is there to be no concession to Ireland?'[60] When the government actually proposed such a compromise, and with most advanced
Nationalist papers shut down, the *Independent* led the campaign against
the 'hateful and pernicious' Irish party decision to support it.[61] Two or
three pages daily were devoted to denunciations of the proposals by
local government bodies and newspapers. 'Against Exclusion – Irish
Press Emphatic – Chorus of Condemnation...The entire Nationalist
Press of Ireland is uncompromisingly determined to resist the exclusion
of any part of Ulster, with the exception of what may be called the
"tied" journals...extremely few and unimportant – which maintain dis-
creet silence'. The *Independent* claimed the indignant letters which filled
several columns daily represented only a fragment of those received.[62] It
did, however, print letters from supporters of the proposal.[63]

It complained that while pretending to consider the terms, the Irish
party secretly endorsed 'the national theft' and set about carrying it by
the dark arts of cajolery and wirepulling.[64] The *Independent* demanded a
'broad and generous' Home Rule measure for an undivided Ireland,
and suggested Unionists might be offered extra parliamentary representation.[65] It commented bitterly that the party's negotiators had not got
all-Ireland Home Rule because they would not demand it,[66] and that
after committing the 'fatal blunder' in 1914 of agreeing 'at Mr Lloyd
George's breakfast table' to optional exclusion of four counties, the IPP
were now presenting the Unionists with two additional counties as a
reward for their 'sacrifice' and exerting their strength to squelch the
protests of the nation; it was just as well that the Unionists had not held
out for nine counties.[67] It expressed retrospective regret that the
country had been restrained by misguided loyalty from protesting 'with

THE UNITED SMASH 'EM UPS.

"We won't have it; we won't have it."

Scene—Shows the ring of wreckers dancing around the pole of Temporary Arrangement.

O'Brien.—Lloyd George's cherished action
May peace in Ireland make,
So once again to faction
Does rotten Cork awake.

(Chorus.)

Ring a ring of wreckers, oh,
Diehards, frauds and checkers, oh,
Geese and foxes here combine
Fast Home Rule to undermine.

Healy.—By House of Lords I mean to stick
This scheme to circumvent,
A limb of Cork is bound to kick
Against dismemberment.

Lansdowne.—With this dissent I'm overjoyed,
For if this measure fails,
Behind the broken scheme of Lloyd
May follow crowded jails.

Murphy.—On matters turfy old William Murphy
Bestows a lot of care;
No soil or grass we should let pass
But keep like penny fare.

Small Boy.—Taffy was a Welshman, Taffy was a thief,
Taffy would ensnare us with pretence of relief.
If we would save our bacon Taffy off must stay,
For, like old Daddy Aiken, he'd steal a lump away.

Alf Fox.—I stand for Ireland all intact
With alien spite and Ulster fact,
And so with joy I hail a split
That British bonds may closer knit.

S. Unionist.—If we Home Rule away could drive,
Oh how we'd hold our station,
And on tame toleration thrive
And green conciliation.

Diehard.—Where cant and sham do weakly rage
With feelings soft and green
The Diehard finds a proper stage
For anti-Irish spleen.

P.L.G.—No ring of wreck or discontent
Could be complete in grumbles
Without a type to represent
Some gas-inflated Bumbles.

A. M. W.

Leader cartoon by Tom Laler: 'Alf Fox' represents the *Irish Times*
Source: Courtesy of the National Library of Ireland

vehemence' against the concessions of 1914. Devlin's claim that acceptance of partition now would prevent the creation of a Unionist-
controlled executive in the excluded area were dismissed out of hand.[68]
'It is no wonder that we are seriously confronted with the creation of
an Irish Alsace, and that Sir Edward Carson is the winner. The man of
grit and backbone always scores'.[69] Brewster updated his 1914 cartoon
to show Lloyd George spoiling the 'Home Rule coat' by cutting off its
Ulster tail.[70]

Rumours circulated among Redmondites that Murphy wished to
displace Redmond. The *Independent* replied that Murphy had no parliamentary ambitions, or he would have crawled to Redmond like the
jobhunters. Murphy was also ridiculed by D.P. Moran's *Leader*, which
supported the scheme as the best deal available; Moran argued that with
no coherent alternative organisation available, rejecting the IPP would
reduce Nationalist Ireland to helpless chaos.[71] The *Leader* cartoonist,
Tom Lalor, depicted Murphy as Don Quixote joined in an unholy
alliance with Unionist diehards and contrasted his professions of patriotism with the *Independent's* lukewarmness towards the Gaelic League and
coverage of dubious Dublin music-halls.[72]

Past statements by Redmond and his lieutenants calling partition
'an abomination and a blasphemy' only acceptable to 'degenerate
Irishmen' were reprinted prominently, in a manner previously reserved
for 'Larkinisms' during the 1913–14 lockout.[73] The Redmondites were
accused of being bribed by the prospect of official salaries, and compared to the MPs who passed the Union.[74] Lehane published articles
on the administrative problems involved in partition, calling it 'imprac-
ticable and unworkable'.[75] A 'special representative' toured Ulster reporting widespread Nationalist opposition to the scheme.[76] Dillon told
T.P. O'Connor that several *Independent* agents were touring Ulster
encouraging opposition and promoting the paper.[77]

The paper pointed out angrily that while Unionist leaders told their
followers partition would be permanent, northern Nationalists were
assured by the Irish party and their 'Government Treasury organ' that it
would be temporary.[78] The *Independent* accused the Irish party leaders
of deliberate 'bamboozlement':

> The flag of partition, dyed with an 'abomination and a blasphemy', is held
> aloft for our reverence. This unclean thing, so accursed two or three years
> ago, is now to represent the fruition of our hopes. Every good and genuine
> Irishman must despise it, and in the interests of their country and its reputa-
> tion, and in vindication of their own manhood, we ask the people to
> trample upon it....Even if the agreement be regarded as provisional

now…the six counties…will be enabled to appear before the Imperial Conference as a separate unit whose right to live apart from the rest of Ireland has been acknowledged.[79]

There were already signs that the *Independent* was benefiting from discontent with the party. Fr M.J. Devine of Rathcoole declared that Redmond had produced

> an absurd bungling concoction from his official organ offering a theory that the *Independent* in some mysterious fashion caused the revolt.…An attempt is being made to muzzle Nationalist opinion in the North – the Party 'henchmen' are busy, but, thanks to the indefatigable efforts of powerful agencies like the *Irish Independent* everything promises that the day of the Party's dictatorship is well nigh spent.[80]

Healy predictably complained that he and O'Brien, who were also opposing compromise on partition, were unfairly treated by Harrington because their speeches were not reported in full. Murphy retorted that if Harrington had run the *Independent*, as Healy wanted, on the same lines as Dennehy ran the *Independent and Nation* 'in which money was poured as into a bottomless pit' there would be no *Independent* and Healy would face the tender mercies of the *Freeman*.[81]

The partition proposals were eventually approved at a Belfast convention of Ulster Nationalists, where much of Devlin's speech was devoted to attacking Murphy and the *Independent*. The paper, which had repeatedly predicted the convention would not be fairly conducted, reported accusations of packing and vote rigging made against the leadership by the anti-partition minority (centred in Fermanagh and Tyrone). 'It is absurd, therefore, to describe this monstrosity as a settlement by consent'. The performance of the IPP leaders was contrasted with Carson, who showed 'downright determination has its reward'.[82] The new province should be called 'Georgia' (after Lloyd George).[83] When the proposals were further watered down by the government to appease diehard Unionist Cabinet members and negotiations collapsed, the *Independent* declared the IPP leaders had been treated like 'children'. Asquith was 'a discredited and mere huckstering politician…a wily trickster' whose behaviour vindicated the *Independent's* warnings against Liberal trickery. The disaster came from the abandonment of independent opposition by the Irish party; Ireland needed uncompromising negotiators like Parnell rather than 'beggars' and 'jobhunters'.[84] 'Only full Colonial Home Rule can finally and satisfactorily settle the Irish question'.[85]

The primary responsibility for the breakdown of the settlements rested with the diehards among the Conservative Cabinet Ministers; but the *Independent* certainly contributed to the outcome by rallying opposition, highlighting the differences between Nationalist and Unionist expectations, and helping to pressurise the IPP leaders into statements which limited their 'wriggle room.'

Seeking a solution

The aftermath of the 1916 Rising further strengthened the *Independent's* position as leading newspaper of Nationalist Ireland. The *Freeman's Journal*, undercapitalised and with traditions of long-winded news coverage, found it harder to adapt to war conditions than the condensed *Independent*; now its association with the crumbling IPP led many readers to desert it for its rival. Harrington's restraint to Murphy's calls to attack the Irish party had rested less on ideology than on fear that the paper would fall victim to a political boycott; now it was the beneficiary of a boycott. The *Independent* benefited from the change in Irish public opinion, but could not direct it; it reinforced Murphy's attempts to move elite opinion towards a Dominion settlement, but could not create a political force capable of putting such a settlement into practice.

The paper continued to support the war. It paid tribute to the Ulster Division ('Ulster Charge – Stirring Story of heroism – A Terrible Ordeal') as well as the exploits of the 16th Irish Division at Guillemont and Guinchy (though it complained the former received more publicity than the latter.) As Sinn Féin coalesced in 1917 the *Independent* argued that its victories did not represent a mandate for separatism but a revolt against IPP incompetence; the paper endorsed Archbishop William Walsh's claim during the Longford by-election that Ireland was 'practically sold', and contrasted Redmondite disavowals of partition in 1917 with their actions during the Lloyd George talks.[86] The paper continued to present Carson as Lloyd George's evil genius, raised to the War Cabinet 'as a reward for his services in trying to dismember Ireland and an encouragement to the partitionists'.[87] It protested that official arms raids on Nationalist volunteers were not extended to the UVF.

Murphy was a member of the 1917–18 Irish Convention, where moderate Nationalists and Unionists tried to reach a compromise settlement. He advocated Dominion Home Rule but found himself isolated most of the time. Autocratic and accustomed to command, Murphy chafed at the inconclusive discussions and the preponderance of Nationalist and Unionist party activists.

Convention proceedings were supposedly confidential, but while Irish papers were forbidden on pain of suppression to report the debates, these appeared in British papers circulating freely in Ireland. At one point, wishing to publish in the *Independent* an analysis of the Irish financial situation submitted to the Convention by the Irish-born Liberal MP Thomas Lough, Murphy warned Harrington 'You might refer to the Defence of the Realm Order relating to the publication of Convention proceedings and if you think it would transgress the order it should not of course be published'.[88] In March 1918 he told Harrington that Stephen Gwynn, one of the pro-compromise faction in the Irish party delegation, complained about a pro-Sinn Féin letter in the *Independent* attacking Gwynn and J.J. Clancy for their willingness to give up customs:

> I explained that the Editor was most particular in not publishing editorially any matter that would indicate any knowledge of the proceedings of the convention...there was of course a prohibition against publication which the English Press were freely transgressing. You might ask Mr Rice and Mr Lynch to be careful in regard to this matter, as I am the only newspaper proprietor at the Convention.[89]

Murphy helped to organise a split within the Nationalist representation, frustrating the efforts of Redmondites and Midletonite Unionists to broker a settlement involving surrender of customs (though not excise) by the new Irish Parliament.

In the run-up to the 1918 general election, the *Independent* continued to attack the IPP as Liberal stooges, denounce federalist proposals as fraudulent, and compare Carson to the Bolsheviks. It attributed the defeat of the IPP to its 'humbug and corruption'. At the same time, Murphy maintained backstairs contact with the Government; the *Independent* predicted the new Lord-Lieutenant, Viscount French, might be prepared to offer concessions. After Murphy's death on 26 June 1919 the *Independent* continued to advocate his policy, claiming the mandate given by the 1918 general election would be fulfilled by a Dominion settlement. The paper welcomed Northcliffe's advocacy of Dominion Home Rule for Ireland, wishing 'more power to his elbow' if he was sincere.[90] However, it criticised the Northcliffe-owned *Times'* advocacy of partition and attacked the *Freeman's Journal* for insufficient zeal in denouncing it.[91] It gave respectful coverage to pro-Dominion groups such as the Irish Dominion League founded by Sir Horace Plunkett and Parnell's biographer Capt Henry Harrison. The *Independent* was, however, extremely critical of a breakaway group led by Gwynn, now Irish correspondent for the *Observer.* Gwynn's claims that Nationalists did not understand Ulster, some form of partition was inevitable in the short term, and the Better Government of Ireland act might be acceptable if amended were dismissed as the work of 'an effete politician', whose 'fantasies' might unfortunately be mistaken in Britain for serious expressions of Irish opinion.[92]

Irish advocates of Dominion Home Rule had some effect on elite opinion in Britain. In Ireland they were widely dismissed as 'West British' notables without mass support, undermining the Dáil by encouraging British fantasies that 'moderate Nationalists' might work a solution independently of Sinn Féin 'gunmen'. It was considered unlikely that Britain would concede Dominion Home Rule, or observe it if conceded. The unfortunate negotiating experiences of the Redmondites and the intensifying bloodshed of the Anglo-Irish conflict caused many Sinn Féiners to look on compromise as evil and those who advocated abandonment of the Republic as betraying the martyrs.

Towards dominion status – and partition

As the situation in Ireland deteriorated, Lloyd George's Coalition government tried to impose its own Irish settlement. As a first step it brought forward its own Home Rule legislation. The Long Committee report of December 1919 proposed a federal structure as the basis for the Better Government of Ireland act, which passed through Parliament in 1920, while Ulster was consumed by sectarian violence. Its provisions were a dead letter in Southern Ireland, but by removing the new Northern Ireland statelet from the equation, it opened the way for the Dominion settlement of the December 1921 Anglo-Irish Treaty. Nationalists had gained sovereignty but lost on partition.

The Long Committee's proposals, variously described by its advocates as federal, semi-federal, and Dominion – 'a most peculiar blend' were dissected by the *Independent* to show how far they fell short of Dominion status; the proposed Council of Ireland was dismissed as 'a mere academic debating society' and the proposals put forward by Long to heal the '"chronic wound" of Irish discontent' were described as 'a poison, or irritant called partition…slightly diluted [and christened] self-determination'.[93] The Better Government of Ireland bill was 'such a negation of the principles of self-government and democracy that the Irish people, unless bereft of all self-respect and dignity, could not give it a moment's serious consideration'. The Council of Ireland would 'give a permanent veto to the Carsonites…designed to divide and conquer Ireland…they who agreed with the proposal of President Wilson that the world should be made safe for democracy, accede to the claim of a privileged Irish minority to rule the majority'; the financial provisions were 'a swindle upon Ireland'.[94]

The newspaper proclaimed Dominion Home Rule with no partition the minimum Ireland would accept. 'Irish Partition and Plunder Scheme – Meets with Arctic Reception – Nobody Wants It – Imposture Rejected by Irish Press'.[95] Asquith was accused of 'humbug and hypocrisy' for belatedly advocating Dominion Status for Ireland when he could no longer grant it. Bonar Law's declaration that Dominion Status was impossible because it would produce an Irish republic provoked the *Independent* to ask if Plunkett would be deported for advocating Dominion Status; it added that the author of the Blenheim speech was 'imposing on Ireland to-day a Prussian militarism and despotism'.[96] Gordon Brewster regularly portrayed Lloyd George in jackboots and a spiked helmet.

The *Independent* quoted Smuts' denial that Dominion Status inevitably meant secession from the empire and pointed out that Britain had allowed the Dominions greater autonomy as compared to their pre-war status. They were now free to declare war of their own volition, join the League of Nations separately and appoint ambassadors. 'They will act as allies only when [Britain] has right on her side. If they cannot side with her they will remain neutral…England recognises that the Colonies cannot be kept in leading strings forever…Only in Ireland is the demand for self-government branded by England as a crime'.[97] It cited denunciations of the bill by William Jellett (the ultra-Unionist MP for Trinity College Dublin), and the Home Ruler Revd J.B. Armour (presented as speaking for a large minority of Presbyterians) as proof that nobody wanted the bill. 'In the Local Government elections [which produced nationalist majorities on many councils in south and west Ulster, including Fermanagh and Tyrone County Councils, and a strong Labour-Nationalist contingent on Belfast Corporation] Carsonism has been killed in Ulster…if a plebiscite were taken it is doubtful whether even two counties would accept partition'.[98]

Carson was described as Lloyd George's puppet-master and proclaimed the 'evil genius of the British Empire'.[99] An *Independent* editorial complained that if Nationalists were court-martialled for making speeches likely to disturb the peace, Carson should have been court-martialled for a 'truculent and bigoted outburst' at Belfast on 12 July 1919, which compared Plunkett to Lundy.[100] When Carson spoke sectarian riots had already broken out in Derry city. The *Independent* attacked the government's lukewarm response to the Derry situation and called for the 12 July celebrations to be banned 'to protect the Catholics and Nationalists of Ulster from wanton attacks...nothing short of a miracle can prevent bloodshed'.[101] After Carson's speech rioting spread to Belfast, continuing well into 1922. The ensuing horrors received extensive coverage in the *Independent*. The formation of the B-Specials was denounced as 'First Partition Move: Arming Carsonite Forces; Outrageous Step...Dire Prospects'.[102]

The final ratification of the Better Government of Ireland act was denounced as 'the greatest sham of the century'.[103] The opening of the Northern Ireland Parliament was 'Belfast Comedy – The Swearing-In of the Six-County Parliament – Performance Falls Flat – Unenthusiastic Crowds'. An editorial predicted that only jobhunters would benefit from the new institutions.[104] 'Toll of Death Celebrates Belfast Parliament' declared a subsequent issue,[105] while Lord Londonderry's proposals to extend state education were described as an 'education pogrom' against Catholic schools.[106]

The *Independent* welcomed the Truce, declaring Orange Ulster the only dark spot. It subsequently raged that the British were tolerating the coercion of Fermanagh and Tyrone. While martial law had been enforced in the south Ireland, no such measures were taken against an 'organised massacre of the Belfast minority'.[107] During the ensuing months it repeatedly called for Dominion status. When talks broke down temporarily over Lloyd George's insistence that Ireland must remain within the empire, it told readers peace was still possible and praised Smuts for publicly advocating an Irish Dominion.[108] It repeatedly urged delegates to abandon their insistence on a republic and concentrate on avoiding partition. During the final stages of the Treaty negotiations it said they must be pushed to a conclusion; a new war would be 'disastrous'.[109] De Valera and his followers later alleged that the newspaper shared responsibility for the delegates' final decision to accept a dominion settlement; this set the stage for the *Independent's* subsequent rivalry with another dominant political party (Fianna Fail) and its 'kept newspaper' (the *Irish Press*).

The *Independent* immediately welcomed the Treaty as 'the best possible settlement' and congratulated the delegates, predicting that Northern Ireland would see sense and come in as a business proposition, rather than facing a crushing financial burden. It emphasised how far the Treaty went beyond the Better Government of Ireland act, claiming that the new measure practically undid partition and raised 'one of Europe's oldest nations' from a mere local body for 'Southern Ireland' to a Dominion and equal partner in the Commonwealth. Its London correspondent declared that the plenipotentiaries won this great victory by making it clear to their British counterparts that they were determined to stick to their ideals and prepared to die for them (an implied contrast to Redmond) .[110] The next day's editorial noted 'A Regrettable Development': Eamon de Valera's pronouncement against the Treaty.

The *Independent* continued to highlight the plight of Belfast Nationalists while the South debated the Treaty (partly to offset British Conservative press coverage of growing unrest in the new state and the plight of southern loyalist refugees.). It carried regular casualty lists, accusing the Craig government of acquiescence in loyalist butchery and seeking 'to convince the world that the victims of Orange fanaticism are really responsible for their own deaths'.[111]

One horror followed another: 'Orange Fiends Fire into Hospital – The Lowest Infamy Yet – Patients' Plight – Shelter Sought Under Beds – Wholesale Evictions'.[112] The *Independent* complained that while British troops could repel Irish Republican Army incursions at Belleek, there was no sign of drastic action against the sectarian killers. Scathing comparisons were made between British official concern over the massacre of Armenians and obliviousness to the horrors perpetrated in the North.[113] It publicised the plight of the numerous Catholic refugees who fled south, arguing that since the British government rightly compensated loyalists who fled Ireland after such incidents as the West Cork massacre, they should help these people who were, nominally, British subjects.[114]

The outbreak of the Civil War finally diverted the *Independent*'s attention from Belfast. Although in later years it continued to criticise the Northern Ireland government as a ramshackle arrangement propped up by bigotry and subsidies, whose financial plight vindicated Murphy's prediction that Home Rule without fiscal autonomy would breed wasteful irresponsibility, the newspaper's primary focus would be on the affairs of the new Free State. Its coverage of the Ulster Crisis, however, remains an useful source for the discontents of Edwardian Nationalism and the way in which these fuelled Nationalist reluctance to compromise on partition. It also displays how the decay of IPP control over Catholic-Nationalist civil society allowed the development of a new form of newspaper based on consumerism rather than party political allegiance, and how this 'new journalism' was itself constrained by a highly-politicised society. Readership could not be translated straightforwardly into power; the newspaper proprietor could help to focus discontent, but ultimately could not direct it.

Appendix

Some Irish Independent sales figures, 1909–22

Certified by Craig Gardner – published in *Irish Independent* advertisements.

1909	Mar	n.a.	Sept	42,526
1910	Mar	47,614	Sept	49, 652
1911	Mar	51,416	Sept	54,300
1912	Mar	54,207	Sept	55,832
1913	Mar	58,327	Sept	59,699
1914	Mar	66,179	Sept	106,908
1915	Mar	92,497	Sept	98,156
1916	Mar	92,497	Sept	n.a.
1917	Mar	97,532	Sept	n.a.
1918		n.a.		
1919		n.a.		
1920	Mar	125,987	Sept	n.a.
1921	Mar	142,595	Sept	122,443
1922	Mar	119,335		

12

The Conserving Crowd: Mass Unionist Demonstrations in Liverpool and Tyneside, 1912–13

D.M. Jackson and D.M. MacRaild

The popular campaign against the Third Home Rule bill in the major northern British cities has escaped the attention of most historians.[1] Such neglect relates to a perceived lack of importance attached to the issue of Ireland's constitutional status by 1912. Driven by what some have perceived as the 'Crisis of Conservatism'[2] and others have dubbed the 'apathy of Great Britain',[3] it has become commonplace to infer from scanty evidence that, unlike in 1885–86, the populace of the larger island cared little for the political struggle that so exercised their counterparts in the 'sister isle'. Yet during the high water mark of constitutional opposition to a Dublin Parliament, the cause of Protestant Ulster, as it was portrayed, actually mobilised hundreds of thousands of supporters outside of Ireland, particularly in the industrial areas of northern England. Large Irish communities helped to shape the particular politics of such towns and cities; whilst a degree of turbulence may also have been a function of the staunch factionalism of urban politics. Whatever the cause, the politics crowds came out in force to denigrate the potential disintegration of the United Kingdom. The fact that there was no general election in this period ensured additional importance for this series of massive popular demonstrations against Home Rule. Two of the largest of these took place in Liverpool in 1912 and Wallsend-upon-Tyne in 1913, and provide the main focus of this study. Drawing upon detailed press accounts from both locations, as well as exceptionally rare manuscript records of Orange Order activity in Tyneside and County Durham, this chapter seeks to explore the emotional and political affinities of the ordinary members of the protesting Unionist crowd. The assessment of such activities amidst two different political cultures – radical-liberal Tyneside and Tory Liverpool – enhances the discussion that follows.

I

When there are precious few manuscript resources, and a total absence of oral testimony, press reports of crowd action can provide useful evidence of how common people felt about important issues such as Home Rule. Yet we must tread carefully. In the past some historians have unhelpfully conflated crowds with riots.[4] Despite acknowledging the conservatism of eighteenth and early nineteenth century crowds, such approaches only led to a questionable teleology that saw 'the machine wrecker and rickburner [giving] way to the trades unionist and labour militant of the new industrial society'.[5] Furthermore, many labour historians have shown a primary concern for crowds who demanded change: in such studies, the crowd had at least the potential for violence and sought to break up, not maintain, orthodoxies. Yet this perspective is of little use to us as the mass meetings in Liverpool and Wallsend were undoubtedly 'conserving crowds', that saw in the defence of the Union a bundle of ideas that included the *maintenance* of prosperity, national security, and the continued ascendancy of the Protestant faith.

It would be more profitable therefore to turn to the work of Mark Harrison who has distilled and re-assessed some of the most important recent thinking on the subject of crowds. He has convincingly argued that nineteenth century crowds were in point of fact rarely violent, and that their function lay in their role as 'vehicles for the expression of cohesion', and for crowd members to perceive themselves as 'bearers of messages' and to be accepted as such.[6] The work of David Cannadine has also demonstrated the utility of applying techniques from other disciplines to the study of public ritual, but without becoming bogged down in theory.[7] Through his concept of 'circularity' Cannadine has provided perhaps the best definition of the importance of ritual in this period, albeit in a different context: 'it may well be that these spectacles were not just the expression of this sense of community: perhaps they were the community'.[8] This new methodology is applied to the study of Edwardian anti-Home Rule demonstrations to elicit the complex meaning of those events. It may well be that the only way that support for Ulster could be articulated was through participation in extravagant public parades and rallies. In such a context, the most effective ways of making their case was by expressing the continued dominance of their own urban territory, by taking to the streets. For, as one historian of the Orange Order has argued, 'claiming physical space entailed also claiming political and ideological space'.[9]

II

Between 1912 and 1914 the campaign to oppose Home Rule gathered pace under Carson's the energetic leadership. This movement gained support on both sides of the Irish Sea and in recognition of this Carson, Andrew Bonar Law, and other notable Unionists undertook a rigorous schedule of public engagements not just in Ulster, but also throughout the rest of the United Kingdom. This campaign was designed to pressure the government into at least calling a general election, but it also acted as a means of conveying to the Liberals that they were intractably serious in the opposition to the creation of a Dublin Parliament. It was no surprise therefore that following the signing of the Ulster Covenant in Belfast Carson and his Ulster coterie were to travel to England, via the Mersey, to scour the country for further support. Their peregrinations took in Liverpool, the only English city with a comparable sectarian culture to Belfast. When Carson's intended movements were broadcast, the Liverpool Workingmen's Conservative Association [LWMCA], whose chairman Archibald Salvidge was known as the Tory 'boss' of Liverpool,[10] decided to lay on an impressive welcome ceremony. The temper of this organisation was well captured by its secretary, James Thompson, who wrote a fiercely-worded letter to the *Liverpool Courier*, in which he saw fit to make a staggeringly bullish claim:

> In the Liverpool district there is the same loyalty, the same determination to fight in the last ditch in defence of the Union as was so remarkably shown yesterday in Ireland, and if it should be necessary for Ulster to 'hold the pass' I can honestly promise from a long and intimate knowledge of the spirit of the people of Liverpool and the surrounding constituencies that *at least 50,000 men will be ready and willing to stand by their fellow Loyalists in Ireland.* We await events, but at the right time the call, if necessary, will be made, and it will not be made in vain.[11]

This bellicose epistle set a foreboding tone, whilst the irresponsible oratory of F.E. Smith, Unionist MP for Liverpool Walton,[12] did nothing

to soothe the febrile atmosphere. Note his claim to a Belfast audience
in 1912 that 'if the Unionists of Liverpool are told that they have no
concern with the quarrel, and that they must stand idly by while the
liberties of Ulster are usurped, the rifles will go off themselves'.[13] This
demagoguery was typical of Smith. No doubt some of his constituents
were prepared to shed blood for the cause: yet the dominant tones of
those two remarkable autumn days in Liverpool were restraint and
decorum.

After an overnight journey from Belfast, Carson's ship, the aptly-
named *SS Patriotic*, steamed into the Mersey at seven in the morning to
be met with even larger crowds than had gathered to see the ship depart
Belfast Lough.[14] Representatives of the LWMCA and the Orange
Order had assembled at preordained locations and, at the allotted hour,
marched, with 'bands playing and banners flying', from all points of the
compass to be at the Pier Head (many took advantage of a specially
arranged tram service).[15] As well as the marchers many sympathisers,
'men and women of all ages and classes' had adopted the role of street-
side observers, so that one could have 'walked on the heads of the
densely packed mass of humanity from Sir Thomas Street to the Pier
head. It was a magnificent display'.[16] Even the Liberal papers were impressed: the *Mercury* noted that 'over 60,000 hardy souls had missed
their breakfast' before tramping through pouring rain 'mostly on foot'
to be present at the Pier Head. There, waiting for them, were a number
of Orange bands *en grande tenue* who entertained the sodden multitude
with 'hymn tunes'. Pastor Wise, Liverpool's most infamous Protestant
demagogue,[17] 'helped the memory of the singers by repeating the first
lines of the verses'.[18]

When Carson and his entourage had disembarked, they were ceremoniously welcomed to the city by Alderman Salvidge who asked
them to accept a formal address. 'The devotion which you have again
and again shown in the cause of Ireland and the unity of Empire', he
declaimed, 'are nowhere more appreciated than in Liverpool'. Salvidge
continued: 'we, the Unionists of Liverpool are equally resolute. We
Unionists of the Port which is connected with Belfast in so many ways,
stand by Ulster in this great struggle for political justice, Imperial unity
and religious liberty'.[19] And in concluding, he presented Carson with
an illuminated copy of the address amid renewed cheering. Carson,
standing bareheaded in the rain, was clearly moved. '[T]hough somewhat tired by his arduous campaign', he was in 'warrior mood'.[20] He
began by paying Liverpool the compliment that having just left the
solemnity of a determined Ulster he had found himself at home 'in

another Belfast'. He then modestly deflected Salvidge's praise by under-lining the significance of those early morning crowds. 'I am nothing in this fight. It is the cause that matters, and it is the cause the men of Liverpool now, and at all times, have sustained'.[21] Before they could leave the Pier Head however the horses of the two main carriages, which included Carson, Salvidge, Smith, and Londonderry were unhar-nessed and the vehicles were then drawn by 'sturdy men to the gaily decorated Conservative Club'. This unusual action was in fact an old English tradition (virtually obsolete by 1912) often associated with urban elections, which signified both literal support and ceremonial welcome.[22] This was made all the more symbolic considering that the occupants of one of the carriages included Lord 'Charlie' Beresford, tattooed admiral and third son of the Marquess of Waterford, and his pet Bulldog, Kora, 'a formidable looking beast' beribboned in red, white, and blue.[23] To many, despite the Irish connections, this bluff seaman was the personification of John Bull: the many popular depic-tions of him gave 'a sense of security: England was safe as long as Lord Charles and the Navy were on guard'.[24] Thus on a morning of symbol-ism the sight of the hero of *HMS Condor's* famous assault on Alexandria and a British Bulldog being towed by working men through the packed streets of Liverpool would have had particular resonance for such a patriotic crowd.

Was all this merely for the consumption of Liverpool and Belfast? In many ways it was; but Carson's arrival on the Mersey was reported in some detail in all the big national dailies with almost as much fervour as the Liverpool press. The *Daily Telegraph*, for example, noted that Salvidge had originally intended that the ceremonies should not begin until the Monday, but that 'local enthusiasm could not be restrained'.[25] The *Times* thought the loyalists of Liverpool were 'the British reserves in support of Ulster'. But, what struck them as most impressive was the almost exclusive proletarianism of the crowds. 'The multitude was com-posed entirely of the working classes', claimed the *Times*, 'thousands of them wore the Orange regalia. The war cries they shouted were those of the democracy of Belfast'.[26] The *Daily Mail* made much of the gath-ering as a public spectacle, stressing the somewhat cacophonous music that accompanied the procession. 'There were brass bands, concertina bands, reed bands and fife bands', and 'Sir Edward Carson's waggonette was pushed and pulled by a hundred willing hands'.[27] The *Pall Mall Gazette* was also impressed by the zeal of the demonstrators, and pointed out that although 'rain had been falling heavily', huge numbers of people – 'numbering not far short of a hundred thousand'[28] – had made their way to the landing stage or had lined the processional route. The Ulster leaders then retired to the comfort of the Unionist Club and the Adelphi Hotel in preparation for the enormous rally that was set to take place in Sheil Park on the Monday evening: one of the biggest political meetings in the history of Britain.

Those who wished to attend the meeting either took advantage of the specially organised tram services, or met at predestined points throughout the city from which they marched in close order to Sheil Park – much as they had done the previous Sunday morning to the Pier Head. Or as the *Times* put it admiringly: 'the labourers after a hard day's work in the sunshine at the docks and along the quays hurried to the three mustering points of the demonstration', and although they realised that it would be gone midnight when they returned home, 'their hearts were in the business'.[29] The first contingent of demonstrators arrived at about a quarter to eight, and for the next hour 'the orderly brigades of working men' arrived steadily with 'their bands their banners and Union Jacks, their regalia and their mottoes'. Their arrival was accompanied by stirring martial music that included old favourites like 'The Red, White, and Blue', 'Derry Walls', 'The Boys of the Old Brigade', and 'The Hero of Trafalgar'. It was an enormous crowd. The *Daily Post* thought the numbers involved to be at least 150,000, and would not have been surprised if the figure had exceeded 200,000. The organ also made much of the symbols displayed by the marchers, some more unorthodox than others: 'Flags, bannerettes, torches, swords, five pointed emblems, flags, caps, handkerchiefs, and occasionally babies were waved overhead amid cries intended to denote fealty to the Unionist leaders, and to the anti-Home Rule cause'.[30] The VIPs – Carson, Smith, Salvidge, Beresford, Londonderry and Viscount Templeton (another Irish landowner) – arrived at Sheil Park just before nine o'clock, and their entrance precipitated more cheering and the singing of 'Rule Britannia' and the national anthem. Although earlier in the evening Pastor George Wise had been welcomed with pyrotechnics, the organisers reserved their heaviest ordnance for the appearance of Sir Edward on the platform: the sight of whom was the cue for the unfurling of a massive Union Flag which was itself lit by the massive electric arc lamps that had been strung across the park, providing illumination on what must have been a pretty dark October evening. Indeed, the *Times* remarked that the multitude was so far spreading 'that their outer ranks were lost in the darkness'.[31]

Salvidge, as chair of the meeting, formally welcomed Carson and his colleagues by declaring that 'the vast mass of Lancashire people gave the lie to the assertion that [Ulster was]…out upon a bluffing expedition' and that if the Nationalists of the south of Ireland wanted to take Belfast they would 'have the men of Liverpool to reckon with'. Carson then rose to speak but was interrupted by a rendition of 'Auld Lang Syne', and he waited patiently for the singing to die down before he began his peroration. His first words were 'Well done Liverpool', at which someone in the crowd shouted, 'Well done Lancashire'. It was a long speech (the *Courier's* transcript of which is littered with regular interpolations of 'cheers', and 'loud cheers') and Carson used the opportunity to launch a snarling assault upon the Liberal government which had told Ulster that 'You really should fall into line with other Irishmen in the South and West', at which Ulster had replied that they had different attitudes to religion and loyalty – but their pleas had been dismissed by the supposedly treacherous government, or as Carson put it they had said 'damn your ideas of religion and damn your ideas of loyalty out you go'. Sir Edward took heart from the support that Liverpool had shown to his countrymen, and maintained that 'if there is a row I'd like to be in it with the Belfast men, and I'd like to have you with them. And I will (loud cheers)'.[32] After a brief speech from Lord Londonderry, F.E. Smith mounted the podium. He then proceeded to make one of his most extraordinary claims: as he calmly informed his audience that he had been speaking to three large Liverpool shipowners that day, and that they had said to him that 'if, and when, it comes to a fight between Ulster and the Irish Nationalists, we will undertake to give you three ships that will take over to help Ulster in her hour of need 10,000 young men of Liverpool'. This was greeted by wild applause, at which 'F.E.' seized the opportunity and asked 'If the cattle maimers are marching on Belfast and you can get the ships to take you there will you come to us?'[33] At which there were loud cries of 'Yes' and 'what about Charlie Beresford for Admiral?'[34]

To conclude the meeting, Sir Charles Petrie then moved the following resolution which was in many ways Liverpool's own Ulster Covenant:[35] 'This meeting of Liverpool citizens; representing all ranks of the Unionist party solemnly pledges itself to unite with Ulster in resisting Home Rule'. This was augmented by the resolve of nation's Orangemen, who through the Grand Master of England, William Watson Rutherford (Tory MP for West Derby in Liverpool), informed the congregation that 'he had a mandate from the whole of the Orange Lodges in England to say they would stand by Ulster in her time of trial'.[36] The high profile involvement of the Orange Order was crucial to interpreting the events of September 1912, in that we must not see this as simply a demonstration in support of the Tory party. Despite successfully utilising their support, the Conservatives could not control the Orangemen, and the lodges would have protested in some form or another over Home Rule whether it was official Unionist policy or not.[37]

A torch-lit procession back into the city centre then followed. As it wove its way through the streets of the city Carson and his lieutenants were cheered by the many thousands of people who had lined the streets and filled the windows of shops and houses with their eager faces. Pride of place in the procession was the 'grandest banner on parade', the 'beautiful white silk emblem' of the West Toxteth Conservative Women's Association, which declared: 'Unionism means Prosperity'.[38] The *Courier* thought that 'the torch light tattoo was a thrilling tableau in the great loyalist drama' – a drama whose chorus was provided by the marchers who sang popular songs of the day including 'Stop Yer Tickling Jock', and 'Dare to be a Daniel'.[39] When Carson's carriage reached the club at eleven o'clock the scene was one of high excitement. The building had been festooned with Union Jacks, and atop its parapets, surmounted by a sparkling crown, were the mottoes 'We Stand By Ulster', and 'We Will Not Have Home Rule'. The *Courier* in a burst of grandiloquence described the theatre of the occasion in a way that only they could:

> One could hear the rumbling tributes of salutation from multitudes who could only participate in the welcome from a distance. Amid such inspiriting surroundings the fearless commander of the Ulster forces and his courageous brother officers witnessed the march past of brigades far more numerous than the valiant hosts who vanquished Britain's foes on the field of Waterloo.[40]

It was estimated that over 40, predominantly Orange, bands took part in the march past, including a pipe band from Edinburgh which carried a placard that read 'Midlothian For Ulster'. Furthermore, Liverpool's hinterland's were also well represented: for apart from the 'Unionist regiments' that came from every ward of the city, there were deputations from Birkenhead, Bootle, Wirral, Wallasey, Widnes and St. Helens.[41] The procession went past the platform at a 'swinging pace', upon which next to Carson stood F.E. Smith who was described as 'the brilliant cavalier of militant Unionism' and Salvidge as 'the Field-Marshall of Liverpool's Conservative Workingmen – the political warriors of the city'. Of this holy trinity none was more impressed than the lantern-jawed Dubliner who had been gratified by this red carpet treatment; or as his earliest biographer put it 'Liverpool sister of Belfast, rough, big hearted, Protestant, Unionist, gave Carson a great welcome'.[42] The reception that most probably invigorated the Ulster leader, 'You have lit the torch of Empire', Carson remarked to the *Courier's* reporter, 'Yes', the pressman replied, 'and by Heaven it shall never be extinguished by the hands of traitors'.[43] The singing of the national anthem brought the demonstration to a close, eight minutes before midnight.

III

Just over a year later, Carson experienced a similarly enthusiastic reception, this time in Wallsend-on-Tyne. It is the obvious parallels between events on Merseyside and Tyneside that throws new light on our understanding of the support 'Protestant Ulster' received outside of the north of Ireland. Notwithstanding the Tories' usually patchy electoral support in the region, the north-east of England was an important arena for Unionist demonstrations in the years before 1914. Although sectarian politics on Tyneside was of a lower order of magnitude than in Liverpool, and while the imprint of north-east Unionism was also not very heavy, it was significant enough for the Unionist party to convene two large demonstrations there as part of its two-year campaign against Home Rule. To be sure, Tyneside cannot be compared in size to Liverpool or its wider environs of Lancashire, but these politicians clearly saw the region as an important centre for their campaigns against the Home Rule bill. The concentration of shipyard workers reliant upon naval contracts, with their strong emotional and literal connections to other similar centres, and the ethnic make-up of those yards, was certainly seen by Bonar Law and others as a source of potential support, and historians have acknowledged the then Conservative party leader's astute reading of the demographic and economic aspects of Tyneside culture.[44] While the press coverage of Tyneside Unionist meetings in the local press may have been more subdued, Orange Lodge reports for that region, in contrast to Merseyside and the north-west, have remained largely extant, and so allow certain insights into the activities of ordinary men and women aligned to the Unionist cause. Although it was usually the case that local press coverage revealed more about Irish politics than did lodge minutes, there were significant exceptions. This was particularly true when Carson's efforts to preserve the Act of Union were in full flow. Then, lodges made regular reference to the anti-Home Rule campaign. Note LOL 812, 'James Gibson Temperance' lodge of Hebburn, which reported:

> Bro Nutt addressing the members, said that it behoved every member of the order to attend his Lodge at this, the most critical time in the history of the Institution, in order to defeat that appalling disaster which would inevitably occur in the advent of Home Rule. The secretary was instructed to send a report to the *Belfast Weekly News* wishing every success to Sir Edward Carson and the Ulster Unionist Council in the determined stand against Home Rule.[45]

Indeed, at the height of the successive Home Rule crises, raising money for Carson became a focal point for lodge activities, as the minutes of LOL 428 'Jarrow Purple Heroes' demonstrated. In October 1913, the lodgemen decided:

> [A]fter discussing the advisability of 432 having a smoker, Bro Todd moved and Bro Rowan second that we hold a social on November 29 in Lodge Room in Hotel, tickets to be 1/- each. Bro Anderson to cater for refreshments at 7d per head and after all expenses paid the surplice [sic] money to be sent to Sir Ed[ward] Carson's Defence Fund.[46]

With 200 tickets printed, the lodgemen clearly anticipated a significant show of support for the concert and the cause.[47]

Thus despite Tyneside's firmly entrenched Liberal credentials, there was a considerable Unionist and Orange constituency in the north-east who were just as perturbed about the disintegration of the kingdom as their compatriots in Ulster and Liverpool. Moreover, just like Liverpool, it seems that there was a core of support for Carson, including some who were ready at least to declare that they would resort to violence to defend their fellow subjects in Ireland. The official minutes of the Hebburn LOL 339 reflect this seriousness:

> Br Cameron gave the brethren all the instructions required and in an enthusiastic manner told the brethren to let nothing prevent them from turning out in full lodge strength to meet Sir Edward Carson the gallant leader of their Ulster brethren, so that Sir Edward could see for himself that the loyalists of England are determined to take their stand with their Ulster brethren, and under his leadership, fight, if required, for their civil and religious liberties.[48]

In some respects, then, it is unsurprising that the Unionist panjandrums should come to the north-east to muster support. In fact, Carson's meeting at Wharton Park Durham on 13 September was important in both regional and national terms. The Orangemen of the region were excited by the thought of Carson coming to their adoptive home,[49] and men such as Lord Londonderry, a close friend and ally of Carson, who chaired the Wharton Park gathering, extended a warm welcome to the Ulster leader.[50] And it was the success of that gathering that may have convinced the Unionists of the support they enjoyed around the Tyne and the Wear, for within a couple of weeks, against a backdrop of many less important, regional meetings,[51] north-east Unionists again announced that Carson, along with Bonar Law, would again be travelling north. Tyneside buzzed with excitement at the prospect of an event that would be huge for the region. The meeting was to be staged at the ice rink in Wallsend – a bustling shipbuilding town on the Tyne, neighbouring Newcastle. Tickets, on sale at from one shilling to a guinea, were evidently soon snapped up.[52] The day's proceedings on 29 October 1913 began with the seventh annual conference of the Northumberland County Division of the National Unionist Association of Conservative and Liberal Unionist Organisations, held at Tilly's Tearoom in Newcastle. Following a night's rest at Lord Ridley's residence at Blagdon, Carson and the Leader of the Opposition were treated to a lunch with 700 guests.[53]

The mass meeting that followed in the evening was one of the biggest events ever seen in the town: the rink, which was described by the *Shields Daily News* as 'possibly one of the largest buildings of its kind in the province', could hold 15,000 persons and there is every reason to believe it was full.[54] One correspondent expressed disbelief that there were 'that many chairs in Wallsend'.[55] More than 500 stewards had been taken on to marshal the crowds, at one point using semaphore to communicate with each other because the venue was so big.[56] The massive arena was festooned in typical style: 'Union Jacks fell from every girder', reported the *Evening Mail*; alongside the flags were placed evocative slogans, or 'War Cries' as they put it, such as 'One King, One Flag, One Parliament', and 'No Surrender'.[57]

The demonstration was lit by 16 arc lamps, much like Sheil Park a year before; and, in another echo of Liverpool, a band amused the audience with patriotic airs like 'Rule Britannia', and the 'Old Brigade', although the *Chronicle* pointed out that 'the majority of the musical selections were Rag-time numbers'.[58] The audience began to gather at least two hours before the motorcade was due to arrive in Wallsend.[59] The decision to attend early was a sensible one as there was stated to have been 30,000 applicants for seats, and 'if all the standing places had been utilised, then it was estimated that there would be 17,000 present'. Moreover, if that was the case then this was the 'largest indoor meeting ever held in the North of England'.[60]

Just prior to the arrival of the Unionist leaders, an announcement was made to the assemblage that 'there must be no further smoking, as the atmosphere was already becoming too thick'. As the smoke cleared, Bonar Law and Carson mounted the velvet draped platform and were greeted with a rendition of 'For they Are Jolly Good Fellows'.[61] Bonar Law spoke first. His rising occasioning 'a great outburst of enthusiasm, the audience cheering and waving hats and handkerchiefs'.[62] He began by reiterating one of his most controversial statements: that if 'the government forces Home Rule on Ulster without the sanction of the electors and Ulster resists, then she will have the support of the whole Unionist party'. The Tory leader spoke for about an hour, and the audience listened with 'breathless interest' before he gave way to Carson, [63] who also spoke for an hour. Carson's most important claim was that any conciliatory offer from the government would be useless, 'unless constant with the [terms of] the Ulster Covenant'. More interesting was the torchlight parade through the streets of the borough that followed the meeting. This grand procession after the meeting was to be the local Unionists' way of welcoming and thanking Carson and Bonar Law for their efforts in the Unionist cause; as one of the members of the Wallsend's 'Enniskillen True Blues' lodge noted approvingly: 'the reception the[y] were to accord to Mr Bonar Bonar Law and Sir Edward Carson [was to be] in the form of a Torch Light Procession'.[64]

Bonar Law and Carson left the rink at 9.30, accompanied by their host, Lord Ridley, and entered an 'open motor landau' to be ceremoniously driven to the borough boundary of Wallsend. This spectacular torchlight procession was headed by a band, and to the delight of those in the leading vehicles, was evidently quite a spectacle: 'There were thousands of persons to give the distinguished visitors another welcome, and both statesmen, hat in hand, acknowledged the cheers that were raised'.[65] This had been an enormous, well-disciplined demonstration, an indication of the size of which is amply illustrated by the length of the motorised procession: 'what with motorcars and other vehicles following inline, must have been fully a mile in length, and was a capital wind-up to the evening's proceedings'.[66]

The local authorities seem not to have been overly worried about the mood of these meetings, for, even if regular press accounts told of riots and injuries in Ulster, Wallsend was no Portadown.[67] There were around 90 policemen on duty, and they liaised beforehand with the organisers to ensure that everything ran smoothly. As it turned out, there was no trouble at the meeting, and the Superintendent of the Wallsend police commented to the press that as well as directing a motorcade of around 140 vehicles through the tight streets of the town, he had had to contend with an estimated crowd of between 7,000 to 8,000 who had been unable to gain admittance to the rink due to a ticketing error.[68] Although many of these people had 'come from a considerable distance', they had 'showed remarkable restraint and went away in a quiet and orderly manner'.[69] In fact, despite the large crowds the tenor of the whole meeting was quiet and orderly – to the chagrin of some correspondents to the local press who would have preferred a more passionate demonstration. In reporting the meeting the rabidly Unionist *Liverpool Courier* put a buoyant spin on the proceedings by asserting that 'the audience listened with responsive gravity and earnestness'.[70] But some disagreed and blamed this subdued atmosphere on Bonar Law himself whose speech, one attendee thought, was 'terse, business-like' and lacking 'the priceless gift of imagination'.[71] What Unionism needed, according to 'Man of the World', was 'The Chancellor of the Exchequer', as Lloyd George's 'Celtic imagination would have portrayed brilliant word pictures that would have fired the souls of the hearers'. While Carson was acknowledged as a man of quality, the writer felt even 'his star is dimmed': not least by his recent bereavement.[72] This is one of the reasons why the same author reckoned that while he had never attended 'a meeting so vast', he also could not 'call to mind any occasion when enthusiasm was so lacking'.[73]

IV

It was the combined decorum and quietude of these demonstrations that makes the crucial point. These peaceful yet grimly determined protests denote the importance attached to the struggle against Home Rule. The meetings in Liverpool and Wallsend were a manifestation of popular inclusive politics; they were not last-gasp meetings of desperate, marginal men and women. Though the politics of Unionism was unpalatable to many, it had certainly involved people in the political process on a scale not seen since the great radical demonstrations of earlier times.[74] This was an issue bigger than party politics: people were genuinely concerned about the disintegration of the union and what they perceived, however erroneously, to be the encroachment of the Catholic Church into British affairs. In this last respect, the Unionist crowds of the 1910s sounded feint echoes of the enormous meetings that had been held to protest against the re-establishment of the Catholic hierarchy in 1851, but which, despite their size and fervour, had engendered relatively little open violence.[75] Similarly, despite the passions aroused by Carson's sojourns away from Ulster there were negligible instances of violent behaviour.[76] This is unsurprising in many respects, as one historian has noted that the worst instances of sectarian violence 'occurred when the Irish question was in abeyance'.[77] And although one author has stressed that the widely held belief in the orderliness of Victorian society is a 'gross misconception' he was quick to acknowledge that even when rioting, nineteenth-century Britons abstained from serious violence, and remained almost instinctively decorous.[78] This was certainly still true in 1912.

Thus by 'reading the crowd' we can discern many similarities of texture in these two gatherings and thereby discover their larger significance; for these demonstrations, although a year apart and taking place in different cities, shared many important themes. The importance of regimented street processions as an expression of cohesion was obvious at Liverpool and Newcastle; but it was also a reflection of a martial ideal that was both admired and promoted by the far right in British politics and by supporters in the press.[79] Furthermore, the aesthetic of both gatherings relied heavily on patriotic symbolism. Union flags predominated, whether they were carried by marchers, or adorned the great meeting halls. When combined with the ubiquitous regalia of the lodgemen these banners would have created vivid splashes of red, white and blue, and orange, bringing colour to a sepia-tinged urban setting in the best traditions of civic pageantry. The Liverpool *Mercury* thought that the parade in their city had enjoyed 'the spectacular benefit of the regalia of the followers of King William';[80] and the Tyneside press echoed this comment a year later, when they declared of the procession through Wallsend that 'the spectacle was a brilliant one'.[81]

The organisers of these events also updated the traditions of carnival by utilising modern technological advances. Note the heightened drama created by the use of 'arc-lights' at both events. We can also observe how the Newcastle demonstration renewed the ancient tradition of cavalcade by deploying motorcars by the score. This ability to choreograph was the particular skill of the Unionist party in this period, as they proved that they had the capacity not only to address their supporters concerns over Ireland, but also to offer them the visceral thrill of participation in parades and ceremonies. Indeed, in many ways this emotive, visual, quality is the most important point. As these events occurred before the days of amplifiers, not many in these great audiences would have heard what was being said. Thus in this respect to ask whether F.E. Smith's claim that 10,000 armed Liverpool men really would sail to Belfast to fight, was endorsed by his audience, or whether the good people of Wallsend really were 'breathless[ly] interest[ed]' in what Bonar Law had to say would be missing the point. It is far more likely that the demonstrators were transported to such rapturous appreciation by a combination of a sense of tribal affirmation, religious fervour, and theatrical histrionics. This was unconsciously acknowledged by Archibald Salvidge's own son, who observed that despite the absence of any amplifiers which rendered the orators inaudible to most 'the lights, the fervour, the bands the hymns, the cheers served to compensate for any deficiency'.[82] What is striking about this is the obvious similarity between the aesthetic and emotional appeal of those Unionist demonstrations in Liverpool and Newcastle, and the peculiar attraction of Fascist meetings in the 1930s.[83] As well as this similarity of appearance, it has also been observed that there was a 'discernible continuity of ideas in the interpretation of the national interest' between the Conservative 'die-hards' of the 1910s and the British Union of Fascists of the inter-war years.[84]

As we have seen the Unionist party could organise an impressive show, but they were aided and abetted in this by the past masters of unofficial public procession, the Orange Order. Their expertise and experience made them key players in these unique melodramas as their disciplined marching, their gaudy banners, and their martial music was all very attractive – and effective, symbolising both power and gravity. Indeed, the genius of the Orangemen was their ability 'to mix carnival with military dignity'.[85] Their value in both a ceremonial sense and in terms of mobilising foot-soldiers was recognised by the Tory establishment, particularly in Liverpool where, by 1915, there were 197 Orange Lodges, a uniquely high number in the non-Irish parts of Britain.[86] The city's Grand Master John Holden had worked closely with Salvidge in organising the demonstration – and, of course, the lodgemen contributed most of the music.[87] The city's Tory leaders recognised their value and they formed a fundamental component of the city's hegemonic Tory establishment. It is no surprise therefore that the Orange Order's representatives loomed large on the Union Jack draped platform in Sheil Park. Their Tyneside colleagues did occupy a much less exalted position, but the local Orange lodge from Wallsend obtained 59 tickets for the event and distributed them among the brethren.[88] It seems that Carson's visit spurred the north-east's

Orangemen into increased lodge activity in late 1913, which included making special arrangements for as many members as possible to sign the separate English Covenant across the Tyne at Hebburn on the following Saturday.[89] Like these Wallsend men, the members of 'Albert the Good' lodge, Consett, also entered into detailed discussions of the covenant. It was agreed that they would all meet on Saturday 8 November 1913 to sign the covenant, while the lodge offers were detailed to have an announcement placed in the local press to herald the event.[90] These were exciting times for the Order. The Home Rule question allowed the Orangemen to flaunt their role as guardians of both the constitution and the empire, because they believed that they 'held some kind of moral high ground by intertwining, almost imperceptibly, vague notions of civil and religious liberty, anti-Catholicism, bible Christianity, loyalty to Crown and Constitution, and political Toryism'.[91]

Women, too, played an important role in all of these demonstrations. This is interesting considering the contemporaneity of the Suffragette movement, for these female enthusiasts espoused a cause that was at best ambivalent, but usually hostile, towards the political rights of women. The amount of female Orange lodges in Liverpool grew enormously before the Great War, from three in 1881 to 43 in 1915.[92] And this was mirrored by the growth of the Liverpool Women's Unionist Federation, who were important enough for a prominent member of the Ulster Unionist Women's Council to come to Merseyside earlier in 1912 to address a large meeting of these same ladies, at which it was noticed, by the Liverpool press, that the applause was most vociferous.[93] Indeed, much contemporary press reportage makes note of this passionate support. In Liverpool, the Times noted that the 'number of women wearing Orange regalia who accompanied their menfolk was remarkable. In Ulster itself no women joined the procession'.[94] The Post, in describing the scenes at the Conservative Club when Carson's carriage arrived remarked that 'generally speaking the women demonstrated more vociferously than the men'.[95] Indeed, there are even reports of Orangewomen accosting an innocent young man on the Mersey ferry the night of Carson's arrival simply for wearing a shamrock-patterned tie.[96] Although there was only relatively little female Orange activity in the north-east,[97] significant numbers of women attended the Wallsend demonstration. Inside the Rink, observed the Shields Daily News, 'a large proportion of the audience was composed of ladies'.[98] The fact was acknowledged by Carson himself who tactfully addressed his appeal for support to 'Englishmen and Englishwomen'.[99] Thus it seems that despite their lacking the ballot, there were remarkable numbers of women involved in Unionist politics or indeed the Orange Order.[100] Although many people in this period saw Ireland as the keystone of imperial unity, it is probable that many women recognised that the Empire's first line of defence ran through the home.[101]

V

What do these demonstrations add to our understanding of Edwardian Britain? First, it can be argued that these anti-Home rule demonstrations provide evidence of the health of a polity in which concepts of community and sectarian allegiance were still paramount: a political culture that many had assumed to be moribund by the end of the Edwardian period. Some would argue that religion, and even locality, as a political determinant was dying before 1914, and that the only residue of that culture was confined to Liverpool. However, even Tyneside, a Liberal bastion which escaped the worst excesses of sectarianism, provided the location for probably the biggest *indoor* anti-Home Rule meeting ever held, certainly the largest Bonar Law ever addressed.[102] So to put it baldly, therefore, it is obvious that Home Rule *did* have resonance outside Ulster, because an English city could turn more supporters out onto the streets than even Belfast itself.

Sometimes, moreover, political rituals could speak louder than political oratory. The regimentation of the marchers, and the martial unity of those platoons of English, Irish and Scots demonstrators on the banks of the Mersey and the Tyne was certainly meant to represent, in loud and clear terms, a belief in the strength of the Union, and, therefore, in the health and strength of Britain, and the Empire. For as one author has stressed 'Ceremony says, "look this is how things should be, this is the proper, ideal pattern of social life"'.[103] What is so interesting is that such an expansive sort of ceremony should be afforded to Carson – an Irish politician – during his trips to Merseyside and Tyneside. Indeed, the level of reverence drew comment from some quarters of the Liberal press. In Liverpool, it was remarked, Carson met with such 'a reception not unworthy of Royalty' that 'no greater heartiness could have been expected if the rightful monarch of these realms had been the object of their tribute'.[104] This is an interesting point: for all this ceremonial feting of Carson represented more than just homage to one man (although a member of the Liverpool crowd had even shouted out 'King Edward the Eighth of Ulster'[105]), because this Irishman encapsulated a raft of ideas that defined Loyalism, namely: Protestantism,

Empire and the Tory party.[106] Therefore this royal analogy is actually quite useful, as the apotheosis of Carson on the streets of Liverpool and Wallsend can signify the same meaning that a royal coronation is designed to convey: in other words 'a series of ritual affirmations of moral values'.[107]

Even if those marchers had not thought too deeply about the larger significance of their actions, or had not cared that much, the symbolism of parades, music, and flags would have provided psychological satisfaction for those serried ranks of Unionists, without which the rhetoric of the platform would have added to relatively little in terms of popular appeal. But this in turn would have fortified those very same people who felt such obvious discomfort over recent plans for the future of Ireland: for crowd activity such as this can act 'as a means of preserving communal identity or recasting it in the face of external pressure and underlying social change'.[108] Between 1912 and 1914 people were being asked how much the Union of the three kingdoms meant to them – a question that was rarely openly considered. Common opposition to anything is often the most potent method of achieving solidarity. And, as Emile Durkheim's integrationist approach would have it, the 'conscience collective' was often a product of crowd assembly 'where the individuals, being closely united to one another, reaffirm in common their common sentiments; hence some ceremonies [such as those afforded the Ulster leaders] do not differ from regular religious ceremonies, either in their object, the results which they produce, or the processes employed to attain those results'.[109] Notwithstanding the Protestant overtones of Orange bands and battle hymns, perhaps we should look beyond that orthodox religiosity to employ the term 'religious' in a broader Durkheimian sense (which he took to mean anything considered *sacred*). What was more sacred to those saturated stalwarts on the Pier Head, or the torchbearers in Wallsend than the Act of Union?

13

The Ulster Volunteer Force, 1910–1920: New Perspectives[1]

Timothy Bowman

Ulster loyalism as a whole remains an under-studied phenomena, and this is particularly evident in the case of the Ulster Volunteer Force between its tentative beginnings in the small paramilitary forces which were formed in 1910, when the Third Home Rule bill was about to be introduced into Parliament and its incorporation into the Ulster Special Constabulary in late 1920. This is somewhat strange given both the size of the UVF in this period (with possibly a peak strength of 110,000 members by July 1914) and the excellent studies recently completed on the IRA.[2] Those working on modern (i.e. post-1966) Ulster loyalism have tried to explain this:

> My guess is that loyalists are neglected because few academics and serious journalists are unionists. The university-educated middle classes have difficulty understanding why anyone would fight for something as insubstantial as patriotism. They can almost understand Irish nationalism, because the geography of the place would suggest that everyone here ought to 'live together'. If, as many are, they are also left-leaning, they will sympathise with what can be portrayed as an anti-imperialist movement. But when the patriotism is something as unfashionable as a desire to remain part of the United Kingdom comprehension fails completely.[3]

Loyalism in the early years of the twentieth century has not been neglected by historians. However, some of this work is rather compromised by the clear political preferences of its authors. To A.T.Q. Stewart, writing in the tradition of Unionist historians with a capital 'U' the formation of the UVF in 1913 was something to be celebrated.[4] His book, published in 1967 would not have been published, one imagines, at least by Faber and Faber, if it had appeared five years later when the recent Northern Ireland troubles were raging. The Ulster Society has maintained this tradition producing celebratory pamphlets on the Larne Gun-running and the formation of the UVF.[5]

Michael Farrell in *Arming the Protestants* from a clear Marxist and, indeed, Republican, perspective outlined his views that Unionists had no right to self determination (whereas this was a basic right for Nationalists) and that the re-establishment of the UVF in 1920 was orchestrated by British Imperialists and Belfast businessmen with no real popular support.[6]

More academic histories concerning the UVF have tended to consider the 'high politics' of the Third Home Rule Crisis and have tended to relegate the UVF to a minor, supporting role and where they have considered it as a military force they have tended to focus on the Larne gun-running of April 1914.[7] An exception is Vivania Morsano's unpublished Ph.D. that claims, 'the UVF has never been recognised as an organisation which cut across the gender divide and helped to change the position of Protestant Ulster women during the early years of the twentieth century'.[8] While women did indeed serve in the UVF this was, as Marsano acknowledges, largely in the non-combatant roles similar to those taken subsequently by women in the British armed forces during the Great War, namely as nurses and clerks and they made up merely some 3,000 of the 100,000 members of the UVF.[9] Only one, Isabel Miller, was a member of the UVF Headquarters Staff and while she may have sat on this in her capacity as Commandant of the South Belfast Ulster Volunteer Medical and Nursing Corps it is noticeable that she acted as the shorthand typist for UVF Headquarters.[10] The Ulster Women's Unionist Council which was formed in this period was certainly not a radical feminist body and when facing the difficult question of whether to raise funds to equip the UVF or to use the money for political work in Great Britain the members of the committee decided to defer to the advice of Sir Edward Carson, who advised them to concentrate on their political work.[11]

The source material for the UVF is very different to that available for the IRA. Those who were involved in the UVF in this period (especially 1913–14) soon seem to have felt some shame or embarrassment regarding their role. Few army officers who were involved mentioned this in their *Who's Who* entries and it was rarely mentioned in obituaries (an exception being Colonel Hacket Pain's in the magazine of the Worcestershire Regiment, when it was stated that he was believed to have organised and carried out the Larne gun-running of 1914).[12] Very few memoirs were written by those who were involved.

This is in marked contrast to IRA veterans who produced accounts such as Tom Barry's *Guerrilla Days in Ireland*, which sold particularly well in the Irish-American market.[13]

Fred Crawford's *Guns for Ulster* and R.J. Adgey's *Arming the Ulster Volunteers* were both published shortly after the end of the Second World War.[14] They concentrate solely on gun-running and their timing is not insignificant, in that Adgey appears to have been motivated by contemporary accusations of profiting by his involvement in the UVF, which recently released records at PRONI clearly show that he did.[15] The Military History Bureau, set up in the Irish Free State in the 1920s invited all IRA members to submit statements of their roles in the Anglo-Irish War, something that the Northern Ireland government did not do with UVF members. Instead, in 1961 Viscount Brookeborough, Northern Ireland Prime Minister, sent out a letter appealing for UVF material to some, 'two hundred old-established Ulster families prominently identified with the anti-Home Rule movement'.[16] The resultant materials deposited in the PRONI, not surprisingly, display considerable lacuna. These materials are particularly strong for North Antrim, Co. Cavan, South Down and Tyrone; this means that areas where Unionists made up a great majority of the population are neglected. Similarly, this bias in the available source material tends to suggest that the UVF was purely organised and lead by local gentry, which was not always the case. Worst of all, the surviving material exhibits a very strong rural bias. However, the lack of source material is partly compensated for by the availability of Royal Irish Constabulary [RIC], Military Intelligence and newspaper reports, but it may partly explain why some historians have tended to over-emphasise the importance and involvement of gentry families in the UVF, especially during 1913–14.

There are a number of issues to address that have either been neglected by previous historians or where a re-interpretation is in order. First, is the issue of the leadership, membership and regionalism of the UVF. Previous historians have tended to view the UVF as little more than a party militia, which was under the authority of the Ulster Unionist political leadership. Ascertaining the relationship between the UVF and UUP is rather complex, given that the papers of Carson and Sir James Craig are not complete for this period, but they do demonstrate that Carson and Craig were not involved in the day-to-day administration of the force. While Paul Bew states that Carson raised the UVF to prevent disgruntled Unionists resorting to rioting, there is really little evidence to support this interesting hypothesis.[17] In contrast the evidence points to the emergence of the UVF as a bottom up rather than top down force in many areas.

By late 1912, extensive drill was taking place in many parts of Ulster, in most cases organised by Orange Lodges or Unionist Clubs. However, a large amount of what could be called 'independent drilling' was going on, led by former soldiers, for example in Omagh, Co. Tyrone where a former Imperial Yeomanry Sergeant, Osbourne Young was reported as drilling around 30 mounted men by October 1912.[18] Two large paramilitary units had been formed in Ulster by the end of 1912 – the Young Citizen Volunteers of Belfast [YCV] and the Enniskillen Horse – both of which were to become UVF units.

The YCV were initially formed at a public meeting at Belfast City Hall on the 10 September 1912. The initial committee was something of a roll call of Ulster Unionists, including figures such as Frank Workman, J. Milne Barbour and Lt Col. W.E.C. McCammond. There were also a few Nationalist members of the committee and much was made of the organisation as a non-political and non-sectarian one. The YCV carried out drill and route marches and originally they appear to have been formed to develop the work of paramilitary youth movements, instil civic pride, act as a force of special constables and to demonstrate popular pressure for the Territorial Force scheme, introduced in Great Britain in 1908 to be extended to Ireland. Eventually, in April 1914 there was something of a split in the YCV. The unit's commanding officer, Lt Col. R.D.P.S. Chichester brought the unit into the UVF which appears to have led to the resignation of some members of the unit, along with ineffectual protests from committee members such as Frank Workman who, while a supporter of the UVF, appears to have seen the YCV as a very different and separate organisation.[19]

The Enniskillen Horse, in contrast, were raised almost solely on the initiative of one person; William Copeland Trimble, the proprietor and editor of the *Impartial Reporter*, a local newspaper with circulation throughout Co. Fermanagh. Trimble formed this unit as he felt that Carson should be provided with a mounted escort when he visited Enniskillen on the 18 September 1912. Trimble pompously, but seemingly truthfully stated, 'no local military gentleman would undertake the command; and sitting in the saddle at Castlecoole gate, troop by troop the men themselves elected Mr Trimble as leader'.[20] Trimble's leadership of this unit, which by mid-September 1912 was almost 240 strong, raises important issues regarding Unionist feeling in Fermanagh in this period and the extent to which leading figures in 'border Unionism' were prepared to accept leadership roles in resistance to Home Rule. Trimble remained as the commander of this force when it was incorporated into the UVF in early 1913.

The UVF did evolve into something of a 'party militia' by 1914 (i.e. no 'independent' loyalist units existed in tandem with the UVF in the 1913–14 period) but this was in the context of a re-united Ulster Unionism, given the end of the Russellite and Sloanite threats to 'official' unionism. Nevertheless, telegrams sent to Carson in July 1914 suggest that some UVF units were flexing their political muscle over the partition issue and were not prepared unthinkingly to follow the Unionist leadership. The Secretary of the UVF in Raphoe wrote, 'East Donegal expect you to stand firm for a clean cut all Ulster' and Viscount Archdale in Fermanagh penned, '3,000 fully armed Ulster Volunteers determined to hold the county for the Union'.[21]

UVF headquarters appears to have been a very small-scale operation and to have exerted little command over the force as a whole.[22] It is clear that local officers did, on some occasions, refute Belfast command. Capt. Arthur O'Neill, commanding units in North Antrim flatly refused to obey an order from Gen. William Adair to provide 1,100 men for service outside their local area, stating that the distance of North Antrim from the UVF reserves in Belfast, Nationalist strength in the area and the general weakness of the UVF in North Antrim made this impossible.[23]

The local leadership was not always the landed gentry of popular myth. Certainly when paramilitary units were formed they were often commanded by former soldiers who had served in the ranks and had relatively menial jobs. Elsewhere there are examples of gentry involvement but not leadership. For example in the Seaforde Company of the 1st South Down Regiment, Maj. William George Forde the local landowner, Justice of the Peace and Deputy Lieutenant of the County clearly was a member of the force and attended drills, but was described as 'attached' in the roll book. Indeed, the commander of this company was Alexander McMeekin, Forde's coachman.[24] Similarly, in the 1st Fermanagh Regiment, F.W. Barton was described as a 'gentleman' in the roll book but served as an ordinary member, whereas his chauffeur, S.E. Crawford was the battalion transport officer.[25] Elsewhere, Desmond Murphy believes that in Co. Donegal and Co. Londonderry the gentry and Protestant clergymen were practically obliged to take command of UVF units as local businessmen were concerned that they would be boycotted if they accepted leadership roles.[26] Certainly in the City of Londonderry UVF units there were very serious problems in securing suitable officers.[27] By contrast, the RIC County Inspector for Antrim stated that 'any businessman who held back would be a marked man and his business would be ruined'.[28] This raises important questions about both the extent to which some gentry were prepared to become involved in the movement and the degree UVF officers were prepared to submit to the command of their social inferiors.

With regard to the membership of the UVF this, as seen above, is difficult to assess for the movement as a whole. Table 13.1 shows the social composition of the 1st Fermanagh Battalion, UVF in 1914 and compares this with Hart's analysis of social composition of the IRA in the 1919–21. The UVF contained fewer skilled working class and lower middle class members that the IRA. The 'other' category in the UVF figures has been left at 0.3 per cent rather than having this rounded down, as this reflects the gentry membership.

It is clear that UVF membership varied considerably from area to area. During the formation of the force in South Down, Capt. Roger Hall wanted Ulster Volunteers to be '*Picked men*, not enrolled only because they signed the Covenant'.[29] However, in the 5th Tyrone Regiment a very different view was taken with battalion orders of November 1913 stating, 'every man who signed the Covenant should be in'.[30] By August 1913 all members of Ulster Clubs and of the Orange Order were urged by Carson to join the UVF.[31] Following this appeal E.C. Herdman, the Commanding Officer of the 1st North Tyrone Regiment issued a handbill stating that all of those who signed the covenant were expected to attend UVF drills; this must, at least, have made a significant impression on those workers at Herdman's Linen Mills in Sion Mills.[32] It is, however, clear that different categories

Table 13.1 *Occupations of members of 1st Fermanagh Regiment 1913–14 and Irish Volunteers in provincial Ireland (figures cover all of Ireland except for the Dublin urban area)*

	UVF	IRA
	1913–14	1917–19
Sample	642	1,437
Farmer/son (%)	57	40
Farm labourer (%)	25	11
Un/semi-skilled (%)	4	9
Skilled (%)	6	16
Shop asst./clerk (%)	2	12
Professional (%)	2	1
Merchant/son (%)	4	7
Student (%)	0	1
Other (%)	0.3	2

Sources: PRONI, D1267/1 and Peter Hart, *The I.R.A. at War 1916–1923* (Oxford University Press, 2003), pp. 113–15.

of membership soon emerged, with Col. Hacket Pain writing to all UVF Divisional, Regimental and Battalion commanders to inform them that, 'arms should only be given to men who, in the opinion of their Battalion Commanders, are fitted in all ways to be entrusted with them'.[33] Therefore, while the UVF expanded in numbers, probably as part of a propaganda exercise, UVF commanders were determined to set up different categories of membership which meant that, in the event of violence, only reliable and militarily efficient men would be entrusted with rifles.

The regional composition of the UVF is a complex issue. However, it appears that early drilling in 1911 and 1912 was largely confined to Counties Fermanagh and Tyrone. Unionists in areas where Protestants were in a small minority do not seem to have been prepared to join the UVF in any significant numbers, until after the Curragh Incident in April 1914.[34] As late as August 1913 the entire Cavan and Monaghan UVF could muster just 2,000 men for a parade where Carson inspected them.[35] Similarly, in areas such as Belfast and North Down, where Unionists were in a very strong majority, heavy reliance seems to have been placed on normal means of political protest through the Ulster Clubs until very late in the crisis.

Much has been made of the involvement of British army personnel, serving and retired, in the UVF. Hew Strachan notes, 'the army's close link with the Ulster Volunteers was confirmed by the fact that 62 per cent of the latter's divisional, regimental and battalion commands were held by former officers.'[36] Yet on closer inspection the UVF in the 1913–14 period could call on something like 60–70 officers or ex-officers, many of them elderly and long retired possessing rather rudimentary skills gained in amateur rather than regular units. Indeed, of the 19 'HQ personnel' only six had military backgrounds.[37]

The motives of ex-regular officers for joining the UVF could be more than a desire to serve 'Loyalism'. While Capt. W.B. Spender, who famously resigned his commission over the Home Rule crisis, stated emphatically that he did not receive any salary for his staff work for the UVF others were not so principled. Lt Gen. Sir George Richardson received a salary of £1,000 plus the services of a valet and free board and lodging as Commander in Chief of the UVF. With the exception of Spender all regular officers who were involved in the UVF waited until their natural retirement to join the force (and there is evidence that some of those in the Headquarters, i.e. Colonels Couchman and Hacket Pain also received salaries). For example Col. Oliver Nugent retired from the King's Royal Rifle Corps in January 1914 and then immediately appears to have become the commander of the Cavan UVF.

Whether these retired offices brought much expertise to the UVF also seems highly debatable. Richardson appears to have been little more than an amiable old buffer, who justified his salary by doing little more than attending periodic parades throughout Ulster and chairing weekly meetings of the UVF HQ. Col. G.H.H. Couchman (formerly of the Somerset Light Infantry), who was the designated commander of all Belfast UVF units, proved to be an ineffectual Brigadier in the Great War and was removed from the command of the 107th Brigade as soon as it arrived in France; its training deemed to have been completely substandard.[38] Ironically, it was to be rural officers, who came to prominence in the UVF as much due to their position as local landowners as their military expertise (unlike those employed at HQ) who were to prove themselves most able in the Great War. Col. Oliver Nugent, of Mountnugent, Co. Cavan ended the war as a lieutenant general while Capt. Ambrose Ricardo, of Sion Mills, Tyrone ended the war as a brigadier general. While many have described Spender as a brilliant young staff officer who threw away a promising career for his Unionist beliefs, his role at HQ appears to have been very marginal and in the Great War he had a chequered career, retiring in 1920 as a Lt Col.[39] The UVF also attracted more than its fair share of 'adventurers'. For example F.P. Crozier, who was employed to command the Special Service Force of the West Belfast UVF. had been forced to resign from the 3rd Loyal North Lancashire Regiment in 1909 for issuing a series of dishonoured cheques.[40]

While some historians have been very complimentary of UVF HQ staff work, the truth is that much of this seems to have been very poor. Crawford made much of the use of the UVF Motorcar Corps during the Larne gun running.[41] However, his account does not tally with that of the UVF commander in County Antrim, Gen. Sir William Adair, who pleaded on the 22 April for any available transport, including horse drawn vehicles to be brought to Larne.[42] Similarly, endless questionnaires were sent out regarding the number of rifles held by local UVF units, which suggests that little care was taken in the distribution of arms in April 1914.

Richardson introduced a regimental system into the UVF structure in late 1913. Partly, this made some sense – it reflected the belief of British army officers in the importance of the regimental system for building morale and it also stressed the presence of the UVF everywhere in Ulster. However, while the system looked good on paper it did little to take account of the reluctance of individual volunteers to leave their own areas and assumed a uniformity of training. By May 1914 this system had given place to a 25,000 strong Special Service Force.[43]

F.X. Martin, a revered figure in the University College Dublin contingent of nationalist historians, first expressed the view that the UVF was a proto-Fascist organisation.[44] Certainly there are some obvious connections with fascism (although definitions of this are varied, to say the least); the mass rallies, colourful oratory and view that 'democracy' had failed. Beyond these trappings of fascism, the hypothesis carries little weight. There are few new policies proposed, no economic 'Third Way'; few social activities (UVF members drill and parade), a continued reliance on parliamentary leaders and procedure and few members of the UVF were the disgruntled lower middle classes or desperate long-term unemployed (until, possibly 1920). On the whole a more useful analogy is Edwardian militarism rather than proto-fascism. There are clear links with the National Service League. As discussed above, two UVF units, the Enniskillen Horse and YCV even attempted up to mid-1913 to become recognised units of the Territorial Force.

The financing of the UVF is an aspect of the force that will always be shrouded in mystery. As funds were hidden and disguised to confound possible contemporary police investigations, it is impossible to ascertain how much money the UVF actually raised and how funds were dispersed. The auditor of the UVF for this period was Stewart Blacker Quinn and his accounts are problematical as historical documents. Quinn clearly stated that during his tenure he had not actually seen the bills and receipts detailed in his accounts. Also, as a member of the Ulster Unionist Council he was much too closely connected with the UVF to provide any sort of independent analysis of its finances.

What is clear is that the Carson Defence Fund failed to raise as much money as its instigators had hoped. Between February 1914 and March 1915 the fund received a creditable, but far from impressive £41,723 16s. 5d.[45] Carson himself stated, in March 1914, 'let those who are well off or comparatively well off, in accordance with the means they have, contribute what they can…The wage earners of our democracy show a fine example in all the inconvenience they are prepared to undergo'.[46] Given that firms such as Workman and Clark Shipbuilders and Robinson and Cleaver's Department Store actually charged the Carson Defence Fund for their services and products supplied it is hard to accept that Belfast businessmen bankrolled the UVF.

The UVF hid their finances in a number of accounts, controlled by Col. R.G. Sharman Crawford, in the Belfast Banking Co. Ltd.. Probably, the UVF had access to something in the region of £100,000 by mid-1914 although this figure remains highly speculative, as it is clear that money was also held in banks in London and Paris.[47]

The grants paid out to individual UVF units appear to have been incredibly low with the force's major expenditure being the salary of Lt Gen. Sir George Richardson, the rental and staffing of the Old Town

Hall in Belfast and, after April 1914, the lease of buildings as armouries. No separate accounts survive regarding the purchase of arms; Stewart suggested that the Larne gun running of April 1914 cost between £60,000 and £70,000.[48] Presumably, much of the money, which the UVF supposedly possessed, was in the form of pledges, rather than hard currency. A compensation fund thus supposedly stood at £1,043,816, largely made up of pledges from Tory peers although UVF Head-quarters had no access to this money, little of which was to be given to the UVF until fighting actually broke out.[49] At the county level the financial situation was desperate. In October 1914 the 2nd Tyrone Regiment had an overdraft of £400.[50]

During the Great War the UVF rapidly experienced a downturn in activity. There is a myth that UVF members rushed to the colours at the outbreak of the Great War. The UVF played an important role in the formation of the 36th (Ulster) Division and obtained the services of the majority of the most active UVF members, particularly amongst the officer corps. But, on the deficit side the UVF appears to have saddled the 36th (Ulster) Division with more than its fair share of incompetent officers, appointed on the basis of their political alle-giances, rather than their military efficiency. It is equally clear that UVF membership did little to boost recruitment rates in rural Ulster.[51]

Nevertheless, the majority of UVF members remained in Ulster during the Great War and in 1914 and 1915 it is clear that attempts were being made to organise the UVF as a home defence force, able to protect Belfast and Counties Antrim and Down from a possible German naval raid. At various times, there appears to have been serious discussion of amalgamating the UVF with either the Territorial Force or the Volunteer Training Corps, a move resisted by both Richardson and, ultimately, Carson as there were fears that the UVF would disappear as a distinct unit and that Ulster Unionists would no longer be able to appoint its officers.[52] The UVF quickly became moribund, after the failure of these proposals and as the rank and file found more financially rewarding ways to aid the war effort. In the immediate aftermath of the Easter Rising just 1,148 UVF members were sworn in as Special Constables, a far from im-pressive figure and these UVF members were all drawn from the Belfast regiments.[53] In May 1916 all drills were suspended and Headquarters Committee meetings become increasingly less frequent through 1917 and 1918. Despite this inactivity the UVF did not officially stand down until 1 May 1919 when Richardson retired as GOC.

However, in early 1920 there was a re-emergence of Loyalist paramili-tary groups due to the Anglo-Irish War. The role of the UVF in 1920 has been ignored by many historians, Charles Townshend makes no reference to them in, *British Campaign in Ireland, 1919–21* and Michael Hopkinson in, *The Irish War of Independence* mentions the development on just four pages. The situation in 1920 paralleled that in 1912 rather than 1913 with the creation of a large number of independent units. For example the Ulster Imperial Guards were formed amongst ex-servicemen working in the Belfast shipyards. Even some of those involved in the pre-war UVF were wary of resurrecting the force. Basil Brooke formed his 'Fermanagh Vigilance' in an attempt to attract Catholic support; while Crawford created his 'Tigers' (as an oath bound society) believing that small, specialist, 'counter-gangs' were required. The UVF proper was re-established in July 1920 under the command of Lt Col. Wilfrid Spender. At the meeting called to revive the force, no representatives were present from Co. Monaghan and indeed the force seems to have drawn most of its strength from Counties Antrim, Down and Belfast.[54]

In September 1920, Craig, now a junior government minister, pushed for the creation of the Ulster Special Constabulary [USC]. In his memorandum to the cabinet, he stated, 'the organisation of the Ulster Volunteer Force should be used *sub rosa* for raising both forces [by this he meant a special constabulary and a special constabulary reserve i.e. what later became the 'B' and 'C' categories of the Ulster Special Constabulary] as was done for raising the 36th (Ulster) Division when the War broke out; otherwise undesirables might enrol and bring speedy discredit on the Force'.[55] Unionists were clear that they wanted the new force to be quite separate from the RIC, Lt Col. Spender stating, 'my limited acquaintance with RIC methods certainly makes me believe that their main policy is to avoid trouble and let sleeping dogs lie, and to look on every dog that is not biting hard, as asleep'.[56] As a result of Ulster Unionist special pleading, the USC was formed in December 1920. This was done in spite of the concerns of Lt Gen. Sir Nevil Macready [G.O.C. Ireland] who feared that the British government was merely arming a poorly disciplined, all Protestant force. Indeed, Macready was concerned that the formation of the USC made civil war highly likely in Ulster and pointed out that it could lead to the stationing of more, not less, British troops in Northern Ireland.[57]

The USC was supposedly formed as the UVF structure was seen as unwieldy and, indeed, what was needed in the circumstances of 1920–22 were small police units with good local knowledge, rather than battalion sized units, but there seem to have been other considerations. The UVF had, it appears, not recruited well outside Belfast. There was also the ability of the USC to absorb other paramilitary groups and, indeed some refugee Southern Loyalists while at the same time, allowing for a 'weeding out' of both the old and unfit, and political extremists. The

USC enabled men to 'define their own patriotism' with the A (full time), B (part-time) and C (reserve) categories.

However, the UVF did survive as a separate force after December 1920. Some of those writing about the relationship between the UVF and USC have contradicted themselves. Wallace Clark in his *Guns in Ulster* stresses the overlap between the UVF and USC but then quotes the District Commander for South Londonderry, Harry Clarke, saying, in January 1921, 'I need men and the younger and wilder they are the better'.[58] Some local historians have suggested that, certainly in part of County Down most of those joining the USC were young men who felt that they had 'missed their chance' by being too young for military service in the Great War.[59] Such conclusions must remain speculative until a full analysis of the USC membership records, held in the PRONI, has been completed.

Still it is clear that, in some shape or form, the UVF survived as a separate force after the formation of the USC. In November 1921 Col. Carter Campbell, commanding the 15th Infantry Brigade, based in Belfast noted, 'the one really disquieting point in the situation is that the Ulster Unionist Clubs, the basis of the old UVF are reorganising, whether they are getting arms or not I cannot at present ascertain'.[60] If the Anglo-Irish talks had not resulted in the Treaty of December 1921, Macready felt that enough of the UVF remained to enable the formation of a new Ulster Division, 15,000 strong for use anywhere in Ireland and that it would be completely separate from the USC.[61] As late as 1923 Crawford was having meetings with James Craig concerning his command of the UVF and the fear that it might fall into the wrong hands. By this time, though, most of the active membership had been accommodated in the USC.[62]

Overall the UVF in this period was more popular and, indeed, more democratic in its organisation than some historians have allowed. Indeed, in many areas it appears that it was retired 'other ranks' rather than the landed gentry who were the drivers behind much paramilitary activity. The UVF was strongly influenced by regional factors, with the initial impetus for its formation coming in areas of Ulster where Unionists were in a slight majority of the population. Reaching its highest membership, of around 100,000 men in late 1913 the UVF appears to have gone into a rapid decline with the outbreak of the Great War and its attempted re-formation in 1920 appears to have been marred with recruiting difficulties. The formation of the Ulster Special Constabulary clearly involved former UVF personnel to some extent, but the exact nature of this involvement will remain unclear until a full study has been completed of the USC personnel records for the period.

14

The Royal Visit to Belfast, June 1921

Gillian McIntosh

Introduction

In the twentieth century royal visits to Northern Ireland have followed clear symbolic strategies. In terms of ceremony, contemporary royal visits have taken place on a more restricted scale, but by examining royal visits retrospectively it is clear that the symbolic importance of a royal visit has remained constant. For instance, when Elizabeth II visited Northern Ireland in April 2000, she did so to present the (soon to be disbanded) Royal Ulster Constabulary with the George Cross at Hillsborough. The use of royalty in this politically symbolic way has a long, often troubled history in the state. Arguably, the need for 'tradition and for order, as met by ceremonials such as these, actually *increased* [sic] as the stability of the state became ever more uncertain'.[1] In 1971, for example, the Northern Ireland government was very anxious that Elizabeth II come to open the Parliament as the highlight of their state's jubilee celebrations, symbolically re-enacting her grandfather's actions in 1921. However, given the high level of civil disturbance the British home secretary advised against it and there was no royal presence. Interestingly, the period in which George V visited Northern Ireland to inaugurate the Parliament was the most violent in the state's history, outstripping the turbulence of the early 1970s. Elizabeth II also visited the state in 1966, a year rich with symbolism being the fiftieth anniversary of both the Easter Rising and the Battle of the Somme, sacred dates for nationalism and unionism respectively. On this occasion, the

Northern Ireland Prime Minister hoped that during her visit the Queen would endorse his policy of 'bridge building' across the community in Northern Ireland. The Queen however did not and the visit, marred as it was by the controversy over the naming of the new Lagan bridge and two incidents when missiles were thrown at the royal cavalcade, was not deemed a success on any level. Visits of the royals during the Second World War, and Elizabeth's coronation visit of 1953 had morale boosting effects and reinforced the state and its government as part of the Union although, again, issues arising from the 1953 visit led both to parades disputes and to conflict over flags contributing, some have argued, to the passing of the 1954 Flags and Emblems Act. Earlier visits such as that in 1932 by the Prince of Wales to open the newly built Parliament buildings Stormont endorsed the state in a high profile way. But it was the visit of George V in 1921 that set the tone for royal visits to the state in the twentieth century and established the template for subsequent visits. This visit was principally symbolic and came at a period of rapid social and political change in Northern Ireland.

Public attitudes to royal visits to Northern Ireland over the twentieth century have followed a distinct pattern but have never been consensual. Such visits have followed traditional forms (visiting significant buildings, meeting the state's political, spiritual and business elites and so on) this being largely a pragmatic necessity – it was always easier for civil servants administering a visit to follow successful precedents. In this way, each royal visit reminded the audience of previous ones, and was in turn reinforced by them. An examination of public attitudes to the visits of monarchy to the state can be related to 'other dimensions of the political outlook of citizens'.[2] Variations of popular response to royal visits can be seen as crudely dividing along political lines, that is Protestant/Unionist enthusiasm for royalty against Catholic/Nationalist indifference or hostility. However, as was evident from the public response to the 1921 visit there are no such easy conclusions. One could generalise that northern Nationalists associated the monarchy with the British state, and resented their visits on the basis that they underlined Northern Ireland's separation from the rest of Ireland, and emphasised the link to Britain through the Crown. Unionists on the other hand found security in the visits of monarchy to the state, and reassurance from the presence of royals, seeing them as a symbol of unity and stability. Of course there was no such simple opposition, and all sections of the community found the pageantry and ritual associated with royal visits, with the novelty and excitement they generated, entertaining, particularly at times of social austerity and political stress. As

James Murphy argues, this was as much an all-Ireland phenomenon as it was a Northern Ireland one.[3] Jay G. Blumler et al suggest that:

> On the one hand, the presence of Monarchy, as the symbolic custodian of national unity and communal values, would serve to lessen antagonism of subjects to the reigning government and ameliorate the aggressiveness of their behaviour in secular politics. On the other hand, the powerlessness of the Crown would shield it from those hostile and resentful impulses that are often directed against authority holders.[4]

In the period from the turn of the century to the beginning of the First World War in 1914 there were a number of royal visits to Ireland 'influenced by threats to British-Irish links arising from the demands for Home Rule and the more distant rumbles about national independence':

> Royal visits were seen as affirmations of support for the Union and were viewed by the government and particularly the Unionist minority as a means of encouraging loyalty to personalities who clearly projected no political or physical threat, while conveying a sense of continuity, solidarity and even benevolence.[5]

Undoubtedly, throughout the twentieth century in a similar way the Unionist government used royal occasions to unite the protestant community behind the figure of the monarch, to reassert their power and status as those in government, and to remind a domestic and foreign audience of their continuing position within the Union (this was of particular importance given the perception of the threatening presence of the Free State). The ritual associated with royal visits was part then of the process of the communalisation of politics. David Cannadine poses the query, 'Do such pageants reinforce community, or hierarchy, or both?'; in Northern Ireland in 1921 the presence of royalty reinforced both, albeit exclusively the Protestant community and the Unionist hierarchy.[6]

In June 1921 King George V and Queen Mary came to Belfast to inaugurate the Northern Ireland Parliament. Although the event had no precedent, the British government drew comparison with the visit of the Duke of York (the future George V) to open the commonwealth parliament in Australia in May 1901. The Imperial Conference had begun in London two days before the Belfast opening, and Dominion leaders 'were anxious to see an end to the war [in Ireland] because of the unwelcome tensions it had caused in their countries', particularly so in the case of Australia.[7] Although ultimately none attended, Craig invited the dominion premiers to Belfast for the inauguration, arguing that their association 'with the Opening of the youngest Parliament within the King's Dominions' would help his efforts to achieve 'a better state of affairs'.[8] (Craig eventually played host to the premiers of Newfoundland, New Zealand, Canada and Australia in the late 1920s and early 30s). The inauguration ceremony itself took a mere 15 minutes, and the visit lasted only five hours; its significance lying principally in the King's subsequently oft quoted appeal to 'all Irishmen to stretch out the hand of forbearance and conciliation, to forgive and forget' which, despite parliamentary statements to the contrary, was part of the British government's evolving policy in Ireland. As with those speeches delivered over the years at Westminster, the King's speech in Belfast was written by the British government, the only contribution of the Sovereign was that it was cast in terms of a personal appeal. It was clear then to most observers that the speech was 'delivered on the advice of his Imperial Cabinet' although the *Morning Post* 'thought that not a few of the passages bore the imprint of His Majesty's own personality'.[9] Although consistently presented by the British government as the monarch's alone, the Belfast speech was written by Sir Edward Grigg, one of Lloyd George's private secretaries, drawing on earlier drafts by General Smuts and Arthur Balfour, and was 'warmly approved by the King'.[10] With home rule newly established in Northern Ireland, the British government's Irish strategy was still hard-line, and included consideration of total martial law and an economic blockade. 'An uncertain policy, characterised by a willingness to move from active coercion in Ireland to the issuance of feelers for a negotiated settlement and then back to an intensified military campaign, is evident from a review of the British government's conduct in Ireland from October, 1920, to late June, 1921 when Lloyd George decided to pursue formal talks with Sinn Fein'.[11] In terms of negotiation with Southern Ireland, the King (cast in the role of honest broker by the British and Northern Ireland government) was prompted to use the speech in Belfast 'for a grand gesture of reconciliation'.[12] This was a modification of the government's previous more hard-line policy, reflected in the claim of the British chief secretary in 1920 that the British government would not rest 'till we have knocked the last revolver from the last assassin's hand'.[13] Significantly, the King's appeal for peace 'gave the government the chance to put itself right in the eyes of its critics and exert political pressure on Sinn Féin, where military pressure had, it seemed, met with failure'.[14] Through him the government found 'the right means of revealing publicly the government's change of front...loyalists would accept from the Crown what they rejected from any other source'.[15]

Although arguably partial to the Unionist side, the King's role as mediator was vital, imbuing the message with greater meaning. The speech 'provided the necessary cover for the risk of restarting talks in Dublin, and within a fortnight a formal truce was agreed'.[16] It was in terms of the 'King's appeal' that Lloyd George made his subsequent overture to Northern Ireland's new Prime Minister, Craig, to attend a conference with Eamon de Valera in London ('We must honour the King's appeal')[17] and those in which Northern Ireland's Prime Minister accepted: 'In view of the appeal conveyed to us by His Majesty, in His Gracious Message on the occasion of the Opening of the Northern Parliament for peace throughout Ireland, we feel that we cannot refuse to accept your invitation to a Conference to discuss how best this can be accomplished'.[18] Cecil Craig's diary confirmed that her husband felt he could not refuse the invitation because it came as a result of the royal appeal, 'and any such refusal would have been much misunderstood in England'.[19] For the Nationalist *Irish News* it was the success of the King's visit itself (when Lloyd George and his ministers 'had made King George V an agent and instrument of their policy of Disruption and Destruction in Ireland') rather than the speech per se which had persuaded them to call a conference in the first place.[20] As Alvin Jackson summarises, the King's speech 'very neatly proved to be both a baptism and a funeral for partition, for the King's carefully formulated address was a public overture to Sinn Féin, which led to the truce of 9 July and sustained pressure on Craig to come to terms with Éamon de Valera'.[21] Through the 1921 visit George V acted successfully as a mediator facilitating conflict resolution (at least temporarily) through information provision. His speech, the key to the success of the visit, was a prime example of the use and success of the 'sound bite' – the 1921 visit is still remembered for the King's appeal for peace, the minutiae of its true origins long forgotten.

On another level the official function of the King's visit was purely symbolic, something underlined by the fact that its official announcement came from James Craig at the first inauguration of the Northern Ireland Parliament by Viscount Fitzalan, the Lord Lieutenant, a fortnight earlier. Additionally, the King did not outline the Northern Ireland government's programme for Parliament; this was also left to Fitzalan to announce the day after the royal visit. The real inauguration of the Northern Ireland Parliament bore little comparison to the pomp and enthusiasm that greeted the monarch. By comparison, the public

response to the Lord Lieutenant's visit was muted, according to the
Daily Mirror:

> Large numbers of troops and police were evident over portions of the route.
> On the right is the guard of honour, supplied by the Norfolk Regiment.
> Taking into consideration the population of Belfast and its immediate
> thickly populated environs, the attendance of spectators was scant and their
> enthusiasm well restrained.[22]

While the inauguration ceremony foreshadowed George V's (in many
ways acting a dress rehearsal for it, particularly in terms of its stringent
security) it was a low-key affair, which the *Irish News* described as 'cold'
and monotonous. The Nationalist paper was predictably negative in its
coverage: 'What struck the observer most was the complete absence of
enthusiasm and the utter lack of interest displayed by the community'.[23]
The paper also took full advantage of Fitzalan's speech in which he said:
'I don't pretend for one moment that this Act, which is the foundation
of your Parliament in Northern Ireland is a perfect Act. In fact,
I believe it wants amendment already, and I shall not be at all surprised
if it is amended in the not very far distant future'.[24] Birkenhead later
rejected the idea that Fitzalan had been announcing any forthcoming
amendment to the act. The *Irish News* was highly critical of the whole
enterprise:

> A majority of the people in the Six Counties of Ulster are to administer
> some of the affairs of all people by virtue of an Act of the British Parliament
> which they did not want, which they 'only accepted' on the advice of a
> Southern Irish lawyer [Carson] who sternly declined to come into the
> Sorbonian bog with them, and which is so rotten that it 'wants amending'
> before it is put into operation.[25]

Highlighting aspects of the growing civil disorder in the city the *Irish
News* columnist 'Granville II' described the job of some of the
'Specials' in Belfast for the inauguration, which was to wash away the
'choice remarks about the Pope' which decorated the (Catholic) Lord
Lieutenant's route to the City Hall, 'the least offensive of these inscrip-
tions was abominable; the majority of them were unspeakable':
'Thoughtfully, they were taken by a pathway removed from the main
scenes of last year's burnings. More courteously still, they were denied
the privilege of seeing for themselves what Belfast's decorators of dead
walls think about the Pope'.[26] As Fitzalan's entry in the *Dictionary of
National Biography* commented: 'A Catholic Viceroy, as an Irishman

remarked, was "no more welcome than a new Catholic hangman", and his difficulties would seem to have been increased rather than lessened by his religion'.[27] The *Irish News* compared the apathy which greeted the Lord Lieutenant with the 'throngs' which could be expected to greet 'Royal representatives,' in this way foretelling for its reading public the type of event the King's visit would be. Revealingly, its editorial set the inauguration of the Parliament in the context of the execution in Dublin's Mountjoy Jail of three men convicted of murdering a policeman and a JP.[28]

Preparations for the royal visit while thorough were understandably sensitive. In early June the Lord Lieutenant, Viscount Fitzalan,[29] wrote to Craig on a 'very important and difficult point...the absence in the programme of any religious service or prayers. This will have to be arranged for somehow. Stamfordham said the King would insist on it. I told him I assumed it had not been arranged for on account of the difficulty due to the different persuasions etc'. Craig was quick to reassure him:

> You need not be uneasy regarding the Opening Prayer. It was left out of the programme first submitted pending settlement here and I have come to the following arrangement. The Primate of All-Ireland (Archbishop D'Arcy), Cardinal Logue, the Moderator of the General Assembly and the President of the Methodist Body, will be officially approached by the Speaker after he is appointed, to each nominate a Chaplain to the House on the understanding that the Prayer to be used is that now read in the Imperial House of Commons (unaltered, though slightly curtailed) The four chaplains to arrange a roster, either week by week, month by month, year by year, or as they may arrange among themselves. This will cover all denominations and obviate the slightest friction.[30]

In the end only the Protestant churches were present at the inauguration to hear the opening prayer.

The royal visit was planned as far back as February 1921, although the official invitation was only sent and made publicly known in June.[31] At an early stage Craig explained to Sir Hamar Greenwood that the visit should take place before July 'because it would be a pity to mix up the Celebrations that begin practically on the 1st. Although no disturbances have ever taken place in consequence of these Celebrations, still the opposition might feel that we had purposely selected that month, and consider it provocative'.[32] The Unionist *Belfast Telegraph* welcomed the visit and assured the King of a loyal reception. The King, they argued, would have opened a southern parliament with 'equal pleasure.'

The speed with which the northern administration had organised itself
and its Parliament was presented stereotypically as a manifestation of
northern identity, 'that energy and determination that are to be found
in Ulstermen the world-wide over'. By comparison, the south's rejection of a parliament was a sign of 'Irish inconsistency'.[33] Days before the
visit the *Belfast Telegraph* sketched previous royal visits to Belfast, including those of Queen Victoria in 1849, the Prince and Princess of Wales
in 1886 and Edward VII in 1903.[34] However, the forthcoming visit was
set in the context, not principally of past royal visits, but of past
Unionist demonstrations which incorporated commemorations of
Ulster's part in the Great War, Covenant Day, the Ulster Division
review and Peace Day, this element of the familiar allowing those
attending the occasion to make a more personal and local connection to
the royal visit. Experience of choreographing these earlier political
demonstrations ensured a well-organised royal visit which was presented
by Unionists as an expression of Ulster Unionism's enduring place
in the empire. This was certainly the context in which Craig
invited Winston Churchill, Secretary of State for the Colonies, to the
inauguration.[35] According to the royal visit editorial of the *Northern
Whig*:

> The Monarchy is the nexus uniting the ancient kingdoms of the British
> Isles. It binds the mother country to the self-governing Dominions, and also
> those tropical possessions whose dark skinned, primitive people are proud to
> live beneath the benignant rule of the Great White King. Under the British
> Constitution a degree of personal liberty is enjoyed which has not been
> attained in the most democratic of Republics. It offers no obstacle to the
> making of the most daring experiments in self-government within the
> Empire; rather does it provide every facility for them.[36]

Such an expression also reflected their relationship to empire; as Jackson
argues, 'they were sentimentally and superficially committed, but…it
often took a more personal connection to transform uncritical sentiment into a more pro-active imperial faith'. While the visit of George
V in 1921 was part of the 'pageant of empire', which the First World
War and the renewed civil unrest in Ireland exacerbated, empire re-
mained merely an adjunct to Unionism.[37] 'Popular imperialism in
Ulster, therefore, had little to do with the objective condition of the
Empire, and a great deal to do with popular political morale; popular
imperialism in Ulster reflected more directly the relationship between
Unionism and the British Crown and the relationship between
Unionism and the rest of Irish politics'.[38] George Boyce maintains that

the British government pensioned off Unionists in Northern Ireland with their own parliament 'because direct rule from Westminster might give the impression that Great Britain was aiding and abetting Ulster in her refusal to unite with the rest of Ireland'.[39] This was not how Belfast's Unionist press saw it, believing that the establishment of the parliament was the end of Ulster Unionism's journey of separation from the rest of Ireland, finally giving it control over its own destiny: 'The coming of his Majesty will be the crowning event in the inauguration of the new Parliament...The King will put the seal on the work so happily begun'.[40]

Craig was of course a consummate past master in stage management, having honed his skills in Ulster's pre-war anti-Home Rule demonstrations. But the royal event did not come cheap as he explained to Greenwood:

> There is also the urgent matter of an Entertainment Fund in connection with the Opening Ceremony. I feel bound to have an official Lunch and a Reception later in the day, and to take personally such steps as are necessary in connection with platforms, gangways in the Docks, and decorations as will be worthy of the occasion. Here again, there is no fund [upon], which I can draw.[41]

Fortunately, Craig had not only the Imperial Treasury to appeal to for money, but also benefited from private donations. In August 1921 he wrote to Walter Long, for instance, thanking him for his donation of three thousand pounds: 'I never anticipated such heavy expenses as have fallen on my shoulders personally in connection with the two "openings" of Parliament & the setting up of our Government'.[42] Money was thus forthcoming and Belfast was bedecked with red, white and blue, with even the straw edging of the royal horses' stalls plaited with red, white and blue ribbons. Lady Craig's diary provides a flavour of the decorations and atmosphere:

> The King and Queen have the most wonderful reception, the decorations everywhere are extremely well done and even the little side streets that they will never be within miles of are draped with bunting and flags, and the pavement and lampposts painted red white and blue, really most touching, as a sign of their loyalty.[43]

According to the *Irish Independent* 500 men were involved in the decoration of Belfast city and the sprucing up of the City Hall itself, 'in consequence of the depression in the building trades in recent weeks, the additional work is at the moment particularly welcome'.[44] But it was not only the decorations which impressed, across the board, the newspapers were dazzled by the range of exotic military uniforms, the fine apparel of the ladies and the profusion of gold brocading. Belfast was not the only focal point for crowds curious to watch the proceedings, with many taking advantage of the slopes of Cave Hill and Bellevue to watch the arrival and departure of the royal flotilla. The banks of Belfast harbour were lined with flag and handkerchief waving enthusiasts. With the day proclaimed a holiday for the state the feeling of a day out was enhanced by those who brought picnics to sustain them. As an indication of the large numbers gathered in the city nurses and members of the ambulance corps lined the royal route (fainting women were singled out in the press as the group most needing their ministrations) while water was supplied by the Irish Temperance Movement and the Water Commissioners, with the help of the Boy Scouts (from whom programmes could also be bought for 2/6d). As with any ceremonial occasion there were also humorous moments: 'The long wait for so many people was passed patiently and good humouredly, cheers being frequently raised for no apparent reason, while any person inside the barriers, whether uniformed or in civilian clothes, no matter what he was, came in for a sally of cheers'. The waiting crowds were treated to an air show by four aeroplanes, 'the airmen seemed to have a wonderful command of the machines, and the display was interesting if a little overdone by the airmen'.[45]

After the ceremonial greeting at the quayside the royal procession made its way via the Albert Memorial, High Street, Castle Place, Donegal Place and Donegal Square North to the City Hall, the route lined by soldiers of the Norfolk Regiment, the Somersetshire Light Infantry, the Royal Ulster Rifles, the Royal Inniskilling Fusiliers and the Royal Irish Fusiliers. Along the route observers had brought chairs, boxes and even small ladders to enhance their view of the procession, while small children were raised on shoulders. At the City Hall the King was greeted by Northern Ireland's elite – members of the Northern Ireland House of Commons and the Senate, as well as others prominent in business and the leaders of the Protestant churches. In the grounds of the City Hall specially constructed stands accommodated nearly three thousand onlookers, the majority of whom were members of the Public Boards, their wives and friends, with a separate section given over to disabled soldiers. The Royal Ulster Rifles formed the guard of honour in front of the City Hall and, as they symbolised Ulster's contribution to the First World War, were singled out for particular cheering by the assembled crowd:[46] 'In them the assembled thousands saluted the Ulster Division, who proved by their courage and devotion to death in those fateful days in France the loyalty of the Imperial province'.[47] Veterans were accorded a special stand in front of the City Hall; George V highlighted the theme of Unionism's contribution to the First World War in his Ulster Hall speech.

Following the King's brief speech (and a sumptuous lunch) at the City Hall the royal procession made its way to the Ulster Hall, scene of so many significant moments in Unionist history, where civic bodies presented loyal addresses. Again, the choreography of the occasion was evident in the Ulster Hall:

> As they moved to the platform the company sang the National Anthem. The first verse was sung by men only, led by the Belfast Philharmonic Society. Female voices gave the first lines of the third verse with organ accompaniment, and then the whole audience joined in singing *fortissimo* the closing lines.[48]

In common with the stands outside the City Hall, this reception was also the exclusive province of the Unionist elite, for instance it was suggested that 'a certain number [of the 2000 seats] should be allocated for distribution by the official Unionist party'.[49] Throughout the coordination of the visit, the Northern Ireland government was alert to its sensitive nature and was keen that the speeches surrounding and during it would be seen to be non-political. For instance, Cecil Craig informed the Executive Committee of the Ulster Women's Unionist Council that their loyal address to the Queen 'must not appear that it was from a Political Organisation'; it was therefore signed by herself and Edith, the Duchess of Abercorn, simply on behalf of the loyal women of Ulster.[50]

The King's speech in the Ulster Hall echoed his earlier appeal for peace, with the addition of a significant local flavour, a tribute to the 36th 'Ulster' division, 'to all who served, men and women alike, and to offer our heartfelt sympathy to those who have suffered by disablement or loss'.[51] Indeed, the *Belfast Telegraph* presented the King's visit as 'in some sense, an expression of appreciation upon the part of his Majesty as to how Ulster played her part in the Great War'.[52] It expressed the hope that 'the mad men and the bad men' who had 'hurried Ireland into frightful excesses, and deluged her in blood, would face the facts like practical men, instead of following the hopeless practice of "chasing the rainbow"'. If they did Ireland within six months might 'be the happiest country in the world'.[53] His duties complete, George V and his entourage then made their way back to the royal yacht and returned to England.

Amidst the strict security the policing of this royal visit symbolised in a broader way the changes in Northern Ireland and the attitude of those who governed the new state. Significantly, the old Irish police force's final ceremonial duty in Belfast was also the occasion of the official high profile endorsement of the 'Specials'.[54] The Royal Irish Constabulary (men chosen exclusively from the six counties of the new state) provided a guard of honour at the quayside where the King's yacht berthed, while their band provided the musical entertainment. At the dock two deputations of shipyard workers (30 from Harland and Wolff and 10 from Workman and Clark) were presented to the royals by H.M. Pollock, Chairman of the Harbour Commissioners and Northern Ireland's first Minister of Finance. This was an interesting gesture, given that the shipyards were a particular site and catalyst for conflict in this period and both companies were singled out for particular criticism and blamed for the expulsion of Catholics in the *Irish News'* royal editorial: 'No man who is a Catholic dares seek to earn a day's employment in the great industrial concerns owned by Harland and Wolff and the English company known as Workman and Clark'.[55] In addition to the Royal Irish Constabulary (helping the army to marshal the routes) the 'A' and 'B' Specials were present in Belfast city centre in large numbers.[56] At Craig's own request they also provided a guard of honour outside the Ulster Hall, the scene of the King's last engagement of the day, accompanied by the band of the Royal Irish Constabulary.[57] For some, special attention was owed to this auxiliary police force because 'they made the election possible, and it is only through them that the laws of the new Parliament can be enforced'.[58] The 'Specials' were established in November 1920 as an auxiliary force to support the Royal Irish Constabulary; drawn from the revived Ulster Volunteer Force they were an almost entirely Protestant force. Partisan and increasingly controversial, they were perceived by the Catholic population 'as little more than Protestant vigilantes', responsible for 'a number of murders of their co-religionists'.[59] That they should have been so selected for royal attention by the Northern Ireland government sent a particularly strong message to Catholics in the new state about the mind set of those who now governed it and them.

For the King personally his willingness to act as a mediator in June 1921 (in a single round of mediation) was rooted in his desire for peace and his previously limited efforts at conciliation in Ireland (which had met with little success) and revealed his understanding of, and arguably bias towards, Ulster Unionism. As early as 1914 he argued that Ulster Unionists would 'never send representatives to a Dublin Parliament whatever the safeguards'. Moreover, he believed that the British army would never force Ulstermen to accept home rule 'upon those who wished only to remain citizens in all respects equal and at one with those in Scotland, Wales or England'.[60] Having agreed to 'create enough peers to push the Parliament Act through the House of Lords' he was of course held responsible by many Unionists 'for the "fact" that the constitution was in suspense, for the fact that Unionists in the Lords could no longer force a dissolution'.[61] This sympathy with Ulster Unionism was perhaps encouraged by his private secretary, Lord Stamfordham, whose correspondence with Theresa, Lady Londonderry, in the period of the Ulster crisis makes it clear that his sympathies were very much with Ulster Unionism; for example, following the anti-home rule demonstration in Ulster in April 1912 he wrote: 'Thank you very much for the Belfast newspaper giving such a full account of Tuesday's marvellous demonstration. It must have set Asquith and Co. thinking how in the name of all that is just, wise, statesmanlike to say nothing of expedient they can force Home Rule upon Ulster'.[62] In September that year, he wrote to say how 'dignified' and 'powerful' he thought the terms of the Solemn League and Covenant were.[63] By the start of 1914 Stamfordham was advocating negotiation: 'Surely then a mutual agreement *alone* can bring peace – and avert the shame of bloodshed. Well! The King will continue to work to that end – but there will have to be much give and take from *all* sides'.[64] With the Buckingham Palace Conference in July 1914, George V drew together the opposing leaders in the conflict in an attempt to reach a settlement, his opening statement echoing Stamfordham's sentiments to Lady Londonderry: 'to me it is unthinkable, as it must be to you, that we should be brought to the brink of fratricidal strife upon issues, apparently so capable of adjustment as those you are now asked to consider, if handled in a spirit of generous compromise'.[65] The conference 'was designed to serve a time honoured purpose of conferences and committees – that of delaying the day of decision. So much it achieved – and no more'.[66] After only three days it broke up, having failed to reach agreement. Despite this the King remained active on Irish affairs, warning his government particularly about the activities of the Black and Tans 'and the policy of authorised reprisals'.[67] In May 1921 'he pointed out to Sir Hamar Greenwood, Lloyd George's chief secretary for Ireland, "that in punishing the guilty we are inflicting punishment no less severe upon the innocent"'.[68] In this he was not alone; in the spring of 1921 'an influential body of political, intellectual and ecclesiastical opinion was ranged against the conduct of government policy in

Ireland'.[69] Despite his partisan position, the King remained the best choice of mediator for all parties given his genuine public commitment to finding a peaceful settlement for Ireland.

As he told Craig on his departure, George V's own advisors were against the Belfast visit, believing that it exposed the King to unnecessary danger.[70] The Craigs were informed that in addition the palace had received 'many letters... begging that Their Majesties should not go over to Ulster'.[71] However, the Lord Lieutenant assured Craig prior to the visit that 'nothing could exceed [the King's] affability and interest in the arrangements and the whole business'.[72] Given that the period 1920 to 1922 was the most violent in the history of Northern Ireland, with 453 deaths, such fears were well founded.[73] And as if to underline the point, 10 days before the royal visit seven people had died in fighting, while the day after the parliament's royal inauguration the IRA blew up the train carrying the king's escort, the 10th Hussars, (who had been singled out for particular praise in the press coverage of the visit) back to Dublin, killing four men and 80 horses. Concerns about the King's safety were not limited to the British authorities; security measures were stringent in Belfast, indeed the city was under continuous curfew from July 1920 to December 1924: 'precautions had been taken of every description, trusted men stationed in each house, and on every roof top, and the closest security of all in the houses, and of course in the streets too. Every alternate policeman faced the crowd, but as there were troops in front, this was not specially apparent'.[74] Additionally, owners and occupiers of buildings in Belfast city centre were ordered to block off access to roofs from eight pm on the eve of the visit until eight am on the day following it. Heightened security was not only in place, but was seen to be so, featuring frequently in journalists' reports.

The King was concerned that his actions in going to Northern Ireland would antagonise Southern Ireland,[75] however on the eve of his trip he was more troubled by speeches in both Houses of Parliament which he felt did not express support for his efforts.[76] This was a point that the *Irish News* was quick to pick up on. However, the Lord Chancellor, Lord Birkenhead, felt that the Prime Minister's invitation to Craig and de Valera would 'dissipate the apparently harsh disparity between the King's appeal' and Birkenhead's own eve of visit speech (which had argued that the British would 'continue the war, at whatever sacrifice, to prevent Irish independence'). Lloyd George argued that it was a positive thing that the speeches had come so closely together, 'in dealing with the Irish,' he said, 'you must shew that you mean to go on'.[77] In the event, the response from the press in the south of Ireland was favourable to the King's speech, while the welcome from Unionist Belfast, where many were reported as having waited eleven hours to see the royals, was enthusiastic; 'I think my speech was appreciated', the King wrote afterwards, 'I never heard anything like the cheering'.[78] A combination of factors enhanced the warmth of the welcome. In elections that spring 40 Unionists were returned to the Northern Ireland Parliament, along with six Sinn Féiners and Nationalists. The Unionists' election success obscured the fact that they had won only two of the four available seats in Armagh, while in Fermanagh and Tyrone 'fifty-seven per cent of the electorate voted against partition and returned four anti-partition candidates'.[79] Both Sinn Féin and Nationalist MPs abstained from Parliament, and were therefore not part of the loyal welcome for the King. In a letter from the secretary to the Northern Ireland Cabinet, W.B. Spender, to Sir Frederick Moneypenny, Belfast's Lord Mayor, Spender informed him that 'Nationalist MPs' had been invited to the inauguration but were unlikely to come.[80] Neither was the Catholic hierarchy present, Cardinal Logue explaining that he had a previous engagement.[81] Despite this level of official Catholic and Nationalist disapproval, this royal occasion provided entertainment and distraction for a cross-section of an increasingly disturbed Northern Ireland.

The response of the Belfast press to the royal visit split along predictable political lines. In general, the Unionist press followed the official line and took the opportunity to endorse a separate Ulster Parliament, whilst at the same time (and to varying degrees) arguing that Southern Ireland could enjoy the same if there were peace. Unsurprisingly, the Nationalist *Irish News* was highly critical of the British government and the visit, while at the same time its pages made little attempt to disguise the enthusiasm and excitement surrounding the occasion. It was particularly critical of the speech itself, arguing in a later editorial that Lloyd George's hand was visible in every sentence. It recognised, however, that the King was playing the part of the honest broker, arguing for his supposedly non-political role and maintaining that he was 'above party feuds and discords, and that the questions which trouble nations and peoples are not things to be thrust under his notice'.[82] (Conversely, the *Belfast Telegraph* predicted that the King's visit would be 'destitute of any political significance').[83] The *Irish News* condemned the King's speech, 'full of vague professions and pious good wishes', arguing that on the eve of the visit the Lord Chancellor had spoken with Lloyd George's 'true voice', 'that war was raging in Ireland, that war would be waged, and that nothing but war need be looked for by Ireland, until she surrendered abjectly and accepted Partition'. The British Prime Minister, the paper concluded, had traded on royalty.[84]

All the main Unionist papers provided special supplements to mark the royal visit. In general they set the visit in the local context of Ulster's political and industrial history. The visit was represented as the last act in the progress of Unionism to separation from the rest of the country although some added a caveat. 'The impressive pageant of yesterday', wrote the *Northern Whig*, 'graced with all the pomp and circumstance proper to a great historic occasion, brings to a close an eventful chapter in the history of Ulster's struggle for her bare rights. That struggle may not be over'.[85] For the *Belfast Newsletter* the King's visit would allow his 'loyal subjects in Belfast' to 'prove beyond all doubt that the heart of Ulster beats true to the Imperial traditions that have always been associated with the province'. Interestingly, the *Newsletter*'s editorial on the eve of the visit began in Irish with the words '*Cead Mile Failthe*' [sic]. The visit was, according to the editorial, a sign to the 'whole world that our acceptance of the new status in no way weakens the link between us and the Crown and that the gift of self-government under our own Parliament does not depreciate our connection with Great Britain and the Empire'. The paper looked positively towards the future:

> The peace and welfare of our country is as dear to us as it is to the most extreme of those who hold different views of the government of Ireland to what we do. Our Parliament will be loyal to the Crown and the Constitution: it will also be loyal to Ireland in that it will seek peace and ensure it by dealing out even-handed justice to all creeds and classes and opinions in legislation and administration. [86]

And expressed the official line that if the rest of Ireland would equally accept the opportunity for peace, 'the way to pacification is thus opened for those who chose to walk in'.

By way of contrast, and taking its tone from a statement issued by the Catholic hierarchy the eve of the visit, the *Irish News* set the opening of the Parliament in the context of what they argued had been a year 'of continuous and intolerable persecution directed against the Catholics of Belfast and the surrounding area'.[87] 'Starting with the victimisation of Catholic workers in the shipyards an intermittent campaign of arson and intimidation of Belfast Catholics lasted from the summer of 1920 until the spring of 1922 when the new Unionist Government was able to exert its control'.[88] They headlined their main coverage of the royal visit: 'Four hours of pageantry and feasting: Verbal Flummery: Not an honest word of hope'. The paper conceded that 'from a spectacular point of view it was an undoubted success...neither money nor pains were spared in the effort, and on the whole the result was very good'.[89] Yet, it reminded its readers that the royals were coming to a 'country torn by disorder and to a city seething with bitter religious hatred and party strife'. They illustrated this by reference to the choice of music which entertained the crowds in Belfast for the visit: 'While the crowd generally abstained from scurrilous party expressions characteristic of Belfast mobs, there were here and there sections whose bigoted feelings could not be suppressed'. For instance, the paper argued, the music chosen by the military bands was not enough to satisfy some loyalists who called for 'The Boyne Water' and 'Kick the Pope'. While during the inspection of the Royal Ulster Rifles 'a regiment which includes a large proportion of Catholic soldiers' a section of the crowd sang 'Derry's Walls,' although interestingly the paper noted it 'lacked general support and the strains died down after a few minutes'. This experience of bands on the street found an echo in a more official way in the organisation of the music played before the royal luncheon in the City Hall; invited from Dublin to perform, H.W. Hopkins, the Director of Musicians in Ireland, was reminded by W.B. Spender, Northern Ireland Cabinet Secretary, that it was 'essential that all the Musicians should be Ulstermen, and should be Loyalists'.[90] Sectarian tension and prejudice was therefore not hard to locate. The *Yorkshire Post* reflected on the partisan nature of the city's decorations: 'Among half-a-dozen arches is one striking archway in Ormeau Avenue, where the drinking fountain forms the central pivot. It bears Orange emblems, and several mottoes, including "Down with Sinn Féin" "Down with traitors"'.[91] This was a predictable and relatively low level of sectarianism which the strict limiting of alcohol with the closure of all licensed premises on the day of the visit (in addition to the heavy military presence) kept in check, contributing to the good behaviour of the crowd.[92]

For both the Unionist and British governments the royal visit was a great success. According to the *Belfast Telegraph* it was unique, 'no sovereign has ever visited Ireland on such a mission'.[93] The visit had a festive holiday air. On its eve, the King's Royal Rifle Corps performed an afternoon of music at Bellevue, while that evening Craig hosted dinner for members of the government at his home at Cabin Hill. Additionally, all the Belfast papers reported crowds of curious onlookers in Belfast city centre viewing the decorations: 'There was a great rush

for the tramcars as the evening advanced, but the evening remained
fine, the majority were content to walk home, taking good care not to
infringe the curfew regulations'.[94] Street vendors did a brisk trade,
according to the *Belfast Newsletter*, in miniature flags, rosettes and 'other
souvenirs of the historic occasion'; while cars, motorcycles and bicycles
were bedecked with 'loyal emblems'.[95] Celebration of the monarchy
was matched by pride in local heroes. Portraits of the King and Queen
were interspersed with those of Craig and Carson; the 'Bank Buildings'
in particular were decorated with a large portrait of the King and
Queen, with portraits of Craig and Carson on either side. Carson,
though, was absent from the royal celebrations, represented instead by
his wife, Ruby. Following the visit, Craig cabled the former Unionist
leader: 'Their Majesties have just left after a magnificent demonstration
of loyalty and affection from tens of thousands of your old followers
who and more especially your friends here the Abercorns, the Rubys
and the Craigs missed their great Leader but he was constant in their
minds and ever will be'.[96] In a letter to Ronald McNeill, who was also
absent from the day, Craig wrote that although she had had a 'tremen-
dous' reception, Ruby [Carson] had 'felt very much the break with the
past'.[97] This 'break with the past' could have been a contributing factor
to Carson's absence, although he claimed pressure of work kept him
from Belfast.

On his return the King was quick to remind his government through
his private secretary 'that the atmosphere created by his speech in
Belfast should not be allowed to evaporate'.[98] Lloyd George assured
Stamfordham that the government agreed; the gamble of sending a royal
messenger had paid off, and letters were subsequently sent to de Valera
and Craig inviting them to a conference with the Prime Minister in
London. Lloyd George informed a Cabinet meeting the day after the
visit that the King's appeal had had a 'favourable reception from the
Irish Nationalist Press' and that de Valera was now 'in a frame of mind
to discuss a settlement on a basis other than of independence'.[99] The
enthusiastic response of the British public to the King's appeal further
persuaded the Prime Minister that 'the time had come for conciliation,
and that public opinion expected him to make the first move'.[100] Still,
Lloyd George remained cautious. He couched his intention to invite
Craig and de Valera to London in terms of being 'fair to the King to
follow up his appeal', before revealing his real thinking to his cabinet
colleagues: 'If he refuses [de Valera], that will strengthen our position
when we come to set up the Crown Colony Government and martial
law'.[101] He was also quick to reassure and flatter the King; the Lord

Chancellor, he told the King, would 'emphasise that what the King had done was His Majesty's action, independent of the Government and thus carrying its own popular appeal'.

> None but the King could have made that personal appeal; none but the King could have evoked so instantaneous a response. No effort shall be lacking on the part of Your Ministers to bring Northern and Southern Ireland together in recognition of common Irish responsibility, and I trust that from now onwards a new spirit of forbearance and accommodation may breathe upon the troubled waters of the Irish question. Your Majesty may rest assured of the deep gratitude of Your peoples for this new act of royal service to their ideals and interests.[102]

This allowed the Prime Minister not only to compliment the King, but also to maintain the myth that the appeal for peace originated with the monarch and not with the government.[103] This was perhaps pragmatic given that the outcome of talks between Nationalists and Unionists in Ireland remained at best uncertain; should they break down, or violence begin again, the prime minister and government (whose Irish policy had been so open to public criticism) would have distance between them and a possibly failed overture for peace. For Craig it was also perhaps a necessary fiction, allowing him to attend the conference in London without overt opposition from Unionists. Certainly, following the King's visit the pressure 'seemed to be off the north and Craig and his ministers were able to make conciliatory speeches, promising just and reformist government within Northern Ireland and offering friendship to the south'.[104]

As Elizabeth Hammerton and David Cannadine maintain: 'The planning, staging and celebration of a ritual is not just a means by which people explain society to themselves: it is also, of itself, an expression, a product, of tensions and conflicts, links and shared assumptions of that society'.[105] That the Unionist government should place so much importance on the renewed presence of the Queen at the jubilee commemoration of 1971 is unsurprising given the history of royal visits to the state in the proceeding fifty years. At key moments in the state's history (in 1921 and at the opening of Stormont Parliament buildings in 1932) the presence of royalty reinforced the Unionist hierarchy and called almost exclusively to the Protestant community to unite behind the monarch and by extension the government (although clearly royal enthusiasm spread across community divides). The 1921 visit was dominated by Northern Ireland's Unionist and Protestant elites; priority was accorded to the Unionist government, industrialists, civic authorities, and Protestant religious leaders (aided by the boycotts of northern Nationalist MPs and the Catholic hierarchy). Additionally, following the addresses of civic bodies in the Ulster Hall, several members of the Unionist elite had honours and titles bestowed upon them. In part this encouraged Unionists to see the visit as 'a loyalist triumph and a logical return for years of bitter patriotism and bloody sacrifice'.[106] But while the King and the British Prime Minister thought the list of those to be honoured was too long,[107] Craig argued that the investiture would placate some who were unhappy with developments and recompense others who would not be rewarded with government positions. Indeed, in a letter to Greenwood in April 1921, Craig made it clear that he had been given a free hand in the matter of offering 'a certain number of Honours in connection with the Opening of the Parliament':

> It is unnecessary to give you the many reasons why this is necessary as Davies is fully alive to the importance of being able to settle differences which arise from time to time in this old fashioned manner. The Prime Minister told me personally that he thoroughly approved and would back up any decision I arrived at.[108]

More significantly, with the symbolic inauguration of the Northern Ireland Parliament in 1921 by the King the embryonic state's position within the empire was made tangible in a high profile way to both a domestic and foreign audience. This was of course aided by the press, which conjured up interest and excitement about the event in the public sphere, and gave the population at large (in particular the Protestant population) a sense of involvement. Additionally, focus on Ulster's part in the Great War, throughout the visit and in the press, allowed Unionists to claim their position in the empire in terms of sacrifice. Ostensibly the visit may have been Lloyd George's way of providing his government with another option in terms of Irish policy, but for Craig and his constituency it was the symbolic endorsement of the new state and new government. In a high profile way, with northern Catholic and Nationalist elites absenting themselves from the proceedings, it underlined the separation of the north from the south, and internally the distance between the Catholic and Protestant communities. This royal ritual united Unionists in a display of strength, while at the same time betraying their continuing defensiveness in the face of serious civil unrest within and without the state.

Chronology of Key Events in the Ulster Crisis

1885

21 Jan.	Parnell at Cork declared that 'no man has the right to fix the boundary to the march of a nation'.
1 May	Irish Loyal and Patriotic Union founded.
9 June	Gladstone's Ministry defeated in the House of Commons.
23 June	Marquis of Salisbury appointed Prime Minster of a minority government. [see 9 June]
25 June	Sir William Hart Dyke appointed Chief Secretary. Redistribution of Seats Act abolished all but nine Irish Parliamentary boroughs. This creates the basis for a territorial Ulster/southern Ireland electoral divide.
27 June	Edward Gibson as Baron Ashbourne became Lord Chancellor of Ireland.
30 June	Henry Herbert, Earl of Carnarvon, sworn in as Lord Lieutenant.
14 Aug.	Purchase of Land Act; Labourers Act; Education Endowments Act.
1 Sept.	Parnell defined the Irish party platform as having 'a single plank' of self-government.
23 Nov.– 9 Dec.	General election; Irish Party won 86 seats.
17 Dec.	Herbert Gladstone announced that his father was converted to home rule, 'Hawarden Kite'.
28 Dec.	Irish Defence Union [protection of landlords] founded.

1886

8 Jan.	Ulster Loyalist Anti-Repeal Union formed from demonstration in Belfast against home rule.
12 Jan.	Parliament opened; Lord Carnarvon resigned.
23 Jan.	William Henry Smith appointed Chief Secretary.
25 Jan.	Irish Unionist Party founded; Col. Edward J. Saunderson chosen as leader.
26 Jan.	Salisbury Ministry defeated in House of Commons (329–250).
28 Jan.	Salisbury resigns.
1 Feb.	Gladstone appointed Prime Minister for third time.
6 Feb.	John Morley appointed Chief Secretary.
10 Feb.	John Gordon, Earl of Aberdeen, sworn in as Lord Lieutenant.
16 Feb.	Catholic bishops expressed approval of home rule; published on 22 Feb.
22 Feb.	Lord Randolph Churchill in Belfast 'plays the Orange Card'.
27 Mar.	Joseph Chamberlain and Sir G.O. Trevelyan resigned from the Cabinet.
8 Apr.	Gladstone introduced Government of Ireland bill.
17 Apr.	Land Purchase bill introduced in the House of Commons.
17 Apr.	Irish Protestant Home Rule Association founded.
3–4 June	Sectarian rioting on Belfast shipyards began summer of disturbances.
4 June	Ulster Liberal Unionist Committee formed.
8 June	Government of Ireland bill defeated on its Second Reading (341–311).
26 June	Parliament dissolved.
1–17 July	General election; Irish Party won 85 seats.
25 July	Salisbury appointed Prime Minister second time.
5 Aug.	The 6th Marquess of Londonderry sworn in as Lord Lieutenant; Sir Michael Hicks Beach appointed Chief Secretary.
25 Aug.	Commission to inquire into Belfast riots appointed.

1887

7 Mar.	Arthur James Balfour appointed Chief Secretary.
28 Mar.	Criminal Law and Procedure bill introduced in the House of Commons.
31 Mar.	Irish Land bill introduced in the House of Lords.

| 18 Apr. | *The Times* published forged facsimile letter of Charles Stewart Parnell's condoning the murder of T.H. Burke in 1882. |
| 15 Oct. | Sir Joseph West Ridgeway appointed Under-Secretary. |

1888

| 5 Nov. | Charter created borough of Belfast a city. [see 20 May 1892] |
| 24 Dec. | Land Purchase Act. |

1890

| 1-8 Dec. | Meeting in Committee Room 15 in which Parnell's Party splits. |

1891

6 Apr.	Irish Unionist Alliance formed from Irish Loyal and Patriotic Union.
5 Aug.	Purchase of Land Act increased facilities for purchase and established Congested Districts Board.
9 Nov.	William L. Jackson appointed Chief Secretary.
Dec.	Workman Clark start their own engine-works at Queen's Island, Belfast.

1892

20 May	First Lord Mayor of Belfast. [see 5 Nov 1888]
17 June	Ulster Unionist Convention in Botanic Gardens, Belfast resolved to have nothing to do with a home rule Parliament.
12–26 June	General election; Liberals largest party, Nationalist return 81.
22 Aug.	Robert Milnes, Baron Houghton, sworn in as Lord Lieutenant; John Morley appointed Chief Secretary.
29 Sept.	Belfast Labour Party formed; first labour party in Ireland.

1893

13 Feb.	Gladstone introduced second home rule bill in the House of Commons. [see 2, 9 Sept.]
21–22 Apr.	Disturbances in Belfast following second reading of home rule bill.
23–30 May	Salisbury visited Ulster.
27 July	Act enabling Belfast Water Commissioners to build reservoirs.

| 2 Sept. | Home rule bill passed in House of Commons (301–267). [see 13 Feb., 9 Sept.] |
| 9 Sept. | Home rule bill defeated in the House of Lords (419–41). [see 13 Feb., 2 Sept.] |

1894

3 Mar.	W.E. Gladstone resigned as Prime Minister.
5 Mar.	Lord Rosebery appointed Prime Minister.
12 Mar.	Rosebery in the House of Lords stated that home rule will only pass when the 'predominant partner', England, approved it.
18 Apr.	Irish Agricultural Organisation Society founded by Sir Horace Plunkett.
26 May	Royal Commission under H.C.E. Childers appointed to examine financial relations between Ireland and Great Britain. [see 28 Mar. 1895, 5 Sept. 1896]
7 Nov.	Reunification of the Northern Presbytery with the Antrim Presbytery.

1895

23 Jan.	Electricity station owned by Belfast Corporation began operation.
9 Mar.	First issue of the *Irish Homestead* edited by George Russell, known as AE as an organ of the Irish Agricultural Organisation Society.
28 Mar.	First report of the Commission on Financial Relations Between Ireland and Great Britain. [see 26 May 1894, 5 Sept. 1896]
21 June	Liberal Ministry defeated in the House of Commons.
23 June	Rosebery resigned as Prime Minister.
25 June	Salisbury appointed Prime Minister for third time.
4 July	Gerald Balfour appointed Chief Secretary.
8 July	Earl of Cadogan, sworn in as Lord Lieutenant.
12–26 July	General election; Salisbury retained office and 82 Nationalists returned.
27 Aug.	Sir Horace Plunkett proposed formation of the Recess Committee.
11 Oct.	Strike by engineers at Harland & Wolff shipyard in Belfast [see 27 Jan. 1896]

1896

27 Jan.	Harland & Wolff shipyard reopened following strike. [see 11 Oct. 1895]
31 Mar.	Poor Law Guardians Act enabled women to be elected as Poor Law Guardians.
5 Sept.	Publication of the report of Royal Commission on the Financial Relations Between Ireland and Great Britain. [see 26 May 1894, 28 Mar. 1895]
6 Oct.	Rosebery resigned Liberal Party leadership.

1898

21 Feb.	Local Government bill introduced in the House of Commons.
29 Mar.	Registration Act gave women and peers the local government franchise.
Mar.	Celebrations of centenary of the rising of the United Irishmen.
12 Aug.	Local Government Act provided for elected county and district councils.

1899

Jan.	First local government elections.
11 Oct.	Boer War began.

1900

30 Jan.	Reunification of Irish party.
3–26 Apr.	Queen Victoria visited Ireland.
29 Sept.– 12 Oct.	General election; Conservatives gain increased majority, Nationalist returned 82 MPs.
9 Nov.	George Wyndham appointed Chief Secretary.

1901

22 Jan.	Death of Queen Victoria; succession of Edward VII.
5 June	Ulster Farmers' and Labourers' Union and Compulsory Purchase Association founded by T.W. Russell.
30 Sept.	Classes commenced at Municipal Technical Institute, Belfast.

1902

31 May	Treaty of Vereeniging ended Boer War.
11 July	Salisbury resigned as Prime Minister.
12 July	Arthur Balfour appointed Prime Minister.
16 Aug.	Earl of Dudley, sworn in as Lord Lieutenant.
18 Aug.	T.H. Sloan, shipyard worker, Independent Unionist and member of the Belfast Protestant Association won the parliamentary by-election for Belfast South (3,795–2,969).
8 Nov.	Sir Antony MacDonnell appointed Under Secretary.
Nov.	Emergence of Ulster branch of Irish Literary Theatre.
20 Dec.	Land Conference convened in Dublin.

1903

3 Jan.	Report of the Land Conference recommended tenant purchase financed by treasury loans.
25 Mar.	Land bill (Wyndham bill) introduced in the House of Commons.
11 June	Independent Orange Order founded in Belfast by T.H. Sloan.
21 July–1 Aug.	Edward VII visited Ireland.
14 Aug.	Wyndham Land Act (Irish Land Act) largest piece of land purchase legislation.

1904

26 Apr.–5 May	May King Edward VII visited Ireland.
25 Aug.	Land Conference dissolved. [see 3 Sept., 20 Dec. 1902, 3 Jan. 1903]
26 Aug.	Irish Reform Association founded by William O'Brien and Lord Dunraven and the latter's scheme of devolved government published.
Nov.	Publication of first issue of *Uladh*, review of Ulster Literary theatre.
2 Dec.	Unionist conference in Belfast; calls for vigilance and resistance to devolution.

1905

3 Mar.	Ulster Unionist Council formed.
5 Mar.	George Wyndham resigned as Chief Secretary.

12 Mar.	Walter Long appointed Chief Secretary.
13 July	Independent Orange Order issued 'Magheramore Manifesto'.
4 Dec.	Arthur Balfour resigned as Prime Minister.
5 Dec.	Sir Henry Campbell-Bannerman appointed Prime Minister. Electric tramways began operation in Belfast.
14 Dec.	Earl of Aberdeen sworn in as Lord Lieutenant; James Bryce appointed Chief Secretary.

1906

13–27 Jan.	General election; Campbell-Bannerman retained office, Nationalists return 83 MPs.
Apr.	Ulster Liberal Association founded.
1 Aug.	Belfast City Hall opened (architect Alfred Bramwell-Thomas).
1 Nov.	Walter Long elected leader of the Unionist Parliamentary Party.

1907

Jan.	James Larkin arrived in Belfast as organiser for the National Union of Dock Labourers.
29 Jan.	Augustine Birrell appointed Chief Secretary.
6 May– late Nov.	Dock strike in Belfast under the leadership of James Larkin.
24 July	Mutiny in support of strikers by the Royal Irish Constabulary in Belfast.
2 Aug.	*Ne temere decree* affecting marriage between Catholics and non-Catholics issued by Pope Pius X.
12 Aug.	Sectarian rioting in Falls Road, West Belfast; army killed four people.
19 Dec.	Joint Committee of Unionist Associations of Ireland founded.

1908

3 Apr.	Sir Henry Campbell-Bannerman, near death, resigned as Prime Minister.
8 Apr.	Henry Herbert Asquith appointed Liberal Prime Minister.
19–20 May	Lindsay Crawford expelled from Independent Orange Order.
July	Sir Antony MacDonnell resigned as Under Secretary.
14 July	Sir James Dougherty appointed Under Secretary.

1 Aug.   Irish Universities Act replaced Royal University with
              National University of Ireland and Queen's University of
              Belfast.

1909

29 Apr.   'People's Budget' introduced by David Lloyd George in
              the House of Commons.
30 Nov.   Lloyd George's Budget rejected by the House of Lords.
10 Dec.   Herbert Asquith at the Albert Hall in London endorsed
              Home Rule as a Liberal policy intention for the next
              Parliament.

1910

15–28 Jan.   General election; Asquith retained office, Nationalists
              returned 82 MPs.
21 Feb.   Sir Edward Carson elected leader of Unionist Party. [see
              4 Feb. 1921]
6 May   King Edward VII died; succeeded by George V.
11 June   General Assembly of Presbyterian church decided to
              co-operate with Church of Ireland and other evangelical
              churches. [see 15 Oct. 1911]
3 Dec.–   General election; Asquith retained office, Nationalists
13 Jan. 1911 returned 84 MPs.

1911

23 Jan.   Ulster Women's Unionist Council founded.
22 Feb.   Parliament bill introduced in the House of Commons.
1 Apr.   *Titanic* launched in Belfast.
7–12 July   King George V visited Ireland.
18 Aug.   Parliament Act restricted power of the House of Lords.
21 Aug.   Irish Women's Suffrage Federation founded.
23 Sept.   Orange Order and Unionist Clubs rally at Craigavon
              House, near Belfast addressed by Sir Edward Carson.
15 Oct.   Joint Committee of Presbyterian Church and Church of
              Ireland met for the first time.
8 Nov.   [see 11 June 1910] Arthur Balfour resigned as leader of
              the Conservative Party.
13 Nov.   Andrew Bonar Law chosen leader of Conservative Party.

16 Dec. Local Authorities (Qualification of Women) Act enabled women to become members of county and borough councils.

1912

8 Feb. Winston Churchill spoke at Celtic Park, Belfast.

9 Apr. Bonar Law at Balmoral, near Belfast, pledged support of British Unionists for Ulster Unionist resistance to home rule.

11 Apr. Asquith introduced third home rule bill in House of Commons. [see 16, 30 Jan., 7, 15 July 1913]

14–15 Apr. *Titanic* sank on maiden voyage.

2 May T.C. Agar-Roberts proposed in the House of Commons exclusion of four Ulster counties from Home Rule. [see 11/13/18 June]

11/13/ Debate in House of Commons on Agar-Roberts motion
18 June for four county exclusion. Amendment defeated. [see 2 May]

29 June Protestant Sunday school excursion at Castledawson, Co. Londonderry, attacked by Ancient Order of Hibernians procession. [see 2 July]

2 July Protestant shipyard workers in Belfast expel Catholics from yards in reprisal for Castledawson attack. [see 29 June]

27 July Speaking at Unionist rally at Blenheim Palace Bonar Law stated there 'are things higher than parliamentary majorities'.

14 Sept. Riot between supporters of Belfast football clubs, Celtic (Catholic) and Linfield (Protestant).

18 Sept. 'Ulster Day' with signing of Ulster's Solemn League and Covenant.

1913

1 Jan. Sir Edward Carson's amendment to Home Rule bill for the exclusion of Ulster from its operation debated and defeated.

16 Jan. Home Rule bill passed in House of Commons (367–257). [see 11 Apr. 1912, 30 Jan. 1913, 25 May 1914]

30 Jan. Home Rule bill defeated in the House of Lords (326–69). [see 16 Jan.]

31 Jan.   Ulster Volunteer Force (UVF) formed.
7 July   Home Rule bill passed in the House of Commons (352–243). [see 11 Apr. 1912; 16, 30 Jan.; 15 July; 25 May 1914]
15 July   Home Rule bill defeated in House of Lords (302–64). [see 11 Apr. 1912; 16, 30 Jan., 7 July]
17 Sept.   Carson at Newry indicated the formation of a provisional Ulster government in the event Home Rule which included Ulster is implemented.
24 Sept.   Standing Committee of Ulster Unionist Council approved establishment of a Provisional Government in the event of Home Rule.
6 Oct.   Irish Women's Suffrage Federation welcomed Carson's promise that women would be granted vote under provisional Ulster government.
14 Oct.   First secret talk between Asquith and Bonar Law on the Home Rule crisis.
6 Nov.   Second secret talk between Asquith and Bonar Law on the crisis.
4 Dec.   Royal proclamation prohibiting importation into Ireland of military arms and ammunition.
10 Dec.   Last secret talk between Asquith and Bonar Law on the home rule crisis.

1914

15 Jan.   Bonar Law announced the end of meetings with Asquith.
4 Mar.   British Anti-Home Rule Covenant launched.
9 Mar.   Asquith announced in the House of Commons that the Third Home Rule bill would be amended.
20–25 Mar.   Curragh incident when 57 officers state unwillingness to coerce north into home rule.
24–25 Apr.   Larne gunrunning by UVF.
12 May   Asquith announces an amending bill on home rule to be brought forward.
25 May   Home Rule bill passed in House of Commons for the third time.
21–24 June   Buckingham Palace Conference to resolve the Home Rule impasse ended in failure.
23 June   Government of Ireland of (Amendment) bill introduced to provide temporary exclusion of parts of Ulster from home rule scheme by county option.

28 June	Austrian Archduke Franz Ferdinand and his wife assassinated in Sarajevo.
8 July	Amendment bill altered by the House of Lords to enable permanent exclusion of Ulster from Home Rule. [see 23 June]
10 July	Provisional government of Ulster met in Belfast.
3 Aug.	Germany declared war on France. In the event of the United Kingdom entering the conflict, John Redmond announced his support and proposed that Irish and Ulster Volunteers be employed in defence of Ireland.
4 Aug.	Belgium invaded by Germany; United Kingdom declared war on Germany.
8 Aug.	Defence of the Realm Act.
15 Aug.	Press censorship introduced.
Aug.	Establishment of 36th (Ulster) Division in part based on the UVF.
15 Sept.	Suspending Act delayed implementation of home rule for one year or the duration of the war.
18 Sept.	Government of Ireland Act.
12 Oct.	Sir Matthew Nathan appointed Under-Secretary.

1915

18 Feb.	Ivor Churchill Guest, Baron Wimborne, sworn in as Lord Lieutenant.
18 Mar	Defence of the Realm Amendment Act.
25 May	Coalition government formed; Asquith remained Prime Minster and Carson joined the Cabinet as Attorney-General for England.

1916

24 Apr.	[Monday] East Rising began. General Post Office and other buildings in Dublin seized by Irish Volunteers and Citizen Army. Proclamation of Irish Republic. Arrival in Dublin of British troops stationed at the Curragh, co. Kildare.
25 Apr.	Martial law declared throughout Dublin city and county. [see 29 Apr.]
26 Apr.	Proclamation suspending in Ireland operation of sect. 1 of Defence of the Realm Act.
27 Apr.	Birrell and General Sir John Maxwell arrived in Dublin, the latter to assume command of the military operation.

29 Apr.	End of the Rising. [see 24 Apr.] Martial law declared throughout the country.
3 May	Birrell resigned as Chief Secretary; Asquith assumed the duties of the office in addition to remaining Prime Minister.
10 May	Asquith announced appointment of a Royal Commission under Lord Hardinage to Inquire into the Irish Disturbances. [see 18 May, 3 July]
12–18 May	Asquith visits Ireland to learn about events at first-hand.
23 May	David Lloyd George given task of negotiating settlement of Irish question.
25 May	Asquith in the House of Commons announced that old system of government in Ireland has broken down.
29 May	Proposals for Irish settlement by Lloyd George shown to Sir Edward Carson and Viscount Midleton.
12 June	Ulster Unionist Council accepted home rule with Ulster exclusion. [see 23, 29 May]
23 June	Convention of Ulster nationalists accepted Ulster exclusion from home rule. [see 23 May]
1 July	Battle of the Somme began with 36th (Ulster) Division sustaining heavy losses throughout offensive. [see 13 Nov]
20 July	Meeting in Derry against partition led to formation of Anti-Partition League (Irish Nation League).
4 Nov.	Lt-Gen. Sir Bryan Mahon replaced Maxwell as Commander-in-Chief of the British Military in Ireland.
13 Nov.	Somme offensive ended.
6 Dec.	Asquith resigned as Prime Minster.
7 Dec.	Lloyd George appointed Prime Minister.

1917

6 Apr.	The United States declared war on Germany.
8 May	Declaration against partition signed by 16 Catholic and 3 Protestant bishops published.
16 May	John Redmond accepted Lloyd George's proposal for an Irish Convention.
21 May	Announcement of a convention of Irishmen of all parties for the purpose of producing a scheme of Irish self-government.
28 May	Sinn Féin declined to participate in the proposed Irish Convention.

25 July	Irish Convention met in Trinity College; Sir Horace Plunkett elected chairman.
25 Nov.	Southern Unionist proposed a compromise to end Irish Convention deadlock.

1918

15 Jan.	Bishop O'Donnell opposed surrender of Irish control of economy; nationalists split on question in the Irish Convention.
6 Feb.	Representation of the People Act enfranchised all men over 21 and some women over 30; Redistribution of Seats Act made constituencies of approximately equal population.
20 Feb.	Southern Unionist Committee formed.
6 Mar.	John Redmond died
12 Mar.	John Dillon elected chairman of the Irish Party.
3 Apr.	Irish Party nominee defeated Sinn Féin candidate in the Tyrone East parliamentary by-election (1,802–1,222).
5 Apr.	Last meeting of the Irish Convention.
9 Apr.	Lloyd George introduced the Military Services bill extending conscription to Ireland. Standing [Catholic] Episcopal Committee protested against conscription proposal.
12 Apr.	Publication of Report of the Irish Convention.
18 Apr.	Military Service Act.
21 Apr.	Nationalists of all varieties signed anti-conscription pledge.
23 Apr.	One-day general strike outside Ulster sponsored by nationalists in protest against conscription.
4 May	Edward Shortt appointed Chief Secretary.
11 May	John, Viscount French, sworn in as Lord Lieutenant.
15 June	Lord Lieutenant French imposes martial law throughout most of the south and west of the country.
20 June	Conscription and Home Rule plans abandoned.
June	Ulster Unionist Labour Associated founded.
5 July	Order proscribing meetings, assemblies or processions in public places.
2 Nov.	Lloyd George declared intention to introduce partition.
11 Nov.	Armistice ended war.
21 Nov.	Parliament (Qualification of Women) Act entitled women to sit and vote in the House of Commons.

2–3 Dec.	John Dillon, Eoin MacNeill and the Lord Mayor of Dublin seek to distribute candidates in 8 Ulster constituencies in order to maximise Catholic vote. The final allocation made by Cardinal Logue on 4 Dec.
4 Dec.	Nomination day for general election; 25 Sinn Féin candidates returned unopposed.
14–28 Dec.	General election; Sinn Féin won 73 seats with Countess Markievicz the first woman elected to the House of Commons.

1919

13 Jan.	James Ian Macpherson appointed Chief Secretary.
21 Jan.	Irish Republican Army unit killed two policemen in Soloheadbeg, co. Tipperary. This act is regarded as opening the 'Anglo-Irish War'.
21 Jan.	Dáil Éireann formed at Mansion House, Dublin.
24 Jan.	Irish Unionist Alliance split; Unionist Anti-Partition League begun.
25 Jan.	Strike by Federation of Engineering and Shipbuilding Trades in Belfast.
3 June	Local Government (Ireland) Act; provided for proportional representation at local authority elections.
28 June	Versailles Treaty.
7 Oct.	British Cabinet Committee appointed to consider Irish self-government.
15 Oct.	Proclamation outlawed Sinn Féin, Irish Republican Army and other organisations.
19 Dec.	Unsuccessful attempt to assassinate the Lord Lieutenant, Viscount French, near Phoenix Park.

1920

2 Jan.	Black and Tans formed.
15 Jan.	Local government elections held under Proportional Representation (Sinn Féin, other nationalists and Labour win control of 172 of 206 borough and urban district councils).
30 Jan.	Mayoral elections; Unionist elected for Belfast, Nationalist in Derry, Labour at Wexford and Sinn Féin candidates in 8 boroughs.

25 Feb.	Better Government of Ireland bill introduced in the House of Commons.
10 Mar.	Ulster Unionist Council accepted Better Government of Ireland bill.
12 Apr.	Sir Hamar Greenwood appointed Chief Secretary.
12 June	County councils and rural district councils elections result in Sinn Féin successes which in Ulster gained control of 36 of the 55 rural district councils.
24 June	Decision to revive the Ulster Volunteer Force [UVF].
19 July	Sectarian violence lasting four days erupted in Derry resulting in 19 deaths.
21–24 July	Sectarian disturbances in Belfast resulted in more than a dozen deaths and the expulsion of Catholic workers from shipyards.
27 July	Auxiliary Division of the Royal Irish Constabulary formed.
6 Aug.	Dáil Éireann sanctioned boycott of goods from Protestant firms in Belfast. [see 21, 24 Jan. 1922]
9 Aug.	Restoration of Order in Ireland Act.
13 Aug.	Anti-Partition League called for settlement on Dominion lines.
23–31 Aug.	Disturbances in Belfast caused c. 30 deaths; curfew imposed on 31 Aug.
2 Sept.	Sir James Craig's demand for a constabulary for Northern Ireland conceded by the British government.
1 Nov.	Enrolment of recruits began in Ulster for Special Constabulary Force. [see 2 Sept.]
23 Dec.	Better Government of Ireland Act provided for two Irish Parliaments, Council of Ireland and permitted Catholics to hold office of Lord Lieutenant.

1921

1 Jan.	Beginning of government sanctioned reprisals.
4 Feb.	Sir James Craig replaced Sir Edward Carson as leader of Ulster Unionist Party.
2 May	Viscount FitzAlan, a Catholic, sworn in as Lord Lieutenant. [see 23 Dec.]
5 May	Craig and de Valera had a secret meeting in Dublin.
13 May	Nominations close for elections to Parliaments of Northern Ireland and Southern Ireland.

24 May	Elections to the two Parliaments; 124 Sinn Féin candidates returned for Southern Ireland.
7 June	Northern Ireland Parliament met and appointed a Cabinet with Craig as Prime Minster.
22 June	King George V formally opened the Parliament of Northern Ireland.
28 June	Southern Ireland Parliament opened and held its only session before being adjourned.
9–15 July	Sectarian disturbances in Belfast following disclosure of draft terms of truce left more than 20 dead.
11 July	Truce between Republican and British forces.
14–21 July	Three meetings in London between Lloyd George and de Valera.
19 Aug.	Cardinal Logue, Archbishop of Armagh, rejected invitation by Northern Ireland Minister of Education, Lord Londonderry, to nominate members to the proposed commission on education.
11 Oct.– 6 Dec.	Anglo-Irish conference in London.
10 Nov.	Lloyd George and Craig conferred in London.
13 Nov.	Arthur Griffith signed document agreeing that Northern Ireland could remain outside a united Ireland if a Boundary Commission was accepted.
17–18 Nov.	National Unionist Association conference in Liverpool approved of the Anglo-Irish negotiations.
19–25 Nov.	Sectarian rioting in Belfast caused 27 deaths.
22 Nov.	Northern Ireland government invested with control of Royal Irish Constabulary and responsibility for law and order.
5 Dec.	Craig announced expansion of Northern Ireland Special Constabulary.
6 Dec.	Articles of Agreement for a Treaty.
7 Dec.	Treaty signed.
12 Dec.	Dublin Committee of the Anti-Partition League accepted the Treaty.
14 Dec.	Carson attacked the Treaty in the House of Lords. 14 Dec. Dáil Éireann debate on the Treaty began. 14 Dec. Local Government (Emergency Powers) Act (Northern Ireland), allowed dissolution of unco-operative local councils.
14–16 Dec.	Westminster Parliament ratified the Treaty.

Notes

Chapter 1   The Ulster Crisis: A Conundrum

1. Alvin Jackson, 'Irish Unionism' in D. George Boyce and Alan O'Day (eds), *The Making of Modern Irish History: Revisionism and the Revisionist Controversy* (London, 1996), p. 120.
2. Declan Kiberd, *Inventing Ireland* (London, 1995), p. 3.
3. Gerard Delanty and Patrick O'Mahony, *Nationalism and Social Theory* (London, 2002), p. 137.
4. See, George Dangerfield, *The Strange Death of Liberal England* (1935).
5. Among many books considering other facets of the crisis, see, Cornelius O'Leary and Patrick Maume, *Controversial Issues in Anglo-Irish Relations 1910–1921* (Dublin, 2004); Jeremy Smith, *The Tories and Ireland: Conservative Party Politics and the Home Rule Crisis, 1910–1914* (Dublin, 2000).
6. See, D. George Boyce and Alan O'Day (eds) *Defenders of the Union: A Survey of British and Irish Unionism Since 1801* (London, 2001).
7. Jim Mac Laughlin, *Reimagining the Nation-State: The Contested Terrains of Nation-Building* (London, 2001).
8. Frank Wright, *Two Lands on One Soil: Ulster Politics before Home Rule* (Dublin, 1996), p. 510.
9. Issues germane to the whole period are considered in D. George Boyce and Alan O'Day (eds), *Ireland in Transition, 1865–1921* (London, 2004).
10. *Parliamentary Debates* [*PD*], 194 (1869), c. 1990.
11. Wright, *Two Lands on One Soil*, p. 432.
12. Alvin Jackson, *Home Rule, An Irish History 1800–2000* (London, 2003), p. 5.
13. An extensive range of data can be found in N.C. Fleming and Alan O'Day (eds), *The Longman Companion to Modern Irish History since 1800* (London, 2005).
14. Wright, *Two Lands on One Soil*, p. 510.
15. See, D. George Boyce, 'Rights of Citizenship: The Conservative Party and the Constitution, 1906–1914' in Alan O'Day (ed.), *Government and Institutions in the Post-1832 United Kingdom* (Lewiston/Queenston/Lampeter, 1995), pp. 215–25.
16. See Alvin Jackson, 'Irish Unionism and the Russellite Threat, 1894–1906', *Irish Historical Studies*, 25 (Nov, 1987), pp. 376–404.
17. For a wider discussion of Parnell, see, D. George Boyce and Alan O'Day (eds), *Parnell in Perspective* (London, 1991).
18. D. George Boyce, 'In the Front Rank of the Nation: Gladstone and the Unionists of Ireland, 1868–1893' in David Bebbington and Roger Swift (eds), *Gladstone Centenary Essays* (Liverpool, 2000), p. 190.

19. *PD*, 304 (1886), cc. 1053–54; for an extended discussion, see, Alan O'Day, *Irish Home Rule, 1867–1921* (Manchester, 1998).
20. *PD*, 304, cc. 1335–36.
21. See Alan O'Day, *Parnell and the First Home Rule Episode, 1884–87* (Dublin, 1986), pp. 187–88; James Loughlin, *Gladstone, Home Rule & the Ulster Question, 1882–93* (Dublin, 1987), pp. 69–80, 146–52, 257–64.
22. Wright, *Two Lands on One Soil*, p. 512.
23. P.J. Cain, 'Wealth, Power and Empire; the Protectionist Movement in Britain, 1880–1914' in P.K. O'Brien and A. Clesse (eds), *Two Hegemonies: Britain 1846–1914 and the United States 1941–2001* (Avebury, 2002), p. 108.
24. Boyce, 'In the Front Rank of the Nation', pp. 97–120.
25. A.V. Dicey, *England's Case Against Home Rule* (London, 1886), pp. 23–24.
26. A.V. Dicey, *A Fool's Paradise: Being a Constitutionalist's Criticism of the Home Rule Bill of 1912* (London, 1913), pp. 113–23.
27. Rodney Barker, *Politics, Peoples and Government: Themes in British Political Thought Since the Nineteenth Century* (London, 1994), p. 116.
28. R.V. Comerford, 'Patriotism as Pastime: The Appeal of Fenianism in the mid-1860s', reprinted in Alan O'Day (ed.), *Reactions to Irish Nationalism, 1865–1914* (London, 1987), p. 28.
29. Samuel Clark, *State and Status: The Rise of the State and Aristocratic Power in Western Europe* (London, 1995), pp. 307–8.
30. Wright, *Two Lands on One Soil*, p. 512.
31. W.E. Vaughan and A.J. Fitzpatrick, *Irish Historical Statistics: Population, 1821–1971* (Dublin, 1978), pp. 51–68.
32. Miroslav Hroch, *In the National Interest. Demands and Goals of European National Movements of the 19th Century: A Comparative Perspective* (Prague, 1996), p. 32. But, see, John Hutchinson, *Nations as Zones of Conflict* (London, 2005).
33. Hroch., p. 200.
34. See, *ibid.*, pp. 33, 209; Jim Mac Laughlin, *Reimagining the Nation-State*, p. 130; Patrick O'Mahony and Gerard Delanty, *Rethinking Irish History: Nationalism, Identity & Ideology* (Basingstoke, 1998), p. 21; Ernest Gellner, *Nations & Nationalism* (Oxford, 1983), pp. 48–49.
35. O'Mahony and Delanty, *Rethinking Irish History*, p. 101. Mac Laughlin, too, believes that 'nationalism in countries like Ireland, Spain and Poland prolonged the political power of the Catholic Church'. *Reimagining the Nation-State*, p. 99.
36. *PD*, 37, (1912), c. 2118.
37. *PD*, 31, (1912), c. 388.
38. *PD*, 91, (1917), c. 454.
39. *PD*, 37, (1912), cc. 2120–21.
40. *PD*, 21, (1911), cc. 84–89.
41. See, *Belfast News-Letter*, editorial 9 June 1917.
42. For example, William Coote MP uses 'Britisher' in Fivemiletown, *Ulster Guardian*, 27 Jan 1917, and 'British' in Enniskillen, *ibid.*, 18 Aug. 1917.

43. John Hutchinson and Anthony Smith (eds), *Ethnicity* (Oxford, 1996), p. 6.
44. For texts on nationalism, see Philip Spencer and Howard Wollman, *Nationalism, a Critical Introduction* (London, 2002); O'Mahony and Delanty, *Rethinking Irish History*; Mac Laughlin, *Re-imagining the Nation-State*.
45. Wright, *Two Lands on One Soil*, p. 432.
46. J. Milton Yinger in Hutchinson and Smith (eds), *Ethnicity*, p. 249.
47. Benedict Anderson, *Imagined Communities: Reflections on the Origin and Spread of Nationalism* (London, 1983).
48. Gellner, *Nations and Nationalism*.
49. See Michael Wheatley, '*These Quiet Days of Peace*': Nationalist Opinion Before the Home Rule Crisis, *1909–1913*, in Boyce and O'Day (eds), *Ireland in Transition*, pp. 57–75.
50. David Fitzpatrick, *Politics and Irish Life, 1913–1921: Provincial Experience of War and Revolution* (Dublin, 1977), p. 101.
51. *Irish Independent*, 24, 31 Dec. 1910.
52. From another perspective amplification of this outlook is Virginia Crossman, '"The Charm of Allowing People to Manage Their Own Affairs": Political Perspectives on Emergency Relief in Late Nineteenth-Century Ireland', in Boyce and O'Day (eds), *Ireland in Transition*, pp. 193–208.
53. E.H.H. Green, *The Crisis of Conservatism: The Politics, Economics and Ideology of the British Conservative Party* (London, 1995); Martin Pugh, *The Tories and the People, 1880–1935* (Oxford, 1985).
54. Mark Harrison, *Crowds and History: Mass Phenomena in English Towns, 1790–1835* (Cambridge, 1988), p. 27.
55. David Cannadine, 'The Context, Performance and Meaning of Ritual: The British Monarchy and the "Invention of Tradition"', Eric Hobsbawm and Terence Ranger (eds), *The Invention of Tradition* (Cambridge, 1983), p. 105.
56. David Cannadine, 'The Transformation of Civic Ritual in Modern Britain: The Colchester Oyster Feast', *Past & Present*, 94 (1984), p. 129.
57. Elaine McFarland, 'Marching from the Margins: Twelfth July Parades in Scotland, 1820–1914' in T.G. Fraser (ed.), *The Irish Parading Tradition: Following the Drum* (Basingstoke, 2000), p. 60.
58. Tom Gallagher, 'A Tale of Two Cities: Communal Strife in Glasgow and Liverpool Before 1914' in Roger Swift & S.W. Gilley, *Irish in the Victorian City* (London, 1984) p. 123.
59. D.C. Richter, *Riotous Victorians* (Athens OH, 1981), p. 163. Indeed in 1866 rioters in Hyde Park were careful to 'avoid the flower beds', p. 54.
60. R.J. Holton, 'The Crowd in History: Some Problems of Theory and Method', *Social History* 3, 2 (1978), p. 222.
61. E. Durkheim, *The Elementary Forms of Religious Life*, trs. Joseph Swain (London, 1915), p. 427.
62. The Master of Elibank quoted in Alan O'Day and John Stevenson (eds), *Irish Historical Documents since 1800* (Dublin, 1992), p. 152.

63. Paul Bew, *Ideology and the Irish Question: Ulster Unionism and Irish Nationalism 1912–1916* (Oxford, 1994), pp. 92–93.

64. Elizabeth Hammerton and David Cannadine, 'Conflict and Consensus on a Ceremonial Occasion: The Diamond Jubilee in Cambridge in 1897', *Historical Journal*, 24, 1, (1981), p. 146.

65. O'Mahony and Delanty, *Rethinking Irish History*, pp. 2, 4.

66. Wright, *Two Lands on One Soil*, pp. 513–15.

Chapter 2   The Political Economy of the Ulster Crisis: Historiography, Social Capability and Globalisation

1. E. Childers, *The Framework of Home Rule* (London, 1911), p. ix.

2. T. Sinclair, 'The Position of Ulster' in S. Rosenbaum (ed.), *Against Home Rule: The Case for the Union* (London, 1912), p. 179.

3. A. Jackson, *The Ulster Party: Irish Unionists in the House of Commons, 1884–1911* (Oxford, 1989), p. 4.

4. D. McCloskey, *Econometric History* (Basingstoke and London, 1987), p. 22.

5. A.T.Q. Stewart, *The Ulster Crisis: Resistance to Home Rule* (London, 1967), pp. 42–44.

6. D.G. Boyce, *Ireland 1828–1928: From Ascendancy to Democracy* (Oxford, 1992), pp. 80–81, 86.

7. *Ibid.*, pp. 89–90; D. Burnett, 'The Modernisation of Unionism, 1892–1914?' in R. English and G. Walker (eds), *Unionism in Modern Ireland: New Perspectives on Politics and Culture* (Dublin, 1996), p. 44.

8. P. Ollerenshaw, 'Industry, 1820–1914' in L. Kennedy and P. Ollerenshaw (eds), *An Economic History of Ulster, 1820–1939* (Manchester, 1985), p. 66.

9. One notable piece of economic analysis that undoubtedly applies to the study of the Ulster crisis is the elementary concept of opportunity cost. Opportunity cost must have come into play when the reallocation of time, money and talent associated with political agitation is considered. For instance, the sizable resources that went into constructing the pavilion for the Unionist convention in Belfast's Botanic Gardens on 17 June 1892 could have been utilised elsewhere, as could the time of the 12,000 male delegates and the further 120,000 spectators. That these people chose to engage in political activity logically implies that other uses of their money, work and leisure time necessarily must have been forgone by their decision to engage in political agitation (of varying degrees of legality). By forgoing these options the economy followed a different path than it would otherwise have followed. If Gibbon's claim that once various crises passed, the various social classes that sponsored Unionism could not create enough enthusiasm for sustaining political popular activity is true, then it suggests that other claims on people's time took priority in times of political stability. P. Gibbon, *The Origins of Ulster Unionism; the Formation of Popular Protestant*

Politics and Ideology in Nineteenth-Century Ireland (Manchester, 1975), pp. 132, 138.

10. C. Ó Gráda, *Ireland: A New Economic History* (Oxford, 1994).
11. *Ibid.*, p. 330.
12. K. Ohkawa and H. Rosovsky, *Japanese Economic Growth* (Stanford, 1972).
13. M. Abramovitz and P.A. David, 'Convergence and Deferred Catch Up; Productivity Leadership and the Waning of American Exceptionalism' in R. Landau, T. Taylor and G. Wright (eds), *The Mosaic of Economic Growth* (Stanford, 1996), p. 50.
14. M. Abramovitz, 'The Elements of Social Capability' in B.H. Koo and D.H. Perkins (eds), *Social Capability and Long-Term Economic Growth* (London, 1995), p. 45.
15. Abramovitz and David, 'Convergence and Deferred Catch Up', p. 34.
16. M. Abramovitz, 'Catching-Up, Forging Ahead and Falling Behind', *Journal of Economic History*, 36 (June, 1986), p. 388.
17. Abramovitz, 'Elements', pp. 30–31.
18. L. Kennedy, 'The Economic Thought of the Nation's Lost Leader: Charles Stewart Parnell' in D.G. Boyce and A. O'Day (eds), *Parnell in Perspective* (London, 1991).
19. Childers, *Framework of Home Rule*, p. 274.
20. *Ibid.*, p. 263.
21. *Ibid.*, p. 260.
22. *Ibid.*, p. 281.
23. *Ibid.*, p. 283.
24. *Ibid.*, p. 305.
25. *Ibid.*, p. 269.
26. Rosenbaum (ed.), *Against Home Rule*.
27. E. Carson, 'Introduction' in *ibid.*, pp. 17–41; Sinclair, pp. 170–82; G. Balfour, 'Unionist Policy in Relation to Rural Development in Ireland', pp. 225–49; A.W. Samuels, 'Possible Irish Financial Reforms Under the Union', pp. 271–82; L.S. Amery, 'The Economics of Separation', pp. 282–95; Anon, 'The Problem of Transit and Transport in Ireland', pp. 332–47.
28. Balfour, *ibid.*, p. 225.
29. *Ibid.*, Amery, p. 286.
30. Balfour, *ibid.*; Amery, p. 286.
31. Carson, *ibid.*, p. 30, Amery, p. 292.
32. Carson, *ibid.*, p. 38.
33. Amery, *ibid.*, p. 293.
34. Anon, *ibid.*
35. Amery, *ibid.*, p. 291; Samuels, p. 277.
36. Sinclair, *ibid.*, pp. 178–79.
37. *Ibid.*, p. 178.
38. H.J. Voth, 'Why Was Stock Price Volatility so High During the Great Depression? Evidence from the Interwar Period', Paper Presented at the

Economic History Society Annual Conference, Trevelyan College, University of Durham, 4–6th April 2003.

39. C.R. Hickson and J.D. Turner, 'The Rise and Decline of the Irish Stock Market', Unpublished Paper, School of Management and Economics, Queen's University Belfast (2004).

40. *Ibid.*, p. 4.

41. *Ibid.*, p. 16.

42. *Ibid.*, p. 23.

43. M.E. Daly, *The Spirit of Earnest Inquiry; The Statistical and Social Inquiry Society of Ireland 1847–1997* (Dublin, 1997).

44. *Ibid.*

45. *Ibid.*, p. 83.

46. *Ibid.*, p. 87.

47. *Ibid.*, p. 85.

48. Given Ulster's vital role in the Irish economy it also seems plausible to suggest that discussion of Ulster would have drawn the Society into debates that bordered on politics. This line of reasoning is given some force as Daly concedes herself that a 1917 paper on the politically contentious issue of 'the Foundations of Colonial Self-Government' was only published after a disclaimer regarding the paper's political content was inserted in the final published version. *Ibid.*, p. 86.

49. Stewart, *The Ulster Crisis.*

50. *Ibid.*, p. 50.

51. *Ibid.*, p. 98.

52. J.J. Lee, *Ireland 1912–1985: Politics and Society* (Cambridge, 1989).

53. *Ibid.*, pp. 6, 14.

54. *Ibid.*, pp. 6, 579–87.

55. *Ibid.*, p. 8.

56. R. English and G. Walker (eds), *Unionism in Modern Ireland: New Perspectives on Politics and Culture* (Dublin, 1996).

57. G. Walker, 'Thomas Sinclair: Presbyterian Liberal Unionist' in *ibid.*, p. 36.

58. *Ibid.*, p. 37.

59. P. Bew, '"The Ulster Crisis": Some Ideological Questions Revisited', in S. Wichert (ed.), *From United Irishmen to Twentieth-Century Unionism* (Dublin, 2004), pp. 159–74.

60. *Ibid.*, p. 159.

61. Gibbon, *The Origins of Ulster Unionism*; A. Reid, 'Skilled Workers in the Shipbuilding Industry 1880–1920: A Labour Aristocracy?' in A. Morgan and B. Purdie (eds), *Ireland: Divided Nation Divided Class* (London, 1980), pp. 111–25; R. Munck, *The Irish Economy: Results and Prospects* (London, 1993).

62. D. O'Hearn, *The Atlantic Economy: Britain, the US and Ireland* (Manchester, 2001).

63. Gibbon, *The Origins of Ulster Unionism*, pp. 143–46.

64. Munck, *The Irish Economy*, p. 20.
65. L. Kennedy, *Colonialism, Religion and Nationalism in Ireland* (Belfast, 1996).
66. Childers, *The Framework of Home Rule*, p. 250.
67. *Ibid.*, pp. 239–41; L.M. Cullen, *An Economic History of Ireland Since 1660* (2nd ed.; London, 1987), p. 167.
68. Cullen, *Economic History of Ireland Since 1660*, p. 167.
69. *Ibid.*, p. 168.
70. *Ibid.*
71. Nevertheless, this line of historical enquiry has been hindered because one is faced with the observation that the official set of national accounts for the years 1938–44 were only issued in 1946. J. Begley, 'Income and Expenditure-Based Approaches to Nineteenth Century GDP Estimates', Working Paper presented to Historical National Income Accounts Group, ESRI, Dublin, 2003, p. 1.
72. *Ibid.*
73. Childers, *The Framework of Home Rule*, p. 241.
74. A. Maddison, *Monitoring the World Economy 1820–1992* (Paris, 1995).
75. N. Butlin, 'A New Plea for the Separation of Ireland', *Journal of Economic History*, 28 (June, 1968), pp. 274–91; C.H. Feinstein, *National Income, Expenditure and the Output of the United Kingdom, 1855–1965* (Cambridge, 1972). See also R. Crotty, *Irish Agricultural Production: Its Volume and Structure* (Cork, 1966) and O'Hearn, *The Atlantic Economy*.
76. K.A. Kennedy, T. Giblin and D. McHugh, The *Economic Development of Ireland in the Twentieth Century* (London, 1988).
77. Ó Gráda, *Ireland: A New Economic History*.
78. J.G. Williamson, 'Economic Convergence: Placing Post-Famine Ireland in Comparative Perspective', *Irish Economic and Social History*, 21 (1994), pp. 5–27.
79. J.G. Williamson, 'Globalization, Convergence and History', *Journal of Economic History*, 56 (June, 1996), pp. 291–92.
80. *Ibid.*, pp. 295–97.
81. F. Geary and T. Stark, 'Examining Ireland's Post-Famine Economic Growth Performance', *Economic Journal*, 112 (October, 2002), pp. 919–36.
82. *Ibid.* p. 920.
83. Geary and Stark, 'Examining Ireland's Post-Famine Economic Growth Performance', p. 931.
84. *Ibid.*, pp. 931–32.
85. Geary and Stark's calculations suggest that British GDP per caput and per worker both grew 0.8 per cent per annum, while Irish GDP per caput grew by 0.9 per cent per annum and GDP per worker grew by 1.1 per cent annually. *Ibid.*, p. 927. They additionally conducted a growth accounting exercise and found that capital accumulation and technical change rather than alterations of labour inputs due to emigration

accounted for the bulk of measurable productivity growth in Ireland. *Ibid.*, p. 931.

86. *Ibid.*, p. 927.
87. *Ibid.*, p. 927.
88. N.F.R. Crafts, 'Regional GDP in Britain, 1871–1911', *Scottish Journal of Political Economy* (forthcoming).
89. *Ibid.*, p. 7.
90. L. Kennedy, 'Ulster' in J. Mokyr (ed.), *The Oxford Encyclopaedia of Economic History*, 5 (Oxford, 2003), p. 143.
91. Abramovitz, 'The Elements of Social Capability', p. 43.
92. Ó Gráda, *Ireland: A New Economic History*, p. 349.
93. C.R. Hickson and J.D. Turner, 'The Trading of Unlimited Liability Bank Shares in Nineteenth Century Ireland: The Bagehot Hypothesis', *Journal of Economic History*, 63 (December, 2003), pp. 931–58.
94. Ó Gráda, *Ireland: A New Economic History*, p. 350.
95. *Ibid.*, p. 357.
96. Ollerenshaw, 'Industry, 1820–1914', p. 66.
97 Stewart, *The Ulster Crisis*, p. 41.
98. G.A. Brownlow, 'Institutional Change in the Two Irelands, 1945–1990: an Application of North's Institutional Economics', Queen's University Belfast Ph.D., 2002.
99. K.H. O'Rourke and J.G. Williamson, *Globalization and History: The Evolution of a Nineteenth-Century Atlantic Economy* (London, 1999); J. Foreman-Peck, *A History of the World Economy: International Economic Relations Since 1850* (2nd ed.; London, 1995); J. Foreman-Peck, 'Introduction' in J. Foreman-Peck (ed.), *Historical Foundations of Globalization* (Cheltenham, 1998), pp. xiii–xxv.
100. K.H. O'Rourke, 'Europe and the Causes of Globalization, 1790 to 2000, *Trinity Economics Paper, No. 1*, (Dublin, 2002), p. 2.
101. O'Rourke and Williamson, *Globalization and History*; Foreman-Peck, *A History of the World Economy*.
102. Foreman-Peck, 'Introduction', p. xxiii, O'Rourke and Williamson, *Globalization and History*.
103. Williamson, 'Globalization, Convergence and History', p. 302.
104. *Ibid.*, p. 295.
105. O'Rourke and Williamson, *Globalization and History*, pp. 16–21.
106. Burnett, 'The Modernisation of Unionism'; G. McIntosh, *The Force of Culture: Unionist Identities in Contemporary Ireland* (Cork, 1999), p. 9.
107. Gibbon, *The Origins of Ulster Unionism*, Burnett; 'The Modernisation of Unionism', p. 42.
108. P.J. Cain, 'Wealth, Power and Empire; the Protectionist Movement in Britain, 1880–1914' in, P.K. O'Brien and A. Clesse (eds), *Two Hegemonies: Britain 1846–1914 and the United States 1941–2001* (Avebury, 2002), pp. 106–15.
109. *Ibid.*, p. 106.

110. Stewart, *The Ulster Crisis*, p. 20.
111. Cain, 'Wealth, Power and Empire', p. 107.
112. *Ibid.*, p. 112.
113. *Ibid.*, p. 108.
114. *Ibid.*, p. 108.
115. J. Charmley, *A History of Conservative Politics 1900–1996* (Basingstoke and London, 1998), p. 27.
116. Ó Gráda, *Ireland: A New Economic History*, p. 313.
117. *Ibid.*, p. 330.
118. N.F.R. Crafts, 'Development History', London School of Economics, Department of Economic History, Working Paper No. 54/00 (2000), p. 12.
119. Brownlow, 'Institutional Change in the Two Irelands'.

Chapter 3   The State and the Citizen: Unionists, Home Rule, Ulster and the British Constitution, 1886–1920

1. The Earl of Selborne, *The State and the Citizen* (London, 1912), pp. 153–55.
2. Rodney Barker, *Politics, Peoples and Government: Themes in British Political Thought Since the Nineteenth Century* (London, 1994), p. 13.
3. A.V. Dicey, *England's Case Against Home Rule* (London, 1886), pp. 23–24.
4. Dicey to James Bryce, 18 May 1886, Bodleian Library, Bryce MSS, 2/82.
5. Dicey, *England's Case*, pp. 232–35, 283, 286.
6. *Ibid.*, pp. 13, 183, 185.
7. A.V. Dicey, *A Fool's Paradise: Being a Constitutionalist's Criticism of the Home Rule Bill of 1912* (London, 1913), pp. 113–23.
8. Dicey, *Introduction to the Study of the Law of the Constitution* (London, 1915 edition), p. xvii.
9. *Ibid.*, p. xvii.
10. *Ibid.*, pp. xxi, xxiii.
11. *Ibid.*, p. xxxviii.
12. *Ibid.*, p. liii.
13. *Ibid.*, p. lv.
14. *Ibid.*, pp. ci–cii.
15. For a discussion of Low and Lowell's analyses see José F. Harris and Cameron Hazlehurst, 'Campbell-Bannerman as Prime Minister', *History*, 55 (1970), pp. 360–83.
16. Selborne, *The State and the Citizen*, pp. 158–59.
17. *Ibid.*, pp. 119–21.
18. Dicey in Sir William Anson et al, *Rights of Citizenship: A Survey of the Safeguards for the People* (London, 1912), pp. 89, 166–67.
19. Lord Lansdowne in *ibid.*, p. viii.
20. *Ibid.*, p. xxix.

21. For a critical view of the Unionists in this crisis see Jeremy Smith, *The Tories and Ireland, 1910–14: Conservative Party Politics and the Home Rule Crisis* (Dublin, 2000).

22. *Ibid.*, pp. 67–8; Robert Blake, *The Unknown Prime Minister: The Life and Times of Andrew Bonar Law, 1858–1923* (London, 1955), p. 130.

23. Selborne, *The State and the Citizen*, pp. 115, 135.

24. Blake, *Unknown Prime Minister*, p. 130.

25. Smith, *The Tories and Ireland*, pp. 21–22; David Dutton, 'His Majesty's Loyal Opposition': *The Unionist Party in Opposition, 1905–1915* (Liverpool, 1992), pp. 82–86.

26. Selborne to Lady Selborne, 19 Jan. 1906 in D.G. Boyce (ed.), *The Crisis of British Unionism: Lord Selborne's Domestic Political Papers, 1885–1922* (London, 1987), p. 42.

27. Same to same, 28 Mar. 1907 in *ibid.*, p. 318.

28. Dicey, *A Leap in the Dark*, p. 177.

29. Dicey *A Fool's Paradise*, p. 105.

30. Dicey, *A Leap in the Dark*, p. 181.

31. *Ibid.*, p. 181.

32. Ruth Dudley Edwards (ed.), *The Best of Bagehot* (London, 1993), pp. 253–56.

33. Quoted in P. Fraser, 'The Growth of Ministerial Control in the Nineteenth Century House of Commons', *English Historical Review*, 75 (1960), pp. 444–63 at p. 445. See also Valerie Cromwell, 'The Losing of the Initiative by the House of Commons, 1780–1914', *Transactions of the Royal Historical Society*, 5th ser, 18 (1968), pp. 1–23.

34. Corinne C. Weston, 'Salisbury and the Lords, 1868–1895', in C. Jones and D. Lewis Jones (eds), *Peers, Politics and Power: The House of Lords, 1603–1911* (London, 1986), pp. 461–87.

35. Dicey, 'On the Brink of the Abyss', *Nineteenth Century*, lxvii (Jan.–June, 1910), p. 785.

36. Selborne to T. Comyn Platt, 19 Sept. 1912 in Boyce, *Crisis of British Unionism*, p. 92; same to Austen Chamberlain, 28 Apr. 1910, *ibid.*, pp. 44–45.

37. Midleton to Selborne, 28 Apr. 1910, *ibid.*, p. 46.

38. C.S. Emden, *The People and the Constitution* (Oxford, 1933), p. 299.

39. F.S. Oliver to Selborne, 27, 30 Mar. 1911 in Boyce, *Crisis of British Unionism*, pp. 53, 56.

40. Lord Hugh Cecil, *Conservatism* (London, 1912), pp. 77–80.

41. Dicey, *Introduction to the Study of the Law of the Constitution*, pp. xli, xliii.

42. Selborne to T. Comyn Platt, 19 Sept. 1912 in Boyce, *Crisis of British Unionism*, p. 92.

43. John Ramsden (ed.), *Real Old Tory Politics: the Political Diaries of Sir Robert Sanders, Lord Bayford, 1910–35* (London, 1985), p. 49.

44. Dicey, *A Fool's Paradise*, pp. 117, 125–26; Richard A. Cosgrove, *The Rule of Law: A.V. Dicey, Victorian Jurist* (North Carolina and London, 1982),

pp. 242–43. See also Dicey's letter in *The Times*, 28 July 1911, where he stressed the importance of 'faith in the rule of law and in the maintenance of constitutional morality'.

45. Dicey, *Introduction to the Study of the Law of the Constitution*, p. 305.
46. R.J.Q. Adams, *Bonar Law* (London, 1999), p. 147.
47. Lord Hugh Cecil, Memorandum of 5 June 1913 in Boyce, *Crisis of British Unionism*, pp. 94–98 (which I originally wrongly surmised as having been written by Lord Willoughby de Broke).
48. J.S. Sandars to H.A. Gwynne, 5 Dec. 1914, Bodleian Library, Dep. 20.
49. Adams, *Bonar Law*, pp. 147.
50. *Ibid.*, p. 151; Dutton, '*His Majesty's Loyal Opposition*', pp. 226–29.
51. Ian F.W. Beckett (ed.), *The Army and the Curragh Incident, 1914* (London, 1986) p. 5.
52. Milner to Selborne, 18 Feb. 1914 in Boyce, *Crisis of British Unionism*, pp. 102–4; see also Willoughby de Broke to Bonar Law, 11 Sept. 1913, House of Lords Record Office, Law MSS, 30/2/10.
53. Cosgrove, *A.V. Dicey*, p. 253.
54. Dicey to Milner, 2 Mar. 1914, Bodleian Library, MS Eng. Hist. C. 689, fols. 127–31.
55. Dicey, 'The Appeal to the Nation', *Nineteenth Century*, lxxv (Jan.–June, 1914), pp. 945–57.
56. Dicey, 'The Enigma still Unsolved? (II): Facts and Thoughts for Unionists', in *ibid.*, p. 719.
57. Dicey to Milner, 6 Mar. 1914, Bodleian Library, Dep. 41, fols. 40–42.
58. *The Times*, 27 July 1914.
59. *Rights of Citizenship*, p. 66.
60. Adams, *Bonar Law*, p. 115.
61. J.A.R. Marriott, 'The Constitution in Suspense', *Nineteenth Century*, lxxv (Jan.–June, 1914), p. 18.
62. Elie Kedourie, *The Crossman Confessions and Other Essays in Politics, History and Religion* (London, 1984), pp. 45–46.
63. For a comprehensive treatment of the federal idea see John Kendle, *Ireland and the Federal Solution: the Debate on the United Kingdom Constitution, 1870–1921* (Kingston and Montreal, 1989).
64. Austen Chamberlain to Selborne, 2 May 1912, in Boyce, *Crisis of British Unionism*, pp. 169–70. Dicey for his part was a strong opponent of federalism; see for example Dicey to Milner, 6 Mar. 1914, Bodleian Library, Dep. 41, fols. 40–42 and 7 May 1914, fol. 120, and his *A Fool's Paradise*, p. 97.
65. Carson to Selborne, 18 Feb. 1918, enclosing a letter from Carson to Lloyd George, 14 Feb. 1918 in Boyce, *Crisis of British Unionism*, pp. 210–12.
66. F.E. Guest to Lloyd George, 3 May 1918, House of Lords Records Office, Lloyd George MSS, F 21/2.20.
67. War Cabinet Minutes, 23 Apr. 1918, National Archives, Cab 23/6.
68. John Kendle, 'Federalism and the Irish Problem in 1918', *History*, 56 (1977), p. 227.

69. War Cabinet Minutes, 23 Apr. 1918, National Archives, Cab. 23/6.
70. First Report of the Committee on Ireland, 4 Nov. 1919, National Archives, Cab 27/68.
71. D.G. Boyce, 'Federalism and the Irish Question', in Andrea Bosco (ed.), *The Federal Idea; Vol. I, The History of Federalism, From the Enlightenment to 1945* (London and New York, 1991), p. 134. The Speaker's Report is 'Conference on Devolution: letter from Mr Speaker to the Prime Minister', Cmd. 692, 1920.
72. Boyce, 'Federalism and the Irish Question', p. 133.
73. Reginald Coupland, *Welsh and Scottish Nationalism: A Study* (London, 1954), p. 327.
74. Conference of Devolution: Letter from Mr Speaker to the Prime Minister', Cmd. 692, 1920, pp. 36–38.
75. Austen Chamberlain, 'The Irish Question and Federalism', prepared for the War Cabinet, 17 June 1918, National Archives, Cab. 24/5; L.S. Amery to Lloyd George, 17 Apr. 1918, House of Lords Record Office, Lloyd George MSS, F 2/1/18; Selborne to Walter Long, 31 May 1918 in Boyce, *Crisis of British Unionism*, pp. 217–18.
76. Coupland, *Welsh and Scottish Nationalism*, pp. 333–34.
77. Barker, *Politics, Peoples and Government*, p. 116.

Chapter 4   The Irish Volunteers: A Machiavellian Moment?

1. The new edition (Princeton, 2003) contains a very useful afterward for those new to the subject.
2. The best general account of the progress of the Volunteers in 1913–14, with particular focus on the negotiations between the Provincial Committee and the leadership of the IPP, can be found in Michael Tierney, *Eoin MacNeill: Scholar and Man of Action, 1867–1945* (Oxford, 1980), pp. 97–166. Also, Charles Townshend, *Political Violence in Ireland: Government and Resistance since 1848* (Oxford, 1983), pp. 256–61, 278–79; F.S.L. Lyons, *Ireland Since the Famine* (London, 1971), and the opening chapter of Joost Augusteijn, *From Public Defiance to Guerilla Warfare: The Experience of Ordinary Volunteers in the Irish War of Independence* (Dublin, 1996). A full account of the incidents surrounding the Howth gun-running episode can be found in Bulmer Hobson, *A Short History of the Irish Volunteers* (Dublin, 1918), pp. 148–67, cf. Report of the 'Royal Commission on the Circumstances Connected with the Landing of Arms at Howth on July 26th, 1914', copy preserved in Hobson Papers, National Library of Ireland [NLI] MS 13, 174 (9).
3. Pocock, *Machiavellian Moment*, p. 554.
4. These machinations can be followed in detail in Matthew Kelly, 'Irish Separatism, 1882–1914', DPhil Oxford 2002, pp. 185–212.
5. See Matthew Kelly, 'The End of Parnellism and the Ideological Dilemmas of Sinn Féin' in D. George Boyce and Alan O'Day (eds), *Ireland in Transition* (London, 2004), pp. 142–58.

6. National Archive, London, Colonial Office, Irish Monthly Police Reports, CO 904/86, Apr. 1912, p. 688.

7. CO 904/88, Nov. 1912, p. 408. For detail see, CO 907/87, June & Aug. 1912, pp. 17, 50, 196, 595.

8. Michael Wheatley, '"These Quiet Days of Peace" – Nationalist Opinion Before the Home Rule Crisis, 1909–1913' in Boyce and O'Day (eds), *Ireland in Transition*, pp. 40–43.

9. Leon Ó Broin, *No Man's Man. A Biographical Memoir of Joseph Brennan – Civil Servant & First Governor of the Central Bank* (Dublin, 1982), p. 20.

10. Paul Bew, *Ideology and the Irish Question: Ulster Unionism and Irish Nationalism* (Oxford, 1994), p. 113.

11. CO 904/93, June 1914, p. 496.

12. MacNeill to Figgis, 12 May 1914, Hobson Papers, NLI, MS 13,171 (3).

13. C. Desmond Greaves, *Liam Mellows and the Irish Revolution* (London, 1971), pp. 58–59 cf. Hobson, *A Short History of the Irish Volunteers* (Dublin, 1918), pp. 18–19. In this IRB head-count Pearse, Thomas MacDonagh and Joseph Plunkett are included, although in Nov. 1913 they had not yet been sworn into the Brotherhood.

14. Namely, Laurence Kettle, John Gore, Tom Kettle, Michael Judge, John Walsh, and James Lenehan. Pearse to Devoy, 12 May 1914 in William O'Brien & Desmond Ryan, *Devoy's Postbag vol. II [DPB II]* (Dublin, 1948), pp. 440–41.

15. David Fitzpatrick, *Politics and Irish Life 1913–1921. Provincial Experience of War and Revolution* (Cork, 1998), p. 86.

16. Clarke to Devoy, 14 May 1914, *DPB II*, pp. 444–46.

17. William O'Brien, *The Irish Revolution and How It Came About* (Dublin, 1923), p. 223.

18. MacNeill to Fr Convery, 2 July 1904, 'In theory I suppose I am a separatist, in practice I would accept any settlement that would enable Irishmen to freely control their own affairs, and I would object to any theoretical upsetting of such a settlement. If the truth were to be known, I think that this represents the political views of 99 out of every hundred Nationalists'. Quoted in Michael Tierney, *Eoin MacNeill Scholar and Man of Action 1867–1945* (Oxford, 1980), pp. 104–5.

19. Martyn to Casement, 10 Dec. 1913, Casement Papers, NLI, MS 13,073 (11).

20. Casement to Moore, 2 June 1914, Moore Papers, NLI, MS 10,561.

21. Reproduced in Dorothy MacArdle, *The Irish Republic* (4th ed, Dublin, 1951) pp. 909–11.

22. For example, see statement by MacNeill and Laurence Kettle, 4 Sept. 1914, demanding the transfer from the government of the material means to defend Ireland as a fulfillment of the manifesto. Also, the circular of 24 Sept. 1914 announcing that Redmond's nominees were no longer members of the committee on the grounds that his Woodenbridge speech was incompatible with the manifesto. NLI Hobson Papers, MS 13,173 (1) & (10).

23. A modicum of autonomy in the foreign arena was among the major advances the form of dominion status allowed by the Anglo-Irish Treaty of 1922 represented over Home Rule.

24. Patrick Maume, *The Long Gestation: Irish Nationalist Life 1891–1918* (Dublin, 1999), p. 167.

25. *Irish Volunteer [IV]*, 14 Feb. 1914.

26. On the 'legend' of Ireland's 'preternatural tendency to disunion and fratricidal strife' see, for example, Hugh A. MacCarten, 'Comrades All!', *IV*, 4 July 1914.

27. Peter Hart, *The IRA and its Enemies* (Oxford, 1998), pp. 237–39, 268–69.

28. *IV*, 4 Apr. 1914.

29. cf. Danny Morrison's notorious summary of Sinn Féin's approach to electoral politics in the 1980s, with 'ballot paper in this hand and an Armalite in this hand'. Quoted in Alvin Jackson, *Ireland 1798–1998* (Oxford, 1999), p. 397.

30. CO 904/194/46, 5 Mar. 1914.

31. Casement to Moore, 9 Apr. 1914, Moore Papers, NLI, MS 10,561. MacNeill was also reassuring: 'Casement is all right. In conversation, he is the deadly enemy of the existing order, as we all are, only that we do not let ourselves go to the same extent. In all matters of action, he is wise and careful, and worthy of the fullest confidence'. NLI MacNeill to Moore, 13 Apr. 1914, MS 10,561.

32. National Archive, London, CAB 37/119/51, 2 Apr. 1914. Cf. the Royal Commission on the Howth gunrunning incidents which described the Volunteers as 'composed of respectable citizens, and all its operations had been conducted without disorder'.

33. Arthur Griffith, 'National Unity. Back to the Base', *IV*, 14 Feb. 1914.

34. Tierney, *Eoin MacNeill*, pp. 107–9.

35. Transcript sent by William Maloney to Hobson, 25 Oct. 1938, in Joseph McGarrity Papers, NLI, MS 17,453.

36. Townshend, *Political Violence*, pp. 248–49.

37. Senia Pašeta, 'Thomas Kettle: 'An Irish Soldier in the Army of Europe'?' in Adrian Gregory and Senia Pašeta (eds), *Ireland and the Great War 'A War to Unite Us All?'* (Manchester, 2002), p. 16.

38. *Ibid.* and *Thomas Kettle* [forthcoming].

39. *IV*, 25 Apr. 1914.

40. Liam de Roiste argued the same, *IV*, 14 Feb. 1914.

41. *IV*, 25 Apr. 1914; R.F. Foster, *Modern Ireland 1600–1972* (London, 1988), p. 477.

42. Kettle continued: 'The objective of this movement is a force of 50,000 or 60,000 trained men, armed with modern rifles, and capable of resisting any attack upon the common liberties of this country'.

43. There was no room for feebleness in the Volunteers. William Royce made the case for the adoption of the kilt as their uniform: 'The only objections that can be made to its adoption as a uniform for Volunteers are those

which will come from the skinny-legged, knick-kneed type for whose faulty or undeveloped "understandings" the pants as a covering are a veritable Godsend'. *IV*, 14 Feb. 1914.

44. cf. Casement to Hobson, 7 Sept. 1909. 'The Irish Catholic, man for man is a poor crawling coward as a rule. Afraid of his miserable soul and fearing the Priest like a Devil. No country was ever freed by men afraid of bogies. Freedom to Ireland can come *only* through Protestants because they are not afraid of any Bogey, (except the Pope, and their fear of him is after all a bit of play acting – he'd have a damned bad time of it in Lurgan if he showed up there!)', Hobson Papers, NLI, MS 13,158 (6).

45. *IV*, 7 Feb. 1914.

46. Michael Laffan, 'In Search of Patrick Pearse' in Máirín Ní Dhonnchadha and Theo Dorgan (eds), *Revising the Rising* (Derry, 1991), p. 128.

47. *IV*, 2 May 1914.

48. *IV*, 4 July 1914. Arms were prohibited from import by Royal Proclamation of Dec. 1913, it was mysteriously rescinded 5 Aug. Between times the Volunteers pressured the IPP to lobby for the lifting of the ban before defying it altogether in July at Howth.

49. Townshend, *Political Violence*, p. 264.

50. A.M. Sullivan, *Old Ireland. Reminiscences of an Irish K. C.* (London, 1927), p. 150.

51. CO 904/23, 'Possession and Carrying of Arms specially Revolvers – corres. 1907–12'.

52. *Irish Catholic*, 7 Nov. 1908.

53. *Weekly Freeman*, 24 Oct. 1908.

54. CO 903/18, 'Firing Outrages in Ireland since the 1st January, 1848', p. 68. Re. analysis of crime statistics cf. Joost Augusteijn, *From Defiance to Guerilla Warfare*, pp. 14–19. More detailed figures are discussed in Kelly, 'Irish Separatism', pp. 229–31.

55. It appears that the police did not include any shots fired as part of the Fenian Rising of 1967 when only 28 indictable offences are recorded, higher only than 1866 in that decade.

56. The only other period when the annual total topped one hundred was 1886–88, coinciding with the Plan of Campaign: respectively 135, 120, 103.

57. 1880–82 Firing at the Person, agrarian: 146, non-agrarian: 126. Firing into dwelling, agrarian: 325, non-agrarian: 89.

58. P.H. Pearse, 'The Coming Revolution' in *Political Writings and Speeches* (Dublin, 1966), pp. 98–99.

59. cf. Joseph Lee, *Ireland, 1912–1988* (Cambridge, 1989), p. 1.

60. CAB 37/119/51, CO 904/93, Apr. 1914, p. 19. Hobson argued the official figures underestimated membership; see his *History Irish Volunteers*, p. 93.

61. Fitzpatrick draws attention to the significance of this 9 May instruction, *Politics and Irish Life*, p. 88.

62. O'Rahilly to Devoy, 6 Apr. 1914, *DPB II*, pp. 425–27.
63. *IV*, 7 Feb. 1914.
64. These figures were evidently collated from police reports.
65. CO 904/91 & 93, Dec. 1913, pp. 613–14, 627, Apr. 1914, p. 19.
66. CO 904/92, Feb. 1914, pp. 216, 219, 222–23, 228.
67. CO 904/93, May 1914, pp. 222–34.
68. CO 904/93, May 1914, pp. 222–30.
69. Casement to Moore, 11 Dec. 1913, NLI Moore Papers, MS 10,561 (3).
70. CO 904/93, June 1914, p. 496.
71. CO 904/120, Apr. 1914, pp. 71–72.
72. Hobson, *History Irish Volunteers*, p. 183.
73. CO 904/94, July 1914, p. 6.
74. Bulmer Hobson, *Ireland Yesterday and Tomorrow* (Tralee, 1968), p. 9.
75. Ruth Dudley Edwards, *Patrick Pearse: The Triumph of Failure* (Dublin, 1977, 1990), p. 179.
76. Ashe to Devoy, 27 Apr. 1914, *DPB II*, pp. 427–29.
77. O'Rahilly to Devoy, 6 Apr. 1914, *DPB II*, pp. 425–27.
78. Maume, *Long Gestation*, pp. 94–95, 125, CO 904/86, Feb. 1912, p. 293. For a lurid account of the origins of the AOH see H.B.C. Pollard, *The Secret Societies of Ireland: Their Rise and Progress* (London, 1922; Kilkenny, 1998).
79. Joseph V. O'Brien, *William O'Brien and the Course of Irish Politics 1881–1918* (Berkeley and Los Angeles, 1976), pp. 187–88.
80. O'Brien, *Irish Revolution*, p. 223.
81. McCartan to Devoy, 20 Feb. 1909, *DPB II*, pp. 376–77.
82. Data from three Colonial Office reports 'Return setting forth the Strength of the Volunteers in Sept. 1914, before the division of the Two Bodies' subsequently known as the National Volunteers and the Irish Volunteers', 'Return setting forth the Strength of the Irish Volunteers and the quantity of arms in their hands in the month of December, 1914', and 'Arms in the Possession of the National Volunteers on the 10th December, 1914'. CO 903/18, pp. 51, 54.
83. The traditionalists include Lyons, *Ireland since the Famine*, p. 330 and Alvin Jackson, *Ireland 1798–1998*, p. 198. Cf. Tierney, *Eoin MacNeill*, p. 154 and comment in Townshend, *Political Violence*, p. 279.
84. CO 904/120, Oct. 1914, p. 114, CO 904/95, Nov. 1914, p. 222.
85. On 4 Oct. Devlin addressed 2,000 Volunteers at St. Mary's Hall, Belfast and McCullough was shouted down.
86. CO 904/120, Oct. 1914, pp. 114–18.
87. CO 904/95, Oct. 1914, p. 10.
88. David Fitzpatrick, 'The Logic of Collective Sacrifice: Ireland and the British Army, 1914–1918', *Historical Journal*, 38, 4 (1995), pp. 1017–1030.
89. 'The mere mention in a newspaper a week or two ago that it was intended to enforce the Militia Ballot act, caused hundreds to rush off to America'. The progress of the war would soon seal off this escape from enlistment. CO 904/95, Oct. 1914, p. 11.

90. *Ibid.*
91. Thanks to Dr James McConnel for this observation.
92. CO 904/95, Nov. 1914, p. 216.
93. CO 904/95, Nov. 1914, pp. 231–33.
94. CO 904/95, Dec. 1914, p. 431.
95. Childers to Casement, 8 June 1914, NLI, MS 36,208.
96. Maume, *Long Gestation*, p. 221.
97. Fitzpatrick, *Politics and Irish Life*, p. 109.

Chapter 5   The Landed Elite, Power, and Ulster Unionism

1. See, John E. Pomfret, *The Struggle for the Land of Ireland, 1800–1923* (Princeton, 1930).
2. Peter Gibbon, *The Origins of Ulster Unionism: The Formation of Popular Protestant Politics and Ideology in Nineteenth-Century Ireland* (Manchester, 1975), pp. 143–46.
3. Alvin Jackson, *The Ulster Party: Irish Unionists and the House of Commons* (Oxford, 1989), pp. 5–6.
4. John Harbinson, *The Ulster Unionist Party, 1882–1973: Its Development and Organisation* (Belfast, 1973), p. 110.
5. Amanda N. Shanks, *Rural Aristocracy in Northern Ireland* (Aldershot, 1988), *passim*; David Cannadine, *The Decline and Fall of the British Aristocracy* (London, 1990), p. 176.
6. Frank Ormsby (ed.), *The Collected Poems of John Hewitt* (Belfast, 1991), pp. 134–5.
7. Max Weber, *The Theory of Social and Economic Organization* (ed. Talcott Parsons) (rep. edn; New York, 1964), pp. 324–58.
8. See, Alan O'Day, 'Max Weber and Leadership, Butt, Parnell and Dillon: Nationalism in Transition', in D. George Boyce and Alan O'Day (eds), *Ireland in Transition, 1867–1921* (London, 2004), pp. 17–34.
9. Jim Mac Laughlin, *Reimagining the Nation-State: The Contested Terrains of Nation Building* (London, 2001), pp. 18–20, 210–26.
10. Frank Wright, *Two Lands on One Soil: Ulster Politics before Home Rule* (Dublin), pp. 476–509.
11. David Spring, 'Landed Elites Compared' in David Spring (ed.), *European Landed Elites in the Nineteenth Century* (London, 1977), p. 6.
12. F.M.L. Thompson, 'Britain', in *European Landed Elites*, pp. 22–3, 37.
13. Samuel Clark, *State and Status: The Rise of the State and Aristocratic Power in Western Europe* (London, 1995), pp. 307–8.
14. Ian Budge and Cornelius O'Leary, *Belfast: Approach to Crisis* (London, 1973), chapters 1–3; David Cannadine, *Lords and Landlords: The Aristocracy and the Towns, 1747–1967* (Leicester, 1980), pp. 387, 406.
15. Henry Patterson, *Class Conflict and Sectarianism: The Protestant Working Class and the Belfast Labour Movement, 1868–1920* (Belfast, 1980), pp. 1–18.

16. Alvin Jackson, *Colonel Edward Saunderson: Land and Loyalty in Victorian Ireland* (Oxford, 1995), p. 47.

17. John Tunney, 'The Marquess, the Reverend, the Grand Master and the Major: Protestant Politics in Donegal, 1868–1933', in W. Nolan, L. Ronayne, and M. Dunlevy (eds), *Donegal, History and Society: Interdisciplinary Essays on the History of an Irish County* (Dublin, 1995), p. 678.

18. Graham Walker, 'Thomas Sinclair: Presbyterian Liberal Unionist', in Richard English and Graham Walker (eds), *Unionism in Modern Ireland: New Perspectives on Politics and Culture* (London, 1996), p. 27.

19. Jackson, *Ulster Party*, pp. 57, 165.

20. William Roulston, 'Landlordism and Unionism in Tyrone, 1885–1910', in Charles Dillon and Henry A. Jefferies (eds), *Tyrone: History and Society* (Dublin, 2000), pp. 741–60.

21. Philip Bull, *Land, Politics and Nationalism: A Study of the Irish Land Question* (Dublin, 1996), pp. 143–75.

22. Jackson, *Ulster Party*, p. 239.

23. Ronald McNeill, *Ulster's Stand for the Union* (London, 1922), pp. 44–5.

24. Jackson, *Ulster Party*, p. 57.

25. Andrew Gailey, 'King Carson: An Essay on the Invention of Leadership', *Irish Historical Studies*, 30 (May 1997), pp. 66–87.

26. Diane Urquhart, 'Peeresses, Patronage and Power: The Politics of Ladies Frances Anne, Theresa and Edith Londonderry, 1800–1950', in Diane Urquhart and Alan Hayes (eds), *Irish Women's History* (Dublin, 2000), pp. 43–59.

27. Buckland, *Irish Unionism: Two: Ulster Unionism and the Origins of Northern Ireland, 1886–1922* (Dublin, 1973), pp. 68–91.

28. N.C. Fleming, *The Marquess of Londonderry: Aristocracy, Power and Politics in Britain and Ireland* (London, 2005), pp. 80–116.

29. C. Wright Mills, *The Power Elite* (Oxford, 1956), *passim*.

Chapter 6   Irish Nationalism in Ulster, 1885–1921

1. I am grateful to CRASSH, the Centre for Research in the Arts, Social Sciences & Humanities, University of Cambridge, for providing a Visiting Fellowship for Easter Term 2004, during which time this essay was completed.

2. For convenience I will normally use the term 'Ulster' in this chapter to mean the large and contiguous area in the north of Ireland approximating to the modern Northern Ireland.

3. *Parliamentary Debates*, House of Commons (13 May 1886), cited in James Loughlin, *Gladstone, Home Rule & the Ulster Question, 1882–1893* (Dublin, 1986), p. 143.

4. 'It is worth noting that the ethnic and the ensuing national identities were mutually more sharply defined (and perhaps also more conflicting) where religion rather than culture stood as the criterion'. Miroslav Hroch, *In the National Interest. Demands and Goals of European National Movements of the 19ᵗʰ Century: A Comparative Perspective* (Prague, 1996), p. 32.

5. *Ibid.*, p. 200.
6. See, *ibid.*, pp. 33, 209; Jim Mac Laughlin, *Reimagining the Nation-State: The Contested Terrains of Nation-Building* (London, 2001), p. 130; Patrick O'Mahony and Gerard Delanty, *Rethinking Irish History: Nationalism, Identity & Ideology* (Basingstoke, 1998), p. 21; Ernest Gellner, *Nations & Nationalism* (Oxford, 1983), pp. 48–49.
7. Ebenezer Howard, *Garden Cities of Tomorrow* (London, 1902 and later eds).
8. Patrick Pearse, 'The Heart's Desire', in *Spark* (April 1916), cited in Ruth Dudley Edwards, *Patrick Pearse: The Triumph of Failure* (New York, 1978), p. 338.
9. O'Mahony & Delanty, *Rethinking Irish History*, pp. 78–79.
10. *Ibid.*, p. 101. MacLaughlin, too, believes that 'nationalism in countries like Ireland, Spain and Poland prolonged the political power of the Catholic Church'. *Reimagining the Nation-State*, p. 99.
11. Evidence to the Royal Commission of Inquiry into the Belfast Riots of 1864 (BPP, 1865), cited in A.C. Hepburn, *A Past Apart* (Belfast, 1996), p. 146. Patrick Dorrian (1814–85) was coadjutor and, from 1865, Catholic Bishop of Down & Connor.
12. This term was used by the Orange leader and Unionist MP William Johnston of Ballykilbeg (1829–1902) who believed that such an institution was necessary to counter 'popery', which he regarded as 'a religio-political system for the enslavement of the body and soul of man'. *Belfast Newsletter*, 15 May 1861.
13. These arguments and terms were first developed by Frank Wright in *The Northern Ireland Conflict: a Comparative Analysis* (Dublin, 1987) and in *Two Lands on One Soil: Ulster Politics before Home Rule* (Dublin, 1996). See esp., *Two Lands*, p. 512.
14. Wright, *Two Lands*, pp. 372–75.
15. See e.g. Report of the Londonderry Riots Inquiry Commission, pp. 17–20 (*British Parliamentary Papers* 1870, vol. XXXII), cited in A.C. Hepburn (ed.), *The Conflict of Nationality in Modern Ireland* (London, 1980), pp. 38–39.
16. This kind of approach to electoral politics had some resonance in several constituencies in the south of Ireland prior to 1885, but after the male franchise extension of that year it continued outside Ulster only in two constituencies in the Dublin area which had large Protestant populations.
17. B.M. Walker (ed.), *Parliamentary Election Results in Ireland, 1801–1922* (Dublin, 1978), passim.
18. See Hepburn, *A Past Apart*, p. 160.
19. M. Arnold-Forster, *The Rt. Hon. Hugh Oakeley Arnold-Forster: A Memoir* (London, 1910), pp. 88–92.
20. See various references in the *Irish News* and in the *Northern Star*, Oct.–Dec. 1903.
21. See esp. Hepburn, *A Past Apart*, pp. 137–56. For similar interpretations see also: Marianne Elliott, *The Catholics of Ulster: a History* (London, 2000), pp. 293–94, 364; Loughlin, *Gladstone*, pp. 123, 221.

22. Catherine Hirst, *Religion, Politics & Violence in 19th Century Belfast: the Pound & Sandy Row* (Dublin, 2002).
23. Ambrose Macaulay, *Patrick Dorrian: Bishop of Down & Connor, 1865–1885* (Dublin, 1987), p. 361.
24. Elliott, *Catholics of Ulster*, pp. 293–94.
25. Walker, *Election Results*, passim.
26. Loughlin, *Gladstone*, pp. 123–25.
27. Walker, *Election Results*, passim; Elliott, *Catholics*, p. 295; Loughlin, *Gladstone*, pp. 246–47.
28. Tim McCarthy (1868–1928) came to Belfast in 1897 as first editor of Devlin's weekly paper, *The Northern Star*, which was run in opposition to the episcopally-controlled *Irish News*. McCarthy later edited William O'Brien's Dublin-based *Irish People*, before returning to Belfast in 1906 as editor of the – by then Devlin-controlled – *Irish News*.
29. Many of this class in Belfast had been educated by the Christian Brothers, a lay teaching order which had been brought into the diocese by Bishop Dorrian – although he later fell into dispute with them. Unlike the secular clergy of Down & Connor the teaching Brothers in Belfast were, at least until the 1880s, all incomers from the nationalist heartlands of southern Ireland. See Hepburn, *A Past Apart*, p. 148.
30. See above, p. 108.
31. Devlin to John Redmond, 22 Jan., 13 & 24 May 1903. Redmond Papers, National Library of Ireland [NLI], 15181/1.
32. One historian of these events even felt it necessary to state that 'the IRB was, of course, more than a group of Belfast republicans translated to Dublin'. L.P. Curtis jr, 'Ireland in 1914', in W.E. Vaughan (ed.), *A New History of Ireland* (Oxford, 1996), 6, p. 180.
33. Jonathan Bardon, *History of Ulster*, (Belfast, 1992) pp. 424, 452–53. For biographical details of Hobson, McCullough, McCartan, Clarke and McDermott see D.J. Hickey & J.E. Doherty, *A Dictionary of Irish History since 1800* (Dublin, 1980).
34. MacEntee's father, James, a prosperous Belfast publican, had been a prominent supporter and city councillor for Bishop Henry's Catholic Association. The family premises in Belfast were burned down by loyalists during the troubles of 1920–22.
35. John Gray, *City in Revolt: James Larkin & the Belfast Dock Strike of 1907* (Belfast, 1985), pp. 36–41.
36. For a discussion of this see A.C. Hepburn, *Contested Cities in the Modern West* (Basingstoke and London, 2004), p. 233.
37. See, for instance, the short memoir by William McMullen (1888–1984), *With James Connolly in Belfast* (n.d., n.p. but probably Dublin, 1951).
38. The intervening third party candidate, A.M. Carlisle, who stood as an independent unionist, was brother-in-law to Lord Pirie, chairman of Harland & Wolff's shipyards. Pirie, though prominent in the (Liberal) Unionist opposition to home rule in 1893, had become disgruntled with

the Conservative and Unionist establishment for personal reasons, and by 1906 was a Liberal Home Ruler. Carlisle's intervention facilitated Devlin's election and was doubtless intended to do so: Devlin (N) 4138, Smiley (U) 4122, Carlisle (Ind.Lib.U) 153.

39. W.S. Churchill to George V, 8 Feb. 1911, cited in R.S. Churchill (ed.), *Winston Churchill, Companion* (London, 1968), II, pp. 1034–35.

40. Cited in *The Hibernian Journal*, XLII (June, 1959), p. 22.

41. *The Irish Worker*, 7 Mar. 1914, cited in Arthur Mitchell, *Labour in Irish Politics, 1980–1930* (Dublin, 1974), p. 45.

42. Lord Riddell, *More Pages from My Diary* (London, 1934), p. 202.

43. T.P. O'Connor to Devlin, 1 Oct. 1913, NLI: Redmond Papers, 15181/3.

44. Devlin at Dundalk, *Times*, 6 Oct. 1913.

45. Devlin to Redmond 12 Nov. 1913, Redmond Papers, 15181/3; Devlin to Dillon 12 Nov. 1913, Dillon Papers, Trinity College Dublin, 6730/164.

46. O'Connor to Dillon, 17 Dec. 1913, Dillon Papers, 6740/617.

47. O'Connor to Dillon, 30 Dec. 1913, Dillon Papers, 6740/219.

48. Denis Gwynn, *The Life of John Redmond* (London, 1932) p. 259.

49. Patricia Jalland, *The Liberals and Ireland: the Ulster Question in British Politics to 1914* (Brighton, 1980). Under the terms of the 1911 Parliament act, the government could only overrule the Lords' veto if, in the second and third years in which a bill was brought forward, it was passed in the same form as had been passed by the House of Commons in year one. Later changes might be introduced with the agreement of the opposition, but no unilateral changes were permitted after year one.

50. Memorandum, 23 Feb. 1914, House of Lords Record Office: Lloyd George Papers, C/20/2/7.

51. *The Times*, 7 Mar. 1914.

52. Austen Chamberlain, *Politics from the Inside* (London, 1936), p. 586.

53. Bardon, *History of Ulster*, p. 443.

54. RIC and DMP reports on the Volunteers' split, 31 Oct. 1914. NLI, MS 15,258.

55. Paul Bew, *Ideology & the Irish Question: Ulster Unionism & Irish Nationalism, 1912–1916* (Oxford, 1994), pp. 139–40.

56. Eric Mercer, 'For King, country and a shilling a day: Belfast recruiting patterns in the Great War', *History Ireland*, 11 (Winter, 2003), pp. 29–33. For the proportion of military voters registered in each parliamentary constituency in Ireland at the time of the 1918 general election see *Whitaker's Almanack*, 1919.

57. Dillon to O'Connor, 20 Dec. 1918, cited in Eamon Phoenix, *Northern Nationalism: Nationalist Politics, Partition and the Catholic Minority in Northern Ireland, 1890–1940* (Belfast, 1994), p. 35; Stephen Gwynn, *John Redmond's Last Years* (London, 1919), p. 239. The day referred to by Gwynn was 24 July 1916, the occasion on which Redmond, in a bitter speech to the House of Commons, had to acknowledge that the party's concessions had proved fruitless.

58. Walker, *Parliamentary Election Results*, p. 185. A third candidate appeared on the ballot paper in South Armagh as an independent Unionist, but secured only 40 votes, a bare 1 per cent of the turn-out.

59. The franchise, previously restricted to male householders, was extended to include almost all males over the age of 21, together with women over the age of 30. In Ireland this increased the electorate from just over 700,000 in 1910 to more than 1.9 million in 1918.

60. Michael Laffan, *The Resurrection of Ireland: The Sinn Féin Party, 1916–1923* (Cambridge, 1999), pp. 165–66.

61. Phoenix, *Northern Nationalism*, p. 52.

62. Patrick Maume, *The Long Gestation: Irish Nationalist Life, 1891–1918* (Dublin, 1999), p. 203.

63. Elliott, *Catholics of Ulster*, p. 300.

64. Laffan, *Resurrection of Ireland*, p. 327; http://www.election.demon.co.uk/stormont.

65. Alan F. Parkinson, *Belfast's Unholy War* (Dublin, 2004), pp. 35, 41.

66. Frank Pakenham, *Peace by Ordeal* (London, 1935), passim.

67. Tim Pat Coogan, *Michael Collins* (London, 1990), p. 333.

68. Enda Staunton, *The Nationalists of Northern Ireland, 1918–1973* (Dublin, 2001), p. 53.

69. Between mid-1920 and mid-1922 the Catholic minority in Belfast, comprising less than one quarter of the population, sustained 257 out of 416 civilian deaths. A.C. Hepburn, *Ireland 1905–1925 vol. 2: Documents and Analysis* (Newtownards, 1998), p. 237.

70. Michael Hopkinson, *The Irish War of Independence* (Dublin, 2002), pp. 156–57.

71. Staunton, *Nationalists of Northern Ireland*, pp. 65, 67, 80.

72. Parkinson, *Belfast's Unholy War*, p. 113.

73. E.g. Author's interview with Thomas Dillon (1884–1971), Professor of Chemistry at University College Galway and joint author of the revised Sinn Féin constitution of 1917, Dublin 1966.

74. Ben Novick, in Joost Augusteijn (ed.), *The Irish Revolution, 1913–23* (Basingstoke and London, 2002), pp. 34–52.

75. Laffan, *Resurrection of Ireland*, p. 128. Devlin had of course worked in, or managed, bars for most of his career before entering Parliament in 1902.

76. Maume, *Long Gestation*, p. 217.

77. Augusteijn (ed.), *The Irish Revolution*, p. 130; *Irish News*, 17 Jan. 1922, cited in Jim MacDermott, *Northern Divisions: the Old IRA and the Belfast Pogroms, 1920–22* (Belfast, 2001), p. 157.

78. Laffan, *Resurrection of Ireland*, p. 232.

Chapter 7   Actions and Views: John Brownlee Lonsdale, Unionist MP, 1900–18 and Party Leader, 1916–18

1. An exception is Alvin Jackson, *The Ulster Unionist Party: Irish Unionists in the House of Commons, 1884–1911* (Oxford, 1989) and also, 'Unionist

Politics and Protestant Society in Edwardian Ireland', *Historical Journal*, 33, 4 (1990), pp. 839–66.

2. 5 Griffith's *Valuation of the Union of Armagh in County Armagh* (Dublin, 1864), p. 27.

3. Information about the Land League from an obituary, *Armagh Guardian* [*AG*], 13 June 1924, although we can note that Lonsdale never referred to this in his speeches.

4. Prospectus of J&J Lonsdale, May 1900, Armstrong papers, Public Record Office of Northern Ireland [PRONI], D3727/E/46/1.

5. *Belfast Newsletter [BNL]*, 14 Feb. 1900.

6. *Northern Whig [BNL]*, 9 June 1924.

7. Jackson, *The Ulster Party*, p. 75.

8. From obituaries, *NW*, 9 June 1924 and *AG*, 13 June 1924.

9. *Return Showing the Religious Denominations of the Population According to the Census of 1881, in Each Constituency Formed in Ulster by the Redistribution of Seats Act*, 1885, H.C., 1884–85, LXII (335), 1, 339.

10. Jackson, *Unionist Politics in Edwardian Ulster*, p. 841; B.M. Walker, *Ulster Politics: The Formative Years, 1868–1886* (Belfast, 1987), pp. 182, 240.

11. *Ulster Gazette [UG]*, 10 Feb. 1900.

12. *NW*, 2 Feb. 1900.

13. Joshua Peel to J.B. Lonsdale, 28 Feb. 1900, Peel papers, PRONI, D889/3//1b/1/310.

14. Peel to Lonsdale, 3 Feb. 1900, *ibid.*, D889/3/1b/1/307.

15. *AG*, 28 Sept. 1900.

16. Peel to Lonsdale, 14 Jan. 1901, Peel papers, D889/3/1b/488.

17. *NW*, 4 Feb. 1900.

18. B.M. Walker 'Landowners and Parliamentary Elections in County Down, 1801–1921' in Lindsay Proudfoot (ed.), *Down History and Society* (Dublin, 1997), pp. 319–20.

19. Peel to Lonsdale, 21 July 1900, Peel papers, D889/3/1b/387.

20. Walker, *Elections in Down*, pp. 319–21.

21. *BNL*, 29 Sept. 1900.

22. *UG*, 6 Oct. 1900.

23. *UG*, 14 Oct. 1905; *AG*, 5 Jan. 1906.

24. *UG*, 31 Oct. 1903.

25. *UG*, 31 Oct. 1903.

26. *UG*, 18 Apr. 1903.

27. *UG*, 10 Nov. 1906.

28. *UG*, 22 Sept. 1906.

29. Peel to David Miller, 9 Jan. 1906, Peel papers, D/889/3/3e/62.

30. William Moore to Reginald Lucas, 25 Nov. 1907, Saunderson papers, PRONI, T2996/6/3; Jackson, *The Ulster Party*, p. 105.

31. *UG*, 29 May and 20 Aug. 1904.

32. Jackson, *The Ulster Party*, p. 105.

33. Alvin Jackson, *Colonel Edward Saunderson: Land and Loyalty in Victorian Ireland* (Oxford, 1995), pp. 152–54.

34. F.S.L. Lyons, 'The Irish Unionist Party and the Devolution Crisis' *Irish Historical Studies*, vi (Mar., 1948), pp. 1–22.
35. Jackson, *The Ulster Party*, pp. 234–39; David Burnett, 'The Modernisation of Unionism, 1892–1914' in Richard English and Graham Walker, *Unionism in Modern Ireland* (Dublin, 1996), pp. 54–55; Graham Walker, *A History of the Ulster Unionist Party: Protest, Pragmatism and Pessimism* (Manchester, 2004), pp. 22–23.
36. *BNL*, 27, 29 Sept., 24 Oct. 1904.
37. *BNL*, 3 Dec. 1904, 4 Mar. 1905.
38. *PD*, 3 Dec. 1904.
39. *PD*, 174, 15 May 1907, c. 937.
40. Peel to Lonsdale, 29 May 1906, D889/3/1c/1540: Tandragee Unionist club to Lonsdale, 28 Mar. 1912, Peel papers, D/889/3/3e/146.
41. *Ibid.*, 9 Sept., 7 Oct. 1911.
42. Peel to Lonsdale, 27 Oct. 1906, *ibid.*, D889/3/1c/1/601.
43. See *PD*, index, 182, 1907, cc. 549–53.
44. *Ibid.*, 174, 7 May 1907, cc. 152–53.
45. *Times*, 5 Nov. 1909.
46. Lonsdale to H.B. Armstrong, 11 Nov. 1911, Armstrong papers, PRONI, D3727/e/46/6.
47. *PD*, xxi, 6 Feb. 1911, c. 84.
48. See Gordan Lucy (ed.), *The Ulster Covenant: A Pictorial History of the 1912 Home Rule Crisis* (Belfast, 1989).
49. A.T.Q. Stewart, *The Ulster Crisis* (London, 1967), p. 77.
50. *PD*, 212 c. 1l.
51. *UG*, 20 July 1912.
52. *UG*, 20 July 1912.
53. See letter from Lonsdale to editor of *UG* about discrimination against Protestants in response to remarks by John Redmond. *Ibid.*, 29 Nov. 1913.
54. *PD*, xxxvi, 2 May 1912, cc. 2124–26.
55. *PD*, xxiv, 24 Apr. 1911, c. 1373; *UG*, 2 Dec. 1911.
56. *PD*, xxxvii, 2 May 1912, c. 2118.
57. *PD*, xxi, 19 Feb. 1912, c. 388.
58. *PD*, xci, 7 Mar. 1917, c. 454.
59. *PD*, xxxvii, 2 May 1912, cc. 2120–21.
60. See reference 3 above.
61. 75*UG*, 20 July 1912; *BNL*, 6 Oct. 1913.
62. *PD*, xlvi, 1 Jan. 1913, c. 446. *UG*, 19 July 1913.
63. *UG*, 4 Oct. 1913.
64. *UG*, 18 July 1914.
65. Lonsdale to Armstrong, 16 Feb. 1914, D3727/e/46/15.
66. *PD*, vol. xxi, 6 Feb. 1911, cc. 84–89.
67. *UG*, 21 June 1913.
68. *Ibid.*, 8 Nov. 1913.
69. *Ibid.*, 18 July 1914.

70. *Ibid.*, 13 May 1916.
71. *Ibid.*, 18 Nov. 1916.
72. *PD*, xci, 7 Mar. 1917, cc. 426–54.
73. *PD*, xciii, 21 May 1917, cc. 2005–8.
74. *BNL*, 9 June 1917.
75. Lonsdale to H.B. Armstrong, 24 Mar. 1918, Armstrong papers, D/3727/e/46/40.
76. *PD*, xcviii, 17 Oct. 1917, cc. 99–101.
77. Lonsdale to Armstrong, 30 Dec. 1917, Armstrong papers, D3727/e/46/35.
78. Lonsdale to Armstrong, 30 May 1918, *ibid.*, D/3727/e/46/42.
79. Lonsdale to Armstrong, 10 May 1918, *ibid.*, D/3727/e/46/49.
80. *PD*, xlii, 24 Nov. 1920, cc. 572–77.
81. *Times*, 9 June 1924; *BNL*, 9 June 1924.
82. *NW*, 9 June 1924.
83. Ronald Mc Neill, *Ulster's Stand for Union* (London, 1922): *PD*, xxxvii, 2 May 1912, c. 219.
84. Thomas Hennessey, *Dividing Ireland: World War 1 and Partition* (London, 1999), p. 123.
85. *UG*, 10 Jan. 1914.
86. *Ibid.*, 18 July 1914.
87. See *BNL* editorial 9 June 1917.
88. For example, William Coote MP uses 'Britisher' in Fivemiletown, *UG*, 27 Jan. 1917, and 'British' in Enniskillen, *UG*, 18 Aug. 1917.
89. *PD*, xlvi, 1 Jan. 1913, c. 444.
90. Two religious issues he drew attention to in 1913 were the sectarian attack on Sunday school children at Castledawson in 1912 and the role of the Ancient Order of Hibernians. *UG*, 19 July 1913.
91. See 'Home Rule from a Protestant Standpoint' by James Craig, *UG*, 30 Sept. 1911.
92. H.A. Doubleday (ed.), *The Complete Peerage* (London, 1940), xiii, p. 272; St John Ervine, *Craigavon*; *Ulsterman* (London, 1949), p. 88.
93. Jehanne Wake, *Kleinwort Benson; the History of Two Families in Banking* (Oxford, 1997), pp. 351, 375.
94. *NW*, 9 June 1924.

Chapter 8   Seeking Conciliation: William O'Brien and the Ulster Crisis, 1911–14

1. *Weekly Free Press*, 8 Mar. 1913.
2. E.g., John Dillon to Edward Blake, 3 April 1904, Blake Papers, National Library of Ireland [NLI], microfilm, P. 4683/514.
3. William O'Brien, *The Irish Revolution and How It Came About* (London, 1923), pp. 31–32.

4. Resolution of All-for-Ireland League, cited in William O'Brien, *An Olive Branch in Ireland and How It Came About* (London, 1910), p. 471.

5. R.B. McDowell, *The Fate of Southern Unionism, Crisis and Decline* (Dublin, 1997), pp. 47–48.

6. *Cork Free Press*, 4 July 1914; Frank Callinan, *T.M. Healy* (Cork, 1996), pp. 464–65.

7. A.J. Ward, 'Frewen's Anglo-American Campaign for Federalism, 1910–21, *Irish Historical Studies* [*IHS*], xv, (Mar., 1967), pp. 256–75.

8. *Hansard* (Commons) [*PD*], 9 Mar. 1914, lix, cc. 929–32.

9. O'Brien to Asquith, 4 Nov. 1911, H.H. Asquith Papers, Bodleian Library, Oxford, MS 36/7–9; also copy in Lloyd George Papers, House of Lords, C/6/11/10.

10. Michael Wheatley, 'John Redmond and Federalism in 1910', *IHS*, 32 (May, 2001), pp. 343–64.

11. O'Brien to Asquith, 4 Nov. 1911, Asquith MS 36/7–19.

12. *Weekly Free Press*, 11 Jan. 1913.

13. O'Brien to Birrell, 10 Nov. 1913, William O'Brien Papers, NLI, MS 913/80–88.

14. *Cork Free Press*, 15 Apr. 1912, and 31 Oct. 1912 for report of O'Brien's speech in House of Commons, autumn 1912; W. O'Brien at an All-for Ireland League meeting, Cork, 1 Mar. 1913, *Weekly Free Press*, 8 Mar. 1913; enclosure to Asquith, dated 22 Jan. 1914, Asquith MS 39/253–5; O'Brien. *PD*, 1 May 1912, xxxvii, cc. 1918–32; 1 Apr. 1914, lx, cc. 1242–54; Craig, 11 Apr. 1912, xxxvi, c. 1478.

15. Plunkett proposal, 27 Jan. 1914, Asquith MS 39/103–110.

16. Two linked explanations for Plunkett's hostility to Frewen and Dunraven are the falling out between Frewen and Plunkett over the former's financially disastrous cattle company venture in Wyoming, with which Plunkett had been involved and for which Dunraven had acted as a backer. Dunraven also had a close relationship with Plunkett's cousin, Lady Fingall, with whom Plunkett was in love, see Trevor West, *Horace Plunkett, Co-operation and Politics* (Washington, 1986), pp. 112–13.

17. Alec Wilson's proposal sent to Asquith, 30 Oct. 1913, Asquith MS 39/13–19; see below, pp. 19–20.

18. Patricia Jalland, *The Liberals and Ireland* (Brighton, 1980), p. 196.

19. O'Brien, 1 Apr. 1914, *PD*, lx, cc. 1242–54.

20. Patrick Maume, *The Long Gestation, Irish Nationalist Life, 1891–1918* (Dublin, 1999), pp. 136–37.

21. Lord Loreburn to W. O'Brien, 12, 19 Aug., 15 Nov. 1913, Michael MacDonagh Papers, NLI, MS 11439/4.

22. Maume, *The Long Gestation*, pp. 136–37.

23. E.g., Lord Midleton to Bonar Law, 11 Oct. 1913, 13 Apr. 1914; Walter Long to Bonar Law, 22 Feb. 1914; Lord Lansdowne to Bonar Law, 10 Oct. 1913, Bonar Law Papers, House of Lords Record Office, MSS. 30/3/20, 32/2/31, 31/3/44, 30/3/16; Frank Callinan, *T.M. Healy* (Cork, 1996), p. 500.

24. Bonar Law's memo. n.d., probably aut. 1913, Balfour Papers, British Library, Add. MS 49730/65–70.
25. Walter Long's report, 22 Feb. 1914, Bonar Law MS 31/3/44.
26. Lord Dunraven to Bonar Law, 8 Sept. 1912, MS 27/2/10, O'Brien, 11 Apr. 1912, *PD*, xxxvi, cc. 1466–74.
27. O'Brien to Dunraven, 24 Aug. 1912, O'Brien MS 8554/2.
28. *Ibid.*
29. O'Brien to M. Frewen, 10 Jan. 1918. O'Brien MS 8557/5.
30. Lord Hythe to Bonar Law, 21 Jan. 1914. Bonar Law 31/2/70.
31. Carson, 13 June 1912, *PD*, xxxix, cc. 1065–79.
32. Loreburn to O'Brien, 19 Aug. 1913, MacDonagh MS 11439/4.
33. Capt. J. White to O'Brien, 30 Aug., 4 Sept. 1913, O'Brien Papers, University College Cork, AS 31–33, 35–36.
34. *Ibid.*, 22 Aug. 1913, AS 22–25.
35. Alec Wilson to Asquith, 30 Oct. 1913, Asquith MS 39/13–19; see above, p. 155.
36. White to O'Brien, 26 Aug. 1913; L. Walsh to O'Brien, 1 Sept. 1913, O'Brien, UCC, AS 30, 34.
37. H.C. Smith to O'Brien, 7 May 1914, O'Brien to Smith, 9 May 1914, *ibid.*, AS 84–86.
38. Dunraven to O'Brien, 2 Apr. 1914, O'Brien Papers, NLI, MS 8554/15; see also: Dunraven to O'Brien, 26 Feb. 1913, MS 8554/14, in which he stressed the importance he placed on keeping federalists and O'Brien's organisation in touch with one another; and Dunraven to O'Brien, 1 Apr. 1914, MS 8554/15, in which he expressed his hope O'Brien would support a federal solution.
39. O'Brien to Dunraven, 3 Apr. 1914, MS 8554/15.
40. Dunraven to O'Brien, 17 Sept. 1912, MS 8554/13.
41. 13 Jan. 1913, MS 8554/14.
42. 22 May 1914, MS 8554/15; see above, pp. 160–61.
43. T.M. Healy to O'Brien, 1 Sept. 1911, 26 Oct. 1913, 1 June 1915, MS 8556/5, /6 & /10; Callinan, *T.M. Healy*, pp. 491–97.
44. O'Brien, *Irish Revolution*, p. 230, O'Brien to Frewen 10, 28 Mar., 26 June 1915; O'Brien to Healy, 22 May 1915, O'Brien MS 8557/5, 8556/9.
45. O'Brien, *Irish Revolution*, pp. 206–8; O'Brien, Address to all Members of Parliament, 13 Aug. 1914, Asquith MS 39/251–2.
46. Lloyd George to O'Brien, 20 July 1917, O'Brien UCC, AS 214; O'Brien to Lloyd George, 18 June, 21 July 1917, Lloyd George Papers, House of Lords, F/41/9/3 and 5; O'Brien to Healy, 3 June; 5, 25 July; 3, 18, 29 Aug. 1917; O'Brien to Dunraven 9, 17 July 1917; Dunraven to O'Brien, 7 July 1917, O'Brien MS 8556/12, 13, 14; 8554/16.
47. O'Brien to Oliver Newell, 14 July 1916, O'Brien UCC, AS 142–4.
48. O'Brien, Address to all Members of Parliament, 13 Aug 1914, Asquith MS 39/251–2.
49. O'Brien's speech at All-for-Ireland League meeting, *Cork Free Press*, 23 Sept. 1912.

50. For texts on nationalism, see Philip Spencer and Howard Wollman, *Nationalism, a Critical Introduction* (London, 2002); Patrick O'Mahony and Gerald Delanty, *Rethinking Irish History, Nationalism, Identity and Ideology* (London, 1998); Jim Mac Laughlin, *Re-imagining the Nation-State: The Contested Terrains of Nation Building* (London, 2001).
51. Jalland, *The Liberals and Ireland*, pp. 69, 262.
52. E. Coyle? of Belleek to O'Brien, 25 Feb. 1927, O'Brien UCC, AU 75.

Chapter 9 'Not a Historical But a Prospective Application'? The 1798 Rising as Recalled in the Irish Popular Press of 1898

1. *Northern Whig*, 14 May 1898.
2. See, Kevin Whelan, "'98 After '98': The Politics of Memory', *The Tree of Liberty: Radicalism, Catholicism and the Construction of Irish National Identity 1760–1830* (Cork University Press, 1996); Nuala C. Johnson, 'Sculpting Heroic Histories: Celebrating the Centenary of the 1798 Rebellion in Ireland', *Transactions of the Institute of British Geographers*, 19, 1 (1994), pp. 78–93.
3. See for example E.S. Herman and N. Chomsky, *Manufacturing Consent: The Political Economy of the Mass Media* (London, 1994).
4. H. Newcomb and P. Hirsch, 'Television as a Cultural Forum: Implications for Research', in W. Rowland and B. Watkins (eds), *Interpreting Television* (London, 1984).
5. Examples, of course, are mostly to be found in institutional histories or biographies. Generalised examples are J. Tunstall, *Newspaper Power* (Oxford, 1996) and D. Weaver and G. Wilhoit (1991) *The American Journalist* (1991, 2nd edn, Bloomington). For Ireland see Hugh Oram's anecdotal *The Newspaper Book: A History of Newspapers in Ireland 1649–1983* (MO Books, 1984).
6. Bartholomew Sparrow, *Uncertain Guardians; The News Media as a Political Institution* (Baltimore, 1999), p. 133.
7. M. Waters, *Globalization* (London, 1995).
8. Benedict Anderson, *Imagined Communities: Reflections on the Origin and Spread of Nationalism* (London, 1983).
9. Ernest Gellner, *Nations and Nationalism* (London, 1983).
10. Jim Mac Laughlin, *Reimagining the Nation-State. The Contested Terrains of Nation-Building* (London, 2001).
11. *Ibid.*, Chapter 7.
12. Such authoritative knowledge was itself taken from a small group of 'experts', notably R.R. Madden, a broadly secular Nationalist, Fr Patrick F. Kavanagh, a Nationalist and Roman Catholic partisan, and Revd R.R. Kane, Orange Order Grand Master, loyalist militant and Gaelic League supporter.
13. *Belfast Evening Telegraph* [*BT*], 4 Apr. (all dates 1898*)*.

14. See the various entries in *The Newspaper press directory and advertiser's guide* (London, 1898).
15. *Freeman's Journal* [*FJ*], 23 May.
16. *FJ*, 23 May.
17. Ibid.
18. *FJ*, 10 May.
19. *Ibid.*
20. See, Senia Pǎseta, '1798 in 1898: The Politics of Commemoration', *Irish Review*, 22 (1998) and R.F. Foster, 'Remembering 1798' in *The Irish Story: Telling Tales and Making it Up in Ireland* (London, 2001).
21. Editorial, *FJ*, 18 Apr.
22. Quoted *FJ*, 2 May.
23. F.S.L. Lyons, *Ireland Since the Famine* (2nd ed., London, 1973), p. 202.
24. For example, *FJ*, 4 Apr.
25. 'The Memory of Tone', Editorial, *FJ*, 17 June.
26. *Ibid.*
27. *FJ*, 17 June.
28. R.R. Madden, *The United Irishmen, Their Lives and Times*, Series 1 (3rd ed., Dublin, 1858), p. 305.
29. For example, *BT*, 4 Apr.
30. *FJ*, 16 May.
31. *Ibid.*
32. *FJ*, 22 Apr.
33. *FJ*, 23 May. Only quite recently has historiography re-politicised the Wexford rebels. Landmark articles were: Louis Cullen, 'The 1798 Rebellion in Wexford' in Kevin Whelan (ed.), *Wexford: History and Society: Interdisciplinary Essays on the History of an Irish County* (Dublin, 1987); Kevin Whelan, 'Politicisation in County Wexford' in Hugh Gough and David Dickson (eds), *Ireland and the French Revolution* (Dublin, 1990).
34. Eamonn Phoenix, *A Century of Northern-Life: The Irish News and 100 years of Ulster History 1890s–1990s* (Belfast, 1996).
35. For example, *FJ*, 12 Apr.
36. *Irish News and Belfast Morning News* [*IN*], 12 Apr. See also, 24 May.
37. *Ibid.*, 9 May.
38. *Ibid.*, 28 May.
39. For example, *ibid.*, 5 Apr., 'Peace or War, the Pope's Mediation'.
40. ''98 Celebrations', Editorial, *ibid.*, 12 Apr.
41. *Ibid.*, 23 May.
42. Andrew Boyd, *Holy War in Belfast* (Belfast, 1987, 1st ed., 1969), pp. 180–81; T.J. Campbell, *Fifty Years of Ulster 1890–1940* (Belfast, 1941), pp. 24–25.
43. *IN*, 7 June.
44. For example, *ibid.*, 24 May.

45. Patrick F. Kavanagh, *A Popular History of the Insurrection of 1798: Derived From Every Available Record and Reliable Tradition* (Cork, 1898). See also, Anna Kinsella, '1798 Claimed for Catholics: Father Kavanagh, Fenians and the Centenary Celebrations' in Keogh, Dáire and Nicholas Furlong (eds), *The Mighty Wave: The 1798 Rebellion in Wexford* (Dublin, 1996), pp. 139–56.

46. *IN*, 31 May.

47. *Ibid.*, 14 June.

48. For example, *ibid.*, 12 May.

49. *Ibid.*, 19 May.

50. J.B. Daly (ed.), *Ireland in '98, Sketches of the Principal Men of the Time, Based Upon the Published Volumes and Some Unpublished MSS. of R.R. Madden* (London, 1888).

51. *IN*, 19 Apr.

52. For example, *FJ*, 7 Apr.

53. As the *BT* tartly noted. 4 Apr.

54. For example, *BT*, 4 June; *Belfast News-Letter* [*NL*], 21 May; *Northern Whig* [*NW*] 7 June.

55. For example, *Irish Times* [*IT*], 2 Apr.

56. For example, *ibid.*, 12 Apr.

57. *Ibid.*, 29 Apr.

58. *Ibid.*, 30 May.

59. *Ibid.*, 24 May.

60. *Ibid.*, 30 May.

61. *Ibid.*, 30, 31 May.

62. *Ibid.*, 30 May.

63. *Ibid.*, 31 May.

64. For example, *NW*, 1 Jan.

65. *Ibid.*, 7 June.

66. *Ibid.*, 9 May.

67. For example, *ibid.*, 7 June.

68. *Ibid.*, 8 June.

69. *Ibid.*

70. *Ibid.*

71. *Ibid.*, 14 June.

72. *Ibid.*, 3 Jan.

73. *Ibid.*, 25 May.

74. *Ibid.*, 8 June.

75. *Ibid.*, 14 May.

76. *Ibid.*, 10 June.

77. *Ibid.*, 25 May.

78. *Ibid.*, 8 June.

79. *Ibid.*, 25 May.

80. *Ibid.*

81. *Ibid.*, 8 June.

82. *Ibid.*
83. *Ibid.*, 3 Jan.
84. *NL*, 5 May.
85. *Ibid.*, 21 May.
86. *Ibid.*
87. *Ibid.*
88. *Ibid.*
89. *Ibid.*
90. *Ibid.*, 10 June.
91. 'A Protest', by L.O.L. 247, *ibid.*, 11 June.
92. See its reference in the appendix of Marie-Louise Legg, *Newspapers and Nationalism: The Irish Provincial Press 1850–1892* (Dublin, 1998), p. 182.
93. For example, *BT*, 28 May.
94. *Ibid.*, 4 Apr.
95. *Ibid.*, 21 May.
96. A statement from Revd R.R. Kane, Grand Master of the Orange Lodge of Belfast, approvingly cited in *ibid.*, 2 June.
97. *Ibid.*, 9 June.
98. *Ibid.*, 2 June.
99. *Ibid.*, 21 May.
100. Quoted *ibid.*
101. *Ibid.*, 4 Apr.
102. *Ibid.*
103. *Ibid.*, 5 Apr.
104. *Ibid.*
105. *Ibid.*, 4 Apr.
106. *Ibid.*
107. J.E. Redmond, *Historical and Political Addresses* (Dublin, 1898), p. 174.
108. *BT*, 3 May.
109. *Ibid.*, 2 June.
110. *Ibid.*, 21 May.
111. *Ibid.*, 23 May.
112. *Ibid.*
113. For example, *ibid.*, 2 June.
114. *Ibid.*, 6 June.
115. *Ibid.*
116. *Ibid.*, 2 June.
117. *Ibid.*, 6 June.
118. For example, *FJ*, 2 May; *IT*, 30 May; *NL*, 7 June.
119. *FJ*, 24 May. 'He did not possess the gifts that make the popular writer'.
120. *Ibid.*, 6 June.
121. *Ibid.*, 7 Apr.
122. *BT*, 5 Apr.
123. *Ibid.* Sidney Lee (ed.), *Dictionary of National Biography* (London, 1894), 37, pp. 137–38.

Chapter 10 'Ireland is Out for Blood and Murder': Nationalist Opinion and the Ulster Crisis in Provincial Ireland, 1913–1914

1. The mayor of Sligo, John Jinks, addressing the Sligo Guardians on 1 Aug. 1914, *Western Nationalist* [*WN*], 8 Aug. 1914.
2. This paper is based upon Chapter 9 of *Nationalism and the Irish Party: Provincial Ireland, 1910–16* (Oxford, 2005) and is published by permission of the Oxford University Press.
3. See Michael Wheatley, '*These Quiet Days of Peace': Nationalist Opinion Before the Home Rule Crisis, 1909–1913*, in D. George Boyce and Alan O'Day (eds), *Ireland in Transition, 1867–1921* (London, 2004), pp. 57–75.
4. Kettle speaking at Ardee, 24 May 1914 quoted in J.B. Lyons, *The Enigma of Tom Kettle: Patriot, Essayist and Poet; British Soldier, 1880–1916* (Dublin, 1983), p. 246.
5. The pro-party Nationalist newspapers were the *Leitrim Observer* [*LO*], *Longford Leader* [*LL*], *Roscommon Journal* [*RJ*], *Roscommon Messenger* [*RM*], *Sligo Champion* [*SC*], *Sligo Nationalist* [*SN*], *Strokestown Democrat* [*SD*], *Western Nationalist*, *Westmeath Examiner* [*WE*] and *Westmeath Independent* [*WI*]; the anti-party Nationalist papers the *Midland Reporter* [*MR*] and *Roscommon Herald* [RH]. The independent papers were the *Leitrim Advertiser* [*LA*] and *Longford Independent* [*LI*]; the Unionist papers the *Longford Journal* [*LJ*], *Sligo Independent* [*SI*], *Sligo Times* [*ST*] and *Westmeath Guardian* [*WG*].
6. See Jim Mac Gaughlin, *Re-imagining the Nation-State: The Contested Terrains of Nation-Building* (London, 2001), pp. 187–205.
7. *SC*, 29 Nov.
8. *Ibid.*, 27 Sept.
9. *SN*, 27 Sept.
10. *RH*, 27 Sept.
11. *SC* did carry a Press Association story on 15 Nov. about arms shipments to Ulster from Birmingham, but was alone in doing so.
12. *LL*, 23 Aug.; *WI*, 30 Aug.
13. *RM*, 15 Nov.
14. *MR*, 28 Aug.; 4, 11 Sept.; *RH*, 30 Aug.; 6, 13 and 20 Sept.; 4 and 11 Oct.; 15 and 22 Nov. The tirades of Jasper Tully were enlivened by his denunciation of George Russell ('AE', a supporter of the strikers) as 'this dipthong of an editor'. *RH*, 11 Oct.
15. *MR*, 11 Sept.
16. *RM*, 20 Sept.; *RM* and *WE*, 27 Sept. Hayden owned the *RM* in Roscommon town and the *WE* in Mullingar. The political and newspaper rivalry of the Hayden and Tully families straddled Counties Roscommon and Westmeath for over 50 years.
17. See, *SI*, 20 Sept. and 27 Dec.; *WI*, 27 Sept.; *SC*, 4 Oct.; *LA*, 30 Oct.; *LJ*, 1 Nov.; *MR*, 20 Nov.; *RH*, 22 Nov.

18. *WN*, 11 Oct.
19. *SC*, 11 and 18 Oct.
20. *RH*, 11 Oct.
21. Farrell speaking to the South Longford UIL executive on 26 Oct., *LL*, 1 Nov.
22. *SI, ST*, 11 Oct.
23. *RM*, 18 Oct.
24. *SC*, 25 Oct.
25. *WI*, 1 Nov.
26. *SI*, 1 Nov.
27. See the leader 'English Intrigues', *RH*, 1 Nov.
28. *WN*, 1 Nov.
29. *LA*, 30 Oct.; *LJ*, 1 Nov.; *MR*, 20 Nov.; *RH*, 22 Nov.
30. *WI*, 1 Nov.
31. *MR*, 23 Oct.
32. F.X. Martin, 'MacNeill and the Foundation of the Irish Volunteers', in F.X. Martin and F.J. Byrne (eds), *The Scholar Revolutionary: Eoin MacNeill 1867–1945 and the Making of the New Ireland* (Shannon, 1973), p. 123.
33. *Ibid.*, p. 128.
34. *WI*, 25 Oct.
35. *Irish Independent*, 25 Oct; *LA, RJ, WE*, 1 Nov. Interestingly, Tully's papers did not carry the story, for all his active promotion of Volunteering soon afterwards. It is not clear whether his non-coverage of Athlone events was due to the participation of Irish party men, or because he simply did not believe the *WI* reports.
36. *RH*, 1 Nov.
37. *Ibid.*, 29 Nov.
38. *Ibid.*
39. *MR*, 20 Nov.
40. *WN*, 22 Nov.
41. *WI*, 29 Nov.
42. See, *MR*, 20 Nov.; *WN*, 22 Nov.; *RH, WI*, 29 Nov. The anti-Prussian Jasper Tully in the *RH* envisaged the need to defend against both Ulstermen and Germans.
43. *SC*, 29 Nov.
44. Muldoon to Horgan 16 Dec. 1913, quoted in J.J. Horgan, *From Parnell to Pearse: Some Recollections and Reflections* (Dublin, 1948), p. 229.
45. Stephen Gwynn, *John Redmond's Last Years* (London, 1919), p. 91.
46. Arthur Lynch MP, *Ireland: Vital Hour* (London, 1915), p. 185.
47. Cabinet paper Apr. 1914, 'Irish Volunteers', Augustine Birrell MS, Bodleian Library, Oxford, Dep 301.
48. See, *WN*, 17 Jan. 1914.
49. *RJ*, 31 Jan.
50. Fitzgibbon speaking at Fairymount, Co. Roscommon, *RM*, 24 Jan.
51. *SD*, 15 Nov. 1913; Crime Special Branch report, Nov. 1913, Public Record Office [PRO], CO 904/119. As the Leinsters paraded through

the town, a crowd headed by the Pipers' Band and the Fianna followed singing national songs. Rival crowds cheered and booed each other and the Pipers' Band continued to play outside when the Leinsters returned to barracks.

52. Oliver Snoddy, 'The Midland Volunteer Force 1913', *Journal of the Old Athlone Society*, 1, 1, (1969), p. 43. Six of the original committee of nine were army reservists who later served in the British army in the war.
53. *WI*, 24 Jan. 1914.
54. Cabinet paper Apr. 1914, 'Irish Volunteers', Birrell MS, Dep 301.
55. *WI*, 20 June.
56. *Ibid.*, 31 Jan. and 28 Feb.
57. Marie Coleman, *County Longford and the Irish Revolution, 1910–1923* (Dublin 2003), p. 69.
58. *LL*, 22 Nov. 1913.
59. *LA*, 8 Jan. 1914.
60. *LL*, 14 Feb.
61. *Ibid.*, 25 Apr. and 18 July.
62. *Ibid.*, 16 May.
63. Devine would stand, and lose, as the Irish party's candidate in the North Roscommon by-election in February 1917.
64. *WN*, 14 Feb.
65. *Ibid.*, 14 Mar.
66. *Ibid.*, 28 Mar.
67. Monthly report of the Roscommon county inspector, Mar. 1914, PRO, CO 904/92; RIC Crime Special Branch report, Apr., CO 904/120.
68. See, *SC*, 29 Nov. and 6 Dec.; *SI*; *ST*, 6 Dec. 1913.
69. *ST*, 6 Dec. 1913.
70. *ST*, 7 Jan. 1914.
71. Monthly report of the Sligo county inspector, Feb., PRO CO 904/92.
72. *SC*, 7 Feb.
73. Cabinet paper Apr. 1914, 'Irish Volunteers', Birrell MS, Dep 301.
74. *SN*, 21 and 28 Feb.
75. A fourth victim died some months later.
76. *WI*, 3 Jan. and 14 May 1913.
77. *LO*, 14 Mar. 1914.
78. *WN*, 28 Mar.
79. *SD*, 9 May.
80. *WE*, 27 June.
81. *LL*, 14 Mar.
82. *WE*, 9 May.
83. Wilfrid Scawen Blunt, *My Diaries, Being a Personal Narrative of Events 1888–1914, Part Two 1910–1914* (New York 1980), 20 June, p. 427.
84. Monthly report of the Longford county inspector, Apr., PRO CO 904/93.
85. Monthly report of the Roscommon county inspector, Apr., *ibid.*

86. *WE*, 16 May.
87. Collated from monthly county inspectors' reports for the five counties for June, PRO CO 904/93.
88. *RJ*, 6 June; *RM*, 6 and 13 June.
89. Collated from monthly reports from the RIC county inspectors for Aug. The county numbers were: Leitrim 48 Volunteer 'branches' and approx 4,000 members; Longford 23 branches; Roscommon 56 branches and 5,583 members; Sligo 38 branches and 4,536 members and Westmeath 43 branches and 4,152 members. To reach the approximation of 20,000 Volunteer members for the five counties, it was necessary to add the first Longford figure for membership cited by the county inspector, of 1,917 members in Jan. 1915. Aug. 1914, PRO CO 904/94, Jan. 1915, CO 904/96.
90. David Fitzpatrick, *Politics and Irish Life, 1913–1921: Provincial Experience of War and Revolution* (Dublin 1977; Gregg Revivals edition 1993), p. 101.
91. Kettle to Gwynn, 15 April, quoted in J.B. Lyons, *The Enigma of Tom Kettle*, p. 243.
92. Fitzpatrick, *Politics and Irish Life*, p. 105.
93. *LO*, 27 June.
94. *WI*, 23 May and 20 June.
95. So much so that there was even a temporary reconciliation between Tully and Devine. In June, Tully went so far as to support Devine's co-option to Roscommon county council. *RM*, 20 June.
96. RIC Crime Special Branch Quarterly reports, 1913 and 1914, PRO CO 904/20.
97. *WI*, 10 Jan.; *LL*, 7 Feb.
98. *RM*, 13 Dec. 1913.
99. Farrell speaking to Clonguish UIL on 30 May, *LL*, 6 June 1914.
100. These newspapers published reports of UIL meetings in Longford, Leitrim, Roscommon and Sligo. Trends in party activity in Westmeath in 1914 cannot be analysed from UIL reports, given the scarcity of party reports in the county's newspapers. The UIL was already seriously damaged in North Westmeath, while the *WI* was not at this time a 'paper of record' for the UIL in the south of the county. Totals for all five papers, combined for each month, cannot be shown because branch reports were often duplicated in more than one paper.
101. UIL National Directory Minute Book 1915, p. 442, National Library of Ireland, MS 708.
102. At the national level, Redmond's takeover was also ineffective. Bulmer Hobson considered it to be 'completely illusory' and control of both central staff and funds was kept entirely away from Redmond's nominees. Hobson, *Ireland, Yesterday and Tomorrow* (Tralee, 1968), p. 51. The re-structured Provisional Committee of the Volunteers, with Redmond's representatives, did not even meet until 14 July *WN*, 25 July.

103. Dillon to Blunt 21 May, Blunt MS, West Sussex Record Office, Chichester, Box 16 Vol. 6.
104. Report of Captain Owen, Roscommon District, 'The State of Ireland', PRO CO 904/227.
105. Reports of Mr. Rice, Castlerea; Mr. Moore, Mullingar; Captain Fitzpatrick, Sligo, *ibid.*
106. Monthly report of the Roscommon county inspector, June, PRO CO 904/93.
107. Farrell, interestingly, again went further than his colleagues and looked to goals beyond Home Rule, when he said of Home Rule that 'we had to begin, we had to get our step on the ladder'. He was speaking to the Longford UIL on 31 May 1914. *RH*, 6 June.
108. Patrick McKenna addressing the Streamstown Volunteers, *WI*, 23 May.
109. *WN*, 30 May.
110. Keaveny speaking at Fuerty, *RM*, 30 May.
111. *LL*, 1 Aug.
112. George Geraghty speaking to the Roscommon town Volunteers, *RJ*, *RM*, 1 Aug.
113. *WN*, 1 Aug.
114. Michael O'Mullane, Henry Monson and John Jinks speaking to the Sligo Volunteers, *SI*, 1 Aug.
115. *WN*, 8 Aug.
116. *SC*, 6 June.
117. *RH*, 13 June.

Chapter 11   The *Irish Independent* and the Ulster Crisis, 1912–21

*   The research on which this article is based was undertaken with the financial assistance of Independent Newspapers.
1. *Irish Weekly Independent* [*IWI*], 14 Oct. 1911; 8 Nov.; *Ind.* 9 Oct., 10 Oct. All future references to *IWI* unless otherwise stated.
2. 20 Jan. 1912; 9 Mar.
3. 9 Mar. 1912; 25 May.
4. 20 Apr. 1912; 27 Apr.
5. 4 Jan. 1913.
6. 24 Dec. 1910; 31 Dec.
7. 7 Jan. 1911.
8. 21 Jan. 1911 (first verse omitted). The cartoon appeared 14 Jan., accompanying a description of 'The Ulster Will Fight Comedy'.
9. 23 Dec. 1911; 13 Jan. 1912; 3 Feb.; 16 Mar.
10. 3 Aug. 1912; 17 Aug.
11. 12 July 1912.
12. 28 Sept. 1912.
13. 5 Oct. 1912.

14. 22 Feb. 1913; 1 Mar.; 14 June.
15. 30 Sept. 1911.
16. 15 June 1912; 22 June.
17. 22 June 1912.
18. 27 Jan. 1912; 3 Feb.; 10 Feb.
19. 17 Feb. 1912.
20. 3 Aug. 1912.
21. 30 Aug. 1913; 6 Sept.
22. 19 July 1913; 2 Aug.
23. 19 July 1913.
24. *Ind.* 29 Aug. 1913.
25. Patrick Maume & Cornelius O'Leary *Controversial Issues in Anglo-Irish Relations 1912–22* (Dublin, 2004), pp. 26–35.
26. *Ind.* 9 Oct. 1913; 10 Oct.; *IWI*, 25 Oct.; 22 Nov.
27. *Ind.* 9 Oct. 1913.
28. 18 Oct. 1913.
29. T.M. Healy to Maurice Healy, 17 Mar. 1914 quoted in Frank Callanan, *T.M. Healy* (Cork, 1996), p. 503.
30. 27 June 1914.
31. *Ind.* 5 Nov. 1914.
32. 28 Feb. 1914.
33. 28 Mar. 1914. Asquith used the phrase 'wait and see' when asked the precise terms of the Amending bill.
34. 2 May 1914.
35. 9 May 1914; 16 May.
36. 6 Dec. 1913.
37. 11 July 1914.
38. *Ind.* 6 Apr. 1914.
39. 28 Mar. 1914.
40. 27 June 1914.
41. 23 May 1914; 30 May.
42. 25 July 1914.
43. 4 July 1914.
44. 1 Aug. 1914.
45. 8 Aug. 1914.
46. *Ind.* 28 Nov. 1914.
47. 29 Aug. 1914; 5 Sept.; 12 Sept.
48. 19 Sept. 1914; 26 Sept.
49. 26 Sept. 1914.
50. 29 May 1915.
51. 12 June 1915; 19 June, 25 Sept., and the maverick Home Rule MP Arthur Lynch quoted 31 July 1915.
52. 23 Oct. 1915; 6 Nov.; 20 Nov.
53. 18 Dec. 1915
54. 29 Apr. 1916; 13 May has a cartoon showing Carson's behaviour as 'Cause' and the ruins of Dublin as 'Effect'.

55. *Ind.* 30 May 1916.
56. *Ind.* 8 May 1916.
57. *Ind.* 5 May 1916.
58. 20 May 1916.
59. *Ind.* 12 May 1916; 1 June.
60. *Ind.* 25 May 1916; 7 June; 8 June.
61. 10 June 1916.
62. Notable correspondents include James Creed Meredith (Protestant UCD graduate, subsequently served on the Dáil and Free State Supreme Courts), Fr David Humphreys (Tipperary maverick prominent in the Plan of Campaign in the late 1880s, subsequently agitated to secure part of Erasmus Smith endowment for Catholic education), *Ind.* 13 June, John Sweetman (Meath landowner and former Home Rule MP who had been second President of Sinn Féin), 15 June; J. O'Connor Power (former IRB activist and Home Rule MP), an t-Athair Peadar O Laoghaire (Gaelic writer), W.L. Cole (prominent Sinn Féin Dublin councillor and fruiterer, later a TD) 19 June 1916, and the Coleraine-based ex-MP Patrick McGilligan (father of the future Free State minister), who declares 'three-fourths of Ulster Nationalists repudiate the leadership of Redmond [and]...the selling of Ulster', 28 June 1914.
63. *Ind.*, 13 June 1914 (Col Maurice Moore); 14 June (Robert Lynd); 16 June (Col Maurice Moore, William O'Malley MP).
64. *Ind.*, 19 June 1916.
65. 10 June 1916.
66. 17 June 1916.
67. *Ind.*, 15 June 1916.
68. *Ind.*, 14 June 1916; Eamon Phoenix, *Northern Nationalism: Nationalist Politics, Partition and the Catholic Minority in Northern Ireland* (Belfast, 1994) emphasises this as crucial to Devlin's support for the proposals.
69. *Ind.* 16 June 1916.
70. 10 June 1916.
71. *Leader*, 1 July 1916.
72. *Leader*, 22 July 1916.
73. *Ind.* 12 June 1916; 13 June; 14 June; 15 June; 16 June.
74. *Ind.* 15 June 1916.
75. *Ind.* 16 June 1916; 17 June; 19 June.
76. *Ind.*, 14 June 1916.
77. Dillon to T.P. O'Connor, 20 June 1916, Dillon Papers, Trinity College Dublin, MS 6741/324.
78. *Ind.* 14 June 1916; 16 June.
79. 24 June 1916.
80. 24 June 1916.
81. Callanan, *Healy*, p. 485.
82. 1 July 1916.

83. 15 July.
84. 7 Oct. 1916.
85. 5 Aug. 1916.
86. 12 May 1917; 26 May; 18 Aug.
87. 21 July 1917.
88. Murphy to Harrington, 3 Jan. 1918, Harrington Papers, National Archives of Ireland, 1052/4/34.
89. Harrington Papers 1052/4/36, Harrington to Murphy, 19 Mar. 1918. Murphy attaches a clipping of the offending letter by 'Tulchan' from *Independent*, 18 Mar. 1918. (The convention is implicitly compared with a 'tulchan' – a dead calf's skin stuffed and brought into contact with the cow so she will think her calf is alive and continue to lactate.) J.A. Rice edited the *Evening Herald*: P.J. Lynch edited the *Sunday Independent* and *Weekly Independent*.
90. 21 June 1919.
91. 2 Aug. 1919; 9 Aug.
92. 18 Oct. 1919; 26 Nov. 1921. Gwynn had contacts with the imperial federalists of the Round Table group, and influenced the drafting of the Better Government of Ireland Act through Lloyd George's adviser Philip Kerr (subsequently Lord Lothian). G.K. Peatling, *British Opinion and Irish Self-Government, 1865–1925: From Unionism to Liberal Commonwealth* (Dublin, 2001), pp. 122, 154.
93. *Ind.* 11 Nov. 1919, p. 4.
94. *Ind.* 28 Feb. 1920; 1 Apr.
95. *Ind.* 1 Mar. 1920.
96. *Ind.* 31 Mar. 1920.
97. *Ind.* 4 June 1920.
98. *Ind.* 10 June 1920.
99. 4 Sept. 1920.
100. 19 July 1919.
101. *Ind.* 26 June 1920; 30 June.
102. 18 Sept. 1920.
103. 18 Dec. 1920.
104. 11 June 1921.
105. 18 June 1921.
106. 4 June 1921.
107. 16 July 1921; 23 July; 3 Sept.
108. 30 July 1921; 20 Aug.
109. 24 Sept. 1921; 5 Nov.
110. 10 Dec. 1921; 17 Dec.
111. *Ind.* 20 Mar. 1922.
112. *Ind.* 6 June 1922.
113. *Ind.* 5 June 1922.
114. *Ind.* 26 May 1922; 2 June (photographs of refugees).

Chapter 12   The Conserving Crowd: Mass Unionist Demonstrations in Liverpool and Tyneside, 1912–13

1. For instance, the most important study of civic politics in Liverpool, Britain's most sectarian and Orange city, devotes only two pages to the crisis of 1912–14. See P.J. Waller, *Democracy and Sectarianism: A Social and Political History of Liverpool, 1868–1939* (Liverpool, 1981), pp. 267–69.
2. E.H.H. Green, *The Crisis of Conservatism: The Politics, Economics and Ideology of the British Conservative Party* (London, 1995).
3. Martin Pugh, *The Tories and the People, 1880–1935* (Oxford, 1985).
4. For example E.P. Thompson, 'The Moral Economy of the English Crowd in the Eighteenth Century', *Past and Present*, 50 (1971).
5. George Rude, *The Crowd in History 1730–1848: A Study of Popular Disturbance in France and England* (London, 1981), p. 268.
6. Mark Harrison, *Crowds and History: Mass Phenomena in English Towns, 1790–1835* (Cambridge: Cambridge University Press, 1988), p. 27.
7. David Cannadine, 'The Context, Performance and Meaning of Ritual: The British Monarchy and the "Invention of Tradition"', Eric Hobsbawm and Terence Ranger (eds), *The Invention of Tradition* (Cambridge, 1983), p. 105.
8. David Cannadine, 'The Transformation of Civic Ritual in Modern Britain: The Colchester Oyster Feast', *Past & Present*, 94 (1984), p. 129.
9. Elaine McFarland, 'Marching from the Margins: Twelfth July Parades in Scotland, 1820–1914' in T.G. Fraser (ed.), *The Irish Parading Tradition: Following the Drum* (Basingstoke, 2000), p. 60 [pp. 60–78].
10. Salvidge's career is examined in *ibid.*, passim; and, somewhat less impartially in his son's political biography: Stanley Salvidge, *Salvidge of Liverpool: Behind the Political Scene* (London, 1934).
11. *LC*, 11 Apr. 1912.
12. A man described in one famous work as 'the most fascinating creature of his times', see George Dangerfield, *The Strange Death of Liberal England*, first published 1935 (London, 1997), p. 55.
13. *Belfast Weekly News*, 25 Sept. 1912.
14. Around 150,000 people had thronged the streets of Belfast when the Covenant was signed, although Liverpool was a much bigger city. See A.T.Q. Stewart, *The Ulster Crisis: Resistance to Home Rule, 1912–1914* (Aldershot, 1993), p. 66.
15. Revised timetables for which appeared in the press, see *LC*, 28 Sept. 1912.
16. *LC*, 30 Sept. 1912.
17. Wise appears regularly in Neal, *Sectarian Violence* and Waller, *Democracy and Sectarianism*, p. 240.
18. *Liverpool Mercury [LM]*, 6 Oct. 1912.
19. *LC*, 30 Sept. 1912.
20. *Ibid.*

21. These remarks echoed a speech Carson made in the city in 1910, in which he said: 'From Liverpool I take to Belfast a message of courage. Heaven knows, if this nefarious conspiracy goes on and succeeds. I may be asking you for something more (cries of 'you will get it' and 'no Popery')', *LC*, 26 Nov. 1910.

22. See, James Vernon, *Politics and the People; A Study in English Political Culture, c. 1815–1867* (Cambridge, 1993), pp. 83–84. This was often accompanied with a rendition of 'See the Conquering Hero Comes'.

23. *LM*, 6 Oct. 1912.

24. Robert K. Massie, *Dreadnought: Britain, Germany, and the Coming of the Great War* (London, 1992), p. 501. Beresford's customary breakfast greeting at this time was 'Good morning, one day nearer the German war'.

25. *Daily Telegraph*, 30 Sept. 1912.

26. *Times*, 30 Sept. 1912.

27. *Daily Mail*, 30 Sept. 1912.

28. *Pall Mall Gazette*, 30 Sept. 1912.

29. *Times*, 1 Oct. 1912.

30. *Liverpool Daily Post and Mercury* [LDPM], 1 Oct. 1912.

31. *Times*, 1 Oct. 1912.

32. *LC*, 1 Oct. 1912.

33. Some Nationalists in the South of Ireland had taken to punishing Unionist farmers by maiming their livestock.

34. *LC*, 1 Oct. 1912.

35. Interestingly Sir Charles, who was a former Lord Mayor of Liverpool, became closely involved with Oswald Mosley in the 1930s and was one of the British Union of Fascists principal benefactors, Richard Thurlow, *Fascism in Britain: From Oswald Mosley to the National Front* (London, 1998), p. 108.

36. *LM*, 6 Oct. 1912.

37. The crucial role of Orangemen at Sheil Park, and the massive numbers involved, questions somewhat Neal's claim that the crowds of up to 80,000 that Liverpool witnessed in 1876 'constitute the biggest Orange turnout in English history', see: Neal, *Sectarian Violence: the Liverpool Experience, 1819–1914* (Manchester, 1988), p. 184.

38. *LC*, 1 Oct. 1912.

39. A song adopted by George Wise's bible class who then corrupted it to 'Dare to be a Wiseite'. Those more offensive lyrics were:

> Dare to be a Wiseite!
> Dare to Stand alone.
> Dare to be a Protestant,
> And to Hell with the Pope of Rome.
> See Bohstedt, 'Protestant-Catholic Riots', p. 182.

40. *LC*, 1 Oct. 1912.

41. *Ibid*.

42. I. Colvin, *The Life of Lord Carson: Volume Two* (London, 1934), p. 152.
43. *Ibid*.
44. Bonar Law's assessment of the north-east is noted in Jeremy Smith, 'Bluff, bluster and brinkmanship: Bonar law and the third Home Rule Bill', *Historical Journal*, 36, 1 (1986) p. 167.
45. LOL 812 'James Gibson Memorial Temperance', minutes, 27 Jan. 1912. From the 1890s we read that lodges were instructing their secretaries to send lodge reports to the *Belfast Weekly News* [BWN]. See, for example, LOL 387 'Tantobie', minutes, 6 Mar. 1897.
46. LOL 432 'Jarrow Purple Heroes', Jarrow, minutes, 4 Oct. 1913.
47. *Ibid*., 4 Oct.; 1 Nov. 1913. Similarly, the Orangeman of Wallsend LOL 395 donated £1 out of the lodge funds to Carson's defence fund, reported in the BWN, 4 Sept. 1913.
48. Reported in the BWN, 11 Sept. 1913.
49. To create an impressive show of strength, the Newcastle Orangemen agreed to assemble with the rest of Tyneside's Lodgemen at the Central Station before going to Durham to hear Carson speak. BWN, 28 Aug. 1913.
50. Londonderry claimed, during an address to Hetton-le-Hole Unionists, that he was proud that his great-uncle, Castlereagh, 'caused the union which had brought peace and prosperity to Ireland ever since'. *Shields Daily News* [SDN], 29 Oct. 1913.
51. Such as the one at Haltwhistle addressed by Earl Percy, in which he criticised the Liberals for supporting the part of Ireland that had been most disloyal. SDN, Sept. 1913.
52. *Newcastle Evening Chronicle* [NEC], 24 Sept. 1913.
53. *Ibid*.
54. *Shields Daily News*, 20 Sept. 1913.
55. *Newcastle Evening Mail*, 29 Oct. 1913, 'It was explained that they been commandeered from various towns from Newcastle to Whitley [Bay]'.
56. *Shields Daily News*, 30 Oct. 1913.
57. *Newcastle Evening Mail* [NEM], 29 Oct. 1913.
58. *Daily Chronicle*, 30 Oct. 1913.
59. Indeed, it was thought that 60 to 70 cars would be needed to ferry the bigwigs to and fro. in the end, more than 140 vehicles were present. NEC, 29, 30 Oct. 1913; *Shields Daily News*, 30 Oct. 1913.
60. *Newcastle Daily Chronicle* [NDC], 30 Oct. 1913. It was claimed in the *Evening Mail*, that were 'only two larger halls in the kingdom', of which the Albert Hall was probably the largest.
61. *Ibid*., 30 Oct. 1913.
62. BWN, 6 Nov. 1913.
63. *Newcastle Weekly Chronicle*, 1 Nov. 1913.
64. LOL 395 'Enniskillen True Blues', minutes, 25 Oct. 1913.
65. *NDC*, 30 Oct. 1913.
66. *NDC*, 30 Oct. 1913.

67. See, for example, the report on the rioting on the 12 July 1912 in Belfast – the same day as Carson addressed an anti-Home Rule meeting. *Ibid.*, 12 July 1912.

68. SDN, 30 Oct. 1913.

69. *NEC*, 30 Oct. 1913.

70. *LC*, 30 Oct. 1913.

71. *NEC*, 31 October 1913.

72. Carson's first wife, Annette, died in 1913, in the middle of a hectic period in his legal and political careers. He was in involved in a number of high-profile legal cases at same time as he campaigning so tirelessly against Home Rule. So great were his exertions that he collapsed with acute neuritis and missed the third reading of the Home Rule Bill. See Stewart, *Ulster Crisis*, p. 75.

73. Both letters appeared in *NEC*, 31 Oct. 1913. It was not just the region that showed an interest in Carson's speaking tours. This was an age of telegraph technology and stories could be sent about the country with great rapidity, thus adding to speed with which people could be informed and with which actions could develop or change. When Carson spoke in Wallsend, Sir Edward Grey was talking in Berwick-upon-Tweed. With both men saying different things about Home Rule, one local paper was proud to announce how more than 70,000 words from the two meetings were sent down the wire all over the United Kingdom: the last message was typed in at 11.30pm and the despatch just seven minutes late. *NEC*, 1 Nov. 1913.

74. Although the enormous Chartist demonstrations that occurred throughout Britain in the 1830s were never replicated in Liverpool: a Chartist meeting held in the city in 1839 could only muster a crowd estimated at somewhere between 8–15,000, see Kevin Moore, 'This Whig and Tory Ridden Town': popular Politics in Liverpool in the Chartist Era' in Belchem (ed.), *Popular Politics, Riot and Labour*, p. 39.

75. This is discussed in W.L. Ralls, 'The Papal Aggression of 1850: A Study of Victorian anti-Catholicism' in G. Parsons (ed.), *Religion in Victorian Britain*, vol. IV, *Interpretations* (Manchester, 1988), and P. Millward, 'The Stockport Riots of 1852: A Study of Anti-Catholic and Irish Sentiment' in Roger Swift & Sheridan Gilley (eds), *The Irish in the Victorian City* (Beckenham, 1985), pp. 207–25.

76. Although this may have been to do with something the *Manchester Guardian*, 1 Oct. 1912, noticed, for they had never seen so many police officers (a point that was significantly ignored by the Liverpool press): 'a great constabulary army of horse and foot who were present to keep the theological disputants of Liverpool within due bounds'.

77. Tom Gallagher, 'A Tale of Two Cities: Communal Strife in Glasgow and Liverpool Before 1914' in Swift & Gilley, *Irish in the Victorian City*, p. 123.

78. D.C. Richter, *Riotous Victorians* (Athens OH, 1981), p. 163. Indeed in 1866 rioters in Hyde Park were careful to 'avoid the flower beds' (p. 54).

79. One of the great Conservative causes of the Edwardian period was the implementation of compulsory national military service, this is discussed in R.J.Q. Adams, 'Field Marshall Earl Roberts: Army and Empire' in J.A. Thompson and Arthur Meija (eds), *Edwardian Conservatism: Five Studies in Adaptation* (London, 1988). Also, note the frequent use of military analogy in the Tory *Courier's* reports.

80. *LM*, 6 Oct. 1912.

81. SDN, 30 Oct. 1913.

82. Salvidge, *Salvidge of Liverpool*, p. 123.

83. The idea that Liverpool Toryism was a precursor of British Fascism has been noted by among others, Norman Stone in his *Europe Transformed* (London, 1983), p. 127.

84. Thurlow, *British Fascism*, p. 6. Moreover, William Joyce, Lord Haw-Haw, actually thought that Sir Edward Carson was a fascist because of his unbending principles and demagoguery. We are grateful to Colin Holmes for this information, which comes from his forthcoming biography of Joyce.

85. This is discussed further in D.M. MacRaild, *Irish Migrants in Modern Britain, 1750–1922* (Basingstoke and London, 1999), p. 119.

86. Loyal Orange Institution, *Report of Proceedings of the 40ᵗʰ Annual Meeting* ... (Birmingham, 1915).

87. *LC*, 16 Sept. 1912.

88. LOL 395 'Enniskillen True Blues', minutes, 25 Oct. 1913. The full entry read as follows: 'The Grand Secretary wished it to be signed on 2ⁿᵈ November but as there was such short notice it was decided at that meeting to sign it on 9ᵗʰ November at Hebburn. The Brethren to meet at the Argyll Hotel at 2.15 form into a procession and march to the Prespyterian [sic] church where a sermon will be preached to them and sign the covenant in St Andrew's institute at 3.30'.

89. The Grand Secretary wished it to be signed on 2ⁿᵈ Nov. but as there was such short notice it was decided at that meeting to sign it on 9ᵗʰ Nov. at Hebburn. The Brethren to meet at the Argyll Hotel at 2.15 form into a procession and march to the Prespyterian [sic] church where a sermon will be preached to them and sign the covenant in St Andrew's institute at 3.30.

90. LOL 572 'Albert the Good', Consett, minutes, 1 Nov. 1913.

91. For a further discussion of this see D.M. MacRaild, '"Principle, Party and Protest": the Language of Victorian Orangeism in the North of England' in Shearer West (ed.), *The Victorians and Race* (Aldershot, 1996), p. 140.

92. LOI, *Report of the Annual Meeting of the Grand Orange Lodge... 1881* (London, 1881); LOI, *Report of Proceedings of the 40ᵗʰ Annual Meeting...*(Birmingham, 1915).

93. *LC*, 19, 20 Mar. 1912. The distinguished speaker was a Mrs Mercier-Clements, the Assistant Honorary Treasurer of the Ulster Women's Unionist Council.

94. *Times*, 1 Oct. 1912.

95. *Liverpool Daily Post and Mercury*, 1 Oct. 1912.

96. *Birkenhead News*, 2 Oct. 1912.

97. Jarrow and Hebbburn District, for example, had only one lodge until after the war. See Hebburn and Jarrow District (no. 46), minutes, 1907–1922.

98. *Shields Daily News*, 30 Oct. 1913.

99. *NEC*, 30 Oct. 1913.

100. In fact it seems that the only reaction to this rally from the Liberals in the North East was when Charles Fenwick MP addressed a meeting in the small Northumberland mining community of Seaton Delaval, convened by the town's *Women's* Liberal Association, declaring that the Wallsend meeting had left 'a nasty taste in the mouth', *Blyth News*, 1 Nov. 1913.

101. The importance of women and motherhood in the quest for 'national efficiency', an Edwardian obsession, has been discussed in Anna Davin, 'Imperialism and Motherhood', *History Workshop*, 5 (1978).

102. Bonar Law admitted as much in a Newcastle after dinner speech the following day, see *NDC*, 30 Oct. 1913.

103. J. Skorupski, *Symbol and Theory: A Philosophical Study of Theories of Religion in Social Anthropology* (Cambridge, 1976), p. 84.

104. *LM*, 5 Oct. 1912.

105. *Manchester Guardian*, 1 Oct. 1912.

106. Pageantry is an important element in the public life of England. See for example, D. Cannadine, *Class in Britain* (London, 2000), and Linda Colley, *Britons: Forging the Nation* (London, 1994).

107. E. Shills, and Michael Young, 'The Meaning of the Coronation', *Sociological Review*, 1 (1953) p. 67.

108. R.J. Holton, 'The Crowd in History: Some Problems of Theory and Method', *Social History* 3, 2 (1978), p. 222.

109. E. Durkheim, *The Elementary Forms of Religious Life*, trs. Joseph Swain (London, 1915), p. 427.

Chapter 13   The Ulster Volunteer Force, 1910–1920: New Perspectives

1. For a more detailed discussion of this topic and indeed of the other themes raised please see my *Carson's Army: the Ulster Volunteer Force, 1910–22*, to be published by Manchester University Press in 2007.

2. See, for example, Joost Augustine, *From Public Defiance to Guerrilla Warfare: The Experience of Ordinary Volunteers in the Irish War of Independence, 1916–1921* (Dublin, 1996); Richard English, *Armed Struggle: A History of the IRA* (London, 2003); Peter Hart, *The I.R.A. and its Enemies: Violence and Community in Cork, 1916–1923* (Oxford, 1999).

3. Steve Bruce, *The Red Hand: Protestant Paramilitaries in Northern Ireland* (Oxford, 1992), p. 1. See also, Sarah Nelson, *Ulster's Uncertain Defenders:*

Protestant Political, Paramilitary and Community Groups and the Northern Ireland Conflict (Belfast, 1984).

4. A.T.Q. Stewart, *The Ulster Crisis*, (London, 1967).

5. For further details of this organisations aims and objectives see, http://www.ulstersociety.org/

6. Michael Farrell, *Arming the Protestants: The Formation of the Ulster Special Constabulary and the Royal Ulster Constabulary, 1920–1927* (London, 1983).

7. See, Patrick Buckland, *Irish Unionism 2: Ulster Unionism and the Origins of Northern Ireland* (Dublin, 1972); M.T. Foy, 'The Ulster Volunteer Force: Its Domestic Development and Political Importance in the Period 1913–1920', Queen's University Belfast, Ph.D., 1986.

8. Vivania Marsano, '"Those Who Wish For Peace Must Prepare For War." The Ulster Volunteer Force and the Home Rule Crisis of 1912–1914', University of California, Santa Barbara, Ph.D., 1997, p. 7.

9. Diane Urquhart, *Women in Ulster Politics 1890–1940* (Dublin, 2000), pp. 63–64.

10. 'UVF Headquarters Staff Enrolment Forms', UUC papers, Public Record Office Northern Ireland [PRONI], D1327/4/12.

11. Letter Lady Theresa Londonderry to Sir Edward Carson, 10/6/14, Carson papers, PRONI, D/1507/A/6/5 and Diane Urquhart (ed.) *The Minutes of the Ulster Women's Unionist Council and Executive Committee, 1911–1940* (Dublin, 2001), p. 100.

12. Obituary of Brigadier Gen. Sir William Hacket Pain, K.B.E., C.B. *The Green 'Un* (April 1924), pp. 5–6.

13. Tom Barry, *Guerrilla Days in Ireland* (Dublin, 1949).

14. F.H. Crawford, *Guns for Ulster* (Belfast, 1947); R.J. Adgey, *Arming the Ulster Volunteers* (Belfast, n.d. [1947?]).

15. See set of accounts in 'UVF Arms and Ammunition, Disposal of', PRONI, HA4/1/81.

16. *Report of the Deputy Keeper of the Records for the Years 1960–1965* (Belfast, 1968), N.I. Cmd. 521, p. 20.

17. Paul Bew, *Ideology and the Irish Question: Ulster Unionism and Irish Nationalism 1912–1916* (Oxford, 1994), pp. 92–93.

18. Report by Constable T. Hynes to County Inspector, Tyrone, 10/10/12, 'Miscellaneous papers regarding "drilling" by civilians in Ulster', PRO, WO141/26. This file appears to have been compiled from RIC reports now held in the PRO, CO904 series.

19. This section is based on the surviving YCV papers held in PRONI, particularly the organisation's minute book, D/1568/2 and Constitution and Bye-Laws, D/1568/3.

20. W.C. Trimble, *The History of Enniskillen with References to some Manors in Co. Fermanagh and other Local Subjects* (Enniskillen, 1921), III, p. 1068.

21. Telegrams, Secretary, Raphoe UVF and Archdale to Carson, 22/7/14, Carson papers, PRONI, D/1507/A/6/33.

22. The minutes of the UVF Headquarters council survive only for the period from Aug. 1914 to 1920. These comments are largely based on UVF

orders for 1913–14 in PRONI, D/1327/4/3, 4–5 and F.P. Crozier, *Impressions and Recollections* (London, 1930), pp. 142–57.

23. Letter Captain Arthur O'Neill to General William Adair, 24/7/14, O'Neill papers, PRONI, D/1238/181.

24. 'Roll book for "H" (Seaforde) Company, 1st South Down Regiment', PRONI, D/1263/4.

25. 'Adjutant's Roll for 1st Fermanagh Regiment', PRONI, D/1267/1.

26. Desmond Murphy, *Derry, Donegal and Modern Ulster 1790–1921* (Londonderry, 1981), pp. 196–97.

27. See UVF Orders, 42, O'Neill papers, PRONI, D/1238/91.

28. 'Report on Condition of Ulster', 26/8/13, PRO, CO904/27/3 cited in Paul Bew, *Ideology and the Irish Question*, p. 93.

29. Circular letter R. Hall to UVF commanders in South Down, undated [February, 1913?], Hall papers, PRONI, D/1540/3/5.

30. 'UVF Tyrone Regiment 5th Battalion Orders', 1/11/13, PRONI, D/1132/6/7.

31. Letter Carson to 'Fellow Covenantors' 7/8/13, PRONI, D/1414/12 and *The Times* 20 Aug. 1913.

32. Printed handbill by 1st North Tyrone Regiment, Oct. 1913, PRONI, D/1414/20.

33. Memorandum by Hacket Pain, 27/6/14, PRONI, D/1238/167.

34. These comments are based on military intelligence reports on drilling in PRO, WO141/4 and RIC reports on drilling, PRO, WO141/26 (the latter file contains reports extracted from files held in the CO904 series).

35. *The Times*, 6 Aug. 1913.

36. Hew Strachan, *The Politics of the British Army* (Oxford, 1997), p. 112.

37. 'Headquarters Staff Enrolment Forms', UUC papers, PRONI, D/1327/4/12.

38. Timothy Bowman, *The Irish Regiments in the Great War: Discipline and Morale*, (Manchester, 2003), pp. 111–16.

39. For a detailed account of Spender's career, see, I.L. Maxwell, 'The Life of Sir Wilfrid Spender, 1876–1960', Queen's University Belfast, Ph.D., 1991.

40. See personal file of Brigadier General F.P. Crozier, PRO, WO374/16997, especially memo of 24/4/30.

41. Crawford, *Guns for Ulster*, p. 56.

42. Letter Adair to Capt. Arthur O'Neill, 21/4/14, O'Neill papers, PRONI, D/1238/72.

43. Memorandum by Col. Hacket Pain, 7/5/14, O'Neill papers, PRONI, D/1238/88.

44. F.X. Martin, '1916: Myth, Fact and Mystery', *Studia Hibernica*, VII (1967) cited in Alvin Jackson, *Sir Edward Carson* (Dublin, 1993), p. 67.

45. 'Sir Edward Carson Ulster Defence Fund, Summarized Statement Showing Position of the Fund as at 31/3/15', PRONI, D/1327/14/6/2.

46. Letter, Carson to R. Liddell, 10/3/14, 'Carson Fund, 1914', UUC papers, PRONI, D/1327/14/5/3.

47. 'Col Sharman Crawford's expenses A/C', [10/12/13–31/3/15], PRONI, D/1327/14/6/2.
48. Stewart, *Ulster Crisis*, p. 245.
49. McNeill, *Ulster's Stand for Union*, pp. 156–57.
50. Note for 22/10/14, 'UVF Headquarters Council minute book', PRONI, D/1327/4/2.
51. See my, 'The Ulster Volunteer Force and the formation of the 36th (Ulster) Division', *Irish Historical Studies*, XXXII, (Nov., 2001).
52. Letter, Richardson to Carson, 5/7/15, PRONI, D/1507/A/13/18 and letter Hugh Mulholland to Carson, PRONI, D/1507/A/13/6.
53. M.T. Foy, p. 214.
54. For discussions of the reformation of loyalist paramilitary groups in 1920 see, Farrell, *Arming the Protestants*, pp. 9–47; Brian Barton, *Brookeborough: The Making of a Prime Minister* (Belfast, 1988), pp. 30–38; Foy, 'The Ulster Volunteer Force', pp. 223–32.
55. 'Appreciation of the Situation in Ulster' by James Craig, 1/9/20, PRONI, CAB5/1.
56. Letter, Spender to Wickham, 22/3/21, PRONI, CAB5/1.
57. Nevil Macready, *Annals of An Active Life* (London, 1924), II, pp. 488–89.
58. Wallace Clark, *Guns in Ulster* (Londonderry, 1966), p. 9.
59. I am grateful to Mr. James Hamilton of Campbell College, Belfast for this reference.
60. 'Rioting in Belfast, August and September 1921', PRO, WO35/88B.
61. Letter, Macready to Sir Henry Wilson (?) 1921, Wilson papers, Imperial War Museum.
62. 'Reports of meetings between Sir James Craig and Lt. Col. F. H. Crawford, 1920–32', PRONI, CAB5/1.

Chapter 14   The Royal Visit to Belfast, June 1921

1. David Cannadine and Simon Price (eds), *Rituals of Royalty: Power and Ceremonial in Traditional Societies* (Cambridge, 1987), p. 8.
2. J.G. Blumler, J.R. Brown, A.J. Ewbank, and T.J. Nossiter, 'Attitudes to the monarchy: their structure and development during a ceremonial occasion', *Political Studies*, 19, 2 (1971), p. 152.
3. See also for instance the complicated relationship of Irish nationalism and royal enthusiasm. James H. Murphy, *Abject Loyalty: Nationalism and Monarchy in Ireland During the Reign of Queen Victoria* (Cork, 2001), p. 290.
4. Blumler et al, 'Attitudes to the monarchy', p. 152.
5. Joseph Robins *Champagne and Silver Buckles. The Viceregal Court at Dublin Castle 1700–1922* (Dublin, 2001), p. 160.
6. Cannadine, *Rituals of Royalty*, p. 4.
7. Deirdre McMahon 'Ireland and the Empire-Commonwealth, 1900–1948' in Judith M. Brown and Wm. Roger Louis (eds), *The Oxford*

History of the British Empire, the Twentieth Century (Oxford, 1999), IV, p. 149.

8. Letter James Craig to Winston Churchill, secretary of state for the colonies, 3 June 1921. Public Record Office of Northern Ireland [PRONI], CAB/6/62. Churchill argued that he himself had only agreed to attend because he thought that the British prime minister would also be attending. Moreover, he felt that unless at least three premiers were willing to go, then none should attend at all. Notes of Cabinet meeting 10 Downing Street, 14 June 1921, Thomas Jones (CH) Papers C. vol. 1 f.32, National Library of Wales. I am grateful to Dr Deirdre McMahon for this reference.

9. *Morning Post*, 24 June 1921. PRONI, D/1415/A/11.

10. Later Lord Altrincham. *Thomas Jones Whitehall Diary: Ireland 1918–25*, Keith Middlemas (ed.), (Oxford, 1971), III, p. 77.

11. Francis Costello, 'Lloyd George and Ireland, 1919–1921: An Uncertain Policy', *Canadian Journal of Irish Studies*, 2 (July, 1988), p. 9.

12. Jones, p. 77.

13. Nicholas Mansergh, *The Unresolved Question, the Anglo-Irish Settlement and its Undoing, 1912–1972* (London, 1991), p. 155.

14. D. George Boyce, *Nineteenth Century Ireland: the Search for Stability* (Dublin, 1990), p. 269.

15. Oliver MacDonagh, *Ireland* (New Jersey, 1968), p. 88.

16. Charles Townshend, *Ireland, the c20* (London, 1999), p. 104. However, according to Foster, it was the 'unpalatable alternative of governing the twenty-six counties as a Crown colony under martial law' and 'the removal of Ulster, that prepared the government for negotiation, rather than, as sometimes sentimentally assumed, King George V's conciliatory speech opening the new Northern Ireland parliament.' R.F. Foster *Modern Ireland, 1600–1972* (London, 1988), p. 504.

17. Lady Craig's diary, 26 June 1921. PRONI, D/1415/B/38/1–162. *The Times*, 23 June 1921 printed Lloyd George's letter to Craig following the visit: 'I hope and believe their influence and example will assist to set the whole of Ireland long upon the path of practical co-operation, which alone can lead to the realisation of Irish ideals and the security of Irish interests. The [Better] Government of Ireland act has put the future of Ireland in the hands of her own people, provided only that Southern Ireland renounces its claim to secession from the Empire'. PRONI, D/1415/A/11.

18. Craig to Lloyd George 28 June 1921, PRONI, CAB/4/6.

19. Lady Craig's diary, 28 June 1921. PRONI, D/1415/B/38/1–162.

20. *Irish News* [*IN*], 27 June 1921.

21. Alvin Jackson, *Ireland, 1798–1998* (Oxford, 1999), p. 340.

22. *Daily Mirror*, 7 June 1921. PRONI, D/1415/A/11.

23. *IN*, 8 June 1921.

24. *BT*, 8 June 1921.

25. 'Beyond this flood a frozen Continent/Lies dark and wilde, beat with perpetual storms/Of Whirlwind and dire Hail, which on firm land/ Thaws not, but gathers heap, and ruin seems/Of ancient pile; all else deep snow and ice, /A gulf profound as that SERBONIAN Bog/ Betwixt DAMIATA and mount CASIUS old,/Where Armies whole have sunk: the parching Air/Burns frore, and cold performs th' effect of Fire.' John Milton *Paradise Lost*, Book Two. *IN*, 8 June 1921.

26. *Ibid.*

27. *DNB 1941–50*, p. 413.

28. *IN*, 8 June 1921.

29. Edmund Bernard Fitzalan-Howard, first Viscount Fitzalan of Derwent, 1855–1947. 'The [Better] Government of Ireland Act, 1920, made it possible, for the first time since the Reformation,' for a Roman Catholic to be viceroy of Ireland, and in 1921, on the advice of Lloyd George, whose respect and affection he had won, Talbot was appointed to that post and raised to the peerage as Viscount Fitzalan of Derwent... In the words of (Sir) Winston Churchill, "Devotion to duty alone inspired him to undertake so melancholy a task" as that of viceroy'. *Dictionary of National Biography 1941–50*, L.G. Wickham Legg and E.T. Williams (eds), (Oxford, 1959), p. 412.

30. Craig to Lord Lieutenant, 3 June 1921. PRONI, CAB/6/67.

31. No signature but from Craig to Greenwood, 15 Feb. 1921. Craig suggested that the royal to be invited should either be the King or the Prince of Wales. PRONI, CAB/6/62. The announcement of the date of the opening of the Northern Ireland Parliament was made 22 Mar. 1921.

32. No signature but from Craig to Greenwood, 15 Feb. 1921. PRONI, CAB/6/62.

33. *Belfast Telegraph [BT]*, 8 June 1921.

34. *Ibid*, 21 June 1921.

35. 'I am daily endeavouring to bring about a better state of affairs, and nothing will contribute more to that end than the association of the Secretary of State for the Colonies and the Prime Ministers with the Opening of the youngest Parliament within the King's Dominions'. Craig to Winston Churchill 3 June 1921. PRONI, CAB/6/62.

36. *Northern Whig*, 22 June 1921.

37. Alvin Jackson 'Irish Unionists and the Empire, 1880–1920: Classes and Masses' in Keith Jeffrey (ed.) *'An Irish Empire?' Aspects of Ireland and the British Empire* (Manchester, 1996), p. 125, p. 138.

38. *Ibid.*, p. 143.

39. Boyce, *Englishmen and Irish Troubles*, pp. 184–85.

40. *BT*, 8 June 1921.

41. Craig to Greenwood, 27 Apr. 1921. PRONI, PM/1/71.

42. Craig to Walter Long, British Library, Long Papers Add Mss 62425 f.124. I am grateful to Dr McMahon for this reference. Long (1854–1924) was a prominent British Conservative, former Chief

Secretary for Ireland and Unionist party leader, and actively involved in the Irish Unionist cause before and during the First World War. Back in Cabinet in 1915 he was part of the group which prevented Lloyd George's efforts to negotiate a settlement of the Irish question based on Home Rule for twenty six counties in 1916. He was, additionally, the Cabinet's 'enforcer' on Irish policy from 1918–20. See, *Oxford Companion to Irish History*, p. 328.

43. Lady Craig's diary, 20–22 June 1921. PRONI, D/1415/B/38/1–162.
44. *Irish Independent*, 16 June 1921. PRONI, D/1415/A/11. There was a high level of unemployment in Northern Ireland in this period: 'On 4 October 1921 the Minister of Labour told the House that the number of unemployed persons in the six counties was 78,000 with 25,000 working short time, while in Belfast alone 45,000 persons were wholly unemployed with 12,000 on short time…This high rate of unemployment, over twenty per cent, exacerbated the political tension'. Patrik Buckland, *Irish Unionism: Two. Ulster Unionism and the Origins of Northern Ireland, 1886–1922* (Dublin, 1973), p. 153.
45. *IN*, 23 June 1921.
46. It was Craig's brother Charles who, having seen them perform in Kensington, suggested the inclusion of the Royal Ulster Rifles in the celebrations: 'Seeing that they are the Ulster Rifles and are a local Regiment, and are connected more closely to Belfast, Antrim and Down than any other Regiment in the Service, I think it would be excellent policy from every point of view if you asked to have them over for the ceremony'. Letter C.C. Craig to Craig 19 May 1921. PRONI, CAB/6/62.
47. *Belfast Newsletter*, 23 June 1921.
48. *The Times*, 23 June 1921. PRONI, D/1415/A/11.
49. PRONI, FIN/30/FC/4.
50. Ulster Women's Unionist Council Executive Committee Minutes, 21 June 1921. Diane Urquhart, (ed.), *The Minutes of the Ulster Women's Unionist Council and Executive Committee, 1911–40* (Dublin, 2001), p. 127.
51. *The Times*, 23 June 1921. PRONI, D/1415/A/11.
52. *BT*, 21 June 1921.
53. *Ibid.*, 23 June 1921.
54. The RIC was replaced in Northern Ireland by the Royal Ulster Constabulary in 1922, under whose control were placed the 'Specials'. 'It was originally intended that a third of the RUC should be Catholics, but the Catholic element in the force quickly declined from a peak of 21 per cent in 1923 to 17 per cent in 1927'. S.J. Connolly (ed.), *Oxford Companion to Irish History* (Oxford, 1998), p. 492.
55. *IN*, 23 June 1921.
56. According to the *Belfast Newsletter*, 22 June 1921, three thousand 'Specials' were drafted in from Newtownards.

57. Craig to Sir Laming Worthington-Evans, Secretary of State for War, 10 June 1921 asking for the RIC and the Special Constabulary to be represented and provide a guard of honour. PRONI, CAB/6/62.
58. Moore-Irvine to Spender, Victoria Barracks, Derry 10 June 1921. PRONI, CAB/6/67.
59. *Oxford Companion to Irish History*, p. 562. Budge & O'Leary, p. 142.
60. Mansergh, pp. 67–73.
61. Buckland, pp. 88–89.
62. Stamfordham to Lady Londonderry, 13 Apr. 1912. PRONI, D/2846/1/5/1–9.
63. Stamfordham to Lady Londonderry, 23 Apr. 1912, *ibid.*
64. Stamfordham to Lady Londonderry, 22 Jan. 1912, *ibid.*
65. Cited in Jonathan Bardon, *A History of Ulster* (Belfast, 1992), p. 447.
66. Mansergh, pp. 74–75.
67. Jones, p. 77.
68. D.G. Boyce, *Englishmen and Irish Troubles. British Public Opinion and the Making of Irish Policy 1918–22* (London, 1972), p. 51.
69. *Ibid.*, p. 81.
70. 'The King said to J. when he was saying goodbye in the yacht, "I can't tell you how glad I am I came, but you know my entourage were very much against it". J replied, "Sir, you are surrounded by pessimists, we are all optimists over here"'. Lady Craig's diary, 22 June 1921. PRONI, D/1415/B/38/1–162.
71. Lady Craig's diary, 17 June 1921. PRONI, D/1415/B/38/1–162. Indeed, many of these threatening letters were forwarded to Craig's government and are deposited in PRONI, PM/1/70.
72. Viscount Fitzalan to Craig 11 June 1921. PRONI, CAB/6/62.
73. I am grateful to Dan Cunnane for these figures.
74. Lady Craig's diary, 22 June 1921. PRONI, D/1415/B/38/1–162.
75. Harold Nicholson, *King George V* (London, 1952), p. 349.
76. Kenneth Rose, *King George V* (London, 1983), p. 239.
77. Jones, pp. 79–80.
78. Rose, p. 239.
79. Buckland, p. 131.
80. Letter from W.B. Spender to Sir Frederick Moneypenny, 3 June 1921, PRONI, CAB/6/60.
81. 'Have heard from His Eminence the Cardinal regretting inability to be present owing to prior engagement'. Telegram James Craig to Stephen Tallents, nd, PRONI, CAB6/62.
82. *IN*, 22 June 1921.
83. *BT*, 21 June 1921.
84. *IN*, 23 June 1921.
85. *Northern Whig*, 23 June 1921.
86. *Belfast Newsletter*, 22 June 1921.
87. *IN*, 23 June 1921.

88. Ian Budge & Cornelius O'Leary, *Belfast: Approach to Crisis* (London, 1975), p. 141.
89. *IN*, 23 June 1921.
90. Spender to H.W. Hopkins, Director of Musicians in Ireland, 9 June 1921. PRONI, CAB/6/67.
91. *Yorkshire Post*, 22 June 1921. PRONI, D/1415/A/11.
92. Newspaper notice of a 'Restoration of Order in Ireland Regulations Order', *BT*, 21 June 1921.
93. *Ibid.*
94. *Northern Whig*, 22 June 1921.
95. *Belfast Newsletter*, 22 June 1921.
96. No date. PRONI, CAB/6/67.
97. Craig to Ronald McNeill, 25 June 1921. PRONI, CAB/6/67.
98. Nicholson, p. 354.
99. Jones, pp. 77–80.
100. Boyce, *Englishmen and Irish Troubles*, p. 181.
101. Jones, pp. 79–80.
102. Lloyd George to George V, cited in Nicholson, p. 352.
103. Rose, p. 239.
104. Buckland, p. 146.
105. Elizabeth Hammerton and David Cannadine, 'Conflict and Consensus on a Ceremonial Occasion: The Diamond Jubilee in Cambridge in 1897', *Historical Journal*, 24, 1, (1981), p. 146.
106. Alvin Jackson *Home Rule: An Irish History, 1800–2000* (London, 2003), p. 200.
107. Denis Henry of the Irish Office told Craig that the King thought the list 'rather a long one,' 2 May 1921. Lloyd George Papers, House of Lords, F/11/3/1–3. I am grateful to Dr McMahon for this reference. 'I am, however, not at all sure that when the PM sees the length of the list of these he may not make a difficulty'. Fitzalan to Craig, 14 June 1921, PRONI CAB/6/62.
108. Craig to Greenwood, 16 Apr. 1921. PRONI, PM/1/71.

Further Reading

General studies

Surveys of British history usually contain sections on Ireland and many specialist works on predominantly British themes similarly give attention to it. These and specialist studies on mainly British themes are only occasionally cited below. Thus, it is vital to consult the Royal Historical Society Bibliography (see below). The most germane general accounts covering all or nearly the whole period are K.T. Hoppen, *Ireland Since 1800* (2nd ed.; 1999), A. Jackson, *Ireland 1798–1998* (1999). M.E. Daly, *Social and Economic History of Ireland since 1800* (1981), B. Girvin, *From Union to Union: Nationalism, Democracy and Religion in Ireland – Act of Union to EU* (2002), P. O'Farrell, *England and Ireland since 1800* (1975) and O. MacDonagh *States of Mind: A Study in Anglo-Irish Conflict, 1780–1980* (1983), the last two being more interpretative essays rather than surveys. Hoppen's treatment is provocative; Jackson's is now the best single volume available; Daly is a useful short economic analysis. Several series provide linking volumes, offering an overview of the era. These include D.G. Boyce, *Nineteenth-Century Ireland* (1990), which makes a readable and original contribution, and D. Keogh, *Twentieth-Century Ireland* (1994). M.G.A. Ó Tuathaigh, *Ireland Before the Famine, 1798–1848* (1972), J.J. Lee, *The Modernisation of Irish Society 1848–1918*, a good study for stimulating discussion among students, J. Murphy, *Ireland in the Twentieth Century* (1975), P. Travers, *Settlements and Divisions: Ireland 1870–1922* (1988), R. Fanning, *Independent Ireland* (1983), and O. Walsh, *Ireland's Independence, 1880–1923* (2002), C.H.E. Philpin, *Nationalism and Popular Protest in Ireland* (1987), which is confined exclusively to articles published in or submitted to *Past & Present*. A. O'Day (ed.), *Reactions to Irish Nationalism, 1865–1914* (1987) and C. Brady (ed.), *Interpreting Irish History* (1994) reprint articles from a broader selection of periodicals. W.E. Vaughan (ed.), *A New History of Ireland, VI: Ireland Under the Union, II, 1870–1921* (1996) along with T.W. Moody and F.X. Martin (eds), *The Course of Irish History* (1967).

Studies extending beyond the present terminal boundaries but useful for the period are R.F. Foster, *A History of Modern Ireland* (1988), *The Irish Story: Telling Tales and Making It Up in Ireland* (2001) and (ed.) *The Oxford Illustrated History of Ireland* (1989). Also valuable are J.C. Beckett, *The Making of Modern Ireland, 1603–1923* (1966), *A Short History of Ireland* (1979), A.T.Q. Stewart, *The Shape of Irish History* (2001), M. Tanner, *Ireland's Holy Wars: The Struggle for a Nation's Soul, 1500–2000* (2001), P. O'Farrell, *Ireland's English Question* (1971), E.R. Norman, *A History of Modern Ireland* (1971), J. Lydon, *The Making of*

Modern Ireland: From Ancient Times to the Present (1998), L.M. Cullen, *An Economic History of Ireland since 1660* (1972) and (ed.), *The Formation of the Irish Economy* (1969), R.D. Edwards, *A New History of Ireland* (1972), L.J. McCaffrey, *Ireland from Colony to Nation State* (1979), R. Douglas, L. Harte and J. O'Hara, *Drawing Conclusions: A Cartoon History of Anglo-Irish Relations 1798–1998* (1998) and *Ireland Since 1690: A Concise History* (1999), M. Cronin, *A History of Ireland* (2001) and J. Coohill, *Ireland: A Short History* (2000), the last is a short volume that admirably considers a long stretch of time. D.G. Boyce, *Ireland 1828–1923* (1992), is an excellent short account, and the equally valuable *The Irish Question in British Politics, 1868–1996* (3rd ed. 1996). The doyen of post-1945 Irish scholars, F.S.L. Lyons, *Ireland since the Famine* (1971) remains a key text. Other books are the interpretative essay by O. MacDonagh, *Ireland: The Union and its Aftermath* (rev. ed., 1977), L.J. McCaffrey, *The Irish Question, 1800–1922* (1968), R. Kee, *The Green Flag* (1972), T.E. Hachey, *Britain and Irish Separatism from the Fenians to the Free State, 1867–1922* (1977), P. Adelman, *Great Britain and the Irish Question 1800–1922* (1996), M. Hughes, *Ireland Divided: The Roots of the Irish Problem* (1994), the last two being brief student-focused studies. Two venerable books are N. Mansergh, *The Irish Question, 1840–1921* (rev. ed. 1975) which is a revision of his 1940 assessment, and; *Nationalism and Independence* (1997) along with P.S. O'Hegarty, *A History of Ireland Under the Union, 1801–1921* (1952). Similarly see, T.A. Jackson, *Ireland Her Own* (1946). The most up-to-date economic history is C. Ó Gráda, *Ireland: A New Economic History 1780–1939* (1994). Also, see T. Browne: *Ireland, A Social and Cultural History* (1987), Charles Townshend, *Ireland: The 20th Century* (1998) and D. Fitzpatrick, *The Two Irelands 1912–1939* (1998). Ulster and Northern Ireland are considered in J. Bardon, *A History of Ulster* (1992), P. Buckland, *A History of Northern Ireland* (1981), D. Harkness, *Northern Ireland Since 1920* (1983), T. Hennessy, *A History of Northern Ireland, 1920–1996* (1997), F. Wright, *Two Lands on One Soil: Ulster Politics Before Home Rule* (1996) while O. Rafferty: *Catholicism in Ulster 1603–1983* (1994), J.D. Brewer and G.I. Higgins, *Anti-Catholicism in Northern Ireland, 1600–1998* (1998), A.C. Hepburn, *A Place Apart: Studies in the History of Catholic Belfast, 1850–1950* (1996), M. Elliott, *The Catholics of Ulster* (2000), P. Brooke, *Ulster Presbyterianism: The Historical Perspective, 1610–1970* (1987) and D. Hempton and M. Hill, *Evangelical Protestantism in Ulster Society, 1740–1890* (1992) trace religious themes. A general account of the women's movement in the twentieth century is L. Connolly, *The Irish Women's Movement: From Revolution to Devolution* (2002). A recent valuable collection of essays is found in D.G. Boyce and R. Swift (eds), *Problems and Perspectives in Irish History since 1800* (2003); a more specialised volume is D.G. Boyce and A. O'Day, *Ireland in Transition, 1867–1921* (2004).

Nationalism is explored in D.G. Boyce; *Nationalism in Ireland* (3rd rev. ed., 1995), J. MacLaughlin, *Reimagining the Nation-State: the Contested Terrains of Nation-Building* (2001), P. O'Mahony and G. Delanty, *Rethinking Irish History:*

Nationalism, Identity and Ideology (1998), T. Garvin, *The Evolution of Nationalist Politics* (1981), S. Cronin, *Irish Nationalism* (1980), T.E. Hachey and L.J. McCaffrey (eds), *Perspectives on Irish Nationalism* (1989) and a classic Marxist analysis, E. Strauss, *Irish Nationalism and British Democracy* (1951). A.S. Green, *The Irish National Tradition* (1921) and *Irish Nationality* (1929) remain vital. Useful short essays are P. Alter, 'Symbols of Irish Nationalism', *Studia Hibernia* (1974) and C. Barrett, 'Irish Nationalism and Art, 1800–1921', *Studia Hiibernia* (1975). For the land question see A.G. Donaldson, *Some Comparative Aspects of Irish Land Law* (1957) and D.J. Casey and R.E. Rhodes (eds), *Views of the Irish Peasantry 1800–1916* (1977). For political ideas see, T. Foley and S. Ryder (eds), *Ideology and Ireland in the Nineteenth Century* (1998) and D.G. Boyce, R. Eccleshall and V. Geoghegan (eds), *Political Thought in Ireland Since the Seventeenth Century* (1993). Institutional development is considered in A.J. Ward, *The Irish Constitutional Tradition* (1994), D.H. Akenson, *The Irish Education Experiment: The National System of Education in Nineteenth-Century Ireland* (1970), N. Akenson, *Irish Education: A History of Educational Institutions* (1969), P.J. Dowling, *A History of Irish Education* (1971), T.J. McElligott, *Education in Ireland* (1966), J.J. Auchmuty, *Irish Education: A Historical Survey* (1937). Other valuable studies include V. Crossman, *Local Government in Nineteenth-Century Ireland* (1994) and *Politics, Law and Order in Nineteenth-Century Ireland* (1996), J.H. Andrews, *A Paper Landscape: The Ordnance Survey in Nineteenth-Century Ireland* (1975) and R.B. McDowell, *The Irish Administration 1801–1914* (1964).

Major works including but extending beyond the above categories are M. Hechter, *Internal Colonialism: The Celtic Fringe in British National Development, 1536–1966* (1975), a significant interpretation, L. Kennedy, *Colonialism, Religion and Nationalism in Ireland* (1996) and C.C. O'Brien, *States of Ireland* (1972) and (ed.), *The Shaping of Modern Ireland* (1960).

Once neglected historiography has assumed importance during recent years and guides include, D.G. Boyce and A. O'Day (eds), *The Making of Modern Irish History* (1996), C. Brady (ed.), *Interpreting Irish History: The Debate on Historical Revisionism* (1994), B.M. Walker, *Dancing to History's Tune: History, Myth and Politics in Ireland* (1996) and *Past and Present: History, Identity and Politics in Ireland* (2000), J.C. Beckett, *The Study of Irish History* (1963), I. McBride (ed.), *History and Memory in Modern Ireland* (2001), and D. Cairns and S. Richards, *Writing Ireland: Colonialism, Nationalism and Cultures* (1988). Also, pertinent, in part, is T. Dunne (ed.), *The Writer as Witness: Historical Studies, XVI* (1987). Important articles are P. O'Farrell, 'Millenialism, Messianism and Utopianism in Irish History', *Anglo-Irish Studies*, II (1976), R.F. Foster, 'We Are All Revisionists Now', *Irish Review* (1986), D.G. Boyce, 'Brahmins and Carnivores: The Irish Historian in Great Britain', *Irish Historical Studies* (1987) and 'The Irish Historians' Role and the Place of History in Irish National Life, *The*

Historian (2002), 'Gladstone and Irish Nationalism: Achievement and Reputation', in D. Bebbington and R. Swift (eds), *Gladstone: Centenary Essays* (2000), A. Jackson, 'J.C. Beckett: Politics, Faith, Scholarship', *Irish Historical Studies* (2002), E. Larkin, 'Myths, Revisionism, and the Writing of Irish History', *New Hibernia Review* (1998).

Other useful literature pertaining to a range of themes is B. de Breffny (ed.), *The Irish World* (1977), special issue on the visual arts in *Éire-Ireland* (Fall 1998/Spring 1999), Crookshank and the Knight of Glin, *Ireland's Painters, 1600–1940* (2002), E.E. Evans, *The Personality of Ireland* (1973), E.R.R. Green (ed.), *Essays in Scotch-Irish History* (1969), A.E. Murphy (ed.), *Economists and the Irish Economy: From the Eighteenth Century to the Present Day* (1984), D. Kiberd, *Inventing Ireland: The Literature of the Modern Nation* (1995), W. Nolan (ed.), *The Shaping of Ireland: The Geographical Perspective* (1986); L. de Paor (ed.), *Milestones in Irish History* (1986), F. Campbell, *The Dissenting Voice: Protestant Democracy in Ireland from Plantation to Partition* (1992), J. Leerssen, *Remembrance and Imagination: Patterns in the Historical and Literary Representation of Ireland in the Nineteenth Century* (1996), P. Jupp and E. Magennis (eds), *Crowds in Ireland, c. 1730–1920* (2000), J.H. Murphy, *Abject Loyalty: Nationalism and Monarchy in Ireland During the Reign of Queen Victoria* (2001), W.J. Smyth and K. Whelan (eds), *Common Ground: Essays on the Historical Geography of Ireland* (1988), J.B. Lyons (ed.), *2000 Years of Irish Medicine* (2000), W.N. Osborough, *Studies in Irish Legal History* (2000), E.G. Hall and D. Hogan (eds), *The Law Society of Ireland, 1852–2002* (2002), J.P. MacKey (ed.), *The Cultures of Europe: The Irish Contribution* (1994), R. Mitchison and P. Roebuck (eds), *Economy and Society in Scotland and Ireland, 1500–1939* (1988), George-Denis Zimmermann, *Songs of Irish Rebellion* (1967) and *The Irish Storyteller* (2001), T. Bartlett and K. Jeffery (eds), *A Military History of Ireland* (1996) and L. Hyman, *The Jews of Ireland* (1972). Also, see, T.W. Freeman, *Ireland* (1969), K. Haddick-Flynn, *Orangeism: The Making of a Tradition* (1999). Additionally, see the excellent series of county histories (Irish Geography Publications) which parallels the Victoria County Histories of England though completed in a much shorter time-span and with none of the financial infrastructure of its sister project. Similarly, the published volumes of the proceedings of the bi-annual conference of Irish historians, published under various additional titles since volume 11 but including the designation *Historical Studies*, contain pertinent contributions.

Reference

Printed compilations of documents include E Curtis and R.B. McDowell (eds), *Irish Historical Documents, 1172–1922* (1943), J. Carty, *Ireland from Grattan's Parliament to the Great Famine, 1783–1850* (1949) and *Ireland from the Great Famine to the Treaty, 1851–1921* (1951), A. Mitchell and P. Ó Snodaigh, *Irish Political Documents 1869–1916* (1989) and *Irish Political Documents 1916–1949*

(1985), A. O'Day and J. Stevenson, *Irish Historical Documents since 1800* (1992), P. Buckland, *Ulster Unionism 1885–1923* (1973), A.C. Hepburn, *Ireland 1905–25* (1998), Josef Altholz (ed.), *Selected Documents in Irish History* (2000), W.D. Handcock, *English Historical Documents, 1874–1914* (1977), A. Hyland and K. Milne (eds), *Irish Education Documents*, 2 vols (1992). There are relevant selections of documents in A.C. Hepburn, *The Conflict of Nationality in Ireland* (1978), G. Morton, *Home Rule and the Irish Question* (1980) and H.J. Hanham, *The Nineteenth-Century Constitution, 1815–1914* (1969).

Other reference works include, C. Brady (ed.), *The Hutchinson Encyclopedia of Ireland* (2000), B. Lalor, *The Encyclopaedia of Ireland* (2003), S.J. Connolly (ed.), *The Oxford Companion to Irish History* (rev. ed., 2004), J.E. Doherty and D.J. Hickey (eds), *A Dictionary of Irish History Since 1500* (1980) and *A Chronology of Irish History since 1500* (1989), B. de Breffny (ed.), *Ireland: A Cultural Encyclopaedia* (1983), A. Eager, *A Guide to Irish Bibliographical Material: A Bibliography of Irish Bibliographies and Sources of Information* (1980), H. Boylan (ed.), *A Dictionary of Irish Biography* (3rd ed., 1998), K. Newman (ed.), *Dictionary of Ulster Biography* (1993), L. McRedmond (ed.), *Modern Irish Lives: Dictionary of 20th Century Biography* (1996), P. O'Farrell, *Who's Who in the Irish War of Independence* (1997), R.S. Harrison, *A Biographical Dictionary of Irish Quakers* (1997), T. Snoddy, *Dictionary of Irish Artists: 20th Century* (1996), K. and C. Ó Cérín (eds), *Women of Ireland: A Biographical Dictionary* (1996), B.M. Walker (ed.), *Parliamentary Election Results in Ireland, 1801–1922* (1978) and *Parliamentary Election Results in Ireland, 1918–92* (1992), W.E. Vaughan and A.J. Fitzpatrick (eds), *Irish Historical Statistics: Population 1821–1971* (1978), W.J. McCormack (ed.), *The Blackwell Companion to Modern Irish Culture* (1999), S. Duffy (ed.), *An Atlas of Irish History* (1997), A.M. Brady and B. Cleeve, *A Biographical Dictionary of Irish Writers* (1985), T.W. Moody, F.X. Martin and F.J. Byrne (eds), *A New History of Ireland*, VIII and IX (1982, 1984); W.G.A. Strickland, *A Dictionary of Irish Artists* (1989), C.A. Haigh (ed.), *Cambridge Historical Encyclopedia of Great Britain and Ireland* (1985), Ruth D. Edwards, *An Atlas of Irish History* (2nd ed., 1981), F.H.A. Aalen, K. Whelan and M. Stout (eds), *Atlas of the Irish Rural Landscape* (1997), H. Oram, *The Newspaper Book: A History of Newspapers in Ireland, 1619–1983* (1983) and M. Glazier (ed.), *The Encyclopedia of the Irish in America* (1999). Useful summaries of the literature can be found in Charles Messenger (ed.), *Reader's Guide to Military History* (2001) and David Loades (ed.), *Reader's Guide to British History*, 2 vols (2003).

Although there is no standard Irish historical bibliography, the *Annual Bibliography of British and Irish History* published since 1975 contain sections on Ireland. A compilation of literature up to 1992 by the Royal Historical Society is available on CD-ROM. Older issues of *Irish Historical Studies* contain an annual listing of literature; two historiographical essays by Helen Mulvey initially published there are reprinted in T.W. Moody (ed.), *Irish Historiography,*

1936–70 and J.J. Lee (ed.), *Irish Historiography, 1970–79* (1981) and though dated are still useful. *Irish Economic and Social History* provides an annual listing of exceptional utility.

Irish and British Unionism

At one level Irish and British Unionism existed from the late 18th century though it was only in the later stages of Victoria's reign that it became organised political force when confronted by nationalism and the attempted Home Rule solution of 1886. From that time it assumed greater coherence, organisation and developed effective means of propagandising its case. A.V. Dicey was an immense factor in the intellectual drive against Home Rule. Unionism, though, was never a monolith. Irish Unionists were split between north and south and within these groupings they were divided by background, economic status and conflicting aspirations. British Unionists were afflicted by similar divisions. In 1886 a section of the Liberal Party seceded and became Liberal Unionists which, if it added to the movement's numerical strength, brought further complexity to politics. Some Unionists were simply opposed to Home Rule, but others sought to bolster the Union through extensive reforms and by conciliating Irish Catholic opinion. This last though exposed fractures within Unionism, for many in both Great Britain and especially in Ireland resented concessions to a group which overwhelming aligned itself against the Union. Once largely unloved by historians, a stream of modern writers have examined the Unionist cause more sympathetically. Although still less studied than nationalists, Unionism has come into its own as an interest of historians.

Sources and documents: P. Buckland (ed.), *Irish Unionism 1885–1923: a Documentary History* (1973), A.V. Dicey, *England's Case Against Home Rule* (new imp. 1973), A.B. Cooke and J.R. Vincent, 'Ireland and Party Politics, 1885–7, I, II and III', *Irish Historical Studies* (1968–69), J.R. Vincent (ed.), *The Later Derby Diaries; Home Rule, Liberal Unionism, and Aristocratic Life in Late Victorian England* (1981), A.B. Cooke, 'A Conservative Party Leader in Ulster: Sir Stafford Northcote's Diary of a Visit to the Province, October 1883', *Proceedings of the Royal Irish Academy* (1975), A.B. Cooke and A.P.W. Malcolmson (compl.), *The Ashbourne Papers, 1869–1918* (1974), A. O'Day and J. Stevenson (eds), *Irish Historical Documents since 1800* (1992).

Books: The literature on Irish Unionism is spearhead by P. Buckland, *Irish Unionism, 1885–1922* (1973) and *Irish Unionism. Vol. 1, The Anglo-Irish and the New Ireland, 1885–1922* (1972), A. Jackson, *The Ulster Party: Irish Unionists in the House of Commons, 1884–1911* (1989) and *Colonel Edward Saunderson* (1995). Other key studies include J. Loughlin, *Ulster Unionism and British National Identity Since 1885* (1995), P. Gibbon, *The Origins of Ulster Unionism* (1975), D. McCartney, *W.E.H. Lecky, Historian and Politician 1838–1903*

(1994), P. Collins, (ed.), *Nationalism and Unionism: Conflict in Ireland 1885–1921* (1994), P. Costello, *Dublin Castle in the Life of the Irish Nation* (2000) and J.F. Harbinson, *The Ulster Unionist Party, 1883–1973*, (1973). The British dimension is treated in C. Shannon, *Arthur J. Balfour and Ireland 1874–1922* (1988), L.P. Curtis jr, *Coercion & Conciliation in Ireland, 1880–92* (1963), P. Marsh, *The Discipline of Popular Government* (1978) and *Joseph Chamberlain* (1994), R. Jay, *Joseph Chamberlain* (1981), A. Gailey, *Ireland and the Death of Kindness: The Experience of Constructive Unionism 1890–1905* (1987), M. Callaghan, *British High Politics and a Nationalist Ireland* (1994), R.A. Cosgrove, *The Rule of Law: Albert Venn Dicey, Victorian Jurist* (1980), H.C.G. Matthew, *The Liberal Imperialists* (1973), E. Pearce, *Lines of Most Resistance: The Lords, the Tories and Ireland, 1886–1914* (1999), J. Smith, *The Tories and Ireland, 1910–14: The Conservative Party, Politics and the Home Rule Crisis* (2001), D. Dutton, *His Majesty's Loyal Opposition: The Unionist Party in Opposition, 1905–1915* (1992) and J. Holmes, *Religious Revivalism in Britain and Ireland, 1895–1905* (2001). For some outcomes, see, L.W. McBride, *The Greening of Dublin Castle* (1991), A. O'Day, *Irish Home Rule, 1867–1921*, A. Jackson. *Home Rule: An Irish History 1800–2000* (2003).

Articles: The historiography can be followed in A. Jackson, 'Irish Unionism' in D.G. Boyce and A. O'Day (eds), *The Making of Modern Irish History* (1996). His other germane works include, 'The Failure of Unionism in Dublin, 1900', *Irish Historical Studies* (1989), 'Unionist Politics and Protestant Society in Edwardian Ireland', *Historical Journal* (1990), 'T.W. Russell, the Tenant-Farmer Interest and Progressive Unionism in Ulster', *Éire-Ireland* (1990), 'Irish Unionism, 1870–1922' in D.G. Boyce and A. O'Day (eds), *Defenders of the Union: a Survey of British and Irish Unionism since 1801* (2001) and 'Irish Unionists and the Empire, 1880–1920: Classes and Masses' in K. Jeffery (ed.), *An Irish Empire? Aspects of Ireland and the British Empire* (1996). See, as well, D.G. Boyce, '"The Marginal Britons": The Irish' in R. Colls and P. Dodd (eds), *Englishness: Politics and Culture, 1880–1920* (1986), '"Rights of Citizenship": The Conservative Party and the Constitution, 1906–1914' in A. O'Day (ed.), *Government and Institutions in the Post-1932 United Kingdom* (1995) and 'In the Front Rank of the Nation: Gladstone and the Unionists of Ireland, 1868–1893' in D. Bebbington and R. Swift (eds), *Gladstone Centenary Essays* (2000), R. Fanning, 'The Unionist Party and Ireland, 1906–10', *Irish Historical Studies* (1966), I. d'Alton, 'A Perspective Upon Historical Process: The Case of Southern Irish Unionism' in F.B. Smith (ed.), *Ireland, England and Australia* (1990) and 'Southern Irish Unionism: A Study of Cork Unionists, 1884–1914', *Transactions of the Royal Historical Society* (1973), J.W. Boyle, 'The Belfast Protestant Association and the Independent Orange Order, 1901–10', *Irish Historical Studies* (1962), A. Megahey, '"God Will Defend the Right" – The Protestant Churches and Opposition to Home Rule' in D.G. Boyce and A. O'Day (eds), *Defenders of the Union: A Survey of British and Irish Unionism Since 1801* (2001), N. Vance, 'The Problems of Unionist Literature: Macaulay, Froude and Lawless' in *ibid.*;

G. Jones, 'Scientists Against Home Rule' in *ibid.*; C. King, 'Defenders of the Union – Sir Horace Plunkett' in *ibid.*, A. Wyatt, 'Froude, Lecky and "the Humblest Irishman"', *Irish Historical Studies* (1975), C.B. Shannon, 'The Ulster Liberal Unionists and Local Government Reform, 1885–98', *Irish Historical Studies* (1973), D.C. Savage, 'The Origins of the Ulster Unionist Party, 1885–6', *Irish Historical Studies* (1961) and 'The Irish Unionists, 1867–86', *Éire-Ireland* (1967), P. Buckland, 'The Southern Irish Unionists, the Irish Question and British Politics, 1906–14', *Irish Historical Studies* (1967), 'The Unity of Ulster Unionism, 1886–1939' *History* (1975) and 'Irish Unionism and the New Ireland' in D.G. Boyce (ed.), *The Revolution in Ireland, 1879–1923* (1988), F. Campbell, 'Irish Popular Politics an the Making of the Wyndham Land Act, 1901–1903' *Historical Journal* (2002), F.S.L. Lyons, The Irish Unionist Party and the Devolution Crisis of 1904–5', *Irish Historical Stidoes* (1948), T. Hennessy, 'Ulster Unionist Territorial and National Identities, 1886–1893: Province, Island, Kingdom and Empire', *Irish Political Studies* (1993), G. Walker, 'The Irish Presbyterian Anti-Home Rule Convention of 1912', *Studies* (1997), A.C. Hepburn, 'The Irish Councils Bill and the Fall of Sir Antony MacDonnell, 1906–7', *Irish Historical Studies* (1971), H. Mulvey, 'The Historian Lecky: Opponent of Irish Home Rule', *Victorian Studies* (1958), B.M. Walker, 'Party Organization in Ulster, 1865–92: Registration Agents and Their Activities' in P. Roebuck (ed.), *Plantation to Partition* (1981) and 'Finnigan's Awake: E.S. Finnigan and Ulster Politics, 1874–1892' *New Hibernian Rreview* (2000). For the British aspect see, J. Loughlin, 'Joseph Chamberlain, English Nationalism and the Ulster Question', *History* (1992), J.D. Fair, 'From Liberal to Conservative: the Flight of the Liberal Unionists after 1886', *Victorian Studies* (1986), Third Viscount Chilston, 'The Unionist Alliance (1886–1895)', *Parliamentary Affairs* (1961), R.E. Quinault, 'Lord Randolph Churchill and Home Rule', *Irish Historical Studies* (1979), P. Davis, 'The Liberal Unionist Party and the Irish Policy of Lord Salisbury's Government, 1886–92', *Historical Journal* (1975), A. Gailey, 'Unionist Rhetoric and Irish Local Government Reform, 1895–9', *Irish Historical Studies* (1984) and 'Failure and the Making of the New Ireland' in D.G. Boyce, *The Revolution in Ireland, 1879–1923* (1988), D. Goodman, 'Liberal Unionism: The Revolt of the Whigs', *Victorian Studies* (1959), P.B. Rich, 'Social Darwinism, Anthropology and English Perspectives of the Irish, 1867–1900', *History of European Ideas* (1994), T.H. Ford, 'Dicey's Conversion to Unionism', *Irish Historical Studies* (1973), D. McCartney, 'Lecky's *Leaders of Public Opinion in Ireland*', *Irish Historical Studies* (1964) and 'James Anthony Froude: A Historiographical Controversy of the Nineteenth Century', *Historical Studies*, VIII (1971), D.T. Dorritz, 'Monkeys in a Menagerie: The Imagery of Unionist Opposition to Home Rule, 1886–1893', *Éire-Ireland* (1977), M. Boran, 'The Ireland that We Made: A Galway Tribute to Arthur J. Balfour', *Journal of the Galway Archaeological and Historical Society* (2002), F.H.A. Aalen, 'Constructive Unionism and the Shaping of Rural Ireland, c. 1880–1921' *Rural History* (1993), and C. Ó Gráda, 'The Greatest Blessing of All': The Old Age Pension in Ireland', *Past & Present* (2002).

The Third Home Rule Bill and the Ulster Crisis

With the return to office of the Liberals at the close of 1905 and the ensuing huge electoral triumph of Sir Henry Campbell-Bannerman's Ministry, the stage was set for a renewal of nationalist expectations of receiving some measure of self-government. Initially, the government sought to placate these aspirations with a limited scheme and other legislation but the dispute with the House of Lords over David Lloyd George's budget in 1909 resulted in the calling of two general elections in 1910. Thereafter Irish party numbers in the House of Commons helped shift the emphasis back to a fresh attempt to introduce Home Rule. In 1912 the Third Home Rule bill made its appearance in an atmosphere where the unlimited veto of the Peers had been curtailed. In these new circumstances, Irish Unionists but especially Unionists in Ulster were intent upon either thwarting Home Rule altogether or, in the case of northerners, exempting themselves from its operation. The Ulster Crisis of 1912–14 proved to be one of the most traumatic episodes in modern Anglo-Irish history. The period and its repercussions has been considered in detail; modern scholars have picked over the bones, often with telling effect.

Documents and sources: R.B. O'Brien (ed.), *Home Rule Speeches of John Redmond* (1910), I.F.W. Beckett (ed.), *The Army and the Curragh Incident, 1914* (1986), and D.G. Boyce (ed.), *The Crisis of British Unionism: Lord Selborne's Domestic Political Papers, 1885–1922*, vol. 1 (1987).

Books: While the Third Home Rule bill can be followed in the biographies of the key participants, the one modern study devoted to it is P. Jalland, *The Liberals and Ireland: The Ulster Question in British Politics to 1914* (1980). Among the many biographies see especially, R. Blake, *The Unknown Prime Minister: The Life and Times of Andrew Bonar Law 1858–1923* (1955), R.Q. Adams, *Bonar Law* (1999) and D.R. Gwynn, *The Life of John Redmond* (1932). G. Dangerfield, *The Strange Death of Liberal England* (1935) continues to be an influential interpretation of the Ulster crisis but the most complete work is A.T.Q. Stewart, *The Ulster Crisis* (1967). Major studies include P. Buckland, *Irish Unionism. Vol. 2, Ulster Unionism and the Origins of Northern Ireland, 1886–1922* (1973) and *Sir James Craig* (1980), J.D. Fair, *British Interparty Conferences: A Study of the Procedure of Conciliation in British Politics, 1867–1921* (1980), T. Denman, *A Lonely Grave: The Life and Death of William Redmond* (1995), P. Bew, *John Redmond* (1996), A. Jackson, *Sir Edward Carson* (1995), E. Majoribanks and I. Colvin, *The Life of Lord Carson*, 3 vols. (1932–36), H.M. Hyde, *Carson* (1953), A.T.Q. Stewart, *Edward Carson* (1981), F.H. Crawford, *Guns for Ulster* (1947), R. Anderson, *Edward, Lord Carson: Architect of Partition* (2001), Sir J. Fergusson, *The Curragh Incident* (1964), A.P. Ryan, *Mutiny at the Curragh* (1956), P. Bew, *Ideology and the Irish Question* (1994), St J. Ervine, *Craigavon* (1949), J.E. Kendle, *Walter Long, Ireland, and the Union, 1905–1920* (1992). For a sweeping interpretation, D. Miller, *Queen's Rebels* (1978).

Articles: Important specialised studies include, P. Jalland, 'Irish Home-Rule Finance: A Neglected Dimension of the Irish Question, 1910–14', *Irish Historical Sudies* (1983) and 'United Kingdom Devolution 1910–14: Political Panacea or Tactical Diversion?', *English Historical Review* (1979), A.J. Ward, 'Frewen's Anglo-American Campaign for Federalism, 1910–21', *Irish Historical Studies* (1967) and 'America and the Irish Problem, 1899–1921', *Irish Historical Studies* (1968), J.D. Fair, 'The King, the Constitution and Ulster: Interparty Negotiations of 1913 and 1914', *Éire-Ireland* (1971), M. Sheffz, 'The Impact of the Ulster Crisis (1912–14) on the British Labour Party', *Albion* (1973), T.C. Kennedy, '"The Gravest Situation of Our Lives": Conservatives, Ulster, and the Home Rule Crisis, 1911–14', *Éire-Ireland*, (2001), G.D. Phillips, 'Lord Willoughby de Broke and the Politics of Radical Toryism, 1909–1914', *Journal of British Studies* (1980), J.E. Kendle, 'The Round Table Movement and "Home Rule all Round"', *Historical Journal* (1968), J. Smith, '"Paralysing the Army": The Unionists and the Army Annual Act, 1911', *Parliamentary History* (1996), 'Bluff, Bluster and Brinkmanship: Andrew Bonar Law and the Third Home Rule Bill', *Historical Journal* (1993) and 'Conservative Ideology and Representations of the Union with Ireland, 1885–1914' in Martin Francis and Ina Zweiniger-Bargielowska (eds), *The Conservatives and British Society, 1880–1990* (1996), J. Gooch, 'The War Office and the Curragh Incident', *Bulletin of the Institute of Historical Research* (1973), A. O'Day, 'Irish Home Rule and Liberalism', in A. O'Day (ed.), *The Edwardian Age; Conflict and Stability, 1900–1914* (1979), R. Fanning, 'The Irish Policy of Asquith's Government and the Cabinet Crisis of 1910' in A. Cosgrove and D. McCartney (eds), *Studies in Irish History Presented to R. Dudley Edwards* (1979) and '"Rats" Versus "Ditchers": The Die-Hard Revolt and the Parliament Bill of 1911' in A. Cosgrove (ed.), *Parliament and Community, Historical Studies*, XIV (1983), A.R. Muldoon, 'Making Ireland's Opportunity England's: Winston Churchill and the Third Home Rule Bill', *Parliamentary History* (1996), A. Bielenberg, 'Entrepreneurship, Power and Public Opinion in Ireland: The Career of William Martin Murphy' *Irish Economic and Social History* (2000), A.C. Hepburn, 'Catholics in the North of Ireland, 1850–1912: The Urbanization of a Minority', in A.C. Hepburn, *Minorities in History* (1978), 'Work, Class and Religion in Belfast, 1871–1911', *Irish Economic and Social History* (1983) and 'The Catholic Community in Belfast, 1850–1940' in M. Engman, F.W. Carter, A.C. Hepburn and C.G. Pooley (eds), *Comparative Studies on Governments and Non-Dominant Ethnic Groups in Europe, 1850–1940, vol. 8: Ethnic Identity in Urban Europe* (1992), D.W. Miller, 'The Roman Catholic Church in Ireland, 1898–1918', *Éire-Ireland* (1968), T. Denman, 'The Red Livery of Shame: The Campaign Against Army Recruitment in Ireland, 1899–1914', *Irish Historical Studies* (1994), M. Laffan, 'John Redmond (1856–1918) and Home Rule' in C. Brady (ed.), *Worsted in the Game* (1989), Alvin Jackson, 'Unionist Mythology, 1912–1985' *Past & Present* (1992), M. Foy, 'Ulster Unionist Propaganda Against Home Rule, 1912–14', *History Ireland* (1996), A. Gailey, 'King Carson: An Essay on the Invention of

Leadership', *Irish Historical Studies* (1996), G. Walker, 'The Irish Presbyterian Anti-Home Rule Convention of 1912', *Studies* (1997), T. Bowman, 'The Ulster Volunteer Force and the Formation of the 36th (Ulster) Division', *Irish Historical Studies* (2001), D.G. Boyce, 'Dicey, Kilbrandon and Devolution', *Political Quarterly* (1975) and 'Edward Carson (1845–1935) and Irish Unionism' in C. Brady (ed.), *Worsted in the Game* (1989), P. Jalland and J.O. Stubbs, 'The Irish Question and the Outbreak of War in 1914: Some Unfinished Party Business', *English Historical Review* (1981), and D. and J. Howie, 'Irish Recruiting and the Home Rule Crisis of August-September 1914' in M. Dockrill and D. French (eds), *Strategy and Intelligence: British Policy During the First World War* (1996). T.W. Moody, 'The Irish University Question of the Nineteenth Century', *History* (1958) looks at one measure of Liberal reform.

Index